ORIGINAL
gangstas

ORIGINAL
gangstas

THE UNTOLD STORY OF DR. DRE, EAZY-E,
ICE CUBE, TUPAC SHAKUR,
AND THE BIRTH OF WEST COAST RAP

BEN WESTHOFF

NEW YORK   BOSTON

Hachette Books

Hachette Book Group

1290 Avenue of the Americas

New York, NY 10104

hachettebookgroup.com

twitter.com/hachettebooks

First Edition: September 2016

Hachette Books is a division of Hachette Book Group, Inc.

The Hachette Books name and logo are trademarks of Hachette Book Group, Inc.

The publisher is not responsible for websites (or their content) that are not owned by the publisher.

Library of Congress Cataloging-in-Publication Data has been applied for.

ISBNs: 978-0-3163-8389-9 (hardcover), 978-0-3163-4486-9 (ebook)

Printed in the United States of America

RRD-C

10 9 8 7 6 5 4 3 2 1

To Mom and Dad, for all their love

CONTENTS

ORIGINAL
gangstas

THE STASH

He was the trash-talking, gun-toting hustler who brought the image of the young Compton street kid—tough, aggressive, and sick of being stepped on—to the mainstream. He rose faster and changed popular music more than almost anyone else, becoming not just a performer, known for his hypnotic rap cadence, but a behind-the-scenes mogul who upset the status quo and enriched himself in the process. He aimed to shock, but his lyrics were only as exhilarating as his life itself. He was a womanizer and a family man, a devoted friend and a brutal adversary, capable of the same type of violence that would come to define the music movement he launched. When he appeared on a 1993 episode of *The Arsenio Hall Show*, the host introduced him as "the godfather of gangster rap."

But back in 1985, before he became known as Eazy-E, he was Eric Wright, the twenty-one-year-old neighborhood drug pusher. While pals from southeast Compton slept off hangovers, Eric would often start his days early. He read the *Los Angeles Times* before putting on a white T-shirt and white tube socks, pulled high above his blue crocus-sack shoes. A pager and opaque sunglasses known as locs completed the look. The days tended to be bright and scorching on South Muriel Avenue, the treeless Compton street he called home. Unlike lots of other poor families in the area, his was stable: Dad worked at the post office and Mom at a Montessori school. Eric, however, didn't fly so straight.

Before leaving home, he stretched his sock's elastic band with one finger and crammed in a roll of bills. "He'd keep $2,000 in his sock at all times," said Arnold "Bigg A" White, a childhood friend. "Eric had stashes of cash everywhere." He kept some in his parents' garage, and even a few dollars in the pockets of his Levi's 501s. But his sock was where he kept the bulk of his traveling cash. If someone hit him up—maybe a homeless guy or someone trying to rob him—he could simply pull out his pockets and shrug his shoulders.

In the last couple of years rap's popularity had exploded in the neighborhood, and Eric sometimes thought about getting into hip-hop. But he kept that idea mostly to himself. He focused on the game. Sure, Eric wasn't the biggest drug dealer in the area, but he was doing well. Freebased cocaine was exploding in Los Angeles. Everyone suddenly wanted the stuff: strung-out women with kids, glassy-eyed old guys walking around, *everyone*. People came to Compton from miles around to get the goods.

Crack would soon wreck the community, but no one really knew where things were headed just yet. Even the police didn't know what to make of this seemingly innocuous, odorless stuff. "They would catch you with crack and just give you a slap on the wrist," said Mark "Big Man" Rucker, Eazy's drug-dealing partner.

The influx of crack money was everywhere. Folks showed off gold chains and drove Nissan trucks—tricked out as lowriders, riding on low-profile tires. But as drug dealing became increasingly lucrative, territory disputes erupted. "Then everybody's trying to expand out," said Vince Edwards, a Compton rapper known as CPO Boss Hogg. "One or two blocks is not enough, we need another neighborhood."

Eric himself didn't get high. He didn't even drink. He told friends he didn't like the taste of malt liquor, but mainly he knew sobriety gave him a mental advantage. At only five foot four or so, he needed people to take him seriously. Though he had money and the gear that came with it—"He had all the tight cars, clothes and all of that," said Lorenzo Patterson, his neighbor who became N.W.A member MC Ren—he was careful not to flaunt his wealth. He stayed low-key, wasn't flashy. He wasn't the type to talk a lot, either. Sporting a Jheri curl and a thin mustache, the man behind the locs was guarded and shy. After all, his line of work put a premium on discretion.

When it came to women, however, Eric was a vivacious seducer. He had a baby boy named after himself with his girlfriend Darnettra, who was pregnant again. And he also had *another* woman pregnant at the same time, named Linda. *I'm Eazy-E, I got women galore / You might have a lot of women but I got much more*, he would later rap.

Before long he took on a steady girlfriend, Joyce, who later bore his fourth child Derrek when Eric was twenty-three. Joyce had diminishing degrees of success trying to keep Eric faithful, and took to calling him the "community dick," because he kept getting caught with other women. One time, Joyce got so angry with him that she threw a lunchbox at Eric's head. Tracy Jernagin later became another of Eric's favorites. But when Eric got her and yet *another* woman pregnant at the same time, Jernagin was furious. "I was hearing, from everyone—that's your boyfriend, but this other girl's pregnant, having his baby right now!" she said. Eric and Rucker, the fellow dealer, engaged in a long-running competition they called "baby races," to see who could get the most women pregnant. Eric would win, fathering ten in total.

Still, Eric bought Jernagin expensive gifts, including Gucci watches and a new 1989 Acura Legend. But when she arrived at his house one night and Eric wouldn't come out, she was sure she'd caught him cheating. Jernagin decided to enact revenge. She backed her Acura halfway up the block in order to get some momentum and aimed it directly at Eric's new BMW 750iL, which was parked on the street. The idea was to get him "to come outside and just face me," she remembers thinking, but things didn't go according to plan. "Somehow my car went up, like it lifted up almost on two wheels," she said. When it landed, it was undrivable. The whole thing is kind of a blur from there. Eric's other woman came out and tried to tangle with her, but eventually Jernagin called Eric's sister to pick her up.

Sets

Eric Wright spoiled his kids, regularly taking them to Disneyland or Chuck E. Cheese's. "When we had an outing or a weekend together, we *all* went," Eric Wright Jr. recalled. "To us, he was the biggest and baddest thing walking."

He could also be a sadistic prankster. He'd draw a gopher out of its hole in his backyard by squirting lighter fluid down in it, and then light the animal on fire and watch it run around. He might take a giant ball of crack and taunt crackheads with it. "What would you do for this?" he'd ask, and then just laugh in his weird way, without opening his mouth very wide. He could be funny and menacing at the same time. "I used to think his voice was crazy," said MC Ren. "He called my brother, and he'd be like 'Heeyyyy Charlie' in his little voice."

Before becoming a dealer, Eric worked some dead-end jobs. He considered going out for the post office like his old man, even taking the civil service test. But that life wasn't for him. "I hate workin' for somebody else," he said. Eric and his family didn't have tons of money growing up, but they never lacked. His parents taught him to be a self-starter (though they probably didn't intend for him to be a drug dealer).

He had a vision to succeed, so when it came to his drug business, he didn't fool around. He only worked with the people he trusted. A typical day might start with him prepping his stash of cocaine in the garage and getting into his boat-length 1973 Chevy Caprice, maroon with a white vinyl top, called a "glass house" for the long mirrors surrounding the cabin. It wasn't the only slick car Eric owned. At various points in the eighties he also drove a Nissan truck, a pink Suzuki Jeep with candy paint, and Volkswagen Bugs, including one of 1960s vintage with "The Freaks Come Out at Night" decaled on the back window, in honor of Brooklyn rap group Whodini's hit song.

Eric would pilot the Caprice less than a mile over to Atlantic Drive, pulling up where East Caldwell Street came to an end. This was a particularly dangerous gang nexus controlled by the Atlantic Drive Compton Crips, with other sets including the Neighborhood Crips, the Kelly Park

Crips, and the Southside Crips all nearby. All wanted to grow their drug businesses. "It was a powder keg," said CPO Boss Hogg.

The Crips were established in South Central in 1969 by muscle-bound teenager Raymond Washington, who enlisted a fearsome high school friend named Stanley "Tookie" Williams. They formed an alliance to battle other local gangs. "I thought, 'I can cleanse the neighborhood of all these, you know, marauding gangs,'" Williams said. "But I was totally wrong. And eventually, we morphed into the monster we were addressing." In 1979, Williams was convicted of murder and was put to death by lethal injection in 2005. Washington, who hated guns but loved to scrap—"Raymond would take his shirt off and fight his ass off all day long," an acquaintance said—was murdered in 1979.

Adopting their signature color blue, in the early seventies the Crips attempted to expand their turf into Compton, which had its own neighborhood sets. Guys living on and around Piru Street, near Centennial High School, banded together to defend themselves, forming the Pirus. The group included Sylvester Scott and Benson Owens, who are credited with founding the Bloods, which enveloped sets including the Brims and the Bounty Hunters from the Nickerson Gardens housing projects in Watts. They took red as their color, owing to the fact that the Pirus were called Roosters, the Bounty Hunters were called Blobs, and the Brims used to put red-stemmed matches in their hats.

Both sects splintered and mutated across the country, and their rivalries (sometimes among their own members) became increasingly bloody. By the time Eric became a young man, the Crips and the Bloods, along with Latino gangs, had divided up Compton between them, and were on their way to taking over the region. It's not hard to understand the appeal; in neighborhoods where there's no work, high crime, and crumbling family structures, joining forces with other disillusioned kids helped create pride and a sense of unity. But along with pride and unity came violence. In 1984 there were about two hundred gangland killings in L.A. County; 1988 saw almost five hundred, and by the early 1990s, an estimated hundred thousand gang members were spread across the county.

It's not entirely clear which Crip subset Eric represented. The gang hadn't yet fully splintered, and really, most of the Crip factions in his part of town liked Eric. It didn't hurt that he sold them high-quality coke, and at great prices. But that didn't make him a serious gangbanger. Sure, he sometimes wore blue, but he didn't do drive-bys and he didn't seek retribution against other sets. That wasn't how he rolled. He was about his money, pure and simple.

Atlantic Drive was the name of an apartment building out of which he sometimes operated, and also the name of its street. The unglamorous, two-story stucco spot housed a few dozen families, but it was especially effective as a twenty-four-hour drug market. Its C-shaped layout prevented most of the units from being seen from the street, which meant interested buyers could approach without fear of police observation. Buyers could get everything from crack and angel dust to weed or sherman—marijuana joints (or Nat Sherman cigarettes) dipped in PCP. Though there was plenty of foot traffic, the building managed to keep something of a low profile. After making purchases, buyers were quickly escorted out. No smoking on the premises. It was the perfect dealing zone.

Gangs were involved with the drug trade, but there was little established hierarchy. "If someone saw you were a hustler, they'd front you some," said rapper J-Dee, who dealt on Compton's Poinsettia Avenue. "It was always on consignment, and everyone had a beeper and one of those big brick phones—you'd put it in your pocket, and your pants fell off."

Dealers would keep their supplies at a stash house, a spot inhabited by a drug addict, whom they'd pay in crack—maybe a gram a day. "We called them the house man or the house lady," said J-Dee, adding that he felt no guilt about selling people such a noxious drug. "Our philosophy was, we didn't put a gun to their head."

J-Dee, who went on to fame as a member of Ice Cube's group, Da Lench Mob, specialized in "curb servin'," selling to people hand-to-hand on the street, like a drive-through Taco Bell. Customers included anyone from McDonnell Douglas employees who drove over from Long Beach to addicts from the neighborhood. He kept his money between his insole and the bottom of his shoe ("that way you could run away with it"), and once he made $1,000 he would take it home and come back fresh.

Eric didn't do deals with just anyone on the street. He sold wholesale, and only to clients he knew, including cousins working out of the Atlantic Drive apartments. If he recognized a number on his pager, he'd call back on a pay phone. Of course you needed to know the codes. For an eight ball (an eighth of an ounce) the page should include an "8." The code for a half ounce, meanwhile, was "12." If something felt off, Eric simply didn't do the deal. One slipup could mean the end. Compton hustlers didn't play around. Eric only had to remember Horace Butler.

The Windfall

Horace Butler was Eric's first cousin, once removed, and the spitting image of the rapper Buffy from The Fat Boys. Schoolmates teased Butler constantly about his weight as a kid. "So he'd been toughened up," his friend Mark Rucker said. "If you kicked him, or tripped him, he'd bust you square in the face."

He lived nearby on Poinsettia, and served as Eric's mentor in the drug game. If you stayed on his good side, Butler was generous. He was secretive, however, and you had to earn his confidence. Eric, though, was his trusted kin. When he was a teenager Butler made him his "runner," charged with delivering dope to the customers after Butler made the deals.

Eric, who'd dropped out of Dominguez High School, hadn't known much about the drug business until then. As a teenager, he'd taken joyrides in stolen cars. He'd done burglaries. He stole color televisions and VCRs. "One time he wanted to give his mother a stolen TV as a present," Bigg A remembered with a laugh. When it came to dealing, though, Eric was a novice. Which is why he was surprised when, one day in 1984, Butler invited him to go for a ride in his truck.

Eric climbed into Butler's ride, a candy-painted GMC truck, chromed out with big rims on its off-road tires. Technically speaking, the truck didn't belong to Butler, but to another guy from the area who'd been sent to jail. The truck had been impounded and the rumor was that it was full of packages of sherman. No one wanted to retrieve it for fear that the police would arrest *them*. But Butler didn't care. He managed to secure the truck's release and the big beautiful GMC was now his. With Eric in tow, Butler drove it to a secret neighborhood location away from prying eyes. Butler looked around, making sure no one was watching, and then reached his hands beneath the side of an abandoned house, retrieving a paper grocery bag. He pulled it open and revealed its contents to Eric: bundle upon bundle of cash, tightly bound by rubber bands into squares. "Keep an eye on this for me," he said, putting it back. Eric didn't know what to make of this, but he quickly consented.

Around that time, Butler was acting strange in other ways, too. Rucker noticed it earlier that week as he worked his drug spot nearby on Glencoe Street, a stone's throw from the home of a mutual friend, Emil Moses, who had just hanged himself in his garage. As police and the coroner dealt with the body, a crowd gathered. Butler and Rucker chatted, lamenting the death for a few minutes, before the latter got down to business. Rucker was in the market for some product. "Do you have some?" he asked.

"Nah," said Butler, surveying the area. "I'm laying low. Taking a break."

"Why is that?"

"Things are kind of funny right now."

The men parted ways, making plans to see each other at Moses's funeral, for which Rucker was to be a pallbearer. He had even rented a suit for the occasion. But Butler wouldn't make it. A few days later, just after midnight, he was driving his truck in mid-city L.A., about to enter onto the 10 freeway with a passenger in tow. As he pulled up to the signal light he was shot seven times by his own passenger, who promptly jumped out.

Its driver now dead, the truck slowly rolled backward, before hitting a pole and coming to a stop. The murder left a trail of questions: Who was this person? Why did he or she murder Horace Butler? Was it about money? The truck? Drugs? Only one truth was known: There would be another funeral in Compton that week.

*   *   *

Butler's death hit Eric hard. "Me and him used to be together every day," he said. "I just happened to go off and do some business with my mother that night, and I wasn't there. I figure I was there, I'd probably be dead right along with him."

Eric would quickly have another shock. When he returned to the abandoned house where Butler had stashed his bag of cash, he found not only the money but parcel after parcel of cocaine as well. Eric quickly realized he was sitting on top of a gold mine—even if you didn't consider the cash, there had to be tens of thousands of dollars worth of product here. He just had to figure out how to unload the stuff.

He immediately got to work. When Rucker arrived not long afterward at Eric's house, Rucker was astonished to find Eric crouched over a small electric stove, trying to figure out how to cook up crack. "Man, where'd you get this from?" Rucker asked.

"I went to get the money," Eric said, "and this was there, too."

Eric's inexperience was quickly evident. He cut a rock and held it up to Rucker, speculating on its value. "This is a twenty, right?"

"Hell no!" said Rucker. The rock was closer to sixty dollars. Rucker proceeded to give him a crash course in how to price crack rocks. From then on Rucker began buying his cocaine from Eric. His prices were great—$1,000 for an ounce, an amount for which others might charge $1,500. Eric even gave him parcels on consignment. He could afford it, considering these inherited wares amounted to pure profit.

In 1985, as the recipient of a windfall, Eric appeared to be riding high. Having invested profits from Butler's stash into his own supplies, he had fine clothes and fancy cars. But he wasn't satisfied; deep down he knew this wasn't the life for him. And so he decided to do something about it.

An Historically Dangerous Place

Day-to-day life in Compton didn't mesh with Hollywood's version of gangland. In the daylight hours of the mid-1980s, the city, located about ten miles south of downtown L.A., still looked like a middle-class suburb. Well-appointed, multicolored bungalows had big yards, iron bars on windows, and wrought-iron fences. Kids rode around on bicycles, clothes billowed on lines, and working-class brown and black people went about their business. Late at night teenagers would race their Suzuki trucks and VW Bugs for cash. But it didn't seem like a war zone.

Beneath the surface, however, bubbled the makings of urban catastrophe—high unemployment, poverty, and infant mortality, and rising gang murders. The recession of the 1970s had been eased by Nixon's Comprehensive Employment and Training Act, a public jobs program that put people in the neighborhood to work. In 1982 Reagan gutted it, making it harder for locals to find jobs.

The police weren't much help, either. Until it was disbanded in 2000, Compton had its own police force, one of the most corrupt in the nation. The city of only 93,000 people had sixty-six killings in 1986 and eighty-five in 1987, more than three times the per capita rate of L.A. as a whole, which was then itself an historically dangerous place. Los Angeles during the eighties counted almost three thousand gang-related killings; a black teen was six times as likely to be murdered as his white counterpart.

Eric Wright's parents arrived in Compton from Greenville, Mississippi, as part of the Great Migration. Los Angeles was the main embarkation point for World War II soldiers headed off to the South Pacific, and following the war, plentiful aerospace jobs drew people from all over the country. (The gorgeous weather didn't hurt.) Eric's parents were among the first black families in Compton; for most of the twentieth century, the city was lily white. For a short time in 1949 George and Barbara Bush lived in a Compton apartment complex while he sold oil-drilling equipment.

Compton was also notoriously racist. Though the Supreme Court outlawed housing racial segregation in 1917, developers and banks continued to systematically enforce it. A real estate broker could lose her license for aiding integration, and Compton was hit harder by this trend than any other part of L.A. Meanwhile, violent vigilante groups sought to hold black families off at the city's border, espousing the slogan, "Keep the

Negroes North of 130th Street." Marvin Kincy, a black Compton native and veteran Piru gang member born in 1950, recalled being told not to cross Wilmington Avenue past seven p.m., for fear of "minutemen and spook hunters." He added that, when he was nine, four young white men in a '57 Ford pulled up asking for directions. When he approached their car they pelted him with rotten eggs and tomatoes.

Following a Supreme Court decision in 1948 that made the systematic discrimination increasingly unworkable, housing restrictions were eased. The Wrights settled in Compton, where Eric was born in 1964. Not far away, the Watts riots followed a year later, after a black motorist was pulled over by a white highway patrolman on suspicion of drunk driving, stoking civil unrest, dozens of deaths, and then-unprecedented property damage. In the aftermath, white flight and factory closings began to change the area. The former Bush residence eventually attracted drug dealers, squatters, and prostitutes, and Compton became one of the most dangerous cities in the country.

Anyone in Los Angeles who wanted a cheap high during the early Reagan years just had to visit South Central's vast open-air drug market called the Track, located on Eighty-First Street between Hoover and Vermont.

Sherman was initially popular, but before long crack cocaine was all the rage. You can only snort so much coke before your nose bleeds, but you can smoke crack all day and still want more. "You saw respectable men turn into crackheads," said Ice Cube. "You saw the nurse up the street with the family turn into a strawberry"—that is, a woman selling herself for the drug.

Initially quite expensive and known as "ready rock"—since it had already been freebased with baking soda and was ready to smoke—crack prices began to fall thanks to the efforts of dealers like South Central trafficker "Freeway" Rick Ross. He sent out guys on mopeds to make deliveries all over the area, and by the mid-eighties was moving, literally, tons of cocaine.

Marvin Kincy saw the effects of crack in Compton firsthand. He was stunned to see a prominent community member—a man who had owned a bank and a car wash—pushing a shopping cart down the street one day. "He smoked his entire empire away."

Little did crack customers know that they were helping fund a Central American war. One of Ross's Nicaraguan suppliers, Oscar Danilo Blandón, received protection from the CIA as he channeled his profits to the rebel Contras, working to overthrow the leftist Sandinista government. The Reagan administration also supported the rebels, and funded them through secret weapons sales to Iran, resulting in the Iran-Contra Scandal. Blandón was eventually arrested and worked undercover for the U.S. government, when he ensnared Ross, who served thirteen years in prison.

In 1989, the Senate foreign relations committee led by John Kerry, then a first-term senator from Massachusetts, released a report concluding that senior U.S. policy makers "were not immune to the idea that drug money was a perfect solution to the Contras' funding problems." The CIA may not have directly funneled crack into the inner city, as is sometimes alleged, but they appear to have turned a blind eye toward it, as it suited their geopolitical aims.

Before crack, gangs weren't particularly profitable. But members quickly realized the big money in the drug game. "They started to say, 'I can have nice cars, I can have a house, I can wear nice clothes,'" said "Freeway" Rick Ross. "So then they got involved." For a while, police were ignorant. They looked for PCP on their raids, not coke. But by 1986 mandatory minimum sentencing guidelines were established, making punishment for crack possession far stricter than cocaine. Blacks weren't using more than whites, but police found it a lot easier to roll up on a group of corner dealers, as opposed to kicking in somebody's Beverly Hills door.

Los Angeles police employed brutal tactics to break up the rising tides of gang membership, drug use, and violent crime. The LAPD's CRASH unit, which stood for "Community Resources Against Street Hoodlums," employed its Operation Hammer, far-reaching sweeps across South Central in which police rounded up and arrested thousands of presumed gang members. (Many were ultimately found to be unaffiliated.) CRASH police often carried a "throwaway" gun or "extra dope" to plant on suspects. "They swallow the dope or throw it away, so we beat them up and use our own," one said. "They're illegal, they're selling dope, so what kind of respect do we owe them? That's wrong, but it's how we thought about it." In January 1988 a twenty-seven-year-old woman named Karen Toshima was killed in Westwood Village, caught in crossfire between rival gangs. Though gang-related murders were nothing new, in the wake of Toshima's killing in a well-off neighborhood, Mayor Tom Bradley and the city council agreed to spring for millions for a surge in patrols.

President Reagan declared the War on Drugs in 1982, and police chief Daryl Gates, head of the beleaguered, understaffed LAPD, took a particularly hard line on drug users. In 1990 he told a Senate committee that those who "blast some pot on a casual basis" ought to be "taken out and shot." One dramatic tool of the Gates administration was the battering ram, an armored tank weighing six tons and bearing a fourteen-foot steel arm that crushed doorways of suspected "rock houses." (It inspired a hit song by Compton rapper Toddy Tee, "Batterram," which includes uncredited production work by a young Dr. Dre.)

In April 1989, just-displaced first lady Nancy Reagan, now living with Ronald in Bel Air, suited up in an LAPD windbreaker and tennis shoes to observe a raid of a suspected South Central drug house, near Main Street and Fifty-First. Alongside Chief Gates she watched as a SWAT team busted in. Reagan, who coined the phrase "Just Say No," said she found the sparsely furnished house "very depressing." Equally depressing, perhaps, was the fact that only one and a half grams of crack were seized, yet fourteen people were arrested. Media accounts of the incident noted that the Nancy Reagan drug rehabilitation center was slated to open later that year in the San Fernando Valley. But that never happened, as Reagan abruptly withdrew her support for it over the summer, scuttling $5 million in donations. Her spokesman explained to the *Los Angeles Times* she was "spreading herself too thin."

Ordinary South Los Angeles residents couldn't be blamed for fearing the cops as much as the criminals. Greg Mack, of hip-hop station KDAY, recalled regular gunfire and "ghetto bird" helicopters constantly overheard at his South Central home, searching for perpetrators. "Because my wife at the time was Hispanic, we always got pulled over," said Mack, who is black. "They always thought I was up to no good, that I was riding around with a girl of a different race like I was a pimp."

"They'd shoot people in the back," MC Ren said. "They beat your ass for nothing."

Nearly every L.A. black man I interviewed for this book has stories like these. Being pulled over for minor (or nonexistent) infractions, being humiliated, being arrested unfairly—it was just a fact of life.

Los Angeles's hip-hop scene rose amid this chaos. The music itself was warm and friendly, at least at first. Local MCs rapped over soft, danceable beats; DJs spun New York rappers' records at clubs and house parties; members of car clubs (say, for Nissan trucks, or VW Bugs) blasted cassette mixes; Venice Beach break-dancers spun on cardboard. Some drug dealers invested their profits in local talent, like Compton hip-hop titan Mixmaster Spade, who learned DJing while attending school in New York and returned home to rock parties and foster emerging L.A. rap talent, including King Tee, Toddy Tee, Coolio, and DJ Pooh. That is, until Spade was arrested following a 1987 shootout with police, who found a giant quantity of PCP on the property.

A hip-hop show at the Long Beach Arena the summer previous descended into chaos. Headliners Run-D.M.C. never performed because a fight broke out. KDAY programmer Greg Mack, on stage, saw a man get thrown over a balcony (he somehow survived). Assailants weaponized broken chair legs and yanked off young girls' necklaces. Security was overwhelmed and dozens were injured. "It was a race riot," said popular DJ Rodger Clayton, who promoted and attended the show. "The Long Beach Insanes had stole a Mexican girl's purse and some Mexican dudes went upstairs, broke in the broom closet and went down and hit up the

Long Beach Insanes. Hit 'em with brooms and mops and sticks with sharp edges on 'em. Then all the black gangs got together, that was out there and they just start whupping every Mexican boy, every white boy, throwing 'em off the second level, whupping they ass and everything."

"Some critics, like Parents Music Resource Center crusader Tipper Gore," *People* magazine noted, "believe there is a subliminal message in rap music—that 'it's OK to beat people up.'"

But reality was more complicated. For many kids hip-hop represented a way out, a constructive way to make a living. Performer Alonzo Williams received a pass because he DJed. "I was in East L.A. doing a backyard party and two Latino gangs got to fighting," he said. "But they called a time-out to stop the fight. 'Let the DJ go home. He's not in this shit, man!' Both gangs helped me load my truck up with my equipment."

CHAPTER TWO

SIR ROMEO

A tall, broad-shouldered high school student in the early eighties, Andre Young was already a ladies' man, making the girls laugh and wowing them with his hip-hop prowess. His DJ group Freak Patrol pumped out jams at parties, and his pop-locking routine during half-time at Fremont High School football games drew cheers. Performed to a breathy, electro beat, the robotic dance featured stutter steps and abrupt stops and starts—"popping" out one's limbs before "locking" them in place. His outfit included rubber-soled, Bruce Lee–style shoes, and a customized, Batman-style black jacket, with a little cape in the back and his nickname "Sir Romeo" ironed on—a play on his middle name, Romell.

Another favorite spot to show off was Eve After Dark, a club near Compton in Willowbrook, frequented by nattily dressed young adults. The meaning of the club's name is a little hard to parse—something to do with original sin—but folks lined up to get in. The disco era wasn't too far gone, and a mirror ball spun above the dance floor while DJs pumped out groovy R&B, funk, rap, and electro.

It was like Eden before the snake. No alcohol was served, just sodas. Club owner Alonzo Williams didn't allow gang attire, preferring his male clientele adhere to the sartorial stylings of Morris Day: slacks, hard-bottom shoes, and a skinny tie. Girls might arrive with their hair in a bun, but then shake it out in the bathroom. "Before they leave they'd wrap it back up and, when they got home would be like, 'Hi, Mom!'" said Lonzo.

Andre's mother would drop him off with his brother Tyree and their friends, and then go home and get some sleep, setting her alarm for one a.m. to come pick them up. Inside the club, Andre might juggle conversations with two or three women at a time, with a wingman running interference so nobody got suspicious.

At age sixteen he had his first child with a woman named Cassandra Joy Greene, a boy named Curtis whom he didn't acknowledge until decades later. He also began talking to a pretty fourteen-year-old student named Lisa Johnson. Raised in South Central, Johnson more recently lived on the west side of L.A. Her dad was out of the picture and her brother had been killed in gang violence. Andre seduced her when she was in ninth grade, she said, but their relationship was controversial from the start. Johnson's mother thought she was too young to be dating, so the pair met secretly.

"Then, one day, I received *that phone call*—the call that all moms of teenagers dread," wrote Andre's mother Verna Griffin in her memoir. Johnson was pregnant.

She started tenth grade at Fremont, but only lasted a couple of weeks. "I was pregnant and they didn't want me on school campus," she said. To make things worse, Johnson's mother was furious at her daughter for the pregnancy. She threw Johnson out of the house.

It was January 1983 when Johnson gave birth to their first daughter, La'Tanya. Johnson was fifteen and Andre was seventeen. "He was a real proud father at the time," Johnson said. Andre's mother let Johnson and the baby live with them for a time; Johnson slept in Andre's bedroom, while he slept in the living room. They also stayed with his grandmother in Willowbrook, not far from Eve After Dark. Sometimes they found themselves crashing at grim motels like the Snooty Fox Motor Inn on South Western Avenue, which rents rooms by the hour.

Before long, however, Andre had gotten another young woman pregnant, named LaVetta Washington. Their girl Tyra was born in May 1984. Johnson was furious. She, too, was pregnant again.

Andre Young's accomplished, elegant mother Verna Griffin has created a clothing line and published her memoir in 2008. She's also tough as nails. One night in Los Angeles when she was a young mother, two men attempted to mug her, rolling up and demanding her purse. "Without hesitation, I pulled out my gun and aimed it at them," she wrote. "They sped away."

She and Andre's father Theodore Young were still in high school when they had him, just months before the 1965 Watts riots. They quickly married at Verna's mother's insistence, and rented a home on 135th Street from Theodore's stepfather. The price was right—eighteen dollars a week—but unemployment pushed Theodore into drug dealing. To Verna's distress, his clients would get high at their home. "The stale odor of marijuana was so strong that not even daily cleaning could get rid of it," she wrote. Not long after, she and Andre moved back into her parents' home in an unincorporated part of L.A. County near Compton. Theodore was soon arrested in a drug raid.

She claimed he beat her during their tumultuous marriage. "If I went to the neighborhood store and stayed too long, he would get physical with me," Verna wrote. "If I engaged in what he considered a prolonged conversation with any of his male companions, he would get physical with me." (I could not reach Theodore Young for comment.) Verna added that he also beat her when she was pregnant with her second child, Jerome La Vonte Young, who died during infancy, from unrelated intestinal pneumonia. He began stalking her so badly that she was scared to leave her house, she wrote.

Smart and resourceful despite dropping out of school after ninth grade, Verna held down low-paying jobs at stores like National Dollar, Sears, and Kmart. Poverty was never far from her young family's door, and they didn't always have access to a phone, a car, or even gas. Verna had yet another boy die in infancy, and she herself nearly died from the birth of Andre's younger brother Tyree when doctors failed to remove her placenta.

She also gave birth to a healthy girl, named Shameka. Constant moving characterized Andre's childhood. At one point the family lived near the Compton airport in a housing project called Wilmington Arms, which the *L.A. Times* later called "so notorious as a drug bazaar that one city councilman says it should be demolished." Verna and her brood moved well over a dozen times, hopscotching among apartments and houses in South Central, Watts, Carson, Long Beach, and Compton, including on Thorson Avenue in the latter city, just a few blocks away from Eric Wright. These neighborhoods were rough, with bullies on the block, burglars at the door, and, once, a man murdered right in front of their house. Another time, Verna recalled, after two nursery school children got into a dispute, their mothers settled things by fighting each other with knives.

They were sometimes on government assistance, and when Andre was eleven, the family suffered a bad car accident. Andre's face was severely cut up by smashed glass. He barely complained even though, more than a month later, he was found to have suffered a broken collarbone. "He handled the pain from his injury so well," Verna wrote. "I wondered if that was because I had taught him the importance of enduring pain."

Tyree and Little Warren

Having finally split from Theodore, Verna met her future husband Curtis Crayon at a beach party. Their relationship soon turned rocky as well. Following their divorce he "harass[ed] me with threats of violence," she wrote, and she procured a restraining order.

But the product of their marriage, son Tyree Du-Sean Crayon, who was three years younger than Andre, would become Andre's greatest supporter and confidant. Tyree played football, basketball, and track, and was the first person in the family to graduate from high school. He found work with an aerospace company and fathered a boy. "My brother was my best friend, and we did everything together. He was just a lot of fun to be around. He walked in, the party got live," Andre said.

Verna married a third time, to a corporate level McDonnell Douglas employee from Long Beach named Warren Griffin Jr. The families joined forces, *Brady Bunch*–style, with all eight kids living under one roof at times. The brood included Warren Griffin III, a quiet, bespectacled kid who would become famous as rapper-producer Warren G.

Warren Griffin Jr. was a Mason, as well as a karate master who taught Andre, Warren, and Tyree how to defend themselves. Some weekends Big Warren loaded the entire squirrelly lot into his Ford station wagon and took them to the drive-in. Verna, meanwhile, developed an interest in fashion design and enlisted the kids for her shows. Clad in *Miami Vice*–style duds, Tyree clowned around on the runway, while Andre spun R&B or jazz on the turntables. "We would all model," Warren G said. Verna eventually got her own store at the Carson Mall, and Andre's new girlfriend Michel'le, an up-and-coming R&B singer, came to help promote it, signing autographs.

The family was thick even through tough times, living off powdered eggs during a McDonnell Douglas strike. Warren G worshipped his older stepbrothers. Andre and Tyree called him "Kibbles," "because my hair was nappy like Kibbles 'n Bits," he said. They hung out at nearby Kelly Park, Eric Wright's gang territory. Kids taunted little Warren because he was originally from Long Beach, and so his stepbrothers taught him how to defend himself. "They would sic me on the little dudes when one of them would get to running off at the mouth," Warren G said. " 'Get 'em, Kibbles!' "

Rap Talker

Owing to bad grades, Andre left Centennial High School, located in Compton, for Fremont, which was in South Central. But even after transferring his academic performance didn't improve, and as a result he was booted from the diving team. Still, his instructors saw promise. "His English teacher said, 'I know he's not a dummy; I watch him play chess at lunchtime and he beats everybody,' " wrote Verna. Skilled at drawing, he enjoyed mechanical drafting, which is used to illustrate HVAC systems in construction and architecture plans. A teacher encouraged him to pursue it, but in the end he dropped out of Fremont. He battled with his mother about his future; she insisted he return to school or get a regular job.

But Andre's great passion was music—damn everything else. Verna should have known better; it was their great bond. She performed as part of an act called the Four Aces, who wrote original compositions for piano, and Andre's middle name Romell was taken from his father's neighborhood singing group, the Romells. Verna boasted a tremendous record collection, and as a child Andre controlled the stylus at her parties. Even before he could read, he learned to recognize 45s by their label colors. "Everybody in my neighborhood loved music," he added. "I could jump the back fence and be in the park where there were ghetto blasters everywhere."

Verna was especially into seventies funk: Earth, Wind & Fire, Parliament-Funkadelic, James Brown, Isaac Hayes. Andre grew up listening to it, too. Attending an L.A. Coliseum concert featuring Parliament-Funkadelic as a fourteen-year-old, his mind was blown. He stood mouth agape as a spaceship descended, and George Clinton led his band in madcap, exuberant fashion. Then and there Andre decided to pursue a life of music. "Before I heard them, I was planning to be a mechanical draftsman," he later wrote in the *Los Angeles Times*. "But P-Funk's music opened my mind up to the idea that there are no barriers except the ones you believe in." The funk became the defining music of his life; the foundation of his creations.

Andre would learn to play piano and read sheet music, but was particularly blessed by an incredible ear for sounds that went together. Upon receiving a mixer one Christmas, he taught himself how to incorporate a component of one song with a component of another. "This was like the ultimate thing to have," Andre said. "Damn a bike, I got a mixer!"

In the seventies and early eighties, DJs were the stars of hip-hop. When rappers joined in, they served largely to hype the turntablists. Ice-T was one of L.A.'s first popular rappers, and his early song "Reckless" is basically an extended shout-out to his DJ, Chris "The Glove" Taylor. *The DJ named Glove has reigned supreme / As the turntable wizard of the hip-hop scene.* "Reckless" is part of the *Breakin'* soundtrack, a 1984 hip-hop film featuring pop-locking galore. The MCs are almost an afterthought; in the credits, Ice-T is listed as the "rap talker."

Early hip-hop was performed mostly live, at parties, and when artists first began recording in studios they worked to re-create the festive atmosphere. As Sugarhill Gang's Big Bank Hank put it: *Hotel, motel, Holiday Inn!* Before long groups like Grandmaster Flash and the Furious Five ushered in sociopolitical themes like on their 1982 hit "The Message," and by the mid-eighties hip-hop with aggressive-sounding backing tracks was in full force in New York. Run-D.M.C. and LL Cool J spat over hard beats, and the MC—rather than the DJ—began to dominate.

But L.A. hadn't gotten the memo. There, the party vibe marched on. A faster-paced, heavily synthesized electro-dance DJ sound, with vocoder-altered robotic vocals, still ruled dance floors. Folks weren't interested in sophisticated rapping so much as getting down.

Popular DJs like Egyptian Lover made what sounds today like techno music. On the turntables, he'd manipulate records to play a drumbeat or song section three times in a row—boom boom boom. Egyptian Lover joined a "mobile DJ" crew called Uncle Jamm's Army, who brought their audio equipment wherever there was a party. Group leader Rodger Clayton had a swagadelic persona and a knack for promotion, signing up kids for mailing lists and sending out postcards.

Uncle Jamm's Army was influenced by Afrika Bambaataa, a pioneering New York DJ and former member of violent Bronx street gang the Black Spades, who broke off to start the hip-hop focused Universal Zulu Nation movement. (At the time of this writing, April 2016, Bambaataa was facing allegations from multiple men that he sexually abused them as minors—allegations he strenuously denied.) His song "Planet Rock," which borrowed from the music of German electronic music pioneers Kraftwerk, became a dance floor spectacular upon its 1982 release. Uncle Jamm's extravagant electronic affairs took a page from Bambaataa's, and were wildly popular in the early eighties, with the group performing at

spots like Veterans Memorial Auditorium in Culver City, before grad-
uating to the L.A. Sports Arena. There they performed before upward
of five thousand kids, girls in bandanas and miniskirts, and young
African-American "mods" dancing in a ska style, wearing trench coats. In
the mode of Run-D.M.C. and the Fat Boys, attending B-boys wore oversized Cazal glasses and thick, braided gold chains known as dookie ropes.

The eardrum-annihilating arsenal was part of the advertising. Uncle Jamm's
flyer for a 1983 Sports Arena show promised "a hundred speakers," which were
stacked like pyramids. Dressed in leather and spikes, coonskin caps, or like
Middle Eastern snake charmers, they'd shoot fog and throw fire. Their DJs
ranks included Egyptian Lover, DJ Pooh, Keith Cooley (the half-brother of
innovative turntablist Joe Cooley), and Bobcat, who returned from a stint on
the East Coast with a mastery of the Philadelphia "transformer" sound, whose
name was taken from the shape-changing Transformer action figures. These
shows were less like concerts and more like what we think of today as raves,
with DJs playing continuous hits to keep the party moving. Though Uncle
Jamm's played rap songs, they did not usually feature rappers, however. "[I]t
would get boring," Rodger Clayton said. "We can put rappers on no more than
two minutes a night because they interfere with the energy level."

Disco Lonzo

Although he could hardly be less gangsta, Alonzo Williams is the unsung
architect of the gangsta rap era. A go-along-to-get-along guy eight years
Andre Young's senior, Williams emerged on the mobile DJ scene spinning
disco and R&B in flamboyant costumes. Raised in Compton and sent
to Catholic school, he was first known as Disco Lonzo, clad in a Super-
man shirt, whistle, construction hat with a siren, and, around his neck,
a gold chain reading "Lonzo" with an attached razor blade to cut up his
cocaine. "He was like Disco Stu from *The Simpsons*," said his collaborator, the Unknown DJ. Lonzo recruited help to set up and break down
(or "wreck") his equipment each night, birthing the name of his group:
World Class Wreckin' Cru, which featured a rotating cast of DJs.

Lonzo's dad hooked him up with the owner of Eve After Dark, and the young entrepreneur began throwing parties there in 1979. He promoted a "super freak contest," in which women could win $100 by doing "extremely erotic moves to make the crowd excited." He even brought in male exotic dancers to a storefront downstairs. They're "a lot less hassle than female dancers," he explained.

Andre Young started coming to Eve After Dark on the weekends, and the club gave him his first break one night in 1982. Somehow maneuvering himself up on stage, he worked two turntables, proceeding to blow the crowd's minds by mixing 1961 doo-wop classic "Please Mr. Postman" by the Marvelettes with Afrika Bambaataa's "Planet Rock." This was long before computer software made this kind of thing easy. "One record is twice as fast as the other. So all of the beats won't match. But it worked," Lonzo said. "That was a masterpiece to pull off."

Andre would manually record songs straight off the radio, and layer them together with a four-track recorder. The crude technique let him bring to life mash-ups he'd imagined. "You might hear 'Oh Sheila' by Ready for the World, but the vocals would be a Prince song and the harmony might be a whole other artist," said KDAY programmer Greg Mack. "People would say, 'Oh, he's not a real DJ.' I'd be like, 'I don't care what you call it, shit sounds good!'"

"[W]here normally you go to a club and the DJs play all the hit records back to back, I used to put on a serious show," Andre said. He began calling himself Dr. Dre, after basketball star Julius "Dr. J" Erving, sometimes tacking on to his handle, "The Master of Mixology." Lonzo paid him fifty dollars per night to perform, and invited him to join the World Class Wreckin' Cru. He also provided him access to first-rate recording equipment, including his top-of-the-line four-track bass and drum machine.

The newly minted Dr. Dre also linked up with KDAY, the Echo Park–based AM station with a fuzzy signal that was the first in the world to play a primarily hip-hop format. He and his Wreckin' Cru colleague DJ Yella created drive-time "traffic jam" mixes, and Dre performed at high school "noon dances" for the station, all over the metropolitan area.

While schoolkids slurped milk and ate sandwiches, he played hip-hop and maybe even some Parliament-Funkadelic, working to get them up and out of their seats.

He became a fixture at Eve After Dark, a teenage turntablist who knew what the crowd wanted but wasn't always willing to play it. He pissed off local Bloods by refusing to play the Bar-Kays song "Freak Show on the Dance Floor," said Anthony Williams, a frequent Eve attendee. "The Bloods loved pop-locking to that song," he said, "but he wasn't going to let anyone tell him what to play."

"When I was coming up, to develop my skills I had to do it the hard way," Dre said. "It was basically on the job training."

"He Just Took Everything"

As Andre's professional possibilities expanded, his personal life became rocky. While Lisa Johnson was pregnant with their second daughter he beat her twice, she claimed in a restraining order application filed in California Superior Court on May 7, 1985. The first time, when she was about six months pregnant, he knocked her back, "causing my head to hit the wall," and striking her "several times," reads her complaint, which also says he hit her again when she was about eight months pregnant. (Dr. Dre, through his attorney, had no comment on Johnson's allegations. If Dre filed documents denying claims made in the restraining order, they were not available.)

The birth of La'Toya in September 1984 didn't smooth things over. A few days before Christmas that year, reads the restraining order, he "hit me in the mouth and bust my lip" at Johnson's mother's house. Then one day in April 1985, Andre came calling to her aunt's home in South Central, where she was then living. He had recently turned twenty, and she was pregnant with their third daughter—Andre's fifth child. She said she didn't want to see him anymore because he "was not helping to take care of our daughter," and he then knocked her down twice, states the document. "If it hadn't been for my cousin Nessa he was going to kick me while

I was on the ground," it continues. "Nessa told him to leave me alone. He jump in his car and left and said 'I'll be back again.'"

Johnson's aunt, who asked me not to use her name, to protect her anonymity, recalled this incident as well. "He hit her upside the head, he was kicking her, he called her all kind of names," she said. "I jumped in. I grabbed him and knocked him off of her, and threw him in the rosebush." Less than two weeks later Andre came back, according to the document: "He had a gun, tell me to come out bitch and saying that he would kill me because I didn't know who I was fucking with."

Johnson's allegations against Andre were never ruled upon in court, because she did not file criminal charges. But her aunt helped her apply for a combined child support order and domestic violence restraining order, and on May 29, 1985, Judge Lee B. Ragins ordered Andre to stay at least a hundred yards away from Johnson, and to pay $200 a month child support for each girl.

He ignored both directives, Johnson claimed. "He didn't do any child support, and he did not stop contacting me," she said, adding that he did not contribute financially to the kids' upbringing until a court compelled him to do so in the nineties, after he'd become a major star with N.W.A, and as a solo artist.

"He messed up her whole life. She has not been the same since. She was a beautiful young lady," said Johnson's aunt. "He just took everything that she had."

"I really did love him," Johnson said. "He was somebody that I looked up to because he had a vision, and I saw him struggle with his art that he wanted to do, and I had faith in this guy. I believed everything he told me."

"He struggled getting money for her, for the kids, but none of us had any money," said Marq "Cli-N-Tel" Hawkins, the fourth member of World Class Wreckin' Cru. "There was a point where the music thing just didn't appear to be happening for us."

In her memoir, Andre's mother accuses Johnson of being, at times, an irresponsible mother, and also of "fabricat[ing] stories to get Andre to respond to her."

Three other women would later accuse Andre of beating them, including a mother of one of his other children.

Surgery

Music was Andre's shelter from the chaos overtaking his life. But though he loved hip-hop, it wasn't clear he could make a living doing it. The Los Angeles scene was still in its infancy, and it wasn't yet creating stars like the East Coast. "People back East didn't know much of what was going on in the West," said The Glove. "Back then, they used to call Los Angeles 'Southern.'"

In 1983 Lonzo brought Run-D.M.C. to Eve After Dark. Dr. Dre was inspired by the performance. But the New York group, clad in leather pants, weren't feeling the local Morris Day styles. "They looked at us like we was a bunch of faggots," said Lonzo.

"Some people from the East Coast wouldn't respect nobody at the time," admitted Afrika Bambaataa. He said *he* respected the West, however, and the feeling was mutual. The World Class Wreckin' Cru borrowed pretty obviously from "Planet Rock" on their track "Planet." *We are the pilots of your shuttle, transporters of love*, they intone, over outer-space synth effects.

The group's settled lineup featured four DJs, who could rap to varying degrees, though Lonzo was hindered by a lisp. (Dre's emulation of LL Cool J earned him the nickname "LL Cool Dre.") Their songs tackled a wide variety of themes: "(Horney) Computer" piggybacked on the cybererotic fixation of the era, while "Gang Bang You're Dead" confronted the ascendant gang culture, their colors, their beverages, and their sartorial styles:

> *You wear red rags, blue rags, and big shoelaces*
> *You drink forty-ounce brews by the cases*
> *You dress so tacky 'til you look like a slob*
> *And you wonder why you can't get a job?*

Cli-N-Tel had the idea to do the song after a friend was killed by gang violence; it was cowritten by Lonzo and Dre, and was one of the first songs

Dre rapped on. "Surgery," meanwhile, was his star turn. With breathy vocals, serious scratching, and a synth line beeping like a heart monitor, it features Andre in lothario mode: *The nurses say I'm cute, they say I'm fine / So you better beware because I'll blow your mind.* He was gradually coming out of his shell, growing comfortable on the mic. But he hated the Cru's emasculating song "Lovers," modeled on LL Cool J's "I Need Love." In it, the singer Mona Lisa shoots down each group member in succession. Still, it became hard to argue when it became their biggest early hit. "Dre and DJ Yella didn't want to do any slow records at first," Cli-N-Tel said. "Me and Lonzo convinced them it would be a good thing. Once they saw the reaction from the girls, goin' crazy, they were like, 'Hell yeah!'"

Form Flattering

West Compton native Antoine Carraby's name became synonymous with his prowess on the turntables. Originally known as Bric Hard, at the suggestion of former Cru member the Unknown DJ, the light-skinned, introverted Carraby took his stage name from a 1981 new wave song called "Yella." Obsessed with Prince, DJ Yella wore paisley designs and performed moves straight out of *Purple Rain.* Laid-back, not one to rock the boat, he kept things light.

Andre and Yella loved chasing women together, and the pair complemented each other well musically. After a Kurtis Blow show, that rapper's DJ, Davy DMX, taught Yella to scratch, and Yella in turn taught Dr. Dre. This was a big deal—not many people on the West Coast were yet scratching, and Dre proceeded to run with the style. "Dre was faster on the turntables than Yella," Cli-N-Tel said. "Yella was more of a blender, and Dre did more of the scratching."

The group's home base was Alonzo Williams's South Central home, where the guys recorded, hung out, and practiced their dance moves. "We would watch ourselves in the reflection of the window and look at ourselves rehearse," Lonzo told me in July 2014. We spoke from his studio, an unattached bungalow behind that same house, where he still lives today, formerly owned by famed bandleader Johnny Otis.

Lonzo had big plans for the group, beginning with the release of their 1985 debut *World Class* on his own label, called Kru-Cut. He also crafted their image. They shot the album's cover in a makeshift studio at the Hollywood offices of Macola Records, which pressed up the work. Andre's mother Verna and one of Lonzo's buddies, a tailor, helped create their custom duds. For the shoot Lonzo donned a black sequined jacket and earrings shaped like stars, while Cli-N-Tel wore a purple satin tuxedo jacket with black sequined lapels, and a white dress shirt unbuttoned nearly to his navel. Yella had a similar purple jacket with shoulder pads, as well as white gloves. Dr. Dre's white, form-flattering, sequined surgical-themed outfit was fashioned from a medical supply store smock. A stethoscope hung around his neck.

Makeup was a must for any self-respecting song-and-dance group of the era (to say nothing of the hair metal bands up on the Sunset Strip). World Class Wreckin' Cru had no professional makeup artist, so those duties fell to the act's manager, Shirley Dixon. She powdered their faces to cut the glare and greased their lips to make them shiny. Dre was painted with blush, and finally, for an extra touch, he and DJ Yella got a smidge of eyeliner. This was the Prince influence again. The Purple One had drastically changed the idea of masculinity in pop music. Besides, even acts like Dre's idols Parliament-Funkadelic wore colorful duds and engaged in wild theatrics. "This was the eighties!" defended Lonzo. "You wore a little bit of makeup."

The Cru looked in the mirror, got the OK from Shirley, and were ready to go.

They posed for photos, bathed in purple light, the smoke machine working double time. Some shots were smoldering, some weren't; Dr. Dre, feeling goofy, clowned around in silly positions. He had no idea these pictures would come back to haunt him.

"I'll tell you what. I never had no motherfucking lace on—that was Yella," Dr. Dre later grumbled.

Dre's production skills accelerated rapidly. He and Cli-N-Tel camped out in the studio for days at a time, enlisting others to bring them food or clean clothes.

The Cru's first show was opening for New Edition at Fremont High School, and they began attracting bigger crowds for their live performances, featuring sweaty dance floor numbers and sexy slow jams. When Eve After Dark closed in 1985, Lonzo began hosting parties at a Compton spot called Dooto's. The Cru played there, as well as the adjacent skating rink, Skateland. Lonzo rocked the keytar. Morris Day and the Time's song "The Bird" inspired one of the Cru's synchronized dance routines—complete with slide steps, hip swivels, and birdlike arm flapping. Decked out in doctor suits of powder blue or purple satin, Dre had fun with it, and crowds dug their energy. "We was appealing to the women back then," said DJ Yella.

With Lonzo steering the ship, the glammed-up smooth operators began performing shows around the country, sharing stages with sexified funk and R&B-leaning acts including the Bar-Kays, Oran "Juice" Jones, and Rick James's Mary Jane Girls. They graduated from headlining skating rinks to playing an early hip-hop event called Fresh Fest at the twelve-thousand-capacity Wembley Arena in London. In 1986 they won a record deal with CBS, complete with a $100,000 advance.

Problems quickly emerged. Cli-N-Tel said he looked into the group's financial records and saw irregularities. It was enough to convince him to leave the Cru before their next album, *Rapped in Romance*, released on the CBS subsidiary Epic. Lonzo admitted he took the greatest share of their $100,000 advance—the others couldn't help but notice his new house and BMW—but insisted it was because he was the investor and label owner, and more sensibly managed his earnings.

When *Rapped in Romance* tanked in 1986 they were dropped by CBS. Things looked bleak. Though their independently released 1987 song "Turn Off the Lights" became their biggest hit, the group was already broken up by the time it got popular. Dr. Dre had had enough. It wasn't just about the money; he'd tired of the group's froufrou image and believed their glossy, pandering ballads were out of touch. He wanted to make hard-edged music like Run-D.M.C., or maybe like Ice-T's new song "6 in the Mornin'." But Lonzo wasn't interested; ballads were their bread and butter.

"They wouldn't do my songs," Dre said. "They said they'd never get on the radio."

Dre knew better. Run-D.M.C. slayed at Eve After Dark. Though they only played for about ten minutes, the show affected him profoundly; their hard-edged rhymes and powerful beats showed him that kick-ass hip-hop could thrill a crowd. And he was certain that *he* could do that.

The California Shake

Around 1986, Eric Wright and a drug-dealing associate fell into a dispute. One of Eric's Volkswagen Bugs was burned to a crisp, right in his parents' driveway, so Eric had the guy's own car burned in response. No one remembers why they were beefing—"It was over either money, or girls," said his partner Mark Rucker—but things were getting out of hand. Even Eric's own crew couldn't be trusted. His runner J.D. was dipping into the supply to get high himself. He even stole Eric's radio right out of his car.

Eric grew frustrated. The stash from his gunned-down cousin Horace Butler had run out, and Eric now had to purchase his drugs from other suppliers like anyone else. What once seemed like easy money had become stressful. Others were now gunning for him, hoping to take his spot. "There was always threats on Eric's life," said his friend Bigg A.

Few knew Eric had another passion in life, which he hoped could get him out of the drug game permanently: hip-hop. With his friend MC Ren he'd go shopping for records at the Roadium swap meet. Held on the sprawling Torrance grounds of a former drive-in movie theater, the swap meet featured booths as far as the eye could see, selling everything from laundry detergent to airbrushed T-shirts. Eric and Ren frequented the stall run by Steve Yano, a Japanese-American, onetime psychology grad student who dropped out to sell music. In earlier days he and his wife Susan had thrown disco parties at their house, but their Roadium shop was now frequented by kids looking for the latest jams. Optimally located directly across from the snack bar, the Yanos hung covers like Michael Jackson's

Thriller from their awning, and played hot cassettes to entice kids. While closing up shop at night they'd set their pegboards on the ground, and kids sometimes break-danced or pop-locked right on top of them.

Eric didn't know it then, but some of the tapes the Yanos played were made by Andre Young. Eric had known Dre casually from the neighborhood, but had no idea about his prowess on the turntables, about how he compiled the hottest rap hits of the day on TDK sixty-minute cassettes, adding in his signature scratches. You might hear the Fat Boys, King Tee, or Rob Base & DJ E-Z Rock. In exchange, the Yanos gave Andre records full of "break beats," drum patterns that he could sample in his own songs.

"He would tell Steve: '*This* is gonna be a hit. You gotta push *these* records,'" Susan Yano said. "And he was always right." Eventually, the Yanos began selling these tapes, with names like *'86 in the Mix*, for ten dollars or so, and they became hot sellers themselves. Sure, it wasn't really legal to hock music they didn't own the rights to, but how else was it going to get out there? Most hip-hop came from New York, and almost nobody else local was selling it. The tapes became so popular that rappers begged to be on them, and Dre began recording artists like Tone Lōc and Young MC.

Dre also put his own songs on the tapes, which particularly impressed Eric. "What *is* this?" he asked one day upon hearing a new track. As Steve Yano explained, Eric finally understood: This was his *neighbor's* music. He promptly bought up all of Dre's music that Yano had on offer, pulling a bundle of bills out of his sock.

"Tell Andre I want to get together," Eric said, and asked for Dre's number. Yano eventually agreed to set up a meeting over the phone. "Next thing I know," Yano said, "those guys are on a three-way call with me at two in the morning. Eric wants to open a record store. I tell him, 'Don't do it. It's a bad business. I can show you how, but don't do it.'"

Instead, Yano suggested, they should start a record label.

Eric brewed on the idea. In the meantime, Dre needed a new benefactor. He wanted to make songs that were harder and more visceral, but needed money to record in the studio. He knew two people who might be willing to help him: One was a local drug dealer named Laylaw Good-man, who worked with him on some early songs, including a spooky, Halloween-themed 1985 track called "Monster Rapping," which was pro-duced by Dre and Lonzo, and rapped by Laylaw in his spookiest Bela Lugosi Dracula voice.

The other was Eric. And so he set about convincing him.

The High Powered Crew

After Lonzo upgraded to a BMW, he gave Dr. Dre his old Mazda RX-7. It was a flashy car, and Dre racked up a series of moving violations, which led to a warrant being put out for his arrest, and him being sent to jail.

When Eric found out about the situation, he called up Lonzo. "Dre's in jail," he said. "Give me some money to get him out." Lonzo had been willing to spring Dre from jail before. But on this occasion he was short on funds, and decided to pay his BMW note instead, giving Dre a chance to stew on his own recklessness in the process. Eric decided to bail Dre out himself, and their bond grew. Dre convinced Eric to invest some of his profits into a music venture.

Dre and Eric, both now in their early twenties, began recording tapes in a makeshift studio in the latter's garage, mixing popular instrumen-tal tracks and their own creations. Their collaborators included DJ Pooh, later famous for cowriting the 1995 film *Friday*. "We didn't want to just make mixtapes. We wanted to make the music that wound up on the mix-tapes," DJ Pooh said. Eric's mother kept them lubricated with Kool-Aid.

Dre and Eric began playing house parties, pool parties, and proms together as a mobile DJ team called High Powered Crew. "We came up with the name because we used to keep money in our pockets," said another member, Horace "Mr. Sheen" Taylor, Eric's cousin. Showcasing rappers and playing songs like Run-D.M.C.'s "My Adidas," they per-formed all over south L.A., from Downey to Lakewood, piloting Eric's old, beat-up Ford truck to gigs, which they called the "California Shake" because it wobbled when it went over thirty-five miles per hour. Dre was clearly the star, while Eric, who could DJ a little bit himself, was the operation's financier. He bought the necessary equipment and divvied up the couple hundred dollars they might receive per event.

Not everybody knew what to make of this pairing—the hardened street cat and the flamboyant entertainer. "I thought he was gay because he wore two earrings," said Mark Rucker, of Dr. Dre. "Eric said, 'He's cool, we're going to do this music thing.'"

Eric took stock. All things considered, he was pretty lucky. Unlike so many others who slanged, he was still alive, and not in prison. Horace Butler's fate weighed heavily on him. "I seen that it wasn't really worth it, it wasn't worth my life," Eric said. "I figured I could do something right for a change instead of something wrong."

But he wasn't about to be under someone else's thumb. Like in his drug business, Eric preferred to operate independently. "I figure if I work for my damn self, I could lay my own fucking rules," he said. Dre again brought up the idea of the two of them starting a record label together.

Eric liked the idea, but his dealing partner looked at him like he was crazy. "What you know about music?" Rucker asked. It was a good point. Eric certainly didn't know how to rap. But the skeptical look on his friend's face turned to gratitude when Eric handed him several ounces of crack. They were his to sell, gratis. Eric was done with all that.

It was settled. Eric and Dr. Dre would make a real go of this thing. Still, the picture wasn't yet complete. For that, they'd need to combine forces with a cocksure South Central kid, one who still rode the school bus every day.

CHAPTER THREE

WE'LL PULL YOUR CARD

O'Shea Jackson's grueling daily school bus ride took an hour or more in the morning, and then another hour in the afternoon. Departing from his family's tidy, one-story, midcentury house on Van Wick Street, he'd finally arrive at high school in the San Fernando Valley. When he got home, he'd head down the block to his friend Sir Jinx's place. O'Shea knew things were on and crackin' if the derelict garage door was held up by a broom.

Outside there was a gang war. But inside the garage was a veritable hip-hop paradise. Sir Jinx, an aspiring young producer in oversized glasses whose real name was Tony Wheaton, had turntables, a DJ booth, and a cassette player hooked up to speakers. In woodshop, he'd even made a coffin-shaped box to house his mixing board and record players. Neighborhood turntablists battled. Break-dancers twisted on checkerboard linoleum. Aspiring producers made beats on Sir Jinx's drum machine, although it wasn't very sophisticated—not surprising, considering he'd procured it from a drug dealer friend who received it as payment from a crackhead.

O'Shea and Sir Jinx lived in an unincorporated part of L.A. County, sandwiched between South Central and Inglewood. In the mid-eighties there were setups like Sir Jinx's garage all over South Los Angeles. From a parent's perspective, hip-hop garages were perfect—close enough to keep an eye on their kids, removed enough so they could sleep at night. An up-and-coming DJ named Battlecat operated out of a garage in western South Central. Just blocks from O'Shea's house, his future Westside Connection colleague WC, and WC's brother DJ Crazy Toones hosted kids in their own garage. On nearby Haas Avenue, in DJ FatJack's garage, aspiring turntablists with names like DJ Slip and Rockin' Tom took their parents' disco records and harvested loops for future tracks.

O'Shea was obsessed with the genre. Its breakout hit the Sugarhill Gang's "Rapper's Delight" mesmerized him as a prepubescent in 1979. *What you hear is not a test / I'm rappin' to the beat.* Later, in his Parkman Middle School typing class in ninth grade, O'Shea discussed hip-hop with a classmate named Terry "Kiddo" Hayward.

"Have you ever tried to write a rap?" Kiddo asked him.

O'Shea shook his head.

"Let's try to write one," Kiddo said. "You write one and I'll write one, and we'll see which one comes out the best."

O'Shea thought for a minute and finally came up with: *My name is Ice Cube and I want you to know / I'm not Run-D.M.C. or Kurtis Blow.* It was the first original line he ever rapped.

His moniker was bestowed by his brother Clyde, a mercurial, protective sibling nine years older. Clyde chastised his little brother for trying to talk to his girlfriends when they called. "He got mad at that, he said he was going to slam me in the freezer one day, turn me into an ice cube," O'Shea said in a 2016 interview with *Wired*. "I said, 'You know what? That's a badge of honor.'"

But O'Shea wasn't exactly suave when it came to rapping. Sir Jinx's garage became his training ground. In a variation on the cypher freestyle circles popular in New York—where MCs stood in a circle and rhymed off the top of their heads, one after another—they practiced performing rhymes in measures, rapping four or eight bars at a time. When one guy finished he passed the mic to the next guy; the trick was smooth transition. Those who couldn't keep the beat ate crow.

Graffiti art lined the garage walls—the boys' attempt to replicate the 1984 New York hip-hop movie *Beat Street*. O'Shea and his friends were obsessed with New York acts like the Beastie Boys, Slick Rick, and Run-D.M.C., even borrowing their big glasses and Kangol hats to go with their Adidas pullovers, Troop jackets, and gold chains. The spot was a blast, free of drugs, alcohol, and gangland foolishness. (O'Shea himself admonished those who smoked weed.) So what if it smelled like poop? Jinx's beloved dog Princess had the run of the place, and the guys found themselves hot-stepping over dog shit. It may have been low-rent, but a bubbling caldron of talent passed under that janky garage door, including Candyman, known for his 1990 *Billboard* Top 10 hit "Knockin' Boots."

For his part, O'Shea was quickly developing the skills that would make him into Ice Cube—a master MC who could tear a verse apart and put it back together.

"It was in his soul," said his friend Cli-N-Tel, from World Class Wreckin' Cru. "There was no snarl back then, that came later. But it was his drive, it was his willingness to do whatever to be better."

"He was really good at storytelling," said Doug Young, N.W.A's promoter. "He had subjects; he had predicates. When you listen to Cube rap, you see the story in your head. He paints the picture."

Though Ice Cube spent hours in Sir Jinx's garage, the inspiration for his raps would increasingly come from the volatile world outside those four walls.

The words "South Central" strike fear in some hearts. But making generalizations about the fifty-square-mile section of Los Angeles is difficult, considering the diversity of its people and landscape. The northwestern section includes the historic West Adams neighborhood and the posh Baldwin Hills, also known as the "black Beverly Hills." Central Avenue boasted a world-class jazz scene in the first part of the twentieth century, while Leimert Park is home to Afrocentric stores and creative nonprofits. It's also the former home base for the Good Life Café, whose Project Blowed open-mic night fostered conscious (yet still badass) groups like Freestyle Fellowship and Jurassic 5.

Housing projects abut colorful, squat residences, while rows of run-down blocks are interrupted by houses with fantastically detailed trim and bars on the windows. There are stately churches and sprawling parks, and you'll find lemon and palm trees—some of the latter as big as water towers—sprouting in front yards. There are Latin minimarkets, barbecue spots, Korean liquor stores, and Mexican-run burger stands. Rusted cars sit permanently on lawns. You can shop at swap meets, independently owned beauty supply stores, moped shops, or out of peoples' garages. Like any poor community, there's a strong secondhand economy.

Realtors working north of Interstate 10 obsessively rename neighborhoods to make them sound appealing. The Los Angeles area I lived in for a time was known alternately as Mid-City, Miracle Mile, mid-Wilshire, and even Picfair Village. But Ice Cube's area was broken down by gang turf, not nicknames. The block of Van Wick Street where he grew up was controlled by the 111 Neighbor Hood Crips, so named for West 111th Street, two blocks to the south. (The gang is also known as N-Hood.) But if you jogged farther south, past Imperial Highway, you were into 115 Neighbor Hood Crips territory. Other Crip subsets were nearby, each carving up areas of maybe ten square blocks or more.

Gangbangers would come right up to you and ask where you were from—and if they didn't like the answer, they'd pound you. You didn't have to *be* a Crip to get your ass kicked for living in a Crip neighborhood. Which is why kids from Cube's block didn't often cross nearby South Van Ness Avenue, into Bloods territory. Even young kids couldn't claim ignorance for long. As a second grader, Sir Jinx remembered plopping down on the bus one day when a girl asked him his "set." "Set?" he said. "What's that?" He found out soon enough.

Still, populated by many gainfully employed residents, Cube and Jinx's street—where, on a clear day, you could see the Hollywood sign—wasn't so bad, at least comparatively. Dane Webb, the former *Rap Pages* editor, described it as "a gang-infested neighborhood, but more upper-crust blue collar, though not 'pinkie-out' upper crust."

"This look like a nice neighborhood, but when it get dark, that's when you hear the gunshots," Cube said. He added that during his childhood his own home was shot up: "There were shells that the police had to pick up, right in the grass."

Juice

Cube was a short, well-built, natural athlete, a standout in both basketball and football. He and his friends played "sideline rack 'em up" football in the street, pitting their section of Van Wick against other local blocks— two-hand touch, though players could knock you out of bounds onto the grass behind the curbs, or even into cars. Cube played in the local Pop Warner league as well, serving as outside linebacker and fullback. His brother Clyde had another nickname for him: "Juice," because his initials, O.J., were the same as retired NFL star O. J. Simpson.

The youngest of four, O'Shea grew up in a close-knit family, and when he came of age his parents bought him a Volkswagen Bug, the trendy car at the time. His parents worked at UCLA, his mother Doris as a custodian and his father Hosea a groundskeeper. Squat, no-nonsense Hosea had a garage full of tools and maintenance equipment, and cut the grass for many in the neighborhood.

Hosea taught Cube to be a leader, he said, while Clyde convinced him gangs were a waste of time. "My brother had been through all that shit so he was like, 'Man, you don't have to do that,'" Cube told *Bomb* magazine in 1993. "It's a trip because I look at muthafuckas from N-Hood now who are killers. I wonder if I didn't have that family structure how I would have turned out."

Cube took his lumps along with everybody else. But sometimes it got much worse. On June 29, 1981, when Cube was twelve, his half-sister Beverly Jean Brown, Hosea's daughter from a previous relationship, was slain by her husband in a botched murder-suicide. Beverly was twenty-two, beautiful, and in the prime of life. She and her husband Carl Clifford Brown had been married for less than two years. According to a *Los Angeles Times* report, following a "domestic dispute" Brown took Beverly hostage inside of their South Central home, on West Fifty-Third Street. "Officers who surrounded the house said they heard muffled shots but continued trying to contact Brown by loudspeaker and telephone. A special weapons and tactics team entered the house after midnight to find Brown wounded and his wife dead." Brown himself died on July 27, 1981, less than a month later.

"He was a wannabe cop," Cube said. "He started out for the LAPD and didn't make it, then went into this depression." Brown was an Air Force sergeant during the final year of the Vietnam War, and then for three more years afterward. According to public records, he and Beverly left behind a young son, only a year and a half old.

In 1970, a judge ruled that the Los Angeles Unified School District was guilty of segregation, and ordered it to fix the problem. In the early eighties, Cube was enrolled in the desegregation busing program and sent to the San Fernando Valley, starting with junior high. His neighborhood schools were problematic; the nearest high school, Washington Preparatory, was a Crips stronghold. William Howard Taft High School, by contrast, was a distant, almost inconceivable place, with eucalyptus trees and retro-futuristic architecture. Boasting a mammoth outdoor sports complex, it borders multimillion-dollar homes, but has also suffered shootings over the years. Sir Jinx briefly went there as well, and described it as a "celebrity school" for rich kids, who pulled up in Porsches. It counts Justine Bateman, Lisa Kudrow, and members of House of Pain as alumni.

Cube was a good student who got As and Bs. He played fullback on the football team, along with his friend T-Bone, a tailback. But music was his real focus. He and Sir Jinx formed a group along with their friends Darrell Johnson (known as K-Dee, for Kid Disaster) and Barry Severe. Severe was dating Cube's sister Patricia. Older with a car, he could drive them to a studio to lay down professional-sounding tracks. They called themselves the Stereo Crew; it was a way to unify themselves, not as gangbangers, but as entertainers. K-Dee said that Cube's first rapping name was Purple Ice, paying homage to both Ice-T and Prince.

Their tracks were unpolished. Severe, now a Sacramento-based parole agent, shared with me three very rare Stereo Crew songs from the early eighties. "They sound so dated," he warned, and indeed they have the clunky drum machines, robotic vocals, and simple scratching common in early L.A. hip-hop. (Not to mention some bizarre squealing guitar solos.) "Bust It Up" is nearly six and a half minutes long. Cube is introduced by the other group members: *The Ice is frozen, the Cube is fire / You will drop as he gets higher.*

But Cube seemed to know what he was doing from the jump, and comes out swinging on a track called "To Reach the Top": *I never use a gun, or a knife / And I'll be at the top for the rest of my life.* He raps quickly and cleanly in his high, prepubescent voice. Even more compelling is the antiviolence anthem "Gangs," which castigates hooligans for robbing old ladies and for not snitching on shooters. Cube's verse is the highlight. In forty-five seconds flat he spins a tragic tale about a .44-toting gang member whose civilian friend is gunned down in a drive-by. The gangster responds by killing the perpetrators, and is sentenced to the electric chair. It's a classic Cube morality tale, somewhat mirroring his role in the film *Boyz n the Hood.*

When you're a teenager, strong convictions come and go. Still, considering the explosive, streetwise material they'd soon produce as N.W.A, it's striking that Cube *and* Dre were disparaging gangs in some of their earliest recordings.

Ice Cube and Dr. Dre linked up after they happened to find themselves living on the same street. Sir Jinx's uncle, Curtis Crayon, was Dr. Dre's stepfather. Dre and his mother Verna would often squabble; she wanted him either in school or working, and low-paid DJ gigs didn't qualify. She kicked him out, and so he moved into his younger cousin Sir Jinx's house.

Cube and his buddies in Stereo Crew were thrilled to have an emerging star on their block, considering World Class Wreckin' Cru's song "Surgery" was building Dr. Dre's name locally. The Stereo Crew members wanted desperately to work with him, but initially Dre wasn't too keen on this rowdy little group. "Man, I don't want to fuck with them," he said. "That's my cousin. He's getting on my nerves."

Eventually Dre gave in and agreed to watch Stereo Crew perform in the garage. He was impressed, especially with Cube, whose talent was undeniable even at age fifteen. Dre and Cube quickly became tight, seeing rap shows, cruising down Crenshaw, hitting the roller coasters at Magic Mountain, or just picking up girls. Despite their age difference—Dre is more than four years older—they had plenty in common, even beyond music. They were both interested in architectural drafting, hated gangs, and, on a deeper level, had experienced the death of a sibling. "I used to ditch school and run around the corner. He'd pick me up," Cube said. "I'd roll with him the whole day, hanging." Even today, when they're together, Cube sometimes seems like Dre's little brother.

Around this time the radio station KDAY sponsored a rap competition, called Best Rapper in the West, with the winner to receive a record deal. Performing in front of judges, Stereo Crew's rhymes killed the competition in the early rounds. But in the finals, held at the Hollywood Palladium, they were foiled by a technical glitch: The DJ cued up their cassette at the wrong spot. "Cube got pissed and went over to the DJ and said, 'What are you doing? You fucking our show up!'" Severe remembered, which probably poisoned the well with the judges. They won second place.

Fortunately the group already had a label connection, Alonzo Williams, whom they'd gotten to know through Dre. Lonzo helped them get a one-song deal with Epic Records, and he and Dre coproduced the track, called "She's a Skag," which came out in 1986. Though largely forgettable, the song has some funny lines. Cube ridicules the object of his desire—the skag, aka a skanky girl—because she refuses his advances. *I said, "I'm Ice Cube from the Stereo Crew,"* he raps. *She looked at her friend and they both said "Who?"*

Cli-N-Tel left World Class Wreckin' Cru before their 1986 album *Rapped in Romance*, at which time Barry Severe took his place. He called himself Master B, but Dr. Dre thought "Shakespeare, the Poet of Love" was a swankier name for a member of their cast of heartthrobs. The remaining Stereo Crew members rechristened themselves C.I.A. At first it stood for "Criminals in Action," but they later softened it to "Cru' in Action." They put out a three-track album on Alonzo Williams's label in 1987. Their Beastie Boys influence was particularly strong—"Ill-Legal" clearly emulates *Licensed to Ill*. They also did parody raps of popular records, turning Run-D.M.C.'s "My Adidas" into "My Penis," and the "Pee-Wee Herman" into the "VD Sermon," the latter a humorous tale of sexually transmitted disease that became a crowd favorite.

In the period directly before gangsta rap, parody raps were all the rage. Compton artist Toddy Tee turned Whodini's "The Freaks Come Out at Night" into "The Clucks Come Out at Night." (Clucks being crackheads, of course.) His hit song "Batteram" served as social commentary on Daryl Gates's preferred urban warfare tool, but it was also a play on rapper Shawn Brown's "Rappin' Duke," itself a sort of hip-hop parody that imagined John Wayne rapping. Notorious B.I.G. references it in "Juicy": *Remember "Rappin' Duke," duh-ha, duh-ha?*

Any radio jock worth his salt made funny versions of radio hits. KDAY morning show DJ Russ Parr's group Bobby Jimmy & the Critters turned Timex Social Club's "Rumors" (*Look at all these rumors / Surrounding me every day*) into "Roaches" (*Look at all these roaches / Around me every day*). The parody craze was surely propelled by the success of Weird Al Yankovic, who debuted in 1983 with songs like "I Love Rocky Road" and "Another One Rides the Bus." Yankovic, after all, grew up in Lynwood, which borders Compton to the north.

It was a kinder, gentler time for hip-hop on the West Coast, and Ice Cube was as goofy as everyone else. That is, until he flipped the script.

Skateland

Roller rinks have long been critical incubators of inner-city music culture. They offer not just good, clean fun and a sugar buzz for knobby-kneed kids, but serve as starter nightclubs for coeds too young to drink. Miami bass DJs including southern rap progenitor Luke Campbell, known for his work with 2 Live Crew, spun records for teens at roller rinks in the eighties. Three 6 Mafia got down at a Memphis rink called Crystal Palace, and rapper Nelly and his group the St. Lunatics first recorded at one called Saints. The reality-inspired coming-of-age film *ATL* features rapper T.I. rolling at Atlanta rink Cascade.

Two skate parks were critical to 1980s Los Angeles hip-hop. The first, Mid-City's World on Wheels, was populated by Crips. The carpet was stained with candy and soda, and images of roller skates with wings graced the walls. As for the hardwood, it glistened. "Jheri curl was popular, and it got so hot in here that by the end of the night the floors would be wet," said Greg Mack, the KDAY programmer. At World on Wheels his Mixmasters DJ crew spun records for live broadcast, transmitting using a specially rigged phone line connection.

Compton's answer was Skateland U.S.A., a cavernous spot that could hold up to two thousand kids for parties or concerts. Skateland was Compton's first roller rink, opening in 1984 after a father-son real estate development team took over a 40,000-square-foot bowling alley that had been burned, stripped of its copper wiring and plumbing, and left with holes in its roof. "The smell of mold was so thick you could cut it with a knife," said owner Craig Schweisinger. He purchased the property dirt cheap with his father. The younger Schweisinger eventually earned the nickname "Craziest White Man in Compton," at least partly owing to the fact that Skateland was housed near West Piru Street, smack dab in the center of Bloods' stomping ground. Events were awash in a sea of red pants and hats; you would rarely see people wearing blue.

"There was one way in and one way out," remembered Sir Jinx. "When you come out, the Bloods lined up, and if they didn't like the way you looked, they would beat the shit out of you."

Schweisinger and his father nonetheless had an altruistic vision for the local kids. They restored the facility, installing a 17,000-square-foot hard maple floor. Once it opened, Skateland attendees had to pass through a pair of metal detectors, which kept the guns out, though they still caught kids with "box cutters, razor knifes, and surgical scissors," Schweisinger said. For a particularly bananas Eric B concert they crammed in 2,600 people, arming a pair of security guards with Uzis. This drew rebuke from the fire and police departments; the latter sent a helicopter and canines.

Dre performed with World Class Wreckin' Cru at the roller rink's grand opening in 1984, and he became a regular there, playing dominoes with DJ Yella and Eric Wright after hours in the snack bar. They worked on their lyrics and practiced in the DJ booth, with Schweisinger warning them not to spill their E&J brandy and Pepsi cocktails on the mixing board.

Dr. Dre and Ice Cube also played an early show at Skateland together, with the former warning the latter that its attendees wouldn't tolerate mediocrity. "I would tell him that with this crowd you'd better get up and rock, because if you didn't, they'd throw these full cups at your ass," Dr. Dre said. They performed dirty parody songs, turning Salt-N-Pepa's "I'll Take Your Man" into "I'll Fuck Your Friend." Dre scratched, while Cube rapped, including an early version of "Gangsta Gangsta."

"It was a rough crowd," Cube said. "I wasn't sure what we had created was gonna work." Despite their trepidation, Skateland loved their act and were riding on every punch line, he added.

The Wreckin' Cru enlisted Cube to help them write tracks, including "Cabbage Patch," which harvested a national dance craze referencing the pudgy-faced dolls. But by 1986 Cube, now seventeen, and Dre, twenty-one, were tiring of novelty songs. Their talents were quickly outstripping their groups.

CHAPTER FOUR

OG

Though he's known today as a gritty West Coast rap pioneer, before he was Ice-T, Tracy Marrow was raised in the well-to-do New Jersey suburb of Summit. In the span of four years both Marrow's parents died of heart attacks, and so during junior high, at the dawn of the seventies, he was sent to live with his dad's sister in View Park, a middle-class part of South Central. But he attended the combustible Crenshaw High School, which, in the early days of gangbanging, featured both the Hoover Crips and their rivals in red called the Brims, who were later enveloped into the Bloods.

"The Crips kept their rag in the left pocket; the Crips pierced their left ear. The Brims did everything in the right. Like a mirror image," Ice-T wrote in his memoir *Ice*. But before long, members of other gangs started transferring, and soon anyone who attended Crenshaw—whether or not they were even *in* a gang—was assumed to represent the Crips, and thus eligible for beat-downs from rivals. Ice-T said West Side Crips leader Stanley "Tookie" Williams sometimes dropped by Crenshaw with his equally muscle-bound comrade Jimel Barnes. "Most days, they dressed identically in farmer overalls with the bib down, showing off their bare chests, shoulders, and arms," Ice-T wrote, adding that, at house parties, they were trailed by young Crips who rubbed baby oil on their muscles, to impress the girls.

Ice-T never formally joined the Crips, but hung around with members he got to know through his girlfriend, who lived in a Hoover Crip neighborhood. Like so many others, he got caught up in gangs' primary appeal: affection. "My aunt never said she loved me," he wrote. "My mother and father were never big on that word. You get to Crenshaw, and you got a male friend saying, 'Cuz, ain't nothin' never fin' to happen to you, homie. You safe, cuz. I *love* you.'"

At age seventeen he moved out of his aunt's home. She agreed to give him the $250 monthly Social Security checks she'd been receiving on his behalf, which gave him enough for a cheap apartment and cans of Chef Boyardee. Before graduating he got his tenth-grade girlfriend pregnant, and he decided to join the army, where he spent four years, serving in Hawaii and becoming an M60 gunner. Upon his release he turned to crime—stealing jewelry, Rolexes, Gucci bags, as well as Pontiacs in which to complete such "licks." As his partners started getting serious prison time, his interest in hip-hop began paying off.

He'd already penned numerous "Crip rhymes," tales of intimidation and triumph performed aloud in front of friends like poems, rather than being set to music:

He said "Fuck a Crip nigga—this is Brim!"
So we pulled out the Roscoe, Roscoe said crack
I looked again the nigga was shootin' back

The pimp turned bestselling writer Iceberg Slim inspired Ice-T's stage name. He and his crew would show up at clubs and "buy the mic," giving the DJ $500 so he could rap all night. After being discovered in 1983 while rapping to impress girls at a beauty parlor called Good Fred—where he got his perm—he agreed to make a single called "The Coldest Rap," spitting all the rhymes he knew at the time. It paid about $250, sold well locally, and enchanted the hip denizens of MacArthur Park underground club Radio. There DJs like The Glove and Egyptian Lover and pop-lockers like Lil' Coco and Boogaloo Shrimp held sway. The spot was the height of trendiness—you couldn't buy booze, but could bring your own in—and it hosted the Cold Crush Brothers, and even Madonna. "Madonna drew us up on stage into her show, was trying to undress us and shit," The Glove said.

The white kids at The Radio knew every word of "The Coldest Rap" by the time Ice-T performed there. He became the club's house MC, pulling up each weekend in his criminally funded Porsche, and appearing in 1984's breakdance-sploitation film *Breakin'*, which was inspired by the venue. In the rather corny film, the Mary Lou Retton–esque lead teams up with street toughs outfitted in studded belts, chains, and spiked wristbands. Following *Breakin'* the club moved to a different venue downtown, and became known as Radiotron.

Another good-vibes spot was Leimert Park's I Fresh, a "rap workshop" partly funded by a state grant. Running from 1984 to 1989, it allowed young MCs to hone their crafts, including South Central rapper Yo-Yo, whose high school English teacher turned her on to the program and who would go on to record with Ice Cube. "She was really good on her feet, bubbly and really creative, right at the tip of her fingers," said I Fresh organizer Ben Caldwell. (Not encouraged, however, was Eazy-E, who refused to capitulate to Caldwell's demands to jettison his misogynist lyrics.) I Fresh later morphed into the famed weekly open-mic session held at the nearby Good Life Café, which spawned the Project Blowed sessions.

Before things got gangsta, I Fresh and Radio characterized an optimistic era in Los Angeles when racially and socioeconomically mixed groups of kids got down together. Even New York's king hip-hop impresario Afrika Bambaataa was impressed with the L.A. scene. "It brought together punk rockers, new wavers, hip-hoppers," he said. "You could hear funk, reggae, all up in one club. It was like George Clinton said, 'One nation under a groove.'"

As for Ice-T, by now he'd developed something of an identity crisis. In the early eighties he wore then-fashionable tight leather getups, spikes, and biker gloves, patterned after New York artists like Melle Mel, from the Furious Five. His early songs weren't very tough.

But one day, while he and his friend Randy Mack were jamming to the Beastie Boys' song "Hold It Now, Hit It," Mack made a bold suggestion.

Ice-T should abandon the "costume" and rap about the real-life details of his recently cast off criminal lifestyle. The resulting landmark 1986 song "6 in the Mornin'" embraced what was happening on the streets of South Central. Named for the LAPD's early-hours battering ram raids, the song's protagonist flees the police, beats women, and mows down adversaries. It soon became a local hit.

Gangster Boogie

The poet and spoken-word performer Gil Scott-Heron, best known for "The Revolution Will Not Be Televised," was undoubtedly influential on early hip-hop, as were politically minded spoken-word groups like The Last Poets and the Watts Prophets. But much of early rap was bawdy entertainment, influenced by the pimpadelic black comedy tradition, which included Rudy Ray Moore's dirty-joke-telling character Dolemite, as well as the proudly scatological comedian and musician Blowfly. You can also see the influence of traditional African-American arts like the insult game the dozens, and toasting, which features braggadocious rhyming stories of a character's exploits.

As the seventies turned into the eighties, disco, raunchy comedy records, and rap all began to merge, and it can be hard to tell the difference. In this vein, an argument could be made that the first West Coast gangsta rap song is an obscure 1980 track called "Badd Mann Dann Rapp," a tale of crazed sex, homosexuality, prostitution, and violence. Its singsongy rap is performed by King Monkey, the alias of comedian Jimmy Thompson.

But it, like most early hip-hop, lacked the hard, percussion-driven sound we came to associate with rap. That would dominate after Run-D.M.C. helped change things with their 1983 song "Sucker MCs," which popularized a sparse, drum machine beat that sounded great out of boomboxes. Run-D.M.C. weren't gangsta rappers, but they influenced the man credited with launching the gangsta sound, Philadelphia's Schoolly D. Born Jesse Bonds Weaver Jr., he was raised in West Philadelphia as one of nine kids, and witnessed a pair of murders growing up. An intimidating presence, he wrote, performed, and pressed up his own records, once brandishing a firearm at a record plant employee he accused of bootlegging his work. The protagonist of his 1984 track "Gangster Boogie" deals weed, macks the ladies, and flashes his 8 mm at a would-be jacker. But the song Schoolly D released the next year, called "P.S.K. What Does It Mean?," is considered the first gangsta rap song. "P.S.K." shouts out Schoolly D's neighborhood gang, Parkside Killers, and follows the exploits of a local troublemaker who's driving around town, smoking weed, and drinking beer.

> *Got to the place, and who did I see*
> *A sucker-ass nigga tryin' to sound like me*
> *Put my pistol up against his head*
> *And said, "You sucker-ass nigga I should shoot you dead"*

Schoolly D didn't initially feature such strong language in his songs, but began gaining attention for his music when he "started talking the way people talk on the streets," he said. "P.S.K." became a phenomenon; it's got an eerie lo-fi quality, with huge drums and vicious scratching reverberating as if throughout a cavernous hall. "My jaw dropped," wrote Ice-T, about the first time he heard it. "I turned to my homey and said, 'Yo, this shit is so dusted!' It sounded different than regular hip-hop. It sounded like you were high."

"P.S.K." inspired Ice-T's "6 in the Mornin'," which sounds even more like the tough hip-hop to come. Produced by the Unknown DJ, an enigmatic early World Class Wreckin' Cru member who refused to let anyone take his picture, it succeeds through its details: our hero's squeaking Adidas, his plush truck, his associate's chiming pager, the march of the battering ram.

> *Got a knot in my pocket, weighing at least a grand*
> *Gold on my neck, my pistol's close at hand*
> *I'm a self-made monster of the city streets*
> *Remotely controlled by hard hip-hop beats*

"I rap about what I know," Ice-T said in 1986. "If I grew up in a nice neighborhood, and lived in a half-million-dollar house, I'd be rapping about gold silverware and maids. But I didn't, I grew up in South Central L.A." At the time he recorded "6 in the Mornin'" Ice-T actually was living in Hollywood, but he remained Adidas-clad, thin, and a bit paranoid, with submachine guns hanging on his apartment wall as a form of decoration.

The song was a revelation. When Ice-T performed it at a South Bronx movie house in 1986, it even went over like gangbusters with New York kingmakers Rakim and KRS-One. "It shocked people when he said: *We beat the bitch down in the goddamn street*," said Afrika Islam, another Ice-T producer. "Back then, people didn't associate Los Angeles with 'hood stories. We thought it was all Hollywood and Malibu Beach." Ice-T would be the first rapper signed to Sire Records, Madonna's label.

Meanwhile, in 1987 KRS-One, Scott La Rock, and D-Nice—together Boogie Down Productions—released an early classic gangsta album, *Criminal Minded*. It featured "The Bridge Is Over," championing their home turf of the South Bronx as the birthplace of hip-hop and dissing Queensbridge rapper MC Shan and his Juice Crew. Other artists from the era also get credit for pushing the boundaries of what could be said on record, like New York rapper Just-Ice, known for his 1986 track "Gangster of Hip Hop," and Oakland rapper Too $hort, whose "Freaky Tales" is a pimp-influenced 1987 account of an insatiable harem. In Los Angeles, Compton impresario Mixmaster Spade was an early archetype for Eric Wright, both as a musician and a businessman.

Led by songs like "P.S.K." and "6 in the Mornin'," street-centric hip-hop was emerging as a plausible alternative to soft electro, and the new sound did not escape the notice of Ice Cube, Dr. Dre, and Eric. "These were the only records we were playing, because they were saying things we could relate to," said Dre.

Tired of all the bland crooning and wimpy party raps on the radio, he and Eric wanted to use the language of the streets to tell tales as rough and wild as their daily life. In 1986 they started getting together at Lonzo's house, often accompanied by a songwriter named Laylaw Goodman—the other moneyman Dre had linked up with to help get his music made. He was known simply as Laylaw, a real street dude with cash to spare, owing to his other profession, the drug business. (Eric, in fact, sometimes obtained dope on consignment from him.) Cube also came with Dre to Lonzo's house, and he and Eric began getting to know each other.

One day Dre played the guys his latest track. It featured a pared down, menacing beat with 808 bass and a long, electro fade-out. But there was also something gleeful and sadistic about it, a high-pitched keyboard riff that was immediately catchy. "What Dre wanted to do," wrote *Los Angeles Times'* Jonathan Gold, who interviewed him in this era, "was to create a signature, a sound so distinctive that he'd always know when people were bumping one of his tracks in their cars."

Cube insisted he had the perfect song for the beat, hard-edged like Eazy was interested in for his label. Called "The Boyz-N-The Hood," it was an epic tale modeled after "6 in the Mornin'." The song's young protagonist is drunk on malt liquor, prone to slapping girlfriends and murdering thieves. Its local references include the character's ride (*I pulled up in my '64 Impala*) and preferred malt liquor (*From the 8 Ball my breath starts stinkin'*), and even the local paper (*Little did he know I had a loaded twelve gauge / One sucker dead,* L.A. Times *front page*). "Now *that's* the way I want the lyrics to sound," said Eric, who added some personal touches to the track, like a verse about his old drug runner J.D., who started smoking crack and stole Eric's radio: *The boy J.D. was a friend of mine / 'Til I caught him in my car trying to steal an Alpine.* Cube recorded a demo version of himself rapping over Dre's beat, which Eric listened to on repeat while driving around in his Jeep.

Eric paid Cube a couple hundred dollars for the song, and then later, when it was blowing up, a Suzuki Sidekick. Their business arrangement was incredibly informal, which would later cause tension. But at the time Cube didn't feel exploited. In fact, by not signing any paperwork, he unknowingly insulated himself. "I never signed my publishing away," he said.

"You Turned This Dude into a Rapper"

Dre met a group called H.B.O., aka Home Boys Only, who were from New York, but in 1986 were staying for a time in Southern California.

They had a Run-D.M.C. vibe, and he agreed to record them. But upon arriving to Lonzo's studio, they didn't stick around for long. Their main historic claim to fame nowadays is that they *passed* on "The Boyz-N-The Hood." "They was like, 'Yo, man, we ain't doing that song, that's a West Coast record,'" Dre said.

"They was like, what are you talking about? What's a 'six-four'?" Cube said.

Having already booked the studio time, Dre and Eric weren't sure what to do. Dre suggested Eric rap the song; he'd memorized Cube's version, after all, and the song was more like his life than anyone else's. He was already a street cat, so why not play one on record? But Eric was timid. "Put your glasses on, cut the lights down," said Dre, motioning to Eric's sunglasses. "Just do it."

Eric gave it a go, but he clearly didn't know what he was doing. His delivery was clunky, his cadence and timing a disaster. But Dre was patient, taking the time to "punch in" each line. He'd have Eric rap a short bit—*Cruising down the street in my '64*—rewind the tape, perform it again, and then stitch together the best takes. It took eight or nine hours, but was worth the wait. Dre's genius was recognizing that, for all his faults, Eric had the goods to be a memorable rapper: a unique voice. Indeed, Eric's squeaky instrument turned out to be both terrifying and calming, foreign and immediately recognizable.

"I looked at Dre in amazement, like: 'You turned this dude into a rapper,'" said Cube.

Still, "Boyz" wasn't an immediate success. They weren't sure at first how to promote it; some doubted it would work at all. A rapper who ran in their circles named MC Chip remembers being shocked after hearing it for the first time, what with all the cursing. "You're thinking, like, 'Damn, how's he gonna get radio play?'"

They would worry about that later. For the time being, now that he was a rapper, Eric needed a rap name. The genesis of the moniker Eazy-E is a bit unclear, but he started using it around this time. Cube says they conceived it at the studio—"It sounded cool and it really described him."

Eazy's childhood friend Bigg A says a pair of music industry brothers (he can't remember their names) gave it to him. "He would sit in their office chair, and they said, 'You really take life easy, you're an easy kind of guy,'" Bigg A said. J-Dee from Da Lench Mob speculates Eazy may have gotten it from the 1984 song "Big Mouth," by Whodini, of whom Eazy was a fan. The track concerns a rumor that has been spread around town:

> *Pam was overheard talkin' to her man*
> *Pam told Cookie what she thought she heard*
> *And somehow Eazy-E had got the word*

Whatever the case, on his very first attempt, he'd made rap history. "The line *Cruising down the street in my '64* created gangsta rap," said Terrence "Punch" Henderson, the president of the label responsible for Kendrick Lamar.

Macola

"I was very blue-eyed," Don Macmillan said. "I trusted everybody."

Perhaps that's why in 1986 he welcomed a Compton drug dealer to Macola, his record-pressing plant. The first thing Macmillan, then in his fifties, noticed about Eazy-E, three decades his junior, was how short he was. Then he realized that the room had emptied out; the other artists who were there to talk business had suddenly vanished.

"He's dangerous," someone told him later.

"You don't even want to talk to him," said someone else. "This guy will shoot you if he looks at you!"

Don himself found Eazy exceedingly pleasant, and in any case Eazy was there on legitimate business: He wanted "The Boyz-N-The Hood" pressed up.

Macmillan was an unlikely hip-hop champion. Born in Victoria, British Columbia, as a young man he drove a tugboat along the Pacific coast, pulling oil and gas barges to service logging camps and villages. He arrived in Los Angeles in 1960, but by the time Eazy-E came knocking he was a white-haired family man who lived in suburban Palos Verdes Estates and enjoyed golf.

Don had developed ties with the black music community in the sixties and seventies while working at a vinyl-pressing plant called Cadet on South Normandie Avenue. The South Central spot made records for artists like Ike & Tina Turner, Etta James, and BB King. In 1983 after Cadet folded, Macmillan bought Macola during a fire sale, and brought with him some of Cadet's artists and employees. Though compact discs would soon take off, cassettes and vinyl still had a bit more life in them. Macmillan and his employees tended to vinyl presses and shrink-wrapping machines in the small, bare-bones plant on a dodgy stretch of Santa Monica Boulevard in Hollywood that they shared with gangs and male prostitutes.

The cluttered plant had ashtrays strewn about and cardboard boxes everywhere—records going out, records being returned. Wearing slacks and a collared sports shirt, a cigarette on his lips, Don gave artists a certain amount of time to collect their records that hadn't sold. But if they didn't, beware: That vinyl was headed straight to the grinder to be pressed into something else.

By the mid-eighties Macola was doing great business with self-starting black artists from south of downtown. What made Macola perfect for their needs was that it was a printing plant, record label, and distributor all in one. Why wait for a major record label to discover you, when you could get your own professional-looking album on the cheap? A thousand dollars got you five hundred records, with Macmillan taking a percentage of sales in exchange for distribution. It was a fair trade: Macmillan had connections with record store–supplying distribution networks around the country (including with Memphis-based Select-O-Hits, whose co-owner Johnny Phillips's uncle Sam discovered Elvis), and so a rapper could bring in his music one day and, quite possibly, have a hit on his hands soon after. "Macola was an open-door policy," said Macola promoter Ray Kennedy. "A lot of people were coming in who normally wouldn't get a chance."

Macmillan's somewhat ad hoc business model hit pay dirt with Greg Broussard, aka DJ Egyptian Lover, a breakout star from Uncle Jamm's Army, the popular L.A. DJ crew who already had their own Macola vinyl, "Dial-A-Freak." Broussard came in to press up his robotic twelve-inch 1984 record "Egypt, Egypt," and returned for five hundred more copies, and then five hundred more. He was selling them himself—out of his car's trunk, at swap meets, wherever—and Don asked to get in on the action, seeding the work through his distribution channels. For Egyptian Lover's full-length *On the Nile* album shoot, Macmillan "costumed Broussard and rented the necessary Egyptian memorabilia," according to a news account, which is hilarious to imagine.

Macmillan soon took his entrepreneurship to the next level by signing 2 Live Crew, then a Riverside, California-based trio of air force reservemen riding the electro wave. Their Macola single "The Revelation/2 Live" gained popularity in South Florida, and so at the invitation of a DJ named Luke Campbell, they performed in Miami and eventually moved there. After Campbell joined the group himself and raunchily recast their image, they broke nationally, going on to define the southern rap sound and soundtrack countless hot tub parties.

Macola eventually released records from a who's who of important California artists, including MC Hammer, Too $hort, Ice-T, and Digital Underground. Their R&B electro group Timex Social Club broke into *Billboard*'s Top 10 with their song "Rumors." The whole time, Macmillan didn't know the L.A. hip-hop scene from Adam. "He couldn't tell a good record from a bad record, at least as far as rap goes," said Macmillan's lawyer Gerald Weiner. His talent was timing, and he was smart enough to let his distributors and vendors tell him what to push.

Still, some found his business dealings shady. Egyptian Lover, Arabian Prince, Rodger Clayton, and others accused him of "bootlegging" albums—printing up extra copies, selling them secretly, and then keeping the proceeds for himself. "I would imagine Don was selling records out the back door," said Chuck Fassert, marketing and sales manager at Macola. A number of Macmillan's associates added that he had ties with a nefarious crew back east, who helped promote World Class Wreckin' Cru's hit "Turn Off the Lights."

The Cru's Lonzo Williams described getting a call from a man with a New York accent who accused him of improperly licensing "Turn Off the Lights." "He said, 'If you were in New York, they'd find you in the Hudson River.'" (Macmillan denied all impropriety and any associations with intimidations.)

"The idea that Don somehow didn't treat people fairly, it's just BS in my opinion," said his lawyer Gerald Weiner, adding: "I will say that I think his accounting department was abysmal. I think if you asked Don at any one moment how many records he'd sold, he wouldn't know."

When I visited him at his Palos Verdes Estates home in March 2015, Macmillan did not dispute this characterization. Now in his eighties, his memory is fading, and he gets around slowly. His right leg was amputated below the knee after an artery burst. He insists he gave his artists a fair deal, producing old contracts to bolster his case. Eazy-E and rapper Ron-De-Vu, for example, signed a deal for a record containing "The Boyz-N-The Hood," "Fat Girl," and other tracks, which paid them a $1,000 advance. Any proceeds were to be split fifty-fifty after Macola took 15 percent of gross receipts as a distribution fee.

It doesn't sound like a horrible deal, though without strict accounting the terms wouldn't have mattered much. Whatever the case, Macmillan undoubtedly helped push these records out into the world. The successful artists usually left to make millions for other labels.

"He was a really nice guy," said Doug Young, a record promoter who had an office at the Macola plant, "that I think was in over his head."

Ruthless

Using his drug-dealing profits, Eazy had ten thousand twelve-inch vinyl copies of "Boyz" pressed up at Macola in early 1987. The vinyl listed his parents' home address on South Muriel Drive, and credited Eazy's new label, Ruthless Records. I've been told the imprint was originally going to be called Rockhouse Records—another name for a dope house. But rapper Yomo, who later signed to Ruthless along with a partner named Maulkie, takes credit for its ultimate moniker, which he said he came up with after seeing a newspaper ad for Danny DeVito and Bette Midler's 1986 movie *Ruthless People*.

Eazy and his crew brought stacks of "Boyz" to record stores and swap meets. On weekends they handed out free cassettes on Crenshaw Boulevard, the spot where kids showed off their lowriders. The buzz was palpable, but reports about its initial sales vary. I've read it sold as many as 200,000 copies in its first months, but no one really knows. One important champion was a local white woman, a hip-hop enthusiast in her early thirties named Violet Brown. She was the director of urban music at Wherehouse Records, a chain with some 1,600 stores at the height of its popularity. Under her direction Wherehouse was the first major retailer to stock "Boyz." "You knew by listening to it what would happen with the record. It caught fire very quick," she said.

She put Eazy's music in stores nationwide. This was rare at the time for West Coast acts, but that was changing. Los Angeles upstart label Delicious Vinyl kicked off in 1987 and soon hit with baritone rapper Tone Lōc, a former gang member turned pop rapper with hits like "Wild Thing" and "Funky Cold Medina." They also had Young MC, a Queens-reared USC grad with smart, inoffensive tracks like "Bust a Move."

These acts got play on KDAY, another crucial outlet for "Boyz." KDAY was the little station that could, broadcasting a muddy AM signal from six towers on a hill between Echo Park and Silver Lake. With call letters likely derived from its strictly daytime broadcast license upon its 1956 birth, it featured personalities such as Alan Freed and Art Laboe in its early, Top 40 days. Since its signal shot straight into South Central, it began playing black artists, and even featured "Rapper's Delight" when it came out in 1979. Though KDAY is often described as the first station to play hip-hop twenty-four/seven, it always included R&B in the mix. In fact, a conservative program director took rap out of rotation in the early eighties, and it didn't return in force until the 1983 arrival of Greg Macmillan, originally from Van Alstyne, Texas. Greg called himself Greg Mack and wore cowboy boots. (He reminded Lonzo of Yosemite Sam.) Upon arriving in L.A. he moved to South Central. "All you had to do was listen to the cars driving by and you could hear what people were into," Mack said.

Attempting to jumpstart ratings Mack put rap on heavy rotation, and it worked. Kids adjusted their antennas to pick up the signal, and Mack took his promotional efforts to the streets. He even began rubbing elbows with gangbangers. "I created such a good rapport with these gang guys they would call me at the station and tell me when someone got dusted," Mack said.

He broadcast live from roller rinks, high schools, and clubs. Attempting to compete with Uncle Jamm's Army, he enlisted tastemaker DJs like Tony G, Julio G, and M.Walk (called "Mixmasters") to perform at events, while Mack's own evening show *High 5* counted down the week's top five records. Between songs, high school kids called in to show off their rhyme skills and shout out their high schools: Crenshaw High, Locke High, Manual Arts. DJ Crazy Toones—Ice Cube's DJ today—remembers listening to the countdowns. The next day he and his brother W.C. would travel to one of the schools, hop the fence, and commence lyrical and pop-locking battles over the lunch hour.

KDAY also sent young rappers like Eazy-E, Ice Cube, Ice-T, MC Hammer, and Candyman out on promotional "tours" around the city—community centers, shopping centers, schools. They wouldn't always perform, sometimes just sign autographs or play basketball with the kids. East Coast acts like Run-D.M.C., LL Cool J, and Big Daddy Kane were enlisted as well, in something of a strong-arm arrangement; Mack tended not to play you on the air unless you did concerts for his station. He attempted to appeal not just to young African-Americans, but Latinos, too, who made up almost half their audience, he said.

KDAY was a godsend for the emerging local rap scene. "KDAY was the one station that you could make a record, walk through the door, hand it to them, and they'd put it on the air," said Ice-T. "Right then!" It was also an important community mouthpiece. Following the 1986 riot at the Run-D.M.C. concert in Long Beach, the station held a Day of Peace, suspending their playlist to take calls and promote nonviolence. The guests included Run-D.M.C. and singer Barry White, a former South Central gangbanger himself. Calls for a cease-fire were observed, at least temporarily.

For all his vision, Greg Mack wasn't initially all that excited about "Boyz." But he heard it every time he went out. And so at his request Eazy made a clean version, and it became their most requested record. Suddenly "Boyz" was everywhere. Eazy gave his first live show at Skateland on September 4, 1987 (C.I.A. opened). He was nervous, but he needn't have been. The eight hundred or so kids in attendance knew "Boyz" by heart and rapped it for him.

Eazy played down his gang affiliation for the concert, probably a smart move considering he was a Crip playing in a Blood stronghold. Instead, he wore his typical street clothes: Raiders gear, jeans, Nikes. He had no idea he was creating a fashion template.

Supergroup

Joseph Nazel edited important black publications like the *Los Angeles Sentinel* as well as porn rags like *Players*. He wrote countless Blaxploitation novels, with titles like *My Name Is Black!* His musically inclined son Kim was raised in Compton and Inglewood and, like so many other kids in the early eighties, idolized Prince, so much so that he began dressing like the Minneapolis icon. He even called himself DJ Prince.

But that all changed while roller-skating one day with a friend. A cute girl skated up beside them and asked their names. "I'm Egyptian Lover," said Nazel's friend, the popular DJ. "I'm DJ Prince," said Nazel. The girl sized him up before coming up with her own, Middle East–flavored moniker. "You should be Arabian Prince," she said, "since you're always with him." And so it was. Like his buddy, Arabian Prince released electro records with spacy, exotic sounds befitting his name.

Arabian Prince began encountering Dr. Dre on the local DJ circuit. Before long they were shopping for records at Roadium, hitting the beach, and chasing women together. They'd even drive all the way out to San Bernardino County to visit members of a saucy, charismatic group of female rappers called J. J. Fad. Dre's love interest was Anna Cash (aka Lady Anna), while Arabian Prince's love interest was Juana Burns (aka MC J.B.). The girls wanted to make a record, but Dre wasn't feeling it. "He was like, 'This is corny,'" remembered MC J.B., then a cheerleader for the Los Angeles Express, part of the short-lived United States Football League.

But Arabian Prince had some studio time at his disposal, and so he helped the ladies put together a pair of tracks, called "Supersonic" and "Another Ho Bites the Dust." The latter is a little-remembered entry in the mid-eighties "Roxanne wars," a series of verbal volleys sparked by a dispute between MC Roxanne Shanté and the group UTFO, who made the song "Roxanne, Roxanne." Despite the fact that J. J. Fad didn't know the players involved or have any reason to be upset with them, they threw out their best insults: *Roxanne Shanté ain't got no hair in her back / She's bald.* "At that time, if you didn't have a diss record, you didn't have anything," said MC J.B. The track didn't go anywhere, but its contagious B-side "Supersonic" began to make some noise. Eazy-E saw them perform it at local club the Casa and left impressed.

Meanwhile, Eazy courted Arabian Prince for a "supergroup" he was planning of his own, which also included Cube (from C.I.A.) and Dr. Dre and DJ Yella (from World Class Wreckin' Cru). Though he had a hot single, Eazy was still unconfident in his rapping abilities, and likely thought it best to surround himself with a group of ringers. It was good timing. Dre and Cube had outgrown their old acts, and so the group—along with Eazy's buddy from the neighborhood MC Ren—met at Arabian Prince's mother's house, on Van Ness Avenue in Inglewood. The plan was to come up with a name. Despite Eazy and Dre's inclinations, it wasn't a foregone conclusion they'd be hardcore. After all, three of their original members—DJ Yella, Ice Cube (aka Purple Ice), and Arabian Prince (aka DJ Prince) idolized Prince.

One thing they quickly agreed on: They wanted to represent where they were from, just like the New York rappers who shouted out their boroughs. Arabian Prince jokingly imagined a cover where the guys were holding guns, with the title *From Compton with Love*. That idea didn't go over so well. Eventually he and Dre began complaining about not getting paid for their production credits. "I feel like a nigga with an attitude," someone said, and before long Eazy suggested "N.W.A—Niggaz With Attitudes." It was a moniker shocking enough to turn heads, with a soupçon of righteous indignation. Cube, told of it later, was definitely down. "Black people taking that word and trying to use it, instead of getting abused by it."

It's a genius moniker in its provocativeness—thrilling some, and making others uncomfortable. "In early interviews, MC Ren took full advantage of the disparity, goading reporters, including me, into repeating a word many of them simply were incapable of even stammering," wrote Jonathan Gold. "If you rose to the bait, you were a racist. If you didn't (I didn't), you were a wuss. There was no middle ground."

Eazy was in charge of the group's decision making. By now he'd quit the drug game entirely, and divided his time between his own solo projects and N.W.A. The group's first EP *Panic Zone*, released in 1987, contains two songs that have gone down in history, and one that hasn't. "8 Ball" is an ode to Olde English 800 malt liquor. *I don't drink Brass Monkey*, Eazy starts off the song, responding to the Beastie Boys' paean for their preferred elixir. (The song also samples the white New York act's "Fight for Your Right.") Notably, neither Eazy nor the song's scribe, Ice Cube, actually drank at the time. Sir Jinx said when Eazy toted a forty-ouncer during performances, it would actually be filled with apple juice.

Like "8 Ball," "Dope Man" was written by Ice Cube, and it foreshadowed the group's sound and image to come. It's the first example of Dr. Dre's use of the "funky worm," the high-pitched, irresistible Moog synthesizer sound whose name was coined by seventies funk group Ohio Players. "Dope Man" alternately glamorizes and condemns the pusher and his lifestyle, ending with a stern warning voiced by Mexican-American rapper Krazy Dee: *You sold crack to my sister and now she's sick / But if she happens to die because of your drug / I'm putting in your culo a .38 slug!*

N.W.A's first single was actually the electro-driven track "Panic Zone," an apocalyptic dispatch from L.A.'s tough neighborhoods.

Ice Cube is from L.A., he's in the panic zone
Eazy-E is from Compton, he's in the panic zone
Arabian Prince from Inglewood, he's in the panic zone

Though it hit locally, the song is barely remembered today. Robotic vocals were already on the way out, displaced by, well, gangsta songs like "The Boyz-N-The Hood."

To capitalize on N.W.A's emerging popularity, Macola put together an album called *N.W.A. and the Posse*. They did so without N.W.A's consent, however, creating a bizarre situation in which the group was badmouthing their own record. "That shit was like some whack shit," MC Ren said.

No matter its provenance, *Posse* actually succeeds as a pretty good compilation album of the group's early works, including the *Panic Zone* tracks, "Boyz," and gag songs like "Fat Girl," with Eazy and Ron-De-Vu riffing on the randy, Rubenesque title character. Misogyny and humor comingle on "A Bitch Iz A Bitch," in which Ice Cube denigrates girls who won't give him the time of day.

I Guarantee You We Will Be Rich

Today, *N.W.A. and the Posse* is probably best known for its cover photo, an eighties time capsule featuring a dozen of the group's affiliates, mean-mugging in a graffiti-covered, trash-strewn Hollywood alleyway near Macola, forty-ounce bottles in hand.

The record also introduced another extraordinary talent, Dallas rapper Tracy Curry, who performs on *Posse* with a group called the Fila Fresh Crew. Their contributions include the ode to liquor "Drink It Up" (a boozy parody of "Twist and Shout") and "Dunk the Funk," a banger showing off Curry's dexterous rapping ability. Such lyrical acrobatics were unlike anything the West Coast had yet seen up to this point, and it turns out Curry was a master songwriter as well.

Curry was introduced to N.W.A via a Los Angeles DJ named Dr. Rock, an early member of the World Class Wreckin' Cru. (Dre had taken Rock's place in the group when the latter departed for college in Austin, and he later became an on-air personality for Dallas radio station K104.) At a Dallas party Rock happened upon Curry performing live. "I was blown away," Dr. Rock said. "I thought to myself, 'This is a guy I've got to get on wax.'" Curry originally called himself Doc, because a rap partner's sister was a lab technician, and he thought he looked good in her coat. He later started calling himself D.O.C., adding the periods to connect himself with N.W.A. For the time being, however, he joined Dr. Rock and a friend named Fresh K in the Fila Fresh Crew. Dre, who recorded tracks with them, some of which ended up on *N.W.A. and the Posse*, was blown away.

"He was like 'Nigga, you the shit,'" D.O.C. said. "'If you come out to the West Coast, I guarantee you we will be rich.'"

D.O.C. soon moved into a Compton house behind Centennial High School, owned by a Dallas acquaintance. Before long, however, Dre scraped enough money together to move out of Sir Jinx's house and into a two-bedroom apartment in the city of Paramount, just east of Compton. DJ Yella was his roommate, and they let D.O.C. crash on the floor of their unfurnished living room, where he didn't have so much as a sleeping bag. But despite the spartan accommodations the guys quickly bonded. "That was my first real connection with Dre—that we both liked to drink," D.O.C. said. In the mornings they'd shake off the fog and drive in to the studio in a battered Toyota Corolla, blasting Public Enemy. Their recording spot was the optimistically named Audio Achievements studios in Torrance. Attached to a Mexican restaurant, it was owned by a genial, long-haired recording engineer named Donovan "the Dirt Biker" Smith.

At the studio D.O.C. was quickly enveloped into the Ruthless fold, and became an unofficial member of N.W.A. His first task was writing lyrics for Eazy-E's solo song "We Want Eazy." It was D.O.C., with help from MC Ren, who began fashioning Eazy into the bawdy gangsta character we know today, and D.O.C. was a major writing contributor to *Straight Outta Compton*, as well.

It was ironic, really. Growing up in Texas, D.O.C. knew nothing about L.A. street culture. He used his naïveté to his advantage. "When I first got to Los Angeles, hip-hop music was a scary thing not only to white America but to middle-class black America. They were afraid of it, they thought it was nigger shit," D.O.C. said, adding that he used Eazy as a "comedian" similar to Public Enemy's Flavor Flav—to deliver serious messages with humor.

Eazy-E's character played off a long-established hood archetype: the heroic dealer, surrounded by the finest trappings and women, conquering enemies but never forgetting where he came from. His melodies were hummable, and his tongue was often in his cheek. As he rapped on "No More ?'s" about the way he conducted business:

Walked in, said: "This is a robbery"
Didn't need the money, it's just a hobby
Fill the bag, homeboy, don't lag
I want money, beer, and a pack of Zig-Zags

N.W.A wasn't just the world's most dangerous group, as they branded themselves. They were also gangstas having fun. With the help of D.O.C. and his songwriting, they became bad guys you couldn't help but root for.

CHAPTER FIVE

I'M NOT GIVING YOU SHIT

Mountain View Estates, a neighborhood of multimillion-dollar homes in the posh suburb of Calabasas, lies within the Santa Monica National Recreation Area. It's a forty-minute drive west from downtown L.A. if there's no traffic (although there always is). Only with an invitation is one permitted past the community's gates, but once the guard waves you through you're greeted by a towering fountain shooting mist into the air. But for a gentle breeze, the sloping streets are still. Occasionally a Lexus or Mercedes exits a driveway. On a bright afternoon in October 2014 few residents are enjoying their suburban splendor, though Central-American workers are beautifying homes and grounds apace. In every direction: tiled roofs, wrought-iron sculptures, and immaculately tended lawns, even during a drought.

With its grandiose swimming setups and soulless architecture, Calabasas is where the rich and famous move to show off how much money they have. Mountain View Estates is just west of Hidden Hills, which has become especially well known in recent years for famous residents, including Kanye West and Kim Kardashian, Jennifer Lopez, and Drake.

For months I'd unsuccessfully pestered Jerry Heller for an interview. When I say I want to see the house where Eazy-E lived—two doors down from his own—to my surprise he gives the guard my name. I take a few photos of Eazy's old pad (big pool, sweeping views, a whimsical statue of two boys on the lawn, one holding a violin) and Heller meets me in front of his three-car garage, which houses a Jaguar and a Volkswagen. Built in 1990, Heller's mock-Mediterranean five-thousand-square-foot house has a Spanish-style roof, big picture window in front, and ornate balcony.

"We can talk but no interview," the former N.W.A manager said in our email. Having no idea what this means, I follow him inside with a mixture of trepidation and curiosity. Everyone and their mother has an opinion about Jerry Heller—he's the subject of more diss tracks than anyone this side of Tipper Gore—and I'm curious to know him as a person. Now in his eighth decade, Heller wears the effects of time and a combative career; his face droops, his white hair has thinned, and he walks tentatively. Clad in white tennis shoes and a blue polo shirt, he immediately takes a call, leaving me to observe the contents of his living room. His table is piled with magazine articles about him and N.W.A, old World Class Wreckin' Cru albums, and an early Eazy-E and Ron-De-Vu record, called "L.A. Is the Place." The modern art on the walls looks expensive, and above the fireplace sits a picture of him and his blond, bosomy, much-younger ex-wife Gayle Steiner; they shared a passion for rescue dogs.

Eventually he winds up his conversation. We talk for a few minutes before he receives another call—something involving the director Jim Sheridan, who he says is slated to adapt his memoir *Ruthless* for film— before finally giving me his attention.

"Could I turn on my recorder?" I ask at one point, to which he responds: "I'm not giving you shit!" He explains that constantly rerun television interviews he did years ago haven't paid him a dime, adding that previous book scribes have done him dirty. (He unsuccessfully sued the author and publisher of the 1998 book *Have Gun Will Travel*, about Death Row Records, which he felt unfairly portrayed him. He is also suing the makers of the 2015 biopic *Straight Outta Compton* for defamation.)

Alternately calm and heated, Heller oscillates between saying he doesn't care what anyone says about him, and vehemently denying various allegations. I eventually wrangle some quotes on the record from him, as well as lots of great background information, and leave the premises thinking him simultaneously cold and quite generous. When my grandmother died a year later, he expressed his condolences on my Facebook page.

This is Heller in a nutshell. More than anyone else in this book, people split right down the middle on him. Many Ruthless Records insiders assert his critical role in the development of its artists; there's a reason, they say, that N.W.A became an international phenomenon, while other gangsta rappers of the era didn't break big. Others practically spit at the mention of his name. N.W.A affiliate turntablist DJ Speed called him, to me, a "crook," and to *HipHop DX*, a "snake." (Heller retorted by calling Speed "a gofer. He took Eric's laundry in.") When Heller appeared on the *Murder Master Music Show* internet radio program in 2013, a caller referred to him as a "shylock." He returned to the podcast a year later, and a different listener called him a "shylock" again.

Ice Cube famously used anti-Semitic language toward Heller, when things soured between them. But in the early days, at least to many artists he courted, his background seemed to imply an ability to make it rain. "He was a white Jewish dude that knew people, and he could get into record companies that we couldn't get into," Arabian Prince said. "It was hard enough getting money out of our own banks."

There's one thing no one disagrees about: With Heller's help, Ruthless Records went from a regional, homegrown success to a national powerhouse.

Heller's father owned a scrap metal business. He loved gambling on sports and hung out with the Jewish mob, eventually landing the family in wealthy Cleveland suburb Shaker Heights. As one of the town's few Jews, Heller felt like an outsider, he wrote in *Ruthless*. After receiving a business degree from USC, he reached great heights in the music industry in the sixties and seventies, acting as agent for artists like Marvin Gaye and Creedence Clearwater Revival, bringing Elton John and Pink Floyd across the pond for their first American tours, and serving as mentor to famed music manager Irving Azoff. Heller also promoted electronic music pioneers Kraftwerk's first U.S. tour, in 1975. Along the way, he partied like the rock stars he accompanied.

But Heller fell off his game in the new wave era. In 1985 he was divorced and sleeping on his parents' sofa in Encino, when he received a call from his friend, music manager Morey Alexander, who'd been hipped to the goings-on at Macola. Heller met with Don Macmillan and Rudy Pardee, one half of L.A. Dream Team, who played Heller the group's hot electro hip-hop single, "The Dream Team Is in the House!" Heller agreed to help manage the group, and was also impressed with J. J. Fad, who were on the Dream Team's label.

After being rear-ended on the freeway and receiving a settlement, Heller moved out of his mother's house, bought a condo in the Simi Valley, and plunged into L.A. urban music in earnest. He hocked records at the Roadium, and agreed to manage acts like the World Class Wreckin' Cru and C.I.A.

In the mid-eighties Heller often used to sit in Macola's lobby and "try to pick up artists" to offer his services as manager, Don Macmillan said. Heller hooked up with rappers and DJs whose talents, he believed, weren't being properly utilized. "I recall, at least a couple of times, producers singing the praises of recording equipment that they had purchased from Toys 'R' Us for two hundred dollars," he wrote.

His reputation was that of a mover and shaker from a previous era. Eazy in particular was dying to meet him, so much so that he paid Alonzo Williams to make the introduction. Which is why, on the morning of March 3, 1987, Eazy-E arrived in front of Macola in his burgundy Suzuki Samurai, with MC Ren in tow. Eazy was dressed to impress: locs, brand-new low-cut Converse All Stars, immaculate white T-shirt, and "a gold watch you could tell was real," remembered promoter Doug Young. Young was there for the meeting, too. He had never met Eazy, but his reputation preceded him.

"How do you know it's them?" Heller asked Young, watching from afar as Eazy and Ren came in.

"Because they look like two gangbangers," Young replied.

Lonzo made the introductions, upon which time Eazy retrieved the cash from his sock to pay him for the service. They proceeded to Macmillan's office, where the conversation was a bit awkward. Heller asked

Eazy if he was the "Dope Man" in the song. Eazy went silent, but Heller continued prying.

"I got a money tree in my backyard," Eazy said finally.

This loosened everyone up, and Eazy went on to explain that he wanted his new group N.W.A to sound tough. "They're going to be hip-hop, they're going to be real street with it," he went on. "But, they're going to represent the way that we talk in L.A., the way that we act in L.A. They're going to promote the L.A. culture."

Heller soon warmed to the group's music, particularly "The Boyz-N-The Hood." He and Eazy decided to go into business together, and they soon met at Cahuenga Boulevard restaurant Martoni's. Also there were Heller's partner Morey Alexander and the other Macola artists they were working with, including Rodney-O & Joe Cooley, Rudy Pardee, Russ Parr, the Unknown DJ, Alonzo Williams, Arabian Prince, and Egyptian Lover.

There was friction about Heller's increasingly close ties to Eazy, whose coarse style was disliked by some of his other clients. According to Heller's account of the evening, he announced he'd thrown his lot in with Eazy's upstart label, and that anyone who didn't join him there would need new representation. Alonzo Williams, however, said just the opposite, that artists including Pardee and Unknown DJ gave *Heller* the ultimatum: "It's either us or Eazy." Whatever the case, Heller and many of his artists parted ways.

Heller's decision to team up with Eazy was hastily made. Heller said Eazy offered him 50 percent of Ruthless, but he insisted on taking only a 20 percent fee.

"Every dollar comes into Ruthless, I take twenty cents," he said he told Eazy. "You own the company. I work for you." Heller would also manage a number of Ruthless acts, including N.W.A, but Eazy was the principal decision maker.

Arabian Prince decided to join the Ruthless crew, but he soon grew skeptical about Heller's proposed arrangement. For one thing, you don't want your manager and your label's manager to be the same person. When it's time to negotiate, after all, you need someone looking out for your interests, and your interests only.

Such an arrangement is not particularly unusual in hip-hop, but it is also "not ethical," said David Kronemyer, an industry analyst and former senior vice president at Atlantic Records. "The artist might want tour support from the label, or a video, or to focus on certain markets where the act is strong. The record company might have a different position on all of these issues." (Heller responded that he didn't manage all of Ruthless's acts, but when he did, he was "always on the side of the artist, so any conflict would have been on his side." He added that in these cases he only took a single commission, and never "double dipped.")

Heller and Eazy's relationship would represent the backbone of Ruthless Records. It was a complicated one—some still don't understand it today—and many tried to get between them. "People callin' me, askin' me, 'Why you got a white man as your manager?'" Eazy said. "It's like, when I was lookin' for a manager, I closed my fuckin' eyes and I said, 'I want the best.' Jerry happened to be the best."

Their relationship was also personal. Heller helped Eazy get his first driver's license and set up his first bank account. Eazy helped Heller find a renewed purpose.

"Eazy loved his dad, but they didn't communicate a lot," said Charis Henry, who later became Eazy's personal assistant. While Eazy's father Richard was introverted, "Jerry was like an active father to him. He would say, 'Jerry's like a dad to me.'"

Dre, focused on music, wasn't much involved with the logistics of setting Ruthless up as a business. But he was initially impressed with Heller as well, owing to the time the manager helped the World Class Wreckin' Cru procure some money they were owed from their record label.

One of Eazy and Heller's first decisions was to sign J. J. Fad. It paid quick dividends.

Having heard their songs recorded by Arabian Prince, Dr. Dre no longer thought they were corny. He reworked "Supersonic" and coproduced their debut album of the same name, featuring a reshuffled lineup.

Eazy intended Ruthless to be the hardest label on the block. But putting out a PG-rated group first made sense. "Jerry and Eric were like, 'We need to come out as a legitimate record label, so let's put out the girls first," said MC J.B. Warner subsidiary Atco Records signed on to distribute the work, which went gold. "Supersonic" became a huge breakout hit in the wake of Salt-N-Pepa's 1988 smash "Push It."

J. J. Fad and N.W.A performed at a charity party for underprivileged children at the L'Ermitage hotel in Beverly Hills on Valentine's Day 1988. It was hosted by hunk Scott Valentine, who played Mallory Keaton's bad boy boyfriend on *Family Ties*. N.W.A performed a "kid-friendly" song— no one can remember exactly what—but J. J. Fad was the main attraction to the teenyboppers.

"Supersonic" was even nominated for a 1989 Grammy for Best Rap Performance—the first year it was given out. J. J. Fad wore custom-made tuxedos with miniskirts to the ceremony. Unfortunately, because that particular award wasn't televised, other nominees including Salt-N-Pepa and eventual winner DJ Jazzy Jeff and the Fresh Prince boycotted the ceremony.

Learning the Techniques and Terminology

Despite J. J. Fad's success, neither Atco nor any other major labels were interested in N.W.A, whose sound and image seemed much riskier. And so, with the group's future in doubt, upon his graduation from high school in 1987, Ice Cube made other plans. Following the advice of a Taft teacher, he took the train to Arizona and spent a year studying architectural drafting, receiving a certificate from the now-defunct Phoenix Institute of Technology.

The other N.W.A members kept plugging, but Cube decided to follow his hip-hop backup plan. He remembers a grueling schedule, and work that demanded intense concentration. "Architectural drafting is all about precision, and learning the techniques and terminology to try to put it to use," he said. "The drawings got progressively harder and harder as the year went on." He credits the experience with helping him learn to live on his own. He still worked on rap, with his friend Phoenix Phil's crew, though they didn't really go anywhere.

He missed his friends back home. "I'd get calls from them, 'We're about to go to Chicago, then we fly to Atlanta,'" he said. "And here I have six months of school left! That was the worst year of my life. My dreams were leaving me behind."

In Cube's wake, MC Ren stepped up. Like the departed rapper, he was a bit younger than the other group members. His older brother was friends with Eazy, and the two families lived only two blocks apart in Compton.

As a kid Ren was a disciple of D.M.C. (not Run, like most), and, like Eazy, Crip affiliated. He'd been accidentally shot in a random act of gang-land violence. As his rap talents developed he joined a beatboxing friend named Chip in a duo called Awesome Crew 2. The underage performers scored a show at Sunset Strip club the Roxy. Realizing Ice-T was in atten-dance their heart rates quickened; he was in the process of putting together his Rhyme Syndicate label, which would include artists like rapper Everlast and the duo Low Profile. Unfortunately, Ren recalled, the whole thing went awry. The DJ got the tempo wrong at one point, throwing off their whole rhythm. "We had to rap so fast. It was fucked up," Ren said.

Ren nearly enlisted in the army, but couldn't leave hip-hop behind. He dazzled Eazy with freestyles in the latter's stucco detached garage, which had evolved into a modest practice space with turntables, drum machines, and a stand-up Asteroids video game console. Ren was a pure spitter, capa-ble of dominating the beat with a little extra mustard. Eazy signed him to a solo deal, but soon realized his strengths as a ghostwriter. Ren penned the tracks "Eazy-Duz-It," "Radio," and "Ruthless Villain," which eventu-ally ended up on Eazy's 1988 solo album, *Eazy-Duz-It*. But the pace of "Ruthless Villain" proved too quick for Eazy's meager rapping skills. "So Dre was like, 'Man, just let Ren say the rap!'" Ren remembered. He was soon invited to join N.W.A.

N.W.A's first ever show was at Skateland, on March 11, 1988. "My home-boy Eazy-E and the whole N.W.A posse is in effect," said MC Ren, giv-ing shout-outs between Eazy's "Boyz" verses; many of the lyrics had been changed to remove curses. The group began playing shows on the road, piling into Eazy's navy-blue Ford Aerostar minivan, and sharing cheap motel rooms. At first they opened up for Alonzo's revamped version of World Class Wreckin' Cru—which was awkward for everyone, considering their disparate styles, and the fact that Dre and Yella had quit the group— but by 1988 had graduated to performing with acts like Salt-N-Pepa, MC Hammer, Heavy D, and UTFO. They got strange looks for their Jheri curl. " 'Who the fuck is y'all niggas?' " they were asked. When Cube returned from Arizona later in 1988, for good, Ren stayed in the group.

Hail Mary

Despite N.W.A's traction on the road, Jerry Heller was striking out with his industry contacts. By late 1987 the group still hadn't landed a record deal. Really, it wasn't too hard to figure out. Black performers like Michael Jackson and Prince may have ruled the pop charts; they were expected to look, talk, and act decent. Innuendo was OK, but N.W.A was too violent, too real.

Rap had gone mainstream less than a decade earlier, and many labels still thought it was a fad. The board chairman of Capitol Records told Heller that N.W.A would never sell. David Geffen expressed concern over how N.W.A was "talking about gays." (Never mind that Geffen Records' white-hot metal band Guns N' Roses would soon employ gay and racial slurs themselves on their 1988 track "One in a Million.")

Eventually Heller threw something of a Hail Mary pass, taking a meeting in August 1988 with Bryan Turner and Mark Cerami of Priority Records. Though they had great distribution, Priority wasn't exactly a major industry force. Their biggest claim to fame was the California Raisins, Claymation dried grapes dreamed up by the state's raisin marketing commission. Singing Motown classics and other nostalgic hits, they were voiced by Buddy Miles, a former Jimi Hendrix collaborator. The act's shifting image was alternately as soul group, trendy B-boys, and quartet of straining turds.

The Raisins eventually sold more than three million copies. It wasn't as much of a fluke as it sounds. Turner and Cerami were former executives at K-Tel Records, repackaging old hits into genre collections advertised on late-night television (*Hooked on Swing, Funky Super Hits*). Heller trusted Priority's ability to market music outside of radio, which was mostly a nonstarter for N.W.A, due to their cussing. And so soon he and the crew met the Priority brain trust in a cigarette-smoke-filled Hollywood conference room.

Eazy, his pagers buzzing in his jean pockets, put his Air Jordans up onto the table, while Ren mean mugged. Eventually Dre arrived with a cassette and played "Gangsta Gangsta," the group's latest track and perhaps their tightest and most on-message yet. It kicks off with a drive-by shooting, and soon police sirens wail. *Drinkin' straight out the eight bottle*, raps Ice Cube over a midtempo beat and funk guitar riff appropriated from Steve Arrington.

> *Do I look like a muthafuckin' role model?*
> *To a kid lookin' up to me: Life ain't nothin' but bitches and money.*

Turner, a Canadian, didn't immediately get it. "I couldn't believe the things they talked about actually happened," he said later. But he became fully convinced after seeing the group perform at a Reseda roller rink. The crowd sung along in unison to "Fuck tha Police," a controversial, officially unreleased anthem that was being given out for free by N.W.A's street teams, comprised of kids spreading out across the city to promote the group. Priority agreed to finance and distribute both Eazy-E's solo album and N.W.A's official debut, under the imprint of Ruthless Records.

"It was the best of both worlds: major-label clout with effective indie distribution," wrote Heller.

"They had marketing people, they had a full staff, they could get records in all the stores. It was almost like a West Coast version of Def Jam," said Wherehouse Records' Violet Brown. "Once Priority got their hands on it, it exploded."

CHAPTER SIX

A LITTLE BIT OF GOLD AND A PAGER

Y ou are now about to witness the strength of street knowledge."
Dr. Dre kicked off N.W.A's landmark 1988 debut album *Straight Outta Compton* with this cocksure mission statement, promising to present, in vivid detail, the culmination of a youth marked by survival tactics and institutional humiliations. Dre, Eazy, Cube, Ren, DJ Yella, and Arabian Prince were the ultimate antiheroes, rock stars prepping America for the post-Reagan era, when good and evil would no longer be so white and black.

It's a dope line, and prescient, too: We did witness it. And we were never the same.

The album's most memorable songs feature an assault of abrasive textures, marching drums, samples fragments, and break beats mined from Roadium swap meet records. *Straight Outta Compton*'s bombastic sound matches its rhetoric. To hear it as a child of poverty was to nod in affirmation; to hear it as person of privilege was to gasp in horror.

MC Ren has called tracks three through thirteen "filler." I don't agree. But the work's greatest power lies in its opening tracks, "Straight Outta Compton" and "Fuck tha Police." Blurring the line between rapper and character, the self-referential protagonists are badasses bearing heavy artillery who recognize corruption and are fighting back. What's most shocking, however, is that they're not so much political soldiers as nihilist, murderous criminals.

America wasn't ready. But it had no choice but to adapt, and the work's charged rhetoric is so ferociously eloquent that it still resonates today: *Police think they have the authority to kill a minority,* Ice Cube raps on "Fuck tha Police," adding:

> *Fucking with me 'cause I'm a teenager*
> *With a little bit of gold and a pager*
> *Searching my car, looking for the product*
> *Thinking every nigga is selling narcotics*

The time for reasoned debate has passed, and he has lost his cool. But Cube's enemies extend beyond just the cops. Anyone who crosses him is fair game for his wrath. As he raps on "Straight Outta Compton":

> *Crazy motherfucker named Ice Cube*
> *From the gang called Niggaz With Attitudes*
> *When I'm called off, I got a sawed-off*
> *Squeeze the trigger and bodies are hauled off*

So what if his benefactor Eazy-E actually *was* guilty of selling drugs? So what if Ice Cube had denounced gangs and wasn't, in real life, the madman he portrayed? The anger and pent-up frustrations he vocalized on behalf of his compatriots was real.

Shouting out Compton wasn't a popular thing to do at the time. But N.W.A was following in the tradition of other rap acts who were proud of where they were from, like Boogie Down Productions, who paid homage to the South Bronx, and Run-D.M.C., from Hollis, Queens. "I think we all was thinking about making a name for Compton and L.A.," said MC Ren. Cube, of course, wasn't from Compton, which made the whole thing a little weird. "But it just felt silly yelling 'South Central' when everyone else was yelling Compton," he said. "And, Compton and South Central is two sides of the same coin, so to speak."

Straight Outta Compton owes its greatest debt to Long Island group Public Enemy, whose own landmark work *It Takes a Nation of Millions to Hold Us Back* came out less than two months earlier, captivating rap fans and hip, politically conscious rock fans alike with a message of black unity, and urging revolt against the power structure. Public Enemy made revolutionary stylings all the rage, and helped usher in hip-hop's "golden era" of the late eighties and early nineties, which also included acts like A Tribe Called Quest and De La Soul. It was a time of Afrocentric positivity and uplifting rhymes, before macho posturing consumed the genre.

N.W.A was simultaneously a part of, and removed from, this golden era movement. More a declaration of anarchy than a disciplined treatise, *Straight Outta Compton* offered little of Public Enemy's tempered positivity. Ice Cube felt an acute sense of responsibility, but Dr. Dre called the idea that the group was political "nonsense." "The black police in Compton are worse than the white police," Eazy-E said. "Chuck D gets involved in all that black stuff, we don't. Fuck that black power shit: we don't give a fuck. Free South Africa: we don't give a fuck. I bet there ain't anybody in South Africa wearing a button saying 'Free Compton' or 'Free California.'"

"Straight Outta Compton" was bold and fresh, but also potentially destructive. "[It] was the best song of that album," said DJ Yella. "It went right to the point. Wasn't no sugarcoating. Nothing. This is where we from. This is how it is. And that was a song that didn't take long to make. A couple of days, that's it." There was little precedent for such brazen, anarchic polemics told in street language. Cube's angry, arrogant character is on the hunt for anyone who'd disrespect him. Eazy-E is dangerous, too, but more cunning, and in it for the long con. The combustible persona of MC Ren, meanwhile, is liable to go off at any time.

It's a potent trio—Dre wasn't yet doing much rapping—and even more remarkable when you realize that Cube and Ren were only nineteen when the album dropped. Born one day apart in June 1969, they were already beginning to peak as performers. They pushed each other during recording sessions. Starting at midnight, they went all night in the studio. Even when finished they might go back and change their verse if the other made a hotter one.

Guilty of Being a Redneck

The album's second track, "Fuck tha Police," has become the most famous protest song in rap history, and perhaps the greatest in history period. A protest against law enforcement's abuse of minorities, "Fuck tha Police" has served as an anthem for protest movements ranging from the 1992 L.A. riots to demonstrations in Ferguson, Missouri, over the 2014 killing of unarmed eighteen-year-old Michael Brown by a white police officer. Hundreds, if not thousands, of rappers have paid homage to it.

Ice Cube gets credit for coming up with the song's concept, and he understood how provocative the message would be. "We was sick of being harassed by the police, just because we was young and black. Daryl Gates had declared a war on gangs," Cube said. "And if you think every black kid is a gang member, that means there's a war on every black kid you see."

Dre wasn't initially down. He liked the idea of the track, but didn't want to exacerbate a personal situation; owing to traffic arrests, in early 1988 he was serving weekend lockup, only let out during the week to work. "He didn't want that song out while he had to go back and forth in the county," Cube said. "But when he was off of that little stint, when I brought the idea back up, he was down to do it."

In his book Jerry Heller wrote that in the fall of 1987, the group members were standing outside Audio Achievements Studios in Torrance when, apropos of nothing, police pulled up and without explanation put the artists on their knees, and demanded to see their IDs. A similar scene is portrayed in the *Straight Outta Compton* film, which then inspires Cube to pen a draft of "Fuck tha Police."

Alonzo Williams suspects a different incident helped shape the song. He recalled hearing about a pre–"Fuck tha Police" joyride taken by Eazy, Dre, and others, in which they shot people's cars with paintball guns on the Harbor Freeway. They were pulled over, had guns put to their heads, and handcuffed before police let them go. "They come back to my house shaking like leaves on a tree on a windy day, damn near crying," Lonzo wrote in his memoir. "'Man, fuck the police!'" Eazy may have been referencing this incident when he gave an account of police harassment, telling a television interviewer he was once "snatched out of my car, guns to my head, on the freeway laid down."

Dre fleshed out the structure of "Fuck tha Police," including a courtroom skit in which an officer is put on trial. As "judge," Dre announces his verdict: "The jury has found you guilty of being a redneck, white bread, chickenshit motherfucker!" The "convicted" policeman, played by D.O.C., yells as he's being dragged out, in his whitest voice: "Fuck you, you black motherfucker!"

Reality Rap

N.W.A's members were a bunch of wallflowers. Dr. Dre, by his own admission, suffers from social anxiety, while Eazy-E could go through entire meetings without saying anything. MC Ren was quiet, Arabian Prince wasn't in the mix for long, and DJ Yella "could be in a room and you'd never know he was there," wrote Alonzo Williams. Cube was the only one you wouldn't call an introvert. But together, the group's music was even more aggressive than Schoolly D or Ice-T. "The mind-set of those guys had changed so much, to the point that I didn't know them anymore," added Lonzo. Convinced that this new style would get people to pay attention, the group inflated gangsta rap into a full-blown hip-hop subgenre in one fell swoop with *Straight Outta Compton*.

Nobody at the time used the term "gangsta rap," however. They preferred "reality rap." "[W]e're telling the real story of what it's like living in places like Compton. We're giving them reality. We're like reporters. We give them the truth. People where we come from hear so many lies that the truth stands out like a sore thumb," Eazy said.

This was not the airbrushed, optimistic black America of *The Cosby Show* or DJ Jazzy Jeff & the Fresh Prince, whose "Parents Just Don't Understand" was a hit that year. "What Jazzy Jeff and rappers like him talk about is phony stuff," added MC Ren. "They're talking about what the white world and the white kids can identify with. If you're a black kid from the streets and somebody is rapping about parents not understanding, you'd laugh at that. You might not have parents or you'd have parents that were into crack or prostitution."

Eazy maintained that making money was the ultimate goal. The music *business* is what pulled Eazy from the dope game—not politics, or, like Cube and Dre, because he was blessed with obvious musical gifts. What Eazy lacked in natural rapping abilities he made up for with vision and marketing savvy: He saw a radio dial crammed with wussy, ineffectual performers, and sought to fill the void. He made no bones about his desire to shock and awe.

In 1993 Dr. Dre famously disparaged *Straight Outta Compton*: "To this day I can't stand that album, I threw that thing together in six weeks so we could have something to sell out of the trunk." In a more recent interview, he said, "Back then I thought the choruses were supposed to just be me scratching."

This is harsh self-criticism from a perfectionist. A more accurate quote might be, "I threw that thing together at an obscure studio on a budget of less than $10,000 and it became one of hip-hop's greatest albums." Indeed, N.W.A quickly conceived and recorded the work at the out-of-the-way Audio Achievements studios in Torrance. Dre and Yella led the album's production, assisted by Arabian Prince and owner-engineer Donovan Smith, and they borrowed both from Public Enemy's sonic pastiche approach, and their bombast. The Long Island group's 1987 debut *Yo! Bum Rush the Show* and its follow-up, *It Takes a Nation of Millions*, employed the dizzying, chopped-sample production of the Bomb Squad, an affiliated production team who brought a new level of complexity to hip-hop beats. But Dre also used live instruments to re-create parts of other folks' records he liked, employing, say, a guitar or a flute player to make it sound like a sample.

Live instrumentation meant Dre could control the instruments' individual levels. "If you have a sample, you can't bring the bass guitar up, or the guitar up, without turning the whole sample up," explained session guitarist and bass guitarist Stan "The Guitar Man" Jones. Dre's perfectly tuned ear, monk's patience, and effective bedside manner fused together a thousand disparate ideas. Eazy may have been writing the checks for the studio sessions, but throughout the recording of *Straight Outta Compton*, everybody knew Dre was the boss. "Dre was like the main ear," said MC Ren. "He'd tell you, 'Try to make it like this.' You'd do it. He'd be like, 'Cool.' Or, 'That's terrible.'"

Some tracks are more original than others. The beat from "Express Yourself" is a near copy of Charles Wright & the Watts 103rd Rhythm Band's 1970 hit of the same name, which Wright was appalled to discover upon the record's release. (Priority Records put him in touch with Ice Cube, who "apologized profusely and I got my royalties," Wright said.) The song features a then-rare example of Dre rapping quickly, and he proves himself a nimble lyricist, though his antidrug message would prove embarrassing to him later: *I don't smoke weed or sess / 'Cause it's know to give a brother brain damage.* Jones said he and Laylaw would smoke weed in the studio and invite Dre to participate, but he always turned them down with a laugh, "like, 'I don't need that shit.'"

Straight Outta Compton is a direct product of Eazy-E's vision. MC Ren made it raw, while Cube gave it its caustic, political edge—the thing for which it's most remembered. Of course, none of this would have mattered if Dre hadn't finely molded its structure.

As for Yella's contribution to *Straight Outta Compton*? On the album he receives a coproducing credit, along with Dre. "I'd be on the board, and he'd be on the drum machine," Yella said. "So I'd go over there and program all the stuff on the machine. We were just like a team. We didn't have to be like, 'I do this, and you do that.' It was like Batman and Robin."

"Yella was good at the technical part," said Dre.

According to Ren, Dre did the heavy lifting, and Yella was more like Dre's "assistant," which is a word others used as well. "He didn't really come up with [concepts], but he did the tedious shit, and allowed Dre to concentrate on helping everyone else," D.O.C. said.

"Yella would be doing editing, as far as splicing different parts of songs together—once they were recorded—on the two-track," said Stan Jones, adding that Dre came up with all the beats.

Straight Outta Compton still sounds fresh today, with the exception of its final track, "Something 2 Dance 2," a throwback to the L.A. electro scene. I like it, and it was a dance floor hit at the time. But it's remembered now as electro's swan song, considering that N.W.A pretty much obliterated the sound. Cribbing from Sly & the Family Stone, it features up-tempo disco grooves, jittery synths, and suggestions to "feel the grove, bust a move!" Though Dre and Yella are credited as the track's producers, and Eazy and Dre as its writers, its textures feel like the handiwork of Arabian Prince, who said he was not properly given credit for that song and others on the album, and that such shenanigans helped fuel his decision to leave the group.

Some have speculated that Arabian Prince was unwilling, or unable, to make the transition from electro to hardcore rap. But he told me the real reason he left N.W.A was because he found Jerry Heller's financial dealings disreputable. "We were selling all these records, and weren't seeing the money we were supposed to be seeing," he said, adding that, unlike the other group members, he was already financially stable owing to his successful DJ career. Though he left the group in 1988, while *Straight Outta Compton* was still being recorded, he contributed a great deal of production work on the album, and is on its cover. He has been unfairly glossed over by history (not to mention whitewashed out of the *Straight Outta Compton* film). It's not clear to me why N.W.A's classic lineup is considered to be Eazy, Dre, Cube, Ren, and Yella, since those five alone never actually made an album together.

"You Think White Kids Would Like This?"

Today, *Straight Outta Compton* is remembered as a game-changing, seismic work that altered not just the hip-hop landscape, but popular music at large. It didn't make much noise upon its release, however. *Rolling Stone* didn't review it, or even write a major story on the band until their second album. Many critics just didn't get it. "Somehow DJs Dr. Dre and Yella... drive the three MCs past their own lies half the time," wrote critic Robert Christgau. Radio play was scant, especially at first. But it had great distribution, and was steadily propelled by word of mouth.

"The more hardcore the rap group was, the more the white kids wanted it," said Wherehouse Records' Violet Brown. "All the areas people thought were lily white—like Utah—were actually areas I sold a lot of albums."

In their hometown N.W.A autograph sessions drew hundreds, and then thousands of fans. A show following their debut's release at Skateland hit capacity with some 2,200 attendees, including hordes of screaming groupies, and limos that whisked them to an after-party at the Bonaventure hotel. Skateland's Craig Schweisinger said the show was so loud that his ears rang for days.

But there were hiccups. They were turned away from their own album party at a Beverly Center club because, reportedly, the doorman thought they were "a bunch of thugs." Around the time of *Eazy-Duz-It*'s release, while performing at Harlem's Apollo Theater the unimpressed, fickle audience booed them and threw things at them. At the Anaheim Celebrity Theatre, a brawl broke out on stage and the cops had to intervene. Attendees reported stabbings.

Straight Outta Compton entered a gathering media storm that had already placed Los Angeles at the center of America's crime epidemic, on the front lines of both the gang and crack cocaine explosions. Earlier in 1988, the Dennis Hopper–directed hit film *Colors* focused on a pair of CRASH unit cops, played by Robert Duvall and Sean Penn, in the middle of an L.A. gang war. "Seventy thousand gang members. One million guns. Two cops," was a tagline. Ice-T performed the theme song, which he credits for really launching his career. Critics at the time lauded the film's supposed realism, but I cringed at the depiction of the black and Latino characters during a recent viewing. The volunteer crime patrol group the Guardian Angels, meanwhile, felt it glorified criminal street life. Accusing Sean Penn of profiting from gang violence, they left an "Oscar award" in the form of a toilet bowl, outside of his Malibu house.

Leaving aside the question of whether music may cause kids to behave violently, N.W.A's undoubtedly affected teenagers everywhere. I was eleven years old when *Straight Outta Compton* was released, and my own group of friends was obsessed with the group and its members as we entered Central High School in St. Paul, Minnesota, a few years later. More so than St. Paul as a whole, the school was racially diverse, with white kids like myself bused in from out of the neighborhood for the International Baccalaureate program.

I initially disliked N.W.A. Raised on the police-are-infallible message of *Dragnet* reruns, "Fuck tha Police" seemed not just wrong to me at first, but gimmicky and insincere. But, as outlaw art often does, it eventually swayed my friends and me. We began to question not just authority, but whether drug dealers and gangbangers were inherently bad people, as we'd been coached. We took from N.W.A's music both the righteous politics and the bombast, but mostly the bombast, mocking cops under our breath, mimicking Eazy-E's sleazy come-ons, pulling our athletic shorts down low, and getting drunk on Olde English. Some of us wore pagers, or bought oversized car speakers with maximum bass. We could only dream of driving "six-fours," though I for one didn't know until later that this referred to a 1964 Impala.

We even threw up signs for our neighborhood "gang," named for our local recreation center and called the Langford Park Posse. The signs required making Ls with both hands, and then twisting the left one ninety degrees clockwise to form a P with the other. Despite the fact that most of us couldn't place Compton on a map, we imagined the city to be both terrifying and the epicenter of cool.

To share these memories now is deeply embarrassing, and I realize how insensitive and ridiculous our teenage actions may sound—attempting to appropriate the cool of people whose lives and backgrounds we could hardly fathom. But it's important for me to impart a sense of just how normal this behavior was in white America at the time. If you'll excuse the terrible term, we weren't "wiggers." Just about everyone we knew imitated L.A. gangbangers—the guys at least, and plenty of the girls, too. "It was a sense of being a badass, of empowering myself to be bigger and tougher than I would normally see myself," my friend Eric Royce Peterson told me, of gangsta rap's appeal.

As it turns out, the white suburban audience that flocked to N.W.A wasn't just a fluke. Dr. Dre was hoping for a reaction like this. One white Ruthless employee who asked that his name not be used, said Dre would sometimes invite him into his Nissan Pathfinder to play him the group's latest work. "You think white kids would like this?" he'd ask.

In Los Angeles in 1991, *Married . . . with Children* star David Faustino, who played Christina Applegate's randy younger brother Bud Bundy, together with a group including Nic Adler, scion of Sunset Strip icon Lou Adler, began putting on a premier hip-hop party called Balistyx, which drew a multiracial teenage crowd and was frequented by Eazy-E, who would pull up in front in his BMW, parking in the red zone. (Never mind the tickets.) Xzibit and will.i.am would freestyle battle, and another future Black Eyed Peas member, Fergie, danced in a cage.

Despite being a wealthy white kid, Faustino had hip-hop credibility largely because his TV character showed genuine love for the genre, even putting up Ice Cube and Nas posters in his bedroom. "My album poster being on Bud's wall was one of the illest moments for me," Nas said. "My whole projects went crazy. It was a sign that I'd made it in a lot of ways."

Another sign was fashion. *Straight Outta Compton*'s success didn't just vanquish the reigning L.A. hip-hop style, it vanquished the reigning L.A. hip-hop wardrobe as well. Eazy-E almost single-handedly ushered out the East Coast aesthetic. So long, dookie ropes and giant glasses. Borrowing from the local gang aesthetic, he wore white T-shirts—brand-new, and often more than one at a time—Dickies khakis, and black ballcaps. One of his favorites said "Compton," and he got it custom made at a Compton swap meet store run by a North Korean immigrant named Wan Joon Kim, which was also one of the first to sell gangsta rap.

The black and silver colors were appropriated by N.W.A from the Raiders, who played in Los Angeles from 1982 to 1994. This became the gear of choice for street cats and wannabe street cats the country over. "We'd go to the Foot Locker in K.C. and it would be Chiefs shit all on the rack and all the Raiders gear would be gone," Ice Cube said.

CHAPTER SEVEN

ALL HELL BREAKS LOOSE

Just a month after *Straight Outta Compton* hit stores, Eazy-E released his own album, *Eazy-Duz-It*. Because of the success of "The Boyz-N-The Hood" Eazy-E, solo artist, was at this point more famous than N.W.A, and the album strikes a different tone than *Compton*—lighter and more coarse at the same time, less Public Enemy and more Dolemite. Though it features Dr. Dre beats and the whole N.W.A cast of characters, it largely eschews *Compton*'s pent-up aggression and bombast for tall tales from the bedroom, humorous kiss-and-tell anecdotes, and testaments to Eazy's toughness.

There are plenty of threats (*If you press your luck, I'll smoke you like that and won't give a fuck*) but the character most comes to life when hyperbolically discussing his own virility. Opener "Still Talkin' Shit" features a peanut gallery of old-timers assessing Eazy's performance ("I told you that nigga was crazy!") as he brags about how well-endowed he is (at least a yard), how many women it takes to satisfy him (at least three), and what he does with vaginas he doesn't have time for (puts them in the freezer).

"Hey Eazy!" asks a female crowd member on "We Want Eazy." "Why you wear your pants like that?"

"I wear my pants like this for easy access, baby."

On the album, Eazy's raunchy jokes sometimes give way to something darker—a glorification of violence against women. *I might be a woman beater, but I'm not a pussy eater,* he raps on "Still Talkin'." In the bank heist tale "Nobody Move," his character attempts to rape a woman, only to discover that she is a he, at which point he sticks a gun up the man's skirt, *because this is one faggot that I had to hurt.*

When the *Los Angeles Times* called him on his misogyny in a 1989 interview Eazy claimed to be simply speaking the language of the streets on the album. "We're not putting down women," he said. "It's just street talk. Women understand that. They like us. They buy our records. They don't think of us as bad guys."

"We're not disrespecting women, we're disrespecting bitches," he added to *Spin*, prompting the question: What's the difference between a bitch and a woman? "A woman is a woman. A bitch is someone who carries herself in a stuck-up way. A bitch is someone who fucks everybody except me."

Like Andre Young, Eric Wright hurt women in real life. His girlfriend Tracy Jernagin told me he once shot her with a BB gun. Similar to the time she smashed up his BMW after finding him with another woman, she again came to his house and suspected him of cheating, she said. He told her to leave and she was returning to her car when he came outside, armed, she said, adding that she believed he was just trying to "scare" her when he pulled the trigger. But the pellet hit her in the head, and she went to the emergency room. Wright didn't accompany her to the hospital. A doctor was forced to cut the pellet out, she said. (N.W.A affiliate DJ Speed corroborated the rough outlines of her story.)

Lisa Johnson, the mother of three of Dr. Dre's children who says Dre beat her, also accused Eazy of beating her. She told me that, while she was seeing Dre in the mid-eighties, a friend of hers was dating Eazy. The four of them were planning to go to Magic Mountain one day, Johnson said, when the two women happened to drive by a car in Compton, inhabited by Eazy and the mother of one of his children.

Johnson's friend was not happy to see Eazy with another woman, and she hopped out of the car. Eazy's two love interests began arguing and "all hell broke loose," Johnson said. Though she said the whole thing was merely a chance encounter, Eazy seemed to believe Johnson brought her friend to the scene to "start shit," she said. "[He] came over to the car where I was and started fighting me and punching me in my nose," Johnson said, adding that her injuries were so bad that she ended up at a Culver City hospital. Johnson's aunt, who asked her name not to be used, said she arrived to the hospital to find her niece's face swollen: "She was at my house for weeks, could barely walk."

In a 1993 Howard Stern interview Eazy himself discussed beating a woman ("kicked her ass") for doing "scandalous things."

America Gets *Footloose*

These incidents weren't publicly known at the time of N.W.A and Eazy-E's rise, but their lyrics nonetheless put them in the cultural crosshairs. Not long after the start of Reagan's second term in 1985, the major record labels agreed to self-apply parental warning stickers on their albums, as advised by Tipper Gore's Parents Music Resource Center—a committee organized to save the children from naughty music. (*Straight Outta Compton* had the sticker, and its second song was printed as "——tha Police.") At this point the country got all *Footloose*. Pop artists across the spectrum were jailed for "indecent" performances, including Skid Row's Sebastian Bach, Bobby Brown, and LL Cool J. An Arkansas sheriff pulled heavy metal and hip-hop tapes from a Walmart. GWAR was told not to swear in concert. Dead Kennedys' frontman Jello Biafra had his home raided by the LAPD and was charged with obscenity for a graphic poster included in his band's album *Frankenchrist*. (The charges were later dismissed.)

In 1989, Gore and her Parents Music Resource Center colleague Susan Baker, Treasury secretary James Baker's wife, equated rap with rape in a piece for *Newsweek*. Discussing the phenomenon of "wilding," they noted that the teenaged accused rapists of a Central Park jogger could later be heard in lockup "singing a high-on-the-charts rap song about casual sex: 'Wild Thing.'" (Tone Lōc's track has nothing to do with rape.)

Perhaps most notorious was the Macola-spawned group 2 Live Crew, now based in Miami. They came under fire for the sexual nature of their

1989 album *As Nasty As They Wanna Be*. A U.S. district court judge deemed songs like "Me So Horny" obscene, leading to arrests of both a Fort Lauderdale store owner and the group itself, following a performance. They were later vindicated by the Supreme Court, and the album sold briskly.

Plenty of people balked at N.W.A, from squeamish mothers confiscating their kids' tapes to the police who refused to work N.W.A concerts. But many liberals were similarly aghast at the group's nonpolitically correct themes and imagery: conquering and degrading women, crushing adversaries. "There is an element of documentary realism about N.W.A's music," wrote Frank Owen of *Spin* in 1990, "but that is largely overshadowed by the gleeful delight the band takes in demonstrating their supposed toughness. In reality, N.W.A have more in common with a Charles Bronson movie than a PBS documentary on the plight of the inner cities."

"In the world N.W.A's records described, all men were amoral brutes [and] self-loathing thugs who reveled in getting drunk and murdering one another," wrote journalist John Mendelshon. "Had virulent white supremacists ghostwritten their stuff for them, who'd have been able to tell the difference?"

Mainstream radio wasn't happening, and even college radio stations weren't sure what to think. A few Bay Area stations banned the group. University of California Berkeley's KALX and San Francisco community station KPOO had been early N.W.A advocates, even hosting them in studio. But the DJs for their hip-hop shows, along with those from Stanford University's KZSU, later struck the group's songs from their playlists, owing to the act's "negative" lyrics and influence over youth. In an April 1989 interview with Ice Cube, KALX DJ Davey D challenged N.W.A's frequent self-characterization as "reporters," wondering if children would be able to understand this nuance. "If you see a movie like *Psycho III*, the person in the movie might be psycho, but kids know what's real and what's not," Ice Cube responded. "Just because there's a monster person in a movie who's psycho and killing people, that don't mean they gonna go psycho and kill people." Davey D noted that he'd polled listeners about whether or not to play the group, and while opinions were mixed overall, "we had younger people calling up and saying, 'Hey, we live in San Francisco and there are Crips up here now' and they don't like it."

"They say it's our fault that there are Crips up there now?" Ice Cube said in response. "There's been violence since the beginning of time. There ain't no such word as 'peace.' There ain't never gonna be peace.'"

Many major retailers refused to stock the album, and MTV refused to play the "Straight Outta Compton" video, on the grounds that it glorified violence. By the late eighties the network was influential enough to break acts by putting them in regular rotation. Though they'd long neglected rap, the show *Yo! MTV Raps*, which debuted in 1988, was changing things. But "Straight Outta Compton" wasn't on it.

Does the music video glorify violence? Even with cleaned-up lyrics, it's certainly provocative, with Ice Cube miming pumping a shotgun, and the crew antagonizing police. But it feels more documentary than incendiary. Set in various parts of Compton, it reenacts the notorious gang sweeps of the area, and is also pretty funny, with Eazy-E taunting the cops from his convertible. No one shoots at police or anyone else.

The MTV ban hit the group hard, as they were betting on the network's huge viewership to propel them. They also publicly complained of hypocrisy: The hair metal craze had men in stretch pants objectifying women just as blatantly. But the station did show N.W.A's next work, "Express Yourself," a hit that pushed boundaries in its own right. Opening with slaves toiling in a field and a child facing a master's whip, it cuts to a shot of the group exploding through a paper banner with the words "I Have a Dream." (In some versions of the video, the message was blurred.) The modern version of the child now found himself behind bars, as Dre rapped lyrics written by Cube: *I'm expressing with my full capabilities / And now I'm living in correctional facilities.*

Way Too Many Police Out Here

In 1989 the 200,000-member-strong national Fraternal Order of Police voted not to provide service at concerts for acts that threatened police.

This was potentially troubling news for N.W.A, who set out on their first national tour hitting dozens of cities that year.

A 1989 *Village Voice* cover story on various attempts to censor N.W.A maintains that the police union likely learned about "Fuck tha Police" from Reverend James C. Dobson's magazine *Focus on the Family Citizen*. An article titled "Rap Group N.W.A Says 'Kill Police'" asked readers to "Alert local police to the dangers they may face in the wake of this record release." Christian right readers sprang into action notifying departments, and police faxed copies of the lyrics to other stations around the country, pushing to cancel shows on N.W.A's tour. They were successful in cities like Milwaukee and Washington, D.C. Toledo minister Floyd E. Rose said police were pressuring black clergymen there to speak on their behalf. But he refused, writing to the police chief there: "I must say that while I do not like the music and abhor the vulgar language, I will not be used to stifle legitimate anger and understandable resentment." The show went on in Toledo (albeit with no help from police), as it did in dozens of other cities including Kansas City, where the acting mayor attempted to cancel N.W.A's concert, telling them: "Take your trash back to L.A." When the show went off as planned, Ice Cube remarked on stage, "We just showed your city council that blacks, whites, Mexicans, and Orientals can get together for a concert without killing each other."

In the cities where they were allowed to perform, N.W.A's stage show was polished and professional. They had backup dancers—if you can imagine that—and Dre would get the crowd hyped with warm-up chants like, "Just throw your hands in the air / And wave 'em like you're on welfare." Eazy, who acted something like the headliner, wouldn't come on stage until about twenty minutes into the show. (Many early shows were billed as "Eazy-E and N.W.A.")

Despite Cube's pleas, this wasn't exactly a goodwill tour, and behind the scenes, life on the road was chaotic. The group was kicked off their first flight for arguing with a flight attendant. While they showed off fake guns on stage, they traveled from city to city with plentiful *real* firearms and munitions. Alonzo Williams went along gun shopping beforehand.

"These guys are buying automatic and semiautomatic weapons to go on tour with," he said. "I'm like shit! What kind of tour you guys going on? Vietnam?"

Heller made sure that one tour bus had only guns, while another had only bullets. Cube insisted they needed the guns for protection—he claimed that in Detroit once with Ice-T, "local gangsters" came calling and "the assault rifles came out." But for all their bravado, they didn't really know how to properly handle guns, said one of Ruthless's bodyguards, Joe Fierro, with Dre wanting to shoot with his hand cocked sideways, "like a gangster."

Though Eazy had an armory's worth of weapons at his disposal, including "rifles with red eyes and night scopes and night vision," he had no expertise beyond "street shooting," said Fierro, a Vietnam veteran whose nickname was KJ Mustafa. So on various tour stops they went to firing ranges, with Fierro showing Eazy how to take apart his weapons and properly care for them. Fierro said he would contact local law enforcement, to try to smooth things over before they arrived in town, and so the group wouldn't inadvertently wander into hostile gang zones.

Despite constant badgering from the media, protesters, local community leaders, and "fake ass Jheri curl wearing preachers," in the words of MC Ren, the group refused to remove "Gangsta Gangsta" and "Straight Outta Compton" from their playlists. They agreed not to perform "Fuck tha Police," but things came to a head on the final night of their tour, on August 6, 1989, at Joe Louis Arena in downtown Detroit, home of the Red Wings hockey team. The concert was headlined by LL Cool J, and featured all-stars including Big Daddy Kane, De La Soul, and Slick Rick. Some twenty thousand fans filled the venue. Rather than boycotting the show, the police presence was robust; DJ Speed, who was performing as D.O.C.'s turntablist, said he was spooked to see cops lining up alongside the stage. "Way too many police out here," he remembered thinking, adding that they had a "command center" downstairs.

"That particular night, all our personnel were working that venue.

There were close to two hundred of us. We were strategically placed," confirmed Detroit police sergeant Larry Courts.

N.W.A's camp specifically promised Detroit police beforehand that they wouldn't perform "Fuck tha Police." But Cube said the group had been besieged that day by fans asking them to perform the song. And so backstage before the show they had a powwow: "Yo, man, should we do 'Fuck tha Police'?" There was no consensus, and Cube assumed the plan was a no-go.

But after they performed "Gangsta Gangsta," the crowd began chanting, "Fuck the police!" After "A Bitch Iz a Bitch," the crowd chanted "Fuck the police!" again. Same thing after "Straight Outta Compton." While Cube was rapping "I Ain't the One" he noticed Dre and Ren speaking near the turntables. Shortly thereafter, Ren motioned toward him. "Wait a minute," Ren said, moving toward the front of the stage.

To the crowd Ren said: "Everybody say, 'Fuck the police!'"

"Fuck the police!" the crowd roared back.

Back by the turntables, Dre looked in Cube's direction. "Come in on two."

Dre counted it down, and Cube came on.

Fuck the police, comin' straight from the underground

"The place went stupid," Cube said. "Then we see about twenty motherfuckers from the back trying to bum-rush the front."

They were undercover police, members of the department's gang squad it turns out, tossing aside chairs. Attempting to shut down the show, they climbed the barricade and began dismantling amplifiers. Suddenly: a pair of pops, which sounded like gunfire. (They were actually firecrackers, according to eyewitnesses, although it's unclear if they were set off by police.)

Cube and Ren ran off stage, with Cube changing his shirt and looking for an exit. The cops made their way backstage, mistakenly pushing their way into LL Cool J's dressing room.

Meanwhile, N.W.A loaded themselves into a van. "Go to the hotel, pack your shit," the group's road manager Atron Gregory told them. "We're going to Canada."

By some accounts the group's frenzied departure from Detroit *did* take them briefly into Canada, but they ended up back at their hotel. The police caught up with them there, and, according to Cube, said they'd be going to jail. "[But] all they did was talk to us," he added. "They told us they wanted to arrest us on stage to front us off in front of everybody to show that you can't say 'Fuck the police' in Detroit." This version of events veers from the *Straight Outta Compton* biopic, where the group members are arrested outside the arena and thrown in a paddy wagon. In reality, however, eighteen concertgoers were arrested outside the venue and charged with misdemeanors. Sergeant Courts later said the decision to shut down the show was a poor one, considering the chaos it caused.

N.W.A shortly returned home to L.A. But not before Cube made the police an offer they could, and did, refuse. "Yo, y'all want to do a song called 'Fuck N.W.A'?" he claims to have said. "We'll produce it."

The Detroit fiasco wasn't the only difficulty the group encountered during that first national tour in 1989. In early June Curtis Crayon—the father of Dre's half-brother Tyree, and their mother Verna Griffin's ex-husband—suffered a heart attack and died. Tyree took the news hard. "I don't think [Tyree] ever fully recovered from the shock," wrote Griffin in her memoir. Though there were some positive signs in his life—he had a new job, and was planning to get married—he regularly faced trouble in the streets. "Everywhere I go, it seems that someone always wants to challenge me to a fight," he said.

On the night of June 25, 1989, little Warren Griffin—that is, Warren G—knocked on Verna's bedroom door. Two white men in suits had arrived, and wanted to speak to her. They broke the news: Tyree was dead. Apparently he'd fought with a gang contingency and, in the scuffle, fatally hit his head on the concrete. He never regained consciousness. "I guess they were fighting and they fell," Dre said. "All of them fell, and my brother was at the bottom."

Dre received word at a truck stop during the N.W.A tour. He fell to his knees and began crying. He immediately flew home from the tour to grieve, help his mother cope, and plan Tyree's send-off. "I thought that everyone in the world who knew Tyree attended the funeral," Griffin wrote. She took care of Tyree's son Cedric while his mother was away in the navy, and Dre promised to support them.

Tyree had been Dre's best friend and biggest supporter, and he was profoundly affected by his death. "After my brother passed away, I had started boozing," he said.

In his 1999 song "The Message," Dre raps *Sometimes I wish I just died with you*, voicing his frustration with God. Tyree's death seems to have inspired a cynicism in Dre that spilled over into his music. Whereas his lyrics had previously been antidrug and antigang, he took a sharp turn in the years after the death. *The one who puts the G in it*, he raps on the same song. *Who you think put me in it?*

Eventually Dre returned and the tour continued, but more trouble soon emerged. Following a July show in Birmingham, Alabama, MC Ren was accused of raping and impregnating a sixteen-year-old girl named Sheila Davis, on the group's tour bus. She did not file criminal charges, but sued Ren, who had just turned twenty, along with Eazy, Yella, and Dre. (Cube was not named.)

The case was originally settled for $350,000, but the N.W.A members refused to pay. One of their lawyers, Louis Sirkin, offered a sworn statement that the musicians didn't approve the settlement, prompting a circuit judge to levy fines of $16 million on the group. This decision was reversed, and the case was scheduled to be retried, but it was resolved definitively out of court in 1993, with the woman, now twenty, telling *The Tuscaloosa News* she was "very happy" with the settlement, which was reportedly $2 million. For his part, Ren was never charged with or convicted of rape.

Davis's lawyer, Gusty Yearout, told *The Daily Beast* in 2015 that the four N.W.A members were polite when he came out to L.A. to take their depositions. That is, with the exception of Eazy. "Eazy-E was kind of a smart-ass during the deposition," Yearout said. "He said things like… Ren would never rape anybody without wearing a prophylactic."

The Business of Censorship

The rape allegation didn't make many headlines. But a few months later, the group found itself caught up in the rap controversy of the decade. On August 1, 1989, Priority Records president Bryan Turner received a piece of mail at the company's offices, printed on Department of Justice stationery:

> A song recorded by the rap group N.W.A. on their album entitled Straight Outta Compton *encourages violence against and disrespect for the law enforcement officer and has been brought to my attention. I understand your company recorded and distributed this album, and I am writing to share my thoughts and concerns with you.*
>
> *Advocating violence and assault is wrong, and we in the law enforcement community take exception to such action. Violent crime, a major problem in our country, reached an unprecedented high in 1988. Seventy-eight law enforcement officers were feloniously slain in the line of duty during 1988, four more than in 1987. Law enforcement officers dedicate their lives to the protection of our citizens, and recordings such as the one from the N.W.A. are both discouraging and degrading to these brave, dedicated officers.*
>
> *Music plays a significant role in society, and I wanted you to be aware of the FBI's position relative to this song and its message. I believe my views reflect the opinion of the entire law enforcement community.*

The letter was signed by FBI chief spokesman Milt Ahlerich.

Ahlerich's message was strange; it didn't accuse the group of breaking the law (they weren't), and it didn't threaten any specific repercussions (which would have likely been unconstitutional). The letter didn't even mention any specific N.W.A songs, though it was clearly referencing "Fuck tha Police."

The FBI, then as now, didn't traditionally weigh in on any art, much less rap lyrics; the First Amendment does a pretty good job of keeping government entities out of the cultural conversation. And it turns out Ahlerich, though speaking on behalf of the FBI, hadn't even heard the song. He'd only read the lyrics. If the letter was intended to make N.W.A nervous, the effort was only partially successful. "I was scared. You kidding? It was the FBI. I'm just a kid from Canada, what do I know?" Priority's Bryan Turner told the *Los Angeles Times*. When the controversy broke, he'd just returned from the Soviet Union, where he was putting together a distribution deal for the label. "I showed it to some lawyers. They said they [the FBI] couldn't do anything. That made me feel better."

Ice Cube apparently took the news a little more lightly: "Oh, I didn't know they [the FBI] were buying our records, too!" he said.

The group kept the letter under their hat for a bit, and it didn't make big news until October, when Phyllis Pollack (who began as a Ruthless Records publicist that year) and Dave Marsh, her partner in an anticensorship organization group called Music in Action, published a *Village Voice* cover story titled "The FBI Hates This Band." The media pounced, and overwhelmingly came down on the side of N.W.A. It was one thing to dislike "Fuck tha Police" or its message (as many journalists did), but it was something else entirely for the government to intimidate artists. The *Los Angeles Times* quoted dissenters including U.S. congressman Don Edwards, a Democrat from San Jose and a former FBI agent: "The FBI should stay out of the business of censorship," he said.

The FBI missive had backfired. "I have to say thanks to that FBI agent that wrote us that letter," Dr. Dre said. "You made us a lot of money." Many believe the governmental scolding was the greatest publicity gift N.W.A could have hoped for. It seemed the parade of gatekeepers who attempted to slow N.W.A down (from the cops to the FBI to MTV to the retailers who wouldn't sell their records) actually did the group a favor. After all, the more you tell kids what they shouldn't be listening to, the more they'll clamor for it. "It made them even more dangerous," Bryan Turner said. "So then kids were like, 'I gotta hear this record. The FBI doesn't want me to hear it!' We probably sold about a million records in conjunction with that letter."

That theory may be overblown. By the time the FBI letter was publicized, *Straight Outta Compton* had already gone platinum, on its way to triple platinum. If not for the suppression, they may have sold much more. In fact, Jerry Heller said that Warner later backed off a big partnership deal with Ruthless after being "spooked" by the letter and the reigning anti–hip-hop sentiment.

Daily Beast writer Rich Goldstein pointed out that 1988 was a huge year for record sales, led by George Michael's *Faith* and the *Dirty Dancing* soundtrack, each of which sold over ten million copies. In those pre-internet days, there weren't very many places to hear about new music, and not many places to buy it. All of N.W.A's publicity was great, but that didn't matter if you couldn't actually consume their songs. "Had *Straight Outta Compton* been played on MTV, listened to on the radio, and been available for purchase in big-box retailers like Walmart, there is a good chance it would have eclipsed the *Dirty Dancing* soundtrack," Goldstein theorized.

Something in My Heart

Ruthless Records wasn't just a vehicle for Eazy-E and N.W.A. Sure, the fledgling label didn't have a huge staff, but they signed a diverse range of artists and maintained a regular release schedule, even when Eazy and company were on the road. One of their early discoveries was an R&B singer from South Central named Michelle Toussaint, who performed under the name Michel'le. She sang in a Baptist church growing up, and as a sixteen-year-old working at May Company at the Fox Hills Mall, carried a tune while folding up clothes. An aspiring rapper heard her in this capacity, and convinced her to come along to his audition with Alonzo Williams. Lonzo agreed about her talent. Her big break came in 1987 when World Class Wreckin' Cru's regular female vocalist, Mona Lisa—the one who told Dre, Yella, and the others that she wasn't ready to be their lover—wasn't available to record their song "Turn Off the Lights."

Lonzo enlisted Toussaint, and the song became the Wreckin' Cru's biggest hit. Dre, who performed on the track with her, began calling her every morning before work, she said, and in late 1987 they began dating. She appeared on his Roadium swap meet tapes, and was soon drafted onto the Ruthless team. Bridging the subgenres of new jack swing and the hip-hop–flavored R&B that would take over in the nineties, Toussaint had impeccable chops and a strong, no-nonsense persona. Her first stage name was Baby. "For two weeks I walked around with a pacifier around my neck," she said. Thankfully it was soon jettisoned in favor of her Frenchified Christian moniker, a tribute to her Creole ancestry.

Michel'le is today thought of as a precursor to Mary J. Blige or Beyoncé. And like J. J. Fad, Michel'le's mainstream-acceptable lyrics and radio-friendly sound helped open doors for N.W.A that would have been otherwise closed. The two acts fed off each other, with Dre and Yella coproducing her 1989 debut *Michel'le* and Dre appearing on her single "Nicety." Both the album and its first single, "No More Lies," went gold. "Dre didn't know how to do R&B, and I didn't know how to rap, so we kinda fused it," she said. She gives him credit for pushing her during demanding studio sessions. Recording her hit song "Something in My Heart" was particularly traumatic. He didn't like what she'd initially brought to the session and began berating her, she said. She started crying, and before long commenced a sort of melodic "moaning," which thrilled him, she went on, as it came from a place of genuine emotion. She then belted out new lyrics, conceived on the spot, which she said dealt with her and Dre's actual relationship: *Baby if we try / Things will get better / No one can tell me different.*

Dre made her dig down, as deep as she could go. "I was talking to him through the booth," she said. "I get why 'Something in My Heart' resonates with people. Because it's real."

The magic of her musical partnership with Dre didn't always translate to real life. He began seeing J. J. Fad's MC J.B. "I busted them in the bed together," Michel'le said. (MC J.B. confirmed this account, adding that the two women have since "put this all behind us and we are cordial with each other.")

Eventually Dre and J.B. broke off, and he and Michel'le became more serious. They got engaged—he gave her an eight-carat rock—though never married. During a tour with MC Hammer in 1990 she found out she was pregnant, and bore Dre's son, named Marcel, in early 1991. She stayed at home with Marcel, and her career slowed. "[Dre] didn't want to see [Marcel], and he didn't want to support him on the right level," she said, adding that she was forced to take him to court for child support. Still he eventually made things right: "When my mom and my grandma died, he came into my son's life. They have a good relationship."

Meanwhile, Michel'le was drawn into the first salvo of what would be later known as the East Coast–West Coast wars. In 1991 Bronx rapper Tim Dog, upset about L.A. hip-hop's rising popularity at the expense of New York's, released an album called *Penicillin on Wax*, which contained a number of out-of-nowhere shots against the Ruthless camp, including attacks against Dre and absurd, disgusting assertions about Michel'le.

But one allegation—that Dre hit her—she would later claim was true. In an interview with *R&B Divas: L.A.* host Wendy Williams in 2013, Michel'le said he broke her nose so badly she needed a nose job. She added that on numerous occasions he gave her a black eye, even shortly before she was supposed to shoot music videos. "It seemed like the day before a video, I would get a black eye and we had to cover it," she said. She stayed with him throughout this time and never called the police because, in her mind, "getting beat was love to me." (Dr. Dre, through his attorney, had no comment on Michel'le's allegations.)

She told me he beat her one time because she cooked dinner and there "wasn't enough chicken." She told VladTV that during another argument he shot at her and missed her by inches. "I had five black eyes. I have a cracked rib, I have scars that are just amazing," she told WWPR's The Breakfast Club in 2015. "I do remember when he first hit me. When he first gave me my very first black eye, we laid in the bed and he cried. He was crying. I was crying because I was in shock and hurt and in pain. I don't know why he was crying, but he said, 'I'm really sorry.' I think that was the only time he ever said he was sorry. And he said, 'I'll never hit you in that eye again, okay?' And I was like, 'Yeah, okay.' And we fell asleep." The couple broke up for good, she said, when he became engaged to his current wife, Nicole Threatt, in the mid-nineties.

"I made some fucking horrible mistakes in my life," Dre told *Rolling Stone* in 2015, addressing the general topic of his violence against women. "I was young, fucking stupid. I would say all the allegations aren't true— some of them are. Those are some of the things that I would like to take back. It was really fucked up. But I paid for those mistakes, and there's no way in hell that I will ever make another mistake like that again."

The Ghostwriter

Around the same time of Michel'le's solo debut, another Ruthless Records artist was emerging as a superstar: D.O.C. After arriving from Dallas he quickly became the silent backbone of the N.W.A operation, ghostwriting lyrics and helping shape songs. Eazy was a fan, and Dr. Dre trusted his instincts more than almost anyone. "He and D.O.C. were two peas in a pod, they were very, very close," said MC J.B.

Dr. Dre has long employed ghostwriters; in interviews he has said that he sees rapping as just another part of a song's sound, not necessarily more or less important than, say, the percussion. Over the years he's enlisted luminaries including Snoop Dogg, Eminem, Jay-Z, Drake, and Rick Ross to write for him. But D.O.C. has long been his go-to guy. Tall and good-looking, though not always comfortable in front of cameras, some have called D.O.C. the West Coast's answer to Rakim, the Long Island rap titan whose complicated rhyme structures altered rap permanently. But D.O.C.'s own dynamic, stutter-step flow is different; he crams whole paragraphs into single lines, varying tempo while somehow maintaining a breezy feel. As a solo performer he goes lighter on the tough-guy stuff than N.W.A, preferring instead to boast about his skills on the mic.

D.O.C. had a go-along-to-get-along attitude, and tended not to rock the boat. "You never saw me in the early videos, never heard about me, but I put a lot of work in," he said. "I felt shitted on, a little bit, but I never complained about it." He received a $35,000 advance for his 1989 debut solo album *No One Can Do It Better*, but almost never signed proper contracts, content to let benefactors like Eazy-E and Dr. Dre provide him with living expenses and other perks.

D.O.C. said he owns little of his proper publishing, that is, royalties for the songs he wrote and performed. One persistent rumor has it that he gave some of it up in exchange for jewelry. Jerry Heller said that story is false, but D.O.C., while concurring that Heller was not involved, said Eazy took advantage of him, giving him a chain, a watch, and a ring in exchange for the rights to a number of songs. "I took about five thousand dollars in jewelry and give him about a million bucks worth of publishing."

But before music industry realities caught up with them, D.O.C. and Dre were having the time of their lives, young men doing their craft at ridiculously high levels. "There's a synergy with Dre and me," D.O.C. said. Dre dedicated himself to the making of *No One Can Do It Better*. Their celebrated collaboration "The Formula" was birthed after Dre and Michel'le went out late one evening, returning in the middle of the night when D.O.C., living at Dre's place, was asleep on the floor. Dre woke D.O.C. up: "I was on my way home and I got caught up in a daydream. It was me and you was bustin' a song called 'Tha Formula' to a Marvin Gaye beat!" Dre played D.O.C. a tape of the song in question—Gaye's "Inner City Blues (Make Me Wanna Holler)"—and then promptly passed out. D.O.C. roused himself and stayed up until five thirty in the morning putting the track together.

The album went platinum, Jay-Z later shouted it out on his 2003 song "Public Service Announcement," and D.O.C. bought a house in the Conejo Valley. He was feeling like a rock star. By late 1989 it began to seem like big paydays were around every corner, including an upcoming tour. The fame and fortune went to his head, and his substance abuse was unchecked. "I was a young man completely out of control," he said.

One night in mid-November 1989, he was filming a pair of videos in East Los Angeles, "Beautiful But Deadly" and "The Formula." In the latter, Eazy and Dre hold rapper tryouts with wannabes with names like MC

Mallet and New Kids in the Hood. But Dre isn't satisfied until, in a haze, he imagines crafting his "perfect rapper" in the lab—D.O.C.

Filming two videos at the same time was a long, arduous process. D.O.C. drank and smoked weed practically all day, running on fumes that night when he finally got into his car to make the long drive to his Agoura Hills home, westbound on the 101. He fell asleep and his car spun out, throwing him through the back window. His car collided with a tree. Once the medics arrived, they couldn't sedate him because they didn't know what drugs he had in his system, he said. Still intoxicated, he fought back as they tried to insert a breathing tube, scarring his larynx.

D.O.C. was taken to Kaiser Hospital, and then Cedars-Sinai. His hospital bills came to more than $60,000, Jerry Heller wrote, which Eazy "paid for out of his own pocket." D.O.C. would make a full recovery but for one, very serious problem: He lost his voice. He could still talk, but it sounded raspy, something like a stage whisper. For a man known for acrobatic turns of phrase, this was a massive blow. "My mother begged me to come home after the wreck but I couldn't, I felt defeated. I was ashamed to go home," he said.

D.O.C.'s voice would never recover. He said an operation to expedite the healing process was botched, though he also blames himself for not following through with his rehab sessions. In the wake of his accident, he descended further into drug and alcohol abuse, which would continue for much of the nineties. "I used to ask Dre for five grand every three or four days for about two years and would get it and then go spend it up on dope," he said. He was drunk at all hours of the day, stumbling around parties, once brandishing a sawed-off shotgun, shirtless and threatening people.

I meet D.O.C. in 2011, over a late dinner at a Mexican restaurant in Sherman Oaks. For someone out of the spotlight for decades, D.O.C. still carries a star quality. He's in good shape, though his voice sounds like he speaks through a smoker's voice box. He charms the restaurant's staff, some of whom he knows from having lived just across the street, the spot chosen for its proximity to one of Dre's preferred studios, Record One.

"I'll get an Arnold Palmer," he says, "so it will look like I'm having a real drink." He's been sober for six months, he adds, and goes on to talk honestly about everything from his accident to his money problems. He doesn't seem to feel sorry for himself, and weaves in ruminations on current projects: mentoring young rappers, a reality show, and possible experimental stem-cell surgery to repair his vocal cords he's hoping to receive from a Barcelona doctor.

D.O.C. now lives in his native Dallas, where he helps raise his daughter Puma, whose mother is R&B icon Erykah Badu. But the week I meet him, he's in town at Dre's invitation to work on *Detox*, the near-mythical album Dre started around 2001, and which he would eventually scrap. D.O.C. was first brought into the *Detox* fold around 2005. But the pair butted heads about money. Dre rented a house for him and paid him a $20,000 annual retainer, he says, but that wasn't enough for him to be comfortable. They also clashed over the album's direction; it was only one chapter in their long, on-again, off-again friendship, which is tangled up in their working relationship.

Their collaborative album *No One Can Do It Better* is a testament to the great work they do together. So are *Straight Outta Compton*, *Eazy-Duz-It*, *The Chronic*, and *2001*, all of which D.O.C. wrote on, and all of which are classics. Still, one can't help but wonder: What if? What if D.O.C. hadn't crashed his car, hadn't lost his voice? Maybe he, like Dre's later stars Snoop Dogg and Eminem, would have taken over mainstream America. "I'm probably one of the best motherfuckers to ever pick up a microphone and spit in it," D.O.C. says, "but you'd never really know that, because I never really got a chance to show you."

Thrill Seeker

Though D.O.C.'s career looked bleak in late 1989, for N.W.A the party was just getting started. Like with many men who get famous at a young age, seduction became a volume game. DJ Yella always seemed to be on the prowl, while Eazy-E had sex with women for pleasure, for sport, and even as practical jokes. Upon Eazy's invitation, Jerry Heller once arrived at the rapper's hotel suite to discuss royalty statements, only to discover him being fellated on the toilet.

"Eazy used to call hisself a thrill seeker, meaning he would just bareback, have sex without condoms," Dr. Dre said in the documentary *N.W.A: The World's Most Dangerous Group.* "So he called me and Cube 'RATS,' Rappers Against Thrill Seekers."

If Dre said he used condoms, he certainly didn't do so religiously, and ended up fathering, by my count, at least ten children. He and Eazy both faced a number of paternity lawsuits, some of which ended with them being forced to pay child support.

Eazy, however, seemed the one most dedicated to hedonism. As the label owner, he was also the best paid, and he treated himself to luxuries like an early, comically oversized cell phone. Eazy also bought a house in Norwalk. In the shadow of the noisy 605 freeway—all the better for, say, a quick escape from the cops—it's a modest, tan, three-bedroom structure in a middle-class area, but not too far from the hood. After word got around that he lived there, neighborhood kids would amass at the front door, remembered Ruthless Records rapper Steffon, and Eazy would happily sign autographs. He bought another house out in the Valley in Westlake Village—the backyard had a waterfall—and got one for Dre just around the corner.

Ice Cube was running at a different speed. He said he practiced safe sex, and had a single paternity case, from 1991, which is sealed, meaning it is unclear if the child was found to be his. In contrast to Eazy and Dre, who were arrested often on allegations ranging from reckless driving to assault, Cube has a clean adult criminal record. While the other guys were sowing their wild oats, he was meeting the woman of his dreams. He and his friend T-Bone spent weekends at the Fox Hills mall, shopping and clowning around, sometimes with future *Friday* stars Faizon Love and Chris Tucker. On these outings, the duo would regularly bump into a beautician from South Central named Kim Woodruff, with whom Cube would try to strike up conversation. "She didn't give me no play," he said.

But one day Cube and T-Bone were driving down Crenshaw, headed to the beach, when they pulled up next to Kim and her cousin at a stoplight. "I looked over and said, 'Cube, that's the girl you're trying to talk to!'" T-Bone recalled. Cube honked the horn and signaled for them to pull over, and they exchanged numbers. It turns out they had the exact same cars—gray Suzuki Sidekicks.

"When Ice Cube met Kim, it was over for every other chick in the city," said Cube's friend J-Dee. "They were the 'it' couple. My girl would be like, 'Cube wouldn't do that to Kim, that shit you're doing to me.'"

N.W.A Money

In 1989, Cube was still living with his parents—doing the dishes and everything. For someone who was an essential part of two hit albums (*Straight Outta Compton* and *Eazy-Duz-It* would sell more than five million combined) this was an unimaginable indignity. By the middle of that year he'd reportedly received $32,700 in album royalties, and a bit less than that amount for the tour.

"I think that he got what someone at his stage of his career would have gotten," Heller insisted. But Cube felt otherwise. "Jerry Heller lives in a half-million-dollar house in Westlake, and I'm still living at home with my mother. Jerry's driving a Corvette and Mercedes-Benz and I've got a Suzuki Sidekick," he groused to *Spin*.

"Jerry has no creative input into the group: he just makes all the fucked-up decisions and gets all the fucking money," he continued. One of those "fucked-up decisions"? Not letting N.W.A appear on an episode of Jesse Jackson's show *Voices of America*, about controversial music, because apparently they wouldn't be paid. "We should have been on that show, getting nationwide exposure and getting people on our side," Cube went on. "When you turn down something like that, you've gotta think that the man doesn't want it for the group. He's just in it for the short term so that he can make as much money as quickly as possible."

Cube felt particularly miffed about the spoils from *Eazy-Duz-It*. Sure, it had Eazy's name on the front, but Ice Cube considered it basically an N.W.A album, since they all had contributed. "Eazy's royalty statement came in. So I just know that this money is about to be broke up five ways, and everybody's gonna get paid," he said. "And dude was like, 'Nah, this is Eazy-E money, we getting N.W.A money.' I'm like, 'Eazy-E and N.W.A's the same thing!' "

In 1989 Cube began talking privately with Patricia Charbonnet, a savvy N.W.A publicist. She had taken a particular shine to him; Eazy and Ren complained that she channeled the majority of interview opportunities his way. She agreed that Cube wasn't getting what he was worth, and advised him to seek out a lawyer.

During N.W.A's 1989 tour, word came down that Priority Records staff would be meeting them in Arizona to present them with plaques, celebrating a million copies sold of *Straight Outta Compton*.

They would also receive $75,000 checks—payment for previous works and an advance on their next album. It was more money than Cube had ever seen in his life. "I needed that money, I wanted that money," he said. But there was a catch. Jerry Heller said they'd have to sign a contract, considering they'd previously functioned on only a handshake-style agreement.

Cube was dubious. Wasn't he entitled to money for work he'd already done, no matter what? At the very least, shouldn't he show the contract to his lawyer? "Jerry told me that lawyers were made to cause trouble," he said.

Cube and his lawyer did attempt to negotiate with Ruthless, to no avail. In the end, Cube didn't sign the contract, and lobbied the other members to abstain as well. But the allure of cash for the twentysomething rappers was too strong. Afterward, there was tension. "Everybody was like, 'Why didn't he sign it?' " said Ren.

As the label owner, Eazy ultimately controlled Cube's payday. But when it came to business, Cube believed Heller pulled the strings, and that he was simply another in a long line of corrupt, white record company men.

"We tried to settle this dispute diligently," said Cube's lawyer Michael Ashburn in early 1990. "We bent over backwards to try and make a financial agreement that was acceptable to both sides. I was surprised how indifferent they were when it came to settling... They gave us a statement showing that Ice Cube had been advanced $32,700. He's owed at least another $120,000, plus his publishing royalties, which he hasn't received a cent on so far. Ice Cube wanted to continue with N.W.A, but he just wasn't getting paid."

When I talked to him, Heller countered that delays between album sales and artist payouts are common, and reasonably noted that Cube has profited millions from *Straight Outta Compton* in the decades since its release. David Kronemyer, a longtime record company executive who worked with Ruthless, seconds this assertion. "It takes a long time and most artists never recoup. Ice Cube did, in fact, recoup in this situation, it just took a long time," he said. Heller claimed both his and Cube's legal teams audited Ruthless's accounting, and that Cube never filed suit.

"If I've been fuckin' everybody, why aren't they suin' me?" Eazy asked.

You Don't Fire Me

By late 1989 Cube was in limbo, unsure whether or not to continue on with the group. He consulted Public Enemy's Chuck D, who encouraged him to stay the course, because he was such a big fan of N.W.A.

The other members of the act made Cube's ambivalence the butt of jokes. Just before the Arizona meeting, when Cube made clear his intentions not to sign the N.W.A contract, they recorded a homemade parody video using Eazy's camcorder. D.O.C. stars as Cube, munching on ice and musing on his brilliance. He receives a call from Heller (playing himself), who implores him to sign the N.W.A contract, offering a Ferrari Testarossa, a Beverly Hills house, and "three white people in my family to carry your clothes to the gig." The Cube character passes, until Heller makes him an offer he can't refuse: a briefcase full of activator for his Jheri curl.

It's not clear if Cube saw this video at the time—it was later released on an N.W.A videotape—but T-Bone said Cube finally came to a decision after being tipped off that Eazy was planning on releasing him. And so, by the end of 1989 he'd made his decision: You don't fire me. I quit.

Some thought Cube was making the mistake of a lifetime. "Everybody was like, 'Go ahead, nigga. Be like Arabian Prince,'" Cube said.

Kim, however, his crucial confidante, told him he should believe in himself and follow his heart. It also helped having Patricia Charbonnet in his corner, whom Cube named as his manager. She quickly began talking with Priority's Bryan Turner about securing him a solo deal.

That Ice Cube only made one album with N.W.A is unfortunate. But the fissure was probably inevitable, considering the group's unholy mixture of youth, fame, and controversy.

"Threat of police action and the FBI letter wore on the group," wrote Jerry Heller.

"All the money and all the fame creates a fog," said Cube. "You can run into each other like helicopters crashing in the desert."

Nobody could have predicted the future—that Ice Cube would give the all-mighty N.W.A a run for its money—but one thing was clear. The kinder, gentler era of hip-hop was over.

By 1988, Rodger Clayton had stopped throwing his giant electro soirees with his mobile DJ crew Uncle Jamm's Army. "It's just too dangerous because of the gangsters," he said. "Ninety-nine percent of the kids are good, but just one kid with a gun can ruin everything." Even bigger was the influence of the gangsta rappers. N.W.A's success would set off an avalanche of tough-talking, street-smart groups, with no subject any longer off-limits, however inflammatory or obscene. The record companies quickly realized just how profitable this style could be, and hip-hop was never the same.

CHAPTER EIGHT

MOST WANTED

Ruthless Records initially operated out of Eazy-E's parents' garage, but around 1988 the label moved into its first formal offices, in San Fernando Valley suburb Canoga Park, a good hour by car from Compton. The Valley, forever stereotyped as a cultural graveyard of soulless commuters and their bubble-headed offspring, is today home to countless rappers, who buy first homes there once they get their record company advance. Unlike Orange County and other Los Angeles suburbs, much of the Valley offers fairly quick access to the city, but it's far enough removed that, say, your distant cousin (*so proud* of all your success) won't drop by unexpectedly.

Those first Ruthless facilities were in a dodgy strip mall, with bums scavenging around the premises, and across the street from a discount food outlet selling expired bread. But in the early nineties, with ten or so artists signed to its roster and flush with cash from the success of N.W.A, Eazy-E, J. J. Fad, D.O.C., and Michel'le, Ruthless graduated to a tony, custom-designed suite in an office park just south in Woodland Hills, a few minutes away from where Ice Cube went to high school.

When I visited the site in 2015, I wasn't sure I had the right location. The building's appearance has probably changed somewhat, since it was retrofitted after the 1994 Northridge earthquake, but the courtyard water fountain remains, and the facilities have a sleek, corporate design. It's hard to imagine a gangsta rap label headquartered there. But that was the point; Eazy and Heller, who were running the show, wanted to be taken seriously, and the office park offered legitimacy, not to mention tranquility.

Gold and platinum records lined the walls. In his office, outfitted with trippy black wallpaper, Eazy played music videos at top volume. But he wasn't often there. On a day-to-day basis you'd find folks like Heller's cousin Gary Ballen (Ruthless's general manager), Heller's nephew Terry Heller (head of security), and secretaries including one with "over-the-top, Dolly Parton boobs," Eazy-E's assistant Charis Henry recalled.

Countless performers were vying for a record deal with the upstart label. One of the new faces at Ruthless was Tairrie B, a white rapper signed to Eazy's sublabel Comptown, distributed by MCA Records. Born Tairrie Beth, she was a twenty-four-year-old, tracksuit-wearing, blond B-girl from the Valley. She'd briefly performed in a girl group, and had lately been working with Quincy Jones III, the son of Swedish supermodel Ulla Andersson and Quincy Jones.

Backstage at an Anaheim N.W.A show in 1989, she was introduced to Jerry Heller by a friend who was an actress. Tairrie recalled their conversation:

"Oh," said Heller. "Are you an actress, too?"

"No," she responded tartly, "I'm a rapper."

"A white girl rapper? You never see one of those. Well, I manage N.W.A. If you're really a rapper and got something we can play, we're looking to sign people."

"Sure, yeah right."

"No, I'm serious, you know, come down to Audio Achievements. We're doing auditions in a week."

Once she let her guard down Tairrie B was psyched about the opportunity, but worried: She only had one song, a demo in which she rapped over Jimi Hendrix's "Foxy Lady." On the appointed day she drove her Volkswagen Jetta down to Torrance to meet the crew, alone. "Everyone was like, you can't go by yourself. They're a bunch of gangsters!" she remembered. But she wasn't dissuaded, and did her best to project confidence. All of N.W.A, along with D.O.C., was present. "They're all looking, like, 'What the fuck is she doing here?'"

"Jerry Heller sent me," she said. "I'm a rapper."

"You got a tape?" Eazy asked. She handed her cassette to him, and he immediately put it into the stereo. As the room fell silent, Tairrie asked herself if she had made a mistake by coming.

Her song played through, from beginning to end, an agonizing few minutes. When it was over, Eazy took out the tape. Nobody said a word.

He handed the cassette back to her. Still not receiving any reaction, she thanked the guys for listening and said it was nice to meet them. Just as she turned to leave, Eazy called out:

"Hey, want a record deal?"

It was a moment straight out of a storybook, and with it Tairrie became the first white female rapper signed to a major deal (as opposed to a singer who rapped occasionally, like Debbie Harry or Teena Marie).

But there was no happy ending. First Tairrie angered Heller, she said, by declining to use him as her manager, opting for a veteran named Linda Martinez. (Heller said he does not recall this.)

She also butted heads with Dr. Dre, who was slated to produce her songs. At that time Dre did almost everyone's albums at Ruthless. But they immediately clashed. Tairrie, Martinez, Eazy, and Dre held a meeting to discuss Tairrie's album in Martinez's car outside of the studio. As Martinez recalls, the conversation went like this:

"Dre has the Midas touch," Eazy said. "Everything he does turns gold or platinum. This is a great opportunity for you."

"But I will tell you one thing," Dre added. "When you go into the studio, keep your mouth shut. I have total creative control."

Tairrie refused. "It's not your record, it's my record," she told Dre.

Dre's bedside manner could have used some work. But he's always insisted upon micromanaging artists, and his track record seemed to justify such an approach—just look what he did with Eazy-E. "People ask me how I come up with these hits, and I can only say that I know what I like, and I'm quick to tell a motherfucker what I don't like," Dre said.

Bruce Williams, who became Dre's assistant, described the process like this: "You'll hear him bark out odd orders. 'Do this.' One unexplained utterance and a knob tweak or two later, and it's 'Do this.' And not one of these rappers be knowin' *what* the fuck is goin' on. In the best of situations, the new, raw cats who don't understand the creative process, who don't understand visionary perfectionism—and who does, really?—just go with what is happening. They don't fight it."

Tairrie B wasn't interested in following orders, however. An assortment of different producers, including herself, Quincy Jones III, Bilal Bashir, and Schoolly D, produced her debut, 1990's *Power of a Woman*, which portrayed her as a quick-rhyming badass, and, in her noir-style, black-and-white video for "Murder She Wrote," the female gangsta counterpart to N.W.A. The album didn't sell nearly as well as previous Ruthless releases, likely owing to Dre's lack of involvement. (Tairrie B says the distributor MCA stopped promoting it after she aggressively confronted a *BAM Magazine* writer who wrote a negative review.)

Before the album even came out, Tairrie clashed with the N.W.A affiliates over its final track. That slot on Ruthless albums was often reserved for shout-outs and guest verses, and for *Power of a Woman*'s finale the crew suggested a track in this vein, she said, called "I Ain't Yo Bitch," in which they would call her a "bitch" and she would respond to the contrary. She didn't like this idea, opting instead for a guest-free track called "Ruthless Bitch," in which she flipped the script and called *herself* a bitch. "Just like the gays own the word queer, I'm going to put power into it and define it so you motherfuckers can stop calling chicks bitches," she told me.

No one else liked the idea. She recorded the song anyway, an eight-minute invective-laced epic that used a sample of Led Zeppelin's "Immigrant Song." It dedicated a verse to attacking Dre:

> *Go back to wearing sequins, 'cause you look like a faggot*
> *World Class? You got no class*

The tension boiled over when the two encountered each other on February 21, 1990, at a Grammys after-party hosted by Epic Records, at a spot called Rex II Ristorante in downtown L.A. Dre had just heard the draft of "Ruthless Bitch," and wasn't a fan. He had been drinking, and approached Linda Martinez, with whom he began flirting. As Martinez recalled: "He put his arm around me and said, 'When are you and I going out?'"

Martinez laughed him off, insisting she was old enough to be his mother. Tairrie, who watched the scene unfold from the venue's mezzanine level, was not amused. She came downstairs and told Dre to get his hands off Martinez, who told her that it was "OK." Nonetheless, Tairrie "just unloaded on him," said Martinez. "I could see him getting angrier and angrier."

"I heard your fucking track," Dre said, in Tairrie's recollection. "Fuck you, bitch!"

"Fuck you, Mr. Ultimate Breaks and Beats," she yelled back, referencing a popular series of vinyl albums containing sample-ready breakbeats.

"One more fucking word," he added, a threat she ignored.

"And he punched me in the eye," she said. "And when I didn't go down, he punched me in the mouth."

"He punched her hard, really hard," added Martinez. "The way a guy would hit another guy. It seemed like it had some real force behind it."

At this point security intervened and they were separated. Tairrie B was not so badly hurt that she had to go to the hospital. "He didn't break my teeth, he didn't break a bone," she said. "I had no scars." But she was absolutely livid. She said she called Eazy, called Heller, and threatened to file charges with LAPD. She called her boyfriend—the rapper Everlast, who would later find success with House of Pain—who responded: "Let me come down there and get my boys."

She dissuaded him from doing this, however. The next day she met with Eazy and Heller. "Eazy got real weird and protective," arranging to make sure she and Dre would not be in the same room together, she said.

"Jerry at first expressed some sympathy for Tairrie, wanted to know if she was OK, but said, 'We cannot let you file charges against Dre,'" said Martinez. "In so many words he said, 'We're going to drop you from the label'" if you file charges. (Jerry Heller denies this.)

And so, Tairrie said, she and Eazy worked out a deal: cash for her silence. "It was a nice amount," she said, declining to be specific. "And I was cool." She adds that the deal was made independently of Heller.

In Martinez's recollection, Eazy waited a while before giving Tairrie the funds, and doesn't believe he explicitly called it hush money. Dre declined comment on the alleged battery.

Before her album was released, Tairrie B was forced to rerecord "Ruthless Bitch," since they couldn't get the rights to the Led Zeppelin sample. On the final version she added another shot at Dre:

You cartoon gangsta, I'm calling your bluff
Hitting a woman? That makes you real tough

In her post-Ruthless years, Tairrie B switched genres completely and became a rock star in a number of acts, including fronting a metal band called My Ruin with her husband, Mick Murphy. Around the time of her fiftieth birthday, she finally returned with a hip-hop album called *Vintage Curses*.

In his memoir, Jerry Heller writes that Michel'le—not Dre—punched Tairrie at the Grammys party (which Michel'le and everyone else I talked to denies)—an assertion that angers Tairrie. She told me she regrets calling Dr. Dre a "faggot."

Her biggest regret is not pressing charges against him. She said her efforts battling domestic violence and working in women's shelters in later years have taught her the importance of speaking up. She's especially remorseful because, a year later, Dre would be involved in an even more brutal attack on a woman, television host Dee Barnes. "I feel like, had I pressed charges, either that wouldn't have happened—he wouldn't have the balls to do that to her—or maybe he could have been put away," Tairrie B said.

A Two-Piece Chicken Wing in the Jaw

Dre's and Eazy's violent, reckless behavior sometimes threatened to sabotage the ascent of Ruthless Records, which was trying its hardest to become a legitimate, big-time player in the music industry. Ice Cube's departure didn't help, either. Still, the imprint managed to stay the course, continuing to produce top-selling records. In 1989 the label signed another gangsta group that would develop a large following, Above the Law, who were nearly as tough as their image. Frontman Greg Hutchinson is known as Cold 187um, referencing the California penal code for murder. (The "um" means "untouchable murder" and is also a pronunciation cue for the number 7, "sevum," similar to how, say, "5th" means "fifth.")

Above the Law hailed from Pomona, California, a thirty-mile drive east from downtown L.A. The group came to Eazy's attention through Laylaw, the brother of group member Go Mack. Rounded out by DJ Total K-Oss, and rapper-producer KMG the Illustrator, the act brought with them their mostly completed debut *Livin' Like Hustlers*, which Dre helped produce. Cold 187um, a rapper and producer who plays trumpet, bass guitar, and piano, worked closely with Dre, and they fed off each other. *Livin' Like Hustlers* features the sinister Moog synthesizer sound that N.W.A is known for. "[W]e'd be doing some music and [N.W.A would] hear it and next thing you know our music would end up on N.W.A's records," said Laylaw.

Above the Law got a big break on the 1990 collaboration "We're All in the Same Gang." Made by a group calling themselves West Coast Rap All-Stars, the track features Dre on production, Michel'le on the hook (*Don't you know we've got to put our heads together?*) and rappers including King Tee, MC Hammer, Tone Lōc, and Ice-T. The offering came on the heels of "Self Destruction," from East Coast supergroup Stop the Violence Movement. Bronx rapper KRS-One spearheaded the project following the murder of his Boogie Down Productions DJ Scott La Rock; though Boogie Down Productions were gangsta rap forerunners, KRS-One became increasingly politically conscious, calling himself "Tha Teacha."

"We're All in the Same Gang" was orchestrated by wheelchair-bound Crips shotcaller Michael Concepcion. Concepcion showed up at an N.W.A show at the Anaheim Celebrity Theatre one night with a swarm of gang members in tow; the only problem was they didn't have any tickets. Eager to nonetheless accommodate them (probably a good idea) Heller and bodyguard Joe Fierro rounded up some passes, and the camps later stayed in touch.

Concepcion solicited Ruthless's assistance for "We're All in the Same Gang," which aimed to broker peace between the various warring L.A. gang factions. Above the Law gets into the spirit, rapping: *It don't depend on the color of a rag / 'Cause if you got what they want you know they gonna take what you have.* N.W.A, however, seem loath to denounce gang culture, rapping that they aren't "ministers" or interested in telling you "what to do," perhaps because gangbangers were a core constituency of their listening audience.

"We're All in the Same Gang" got credit for helping spur the 1992 gang truce—which brought the Crips and the Bloods together just before the L.A. riots—and today survives as a wonderful time capsule of the era. The track helps dispel the myth that these West Coast rappers from across the spectrum, from hard-edged to pop, were so different. MC Hammer's just-released *Please Hammer, Don't Hurt 'Em* was on its way to selling ten million copies, and though some laughed at his giant pants, Ice-T shouted him out on his 1991 album *OG Original Gangster.*

I met Cold 187um in 2014 at a fiftieth-birthday party concert thrown for Eazy-E at a Whittier dive bar. Hutchinson chomped on a cigar and, though the event started late, wore dark, red-tinged shades. Solidly built, he carried an undeniable gravitas and a smile that said "God bless you, but don't think about crossing me." He was swarmed by friends and admirers upon entry; women flirtily placed their hands on his well-developed chest. He still puts out music, but his Instagram page these days is largely dedicated to his "Rock-Boy Honeys," the curvaceous women of his chain of magazines for men.

Cold 187um and Ice Cube were labelmates briefly. But when Cube left Ruthless in 1989, expectations soared for Above the Law, particularly for Cold 187um. As a spark plug, tough-talking rapper, perhaps he could fill Cube's void.

The pair was initially tight. Cold 187um respected Cube's style, and Above the Law's 1990 single "Murder Rap" samples him from "Straight Outta Compton": *Here's a murder rap to keep you dancin'*. But there was a difference: If Cube was rapping stories of the ne'er-do-wells he observed, Cold 187um and his groupmates were describing their own upbringings. "We created Above the Law with street money," Cold 187um said.

With Cube and N.W.A now at odds, Above the Law sided firmly with the latter camp.

During the promotion of *Livin' Like Hustlers*, released in 1990, Above the Law escalated tensions with Cube. In a *Los Angeles Times* interview that April, Go Mack questioned Cube's street credentials. "Ice Cube, how's he going to write about something he's never been through? Ice Cube had a good house, he had both a mother and father with him, he got bused to a good school." He added that Cube's rowdy first-person rhymes were actually about *their* lifestyles.

Cube shrugged off the criticism. "New jacks (poseurs) from Pomona should only talk about the 10 freeway," he told the reporter, Jonathan Gold, referencing the transportation artery that cuts through Above the Law's home base.

Gold today is a *Los Angeles Times* food critic and Pulitzer Prize winner, but back then he covered the emergent L.A. gangsta rap scene before just about anyone else, giving N.W.A its first cover story in 1989, for *L.A. Weekly*. Gold's story on Above the Law got Ice Cube into serious hot water. Cube should have known better than saying something so inflammatory; everyone knows you don't insult a fellow rapper's home turf. But the word "poseurs"—which Cube never actually said—made it a whole lot worse.

Gold told me that his editor insisted upon adding the word to clarify the meaning of "new jacks." Whatever the case, Above the Law didn't enjoy the characterization. Upon the article's publication Eazy called up Cold 187um. "Did you read the paper?" Eazy asked him. "He trying to get his clown on."

"I'm gonna beat your boy up when I see him," Cold 187um responded.

"Don't do it, homie," cautioned Eazy.

Insisted Cold 187um: "I'mma beat his ass."

As it turned out, he would see Ice Cube that very night—April 7, 1990—at the Anaheim Celebrity Theatre, for a show headlined by Above the Law. The 2,500-seat venue was an important one for Ruthless acts, who had a hard time finding places to let them play. The crowd was light that night, but issues arose backstage. Cube was there, doing a magazine interview, and he and Cold 187um exchanged words in the hallway. Initially nothing came of it, and Cube headed toward the dressing room of openers Low Profile. Apparently reconsidering, however, Cube popped back into Cold 187um's dressing room, and addressed him from the doorway.

"I guess he tried to come to my dressing room to apologize to me but I'm thinking he still wanna fight," Cold 187um remembered. "Soon as he stepped in my dressing room he said, 'What's up?' and I give him a right."

"Hutch came at him with a two-piece chicken wing in the jaw, knocked him back," recalled rapper Kokane, an Above the Law affiliate who performed that night. "They started yelling. Hutch said, 'Nigga, don't you ever put our name in your mouth!'"

"He tried to give me something and I give him another left," Cold 187um continued. "And then security rushed us."

"They were throwing punches," said Krazy Dee, the early N.W.A affiliate who witnessed the altercation. "We grabbed Cube and said, 'This isn't the place.'"

Accounts of the damage vary. "Cube had a little scratch on him," his new Da Lench Mob partner J-Dee said. "It wasn't really no fight, was just a little scuffling," said Sir Jinx. Neither of these two members of Cube's posse had been allowed into the theater, however, which is perhaps what prevented the incident from escalating into a full-blown melee.

At the end of the day, Cube was fine, physically. But he knew it was time for reinforcements. "I was like, 'Yo, we can't do business together, but we can still be homies.' I was a little naïve on that tip until I saw that there was true venom there," Cube said.

A Different, Severe Sonic Direction

Upon leaving N.W.A, Cube immediately signed a solo deal with Priority Records—the same company that distributed N.W.A—and got to work. When it came to picking producers for his first album, he chose Public Enemy's beat-making team the Bomb Squad, known for their apocalyptic, postmodern soundscapes, whom he'd gotten to know from shows N.W.A performed with Public Enemy before he left.

The Bomb Squad featured Chuck D, a pair of visionary brothers who called themselves Hank and Keith Shocklee, and Eric Sadler. Following the success of Public Enemy's second album *It Takes a Nation of Millions to Hold Us Back* they were in the midst of crafting the group's next album, *Fear of a Black Planet*, to which Cube contributed and which featured the group's most famous song, "Fight the Power," originally conceived for Spike Lee's 1989 film *Do the Right Thing*.

They were the perfect choice for Cube's solo debut *Amerikkka's Most Wanted*, but they actually weren't his first, or even his second. Cube was hoping to get Dre to produce it, but Ruthless wouldn't allow it, and so in late 1989 Cube headed to New York, hoping to work with Sam Sever, known for his work with 3rd Bass. Cube ventured to the offices of the act's label, Def Jam, but never met up with Sever. Instead, at the offices he ran into Chuck D, who suggested they work together. The Bomb Squad, familiar with Cube through his work with N.W.A, was thrilled with the idea, and looked forward to indulging their more melodic side.

A lot was riding on the collaboration; Cube in particular was anxious to show his detractors in N.W.A he was for real. He began readying the album in early 1990 at a preproduction studio in Public Enemy's home turf of Hempstead, Long Island, bringing notebook upon notebook crammed full of lyrics, including for songs originally intended for Eazy-E or N.W.A, like album-opener "The Nigga Ya Love to Hate." He and the album's coproducer Sir Jinx sparred a bit about its counterintuitive chorus—*Fuck you, Ice Cube!*—because, after all, why would you diss yourself? But this type of bold, chip-on-shoulder rhetoric would help define Ice Cube's solo work. His firebrand character was still repressed, brash, and dangerous, but also seemed to realize there was more to life than "bitches and money." He was on a quest to root out greed, addiction, racism, and other bullshit.

Behind Cube's snarling bravado, what's often overlooked in his work is his pure, driven artistry. He arrived in New York prepared to work his ass off. "I figured he'd be coming into the studio with women and drinking forties. It wasn't like that at all," said Sadler, who gets much of the credit for the sound of *Amerikkka's Most Wanted*.

It developed organically. The producers told Cube to "go find your album," i.e., to dig through the Squad's giant catalog of records and decide which ones he liked. He stayed up late and slept there, zeroing in on funk LPs.

Sir Jinx made sure the album maintained a West Coast flavor. But at the same time it charted a different, severe sonic direction. "Endangered Species (Tales from the Darkside)" samples "Fuck tha Police"—*A young nigga got it bad 'cause I'm brown*—but has a frenetic pace, with stop-and-start samples, and grim pronouncements from Chuck D. The final recordings were done at SoHo's Greene Street Studios, with Cube and his crew living out of a furnished apartment in the Village.

The album's title is a Ku Klux Klan reference, and Cube said it came to him from the television show *America's Most Wanted*. "[T]hat kinda represents the America that we were dealing with [during] Reaganomics," he said, adding that "spelling it like that made the record political, and not just dismissed as a gangsta record."

Released in May 1990 on Priority, *Amerikkka* was a quick seller, though, as with *Straight Outta Compton*, many critics didn't warm to it. Some of that had to do with *Amerikkka*'s most infamous track "You Can't Fade Me," which sees Cube's character learning he has made the "neighborhood hussy" pregnant.

All I saw was Ice Cube in court
Payin' a gang of child support
Then I thought deep about giving up the money
What I need to do is kick the bitch in the tummy

Women are often the antagonists in Ice Cube songs. N.W.A's "I Ain't tha 1" portrays them as manipulative gold diggers. Cube also engaged in what could be called "slut-shaming," and seemed to harbor the downright reactionary viewpoint that women who get pregnant should alone have to deal with the consequences.

"If you're a bitch, you're probably not going to like us," Cube said in a 2015 interview about his use of sexist slurs. "If you're a ho, you probably don't like us. If you're not a ho or a bitch, don't be jumping to the defense of these despicable females. Just like I shouldn't be jumping to the defense of no punks or no cowards or no slimy son of a bitches that's men." On the album Cube gives his protégée, feminist rapper Yo-Yo, a chance to retort on "It's a Man's World," but he doesn't exactly come off humbled.

Despite the misogyny, *Amerikkka's Most Wanted* has gone down as a hip-hop classic, regularly listed among the best rap albums in history. It's probably no exaggeration to say Cube unified the East and West coasts—at least for a time. "I don't think the East Coast and West Coast have ever been as glued [together] as they were on that album," said Chuck D.

To promote the album, Cube had his own call-in line, 1-900-234-CUBE. ("Just $2 per minute. Kids, get your parents' permission.") The work went platinum, and suddenly, one couldn't help wonder if N.W.A didn't need Cube more than he needed them. "Ice Cube has now proven that he was N.W.A's crucial element," wrote David Mills of *The Washington Post*. If you listen to the album carefully you'll notice Cube doesn't diss his former group, but that didn't stop N.W.A from antagonizing him on their EP

100 Miles and Runnin', released on August 14, 1990, just three months after *Amerikkka*. *We started out with too much cargo / So I'm glad we got rid of Benedict Arnold*, raps Dre. Adds Ren: *Only reason niggas pick up your record is 'cause they thought it was us.*

Their follow-up LP *Efil4zaggin* contains the diss track "Message to B.A.," which references the Anaheim Celebrity Theatre fight, accuses Cube of "suckin' so much New York dick," and threatens, "when we see yo ass, we gonna cut your hair off and fuck you with a broomstick."

CHAPTER NINE

ME AND ALLAH GO BACK LIKE CRONIES

On March 2, 1991, construction worker Rodney King was watching basketball at a friend's house. He was recently paroled from prison, after serving time for a conviction on charges he robbed a convenience store of $200. Though abstaining from alcohol had been a condition of his release, that night King was drinking 8 Ball, and had also smoked pot. After the game he departed in his Hyundai Excel, with both his friend and another acquaintance riding along.

King drove west on the 210 freeway. He later estimated his speed to be about eighty miles per hour, though Highway Patrol officer Melanie Singer clocked him at a top speed of more than 110 miles per hour, and attempted to pull him over. Exiting the freeway on Paxton Street in the San Fernando Valley, King refused to stop. Singer and her fellow-CHP officer Tim Singer gave chase, and before long they received backup from LAPD cars and a helicopter. "I knew I'm drinking, I knew I'm feeling buzzed, so I cannot afford to get pulled over, *and* I'm on parole, and I'm black," King later said. "I made a bad decision by running from 'em."

King finally stopped and exited his vehicle in Lake View Terrace, and a group of four LAPD officers took over the arrest. They incorrectly believed him to be high on PCP, due to his sweating, his resistance to Taser darts fired at him, and the strength he displayed while resisting capture. King charged at Officer Laurence Powell, who struck him with a baton, apparently on the right side of King's face, contradicting orders from Sergeant Stacey Koon not to hit him in the head. King fell, but attempted to regain his footing as Powell and Officer Timothy Wind continued striking him, at Koon's direction. Even after King appeared to be subdued, the officers did not cease assaulting him. Powell in particular appeared to relish the blows; of the fifty-six dealt to King, he delivered the majority. (It would later come out that Powell, responding to a domestic call in a black neighborhood earlier that day, compared the dispute to the movie *Gorillas in the Mist*.)

The fourth officer, Theodore Briseno, of Latino descent (the others were white), stomped on King, but at one point attempted to stop the beating. It did little good, as King was left with cuts on his forehead, a broken cheekbone, fractures on the side of his face, a broken ankle, and bruises all over his body. Another officer stepped on King's face even while handcuffs were being applied, and began dragging him—while he was hog-tied and facedown—to the side of the road, before King was finally taken to the hospital in an ambulance. King was never charged in connection with his arrest.

Meanwhile, from the balcony of his nearby apartment, a man named George Holliday videotaped nine minutes of the incident, and sold it to a local television station for $500, who passed the footage along to the LAPD. The four officers were charged with the use of excessive force, and the video ran on a loop on news stations across the country.

That the film stirred widespread public outrage, and would lead to the downfall of police chief Daryl Gates, was little comfort to those who had experienced police brutality themselves. The statistics tell the story; between 1986 and 1990, Los Angeles paid out more than $20 million for excessive-force lawsuits. "Being an LAPD cop is like being in a gang," said an LAPD member. "We earn stripes, do beat-downs, get tattoos, and back each other to the hilt."

That same year David Duke, a former grand wizard of the Ku Klux

Klan, running as a Republican for governor of Louisiana, received nearly 32 percent of the vote in the first round, eventually losing in a runoff. A message had been sent: White supremacy was alive and well.

Many members of the Los Angeles hip-hop community expressed their anger or made songs in response to the Rodney King beating, but Ice Cube was particularly methodical about expressing his outrage. Some of his older siblings had been involved in protests surrounding the Watts riots in 1965, he said, and activism ran in his veins. "All black people are going to be faced with things like that, until we are where we are supposed to be in this society," he said. "So every few generations are going to look to protests in that manner, if things don't change." He also understood the philosophical divide between two forms of protest: the nonviolent, epitomized by Martin Luther King Jr., and the "by any means necessary" approach popularized by Malcolm X. Cube made it clear which side he came down on. "I saw pictures of my family in the streets with picket signs—'Nonviolent Movement'—getting beat and getting wet with a water hose and getting lynched. Now, a nonviolent movement, that's as peaceful as you can get and this country did that to them," he said.

As an artist, he was turned on by Public Enemy's "spitting the truth as they saw it," he said. "It was saying something to young black youth."

Ice Cube wasn't your standard civil rights activist. He started off as a bratty kid who said things to provoke a reaction out of people, like when he performed naughty cover songs at Skateland. But calling out racist attitudes on tracks like "Fuck tha Police" got attention, too, and had itself become marketable, as evidenced by the millions of records he was selling. *Amerikkka's Most Wanted* cemented the idea that it was possible to be successful while simultaneously fighting for what he believed in.

Despite continuing their antipolice rhetoric in his absence, N.W.A became even more apolitical after Cube left. Its members wanted little to do with the ideals of black empowerment. Cube's new affiliates Da Lench Mob, however, walked in lockstep with him. The South Central–based crew chose their name hoping it could serve a dual purpose—both to intimidate and appropriate a term describing violent atrocities committed against black Americans. They were rappers, activists, and tough dudes you shouldn't fuck with, all at the same time.

In the beginning, Da Lench Mob was more of an abstract concept than a specific group. "We was like, 'We need a group of faceless men, so everywhere we go, someone can be a part of your team,'" said Sir Jinx. A bang-'em-up posse that was everywhere, and nowhere, at the same time.

The original crew had more than a dozen members including Cube, Jinx, producer Chilly Chill, Yo-Yo, and Del the Funky Homosapien, a Bay Area–based cousin of Cube's who later forged a remarkable underground solo career and with a group called Hieroglyphics. (He also performed with animated group Gorillaz.) Eventually Da Lench Mob gelled as a three-person group, consisting of Cube's childhood friend T-Bone, Cube's childhood rhyming partner J-Dee, and J-Dee's friend Shorty, who was initially brought on for security after release from Corcoran state prison on a robbery conviction. T-Bone was a graphic artist who'd gone to school in the Valley with Cube, but J-Dee and Shorty were tatted-up Crips. The trio made for an intimidating presence.

They got shouted out on "Jackin' for Beats," a 1990 track from Cube's *Kill at Will* EP. Produced by Chilly Chill, the song features Cube rapping over hot instrumentals from the era, including Digital Underground's "The Humpty Dance." The EP saw Cube's songwriting skills continue to advance, particularly on the atmospheric "Dead Homiez," about the funeral of a murdered former classmate. *Why is that the only time black folks get to ride in a limo?...A single file line about fifty cars long / All driving slow with they lights on.*

South Central Flavor

For many of us, eighties and nineties Los Angeles is just a haze of grainy news clips and music videos you can find on YouTube. For those impacted by the era's crime and mass incarceration, however, the consequences of these years are very much present—family members killed, lost to crack cocaine, imprisoned for life. Three-strike convictions, overzealous drug arrests, and other miscalibrations of justice have had eternal consequences.

In 2015 I visited J-Dee in the California Men's Colony in San Luis Obispo, a series of squat, tan buildings and barbed wire surrounded by stunning green hills and rolling mountain peaks halfway between dry Los Angeles and foggy San Francisco.

J-Dee, whose real name is Da Sean Cooper, has been in this prison since 2004, part of a twenty-nine-years-to-life sentence for the 1993 murder of a man outside of a South Central party.

Cooper, wearing a light blue collared prison shirt, is a dead ringer for Ice Cube, right down to the scowl. "I used to joke that I was Cube's mom's sister's son," he says.

J-Dee himself is the first to say he made devastating mistakes that others are still paying for. He grew up both in Compton with his father, dealing crack on Poinsettia Avenue, and in South Central with his grandmother, near Ice Cube. The "J" in his moniker J-Dee came from his nickname "Weed Junkie"; he couldn't get enough of the stuff. He was a member of the 111 Street Neighborhood Crips, and did a lot of dirt, eventually distributing cocaine on a national basis.

Sir Jinx, who had the *Beat Street* garage, said he and Cube were initially a bit put off by J-Dee, because he was such a serious gangbanger. Indeed, he had little use for the law or respect for the criminal justice system, particularly after his father was murdered in 1986. No one was arrested. "I became angry after that, felt the system failed me and my family," he says.

But concerning the 1993 murder, he maintains his innocence. Though he was at the murder scene, he says, he didn't pull the trigger, and was taken down largely because he refused to turn in the actual murderer. Though plenty of convicts have similar stories, J-Dee isn't alone in maintaining his innocence. "I know J-Dee is innocent. Everyone from the neighborhood knows," T-Bone said. "Even a cop told me, 'We know J-Dee didn't do it, we just want J-Dee to do the right thing,' meaning snitch." But it's not that simple. Owing to gangland's G-code (also known as the no-snitching rule) J-Dee was caught in a catch-22. "If they found out he snitched, someone would try to kill him," T-Bone said.

J-Dee rapped as a kid, but didn't initially run in the same circles as Ice

Cube. In fact, they first met when J-Dee became indignant about hearing his name in Eazy-E's "Boyz-N-the Hood," which he knew was written by Cube. *The boy J.D. was a friend of mine, 'til I caught him in the car tryin' to steal the Alpine.*

What J-Dee didn't know was that Eazy had actually penned that line, about a *different* J.D. When J-Dee approached Cube about the track (J-Dee knew Cube's older sister Pat), Cube cleared up the misunderstanding.

They saw each other now and then, but by the time Cube left N.W.A, J-Dee had a young daughter and had ceased dealing drugs. He'd taken a job as a security guard and was working an in-store event at Wherehouse Records when Ice Cube walked in one day in early 1990. *Amerikkka's Most Wanted* was nearly completed, but there was a problem: The ad-libs on the album sounded too "New York." Sure, Cube had traveled across the country in the dead of winter to record with the Bomb Squad, but they still wanted someone who could give it some South Central flavor. Sir Jinx suggested J-Dee; the same qualities that made them wary of him as a kid—his street life—could be valuable for something like this.

Cube took J-Dee outside the Wherehouse to hear a rough cut of *Amerikkka's Most Wanted* and asked if he was still writing and rapping. Indeed, he was. Cube promptly asked him to come to New York, taking out his checkbook and writing a check for $24,000. "I went back inside and quit on the spot," J-Dee remembers.

Cube's childhood friend Terry Gray, aka T-Bone, was also brought aboard, and the pair headed out to New York. On the album, J-Dee is featured in a skit called "JD's Gafflin'," humorously describing how he used to steal folks' Nissan trucks in the McDonald's drive-through. "Nigga, get your motherfuckin' food, leave it in the car, nigga get out!" In terms of dark humor, it didn't get more South Central than that.

Rolling Deep

As the Marriott Marquis in Times Square prepared to host the 1990 New Music Seminar, the four-star hotel had no idea what was about to hit it.

That July some seven thousand music industry types descended upon the annual conference to network, listen to speakers like experimental musician Laurie Anderson and record executive Irving Azoff, and see performers like Zimbabwean rock group the Bhundu Boys and Ice Cube's protégée Yo-Yo. Cube himself spoke on a panel about the ongoing media controversy over hip-hop lyrics, which was the talk of the conference. Azoff expressed disgust that the industry had agreed to the Parents Music Resource Center's demand for warning stickers on albums. "As the walls go down in Europe, the walls are coming up in America," said Ice-T, speaking about 2 Live Crew's obscenity charges in Florida.

Cube initially hadn't wanted to fly Da Lench Mob to New York, but they talked him into it. They knew the Ruthless crew would be there, too, and wanted to prevent a reprise of the fight at the Anaheim Celebrity Theatre. "The only way you're gonna be respected is if we see them and deal with them, otherwise they're gonna continue to punk you," said Shorty.

"When we run into Above the Law, we gonna kick they ass," J-Dee said.

But there was one problem: Above the Law was rolling *deep* at the seminar, with rapper Kokane and a large contingency of locally based affiliates in tow. But Cube and Da Lench Mob had a big posse as well, including Sir Jinx, Cube's childhood friend DJ Crazy Toones and his partner Coolio, both from the group WC and the Maad Circle. Also on hand was six-and-a-half-foot rapper King Sun, as well as numerous Sun affiliates from the hip-hop activist group Zulu Nation, who had joined them with the intention of providing moral support, not to rumble, said Jinx, adding, "We didn't know it was going to be like West Side Story."

The majority of the seminar passed without incident, other than the sad announcement that Heavy D & the Boyz member Trouble T. Roy had died in a freak accident after a concert in Indianapolis. But just before the final panel, the two Los Angeles crews encountered each other.

"They were like, 'Wassup?'" remembered Cold 187um. "I was like, 'Nuthin', but if you want to make it something, we can make it something.'" His crew went back to the room for reinforcements, and the camps encountered each other again on the Marriott's escalators, one going up, and one going down.

By this time Cube had left to speak on the panel. "We sent Cube out. We told him disappear, we don't want you to get in no trouble, we got this," J-Dee said.

The parties agreed to fight in a bathroom, away from cameras. But they didn't make it, instead squaring off amid the terrified convention crowd, who scampered off. Shorty remembered tossing the first punch at Above the Law's Total K-Oss, and J-Dee took on KMG the Illustrator. "Then the melee exploded," said J-Dee. Something like one of those old-timey saloon fights, chairs were flipped and furniture went flying. King Sun picked up a long banquet table—"like the Incredible Hulk," said Shorty—and smashed people with it. T-Bone lost his Air Jordans in a wrestling match.

"I was fighting with every last one of them, I couldn't even tell you who," T-Bone said. "You'd get hit in the back and before you know it you'd be swinging at someone else."

At some point, Cube emerged from his panel to witness the chaos, but didn't participate in the fight. The squab continued until Ice-T and Afrika Bambaataa emerged and warned them that the police were coming, at which point everyone scattered. T-Bone cut out via a side door and found himself in the middle of Times Square, with only socks covering his feet.

When I talked to Cube about it, twenty-five years after the fact, the incident no longer felt so raw. "I was more upset that we came all the way to New York—finally getting the respect we deserve—and we fucking up their seminar."

Who won the fight? It depends on whom you ask. "Da Lench Mob got they ass rolled up," Kokane told me. "*Rolled* up." N.W.A's track "Message to B.A." claimed that Cube ran off while "the rest of his homeboys got they ass beat."

Not true, counters J-Dee, who maintains that Above the Law were "lumped up" and sought medical attention. Sir Jinx said he got a cherry under his eye, but that nobody was seriously injured. Shorty got kneed in the eye by somebody, and notes that Da Lench Mob's aggression had its intended effect: "After that they left Cube alone."

Cold 187um chalked the whole thing up to young artists feeling the pressure. "We [were] kids," he said. "You're looking at young artists who came up at nineteen and twenty years old in a multimillion-dollar situation."

J-Dee said rapper WC quashed the beef at his listening party the next year. "Hutch and I shook hands and embraced each other. Hutch is a good dude. He said they did that to show loyalty to Eazy," he said. Hutch added that he and Cube later performed together.

"I talked to KMG before he died," in 2012, reportedly of a heart attack, said J-Dee. "We laughed about this."

The first years of the nineties were extraordinarily action-packed and con-sequential for Cube. It wasn't just music. In February 1991 he and Kim Woodruff had their first child—O'Shea Jr., who would portray his father twenty-four years later in the film *Straight Outta Compton*.

Owing to the glacial speed of royalty payments, Cube wasn't seeing suf-ficient money coming in. Preparing for his *Kill at Will* EP, he was count-ing on an advance from Priority to buy his family a house, but instead received a "bullshit excuse."

"That was kind of a misunderstanding we had," said Priority Records cofounder Bryan Turner.

And so, Cube did what we'd all like to do when our bosses jerk us around. Just a few days after his son's birth, he grabbed a baseball bat and his fearsome associates J-Dee and Shorty. They headed over to Priority's offices in Hollywood.

"There was a knock on the glass door," said Priority employee Dave Weiner. "I looked up and it was Ice Cube, and he had [his] homeboys with him. They had their trench coats on and weren't looking too happy." He opened the door and they walked silently past, making their way into Turner's office. About five minutes later, Weiner heard screaming and glass breaking.

Turner hadn't told Cube what he wanted to hear.

Cube smashed an old television and other items. "I had an aluminum bat," Cube said. "It was bent when I left." Cube and his crew soon stormed out, but not before smashing gold and platinum plaques in the lobby.

It wasn't, perhaps, as terrorizing as it seems. "I swear to God, man, I remember him looking around the room trying to look for something to break that wasn't too expensive," said Turner.

Nonetheless, as they returned to their car out back, the fuzz swarmed. "Freeze!" a cop yelled, and the three men put their hands up. They were told to get on the ground.

"There's nothing going on here," Priority's other cofounder Mark Cerami insisted, undoubtedly worried about further alienating one of the label's cash cows. Turner seconded that it was all a misunderstanding. And so the cops let them go. Cerami added that he and Cube met in Marina del Rey the following day and went out fishing. Cerami pledged to make things right.

In the end, Cube's outburst had its intended effect: He got his money, and was able to buy a home in Baldwin Hills. He also got a BMW for Kim. The gift doubled as a proposal. "When she went to go get in the car, she was so happy about the car she almost sat on the ring," Cube said. They married in 1992, at the Marina del Rey DoubleTree Hotel. The festivities weren't too large, befitting an unusual rap star who wasn't too flashy.

Doughboy

For all of his hip-hop success, Cube's true introduction to mainstream America came in July 1991, when he starred in the South Central–set *Boyz n the Hood*, a box-office hit that helped launch an entire subgenre of gritty, inner city films. John Singleton, fresh out of USC film school, became the youngest person, and first African-American, to be nominated for the best director Oscar. Cube had just turned twenty-two. The pair met at a rally for Nation of Islam leader Louis Farrakhan. Singleton said *Boyz* originally had parts for all the members of N.W.A, but that only Cube took his offer seriously. (Eazy, in fact, later disparaged it to *Spin*, saying it "reminds me of a Monday after-school special with cussin'.")

Astonishingly, Cube hadn't acted before. "I thought, at the time, actors had to go to school and learn how to become that," Cube said. "[Singleton] was like, 'Yeah, that's true, but some people have what's called *it*, and I think you got it.'"

Cube's portrayal of the combustible Doughboy—brash, loyal to his friends, and unconcerned with his future—became a film archetype. When it came time to play Doughboy, he drew as always from the real-life characters he knew growing up, the kids in the neighborhood who weren't going to make it to twenty-five. "The only difficult scene was the one where I had to cry—I hadn't cried in eight or nine years," he said. "But I've had lots of friends that've been killed, so I just thought about them and the tears came."

For many viewers the film was their first exposure to the horrors of daily life for many in long-idealized sunny Southern California. Along with *New Jack City*, which was released earlier in 1991 and starred Ice-T as a detective in his first serious role, *Boyz* inspired countless knockoffs, many starring rappers. Despite its clear antiviolence message, the film received a torrent of negative publicity following incidents at early screenings. Two dozen people were injured, and a man at a midnight Chicago showing was murdered. Many Southern California theaters pulled the film. "I didn't create the conditions under which people shoot each other," responded Singleton angrily at a Los Angeles news conference. "This happens because there's a whole generation of people who are disenfranchised."

Through gangsta rap and films like *Boyz n the Hood*, South Central and Compton were quickly entering the realm of myth, as apocalyptic no-man's-lands where it was hardly safe to step out your front door. This would be propagated further by films like *Menace II Society* and groups like Compton's Most Wanted. Such depictions of poverty and chaos remain, to a large extent, South Los Angeles's main export to this day.

No Hog

When Cube wasn't cutting tracks or smashing up record company offices, he was becoming a savvy businessman, a trait that he would, ironically, credit to Eazy-E.

After leaving N.W.A Cube started his own production outfit, Street Knowledge Records. Masterminded along with Patricia Charbonnet, its goal was to release his music and that of new artists. Headquarters were a drab South Central building in the heart of Rollin' 60s gang territory. Inside was quite comfortable, with a big television, a top-of-the-line pre-production studio, and Cube's office. Label affiliates would come and go at all hours of the day and night, either to brainstorm ideas, or simply because the streets got too hot. "That was like our fortress," Shorty said. Cube fostered a stable of artists, including Yo-Yo, a former classmate of Jinx's who founded an activist group called Intelligent Black Women's Coalition, which challenged hip-hop sexism.

Also on Cube's roster was Watts rapper Kam, who combined a street mentality with a Muslim's discipline. He developed an interest in the Nation of Islam through the music of Public Enemy and Trenton, New Jersey, group Poor Righteous Teachers. "I never heard anybody rap like that," J-Dee said. "I stopped eating red meat and pork because of Kam."

Lench Mob member Shorty, meanwhile, was hipped to the Nation's teachings when they toured with Public Enemy in 1990. A friend of his brother's found a cardboard box with dozens of Minister Farrakhan VHS tapes, which Shorty proceeded to devour. "We would smoke weed and just listen to the minister, all day and all night long," he said. Upon joining the Nation he gave up the herb, though, along with booze and pork and even his given name, Jerome Washington. He temporarily became Brother Jerome 3X—Black Muslims traditionally take on the "X" to replace their European "slave" names—and then later was known as Jerome Muhammad.

Cube grew up in the Baptist church, but he took to the Nation's teachings, particularly the idea that it was up to blacks to take back their power and dignity from white suppressors. He was introduced to Farrakhan's teachings from a Public Enemy affiliate called Drew. One Saviours' Day—when Nation members celebrate the birthday of founder Wallace Fard—he flew into Chicago to watch Farrakhan speak, and Farrakhan invited him to dinner afterward at his Hyde Park home, which is called "the Palace" and is the former residence of deceased Nation of Islam leader Elijah Muhammad. It's not far from the Nation's headquarters, called Mosque Maryam, a grand complex topped by the star and crescent symbol, which was purchased in the eighties with a multimillion-dollar loan from Libyan leader Muammar Gaddafi.

Cube went back many times, sometimes bringing Shorty. Dining from a spread that might include salad, bean soup, chicken, and beef (no hog) at a large banquet table alongside foreign dignitaries, they received the minister's counsel. "He would say that since God gave you the platform to speak, give the knowledge to your people, wake them up," Shorty said.

Farrakhan warned that, though "enlightened" hip-hop was currently ascendant, the powers that be would try to silence them. "They don't want our people to know that we were kings and queens, that all the technology came from us," Shorty remembered him saying. "If you rob the people of their culture, religion, and god, you want to keep them as blind as you can." Shorty believes that today's hip-hop climate—"all about buffoonery and foolishness"—is proof that Farrakhan's fears were realized.

Cube began speaking publicly on the Nation's ideals and, on his twenty-second birthday, in 1991, Kam performed a symbolic baptism of sorts, exorcising Cube of the "toxins" in his hair, following in the advice of black pride advocates like Marcus Garvey. Aided by Nation captain Shaheed Muhammad, he cut off Cube's Jheri curl.

Still, you never saw Cube in a bow tie. He never officially joined the Nation. Nor did J-Dee or T-Bone. Though Cube still professes love for Islam—*Me and Allah go back like cronies / I don't got to be fake, 'cause he is my homie*, he rapped in 2008—religion is not his thing. "All I know is, it's one God," Cube told me. "Religion is man-made, it's flawed. I don't follow nobody. I follow my own conscience."

Cube's relationship with the Nation was nonetheless mutually beneficial. Spiritually, the Nation of Islam combines traditional Islam with mystical and biblical teachings, along with the ideals of self-reliance and racial separatism. Following Malcolm X's murder in 1965 the organization reached its greatest heights—perhaps a half million followers. But after the death of Elijah Muhammad a decade later the Nation splintered and its popularity waned, only to be revived in the Farrakhan era. The Nation's rebirth was highlighted by Spike Lee's 1992 epic *Malcolm X* and 1995's Farrakhan-led Million Man March in Washington, D.C. That event probably didn't draw a million people, but it was the largest ever gathering of African-Americans. Bow-tied recruits, from coast to coast, raised money for the organization through the sale of bean pies and *The Final Call* newspaper.

Farrakhan's teachings can be homophobic and misogynist, and his anti-Semitism would contribute to his decline in popularity. (Such sentiment would also tar the career of rapper Professor Griff, a Farrakhan admirer whose 1989 anti-Jewish remarks—while serving as Public Enemy's "Minister of Information"—led to his exile from the group.) But Farrakhan and the Nation were nonetheless a substantial force for good in black America, inspiring thousands of men to give up gangs and drugs. Hip-hop was particularly receptive to such black empowerment messages, with artists including Rakim, Big Daddy Kane, and the Wu-Tang Clan drawn to the teachings of Five-Percent Nation, which celebrates black self-knowledge and was founded by a former Nation of Islam member. (Its name references the small percentage of the population committed to the discipline's teachings.)

Farrakhan didn't distance himself from hardcore rap music like the majority of other public leaders. Having played violin as a child and later recorded as a Calypso singer called the Charmer, he was fond of show business. He's long been drawn to celebrities, developing relationships with everyone from Michael Jackson to Mike Tyson and, more recently, Kanye West. Celebrity affiliation drew attention to the Nation, and the organization often provided security through its paramilitary Fruit of

Islam wing to famous black performers and athletes who couldn't necessarily trust traditional channels.

Many celebrities, in turn, were drawn to Nation of Islam minister Khalid Muhammad. He rose to prominence in the eighties and commissioned a multimillion-dollar mosque in South Central. Known for flashy cars and designer suits, he initiated community-building programs and fearlessly recruited from the most dangerous neighborhoods. Emphasizing that African-Americans had been historically mistreated but were now in control of their own destinies, he became Farrakhan's right-hand man, and greatly inspired Public Enemy and Ice Cube. The latter featured him discoursing on his two-part 1991 sophomore solo album *Death Certificate*, whose cover has Cube standing next to a corpse with an "Uncle Sam" tag hanging off the toe. The inset pictures include Cube reading *The Final Call* with the headline "Unite or Perish," flanked by Fruit of Islam members standing alert to his left, and by Lench Mob members in repose to his right. The album's two halves—the "Death Side" and the "Life Side"— continued this theme of divide, the former "a mirror image of where we are today" and the latter "a vision of where we need to go."

Ready to Mash

For *Death Certificate* Cube jettisoned the Bomb Squad and their pastiche approach in favor of more traditional slabs of chunky, midtempo funk, a production vision led by DJ Pooh, and also featuring contributions from Cube, Sir Jinx, Bobcat, and Rashad. The work was even more controversial than *Amerikkka's Most Wanted*, absolutely unsparing in its critiques of Cube's perceived foes, both personal and institutional. Most notorious is "No Vaseline," directed at his former groupmates and one of the greatest diss tracks ever recorded. The song's good-time bounce only heightens its lyrics' venom, accusing the N.W.A members of being gay and moving to white neighborhoods. They were essentially slaves to the "Jew" Jerry Heller, the track insinuates, offering the suggestion, using the Nation's preferred synonym for white men, the group should *Get rid of that devil real simple / Put a bullet in his temple*.

"[I]t probably hurt and affected me more than anything that's ever been said or done to me," Heller told an interviewer, adding that he faced anti-Semitism growing up. "I think he's not anti-Semitic. I think he did it just because he thought it would sell records."

"I'm pro-black. I'm not anti-anything but anti-poor," Cube insisted when asked about the issue, adding that he worked with many Jewish people in the music industry.

"No Vaseline" was inspired by insult game the dozens, which Cube played growing up. He actually recorded the track much earlier and wasn't sure he was going to release it at all, but after N.W.A fired at him on their EP he felt obliged, in the grand hip-hop tradition, to come back a hundred times harder.

For the former underdog Cube, it was a knockout blow. N.W.A never responded, but Ren in particular was pissed. "I was ready to mash," he said, adding that when he showed up at a party where "No Vaseline" was playing he demanded they turn it off. As for Cube and Dre's relationship? They never discussed the song, Cube said.

Another *Death Certificate* lightning rod was "Black Korea," which highlighted tensions between Los Angeles blacks and Korean shop owners. The song came on the heels of the March 16, 1991, killing of Latasha Harlins, an unarmed, fifteen-year-old African-American girl. Harlins was shot to death at a South Central liquor store following a brief scuffle with owner Soon Ja Du, who falsely believed Harlins was shoplifting a bottle of orange juice. Charged with murder, the ailing Du was convicted only of manslaughter, and did no prison time, creating widespread outrage in Los Angeles.

The city then had more than three thousand liquor and convenience shops owned by Korean immigrants, many of whom used an old-world system for pooling funds to raise capital. In 1990, nine different shop employees had been killed during armed assaults, and many owners lived in fear. At the same time, their black customers felt victimized by harassment and stereotyping. During the summer of 1991 numerous South Central stores owned by Koreans were firebombed, including three on the evening of August 17, 1991, among them Empire Liquor Market Deli, where Harlins was killed.

"Black Korea" is less than a minute long, but contains a multitude of epithets, blasting shop owners for assuming customers were shoplifting, and threatening: *So pay respect to the black fist / Or we'll burn your store right down to a crisp.* In "Black Korea" Cube threatens to boycott the stores, but the song actually inspired a boycott of him. The target was the malt liquor he was endorsing, an upstart brand called St. Ides, which was eager to displace "8 Ball" as the favored cheap urban high-alcohol beer. DJ Pooh was in charge of crafting a series of commercials for the beer, and so he signed up gangsta stars including Cube, who urged viewers to *Get your girl in the mood quicker / Get your jimmy thicker / With St. Ides malt liquor.* All told St. Ides received endorsements from a who's who of the early nineties hardcore rappers, including Geto Boys, Notorious B.I.G., Tupac Shakur, Dr. Dre, and Snoop Dogg.

Following "Black Korea," the Korean American Grocers Association (KAGRO), which represented thousands of Southern California stores, insisted the malt liquor brand's owners, McKenzie River, remove Cube from their ads. The company refused, stores pulled the brand, and eventually McKenzie agreed to KAGRO's demands. Cube soon apologized, met with KAGRO's Southern California president, and worked to open a dialogue between blacks and Koreans. He eventually won back his endorsement deal, agreeing to donate money to charity.

There's no doubt the controversy spurred sales. *Death Certificate* made it to number two on the Billboard 200, going platinum like *Amerikkka.* This despite the fact that Jewish activist organization the Simon Wiesenthal Center called on record store chains to remove it from their shelves, and many critics trashed it. *The Village Voice*'s Robert Christgau called Cube "a straight-up racist simple and plain, and of course a sex bigot too." *Billboard* accused the album of "hate-mongering," and the Guardian Angels, the group who left the toilet bowl in front of Sean Penn's house, compared Cube to David Duke.

Speaking on these controversies many years later he lamented "not being as informed as I thought I was at the time." One shouldn't forget that Cube was barely old enough to drink while all this was going on. That doesn't absolve him, but at least Cube faced his critics. In 1992 he was interviewed at his Street Knowledge office by Angela Davis, a former Black Panthers associate and radical feminist, who took him to task about his sexist lyrics, which are all over *Death Certificate*. ("Givin' Up the Nappy Dug Out," in addition to employing long-expired slang, kicks off, *Your daughter was a nice girl, now she is a slut.*) "How do you think black feminists like myself and younger women as well respond to the word 'bitch'?" she asked. "The language of the streets is the only language I can use to communicate with the streets," he responded.

This seems like Cube wanting to have his gangsta rap cake and eat it, too. He elaborated on his charged language further in *Death Certificate*'s liner notes: "The reason I say nigga is because we are mentally dead in 1991. We have limited knowledge of self, so it leads to a nigga mentality. The best place for a young black male or female is the Nation of Islam. Soon as we as people use our knowledge of self to our advantage we will then be able to be called blacks."

As a work of art, *Death Certificate* is one of a kind: simultaneously bigoted and socially conscious, misogynistic and uplifting. The result is an extremely compelling listen that stands with *Amerikkka's Most Wanted* among the top three or four dozen rap albums ever made.

Cube's rapping is self-assured, hugging the beats, never seeming to strain. His storytelling is more evocative than ever, due both to his developing writing talents and his new company. Now that Eazy wasn't around to share his street stories, Cube turned to his Da Lench Mob partners for material. "On tour nobody had cell phones, no satellite hookups, we'd hear these J-Dee and Shorty stories, because they're real as a motherfucker," Sir Jinx said, adding that thematically much of *Death Certificate* is "mourning" their tough lives.

This is especially evident on "My Summer Vacation," about an L.A.

drug-dealing crew that sets up shop in St. Louis when the police heat gets too strong. They take over a local block, killing its former proprietors and raking in profits before the St. Louis contingency fights back and the justice system catches up with them. It's not nearly as gleeful as "The Boyz-N-the Hood," and has greater attention to detail. It's based in truth. In the eighties, Southern California dealers fanned out around the country, taking their gang allegiances with them. "It started spreading like a virus," said "Freeway" Rick Ross. Some were driven out of their adopted territories, but others integrated successfully, leading to strange situations in which midwestern gangbangers were, as Cube puts it in the track, "dyin' for a street that they never heard of." DJ Quik's 1992 song "Jus Lyke Compton" also explores this phenomenon.

The song came out of conversations between Cube, J-Dee, and Shorty. J-Dee, who had sold cocaine in cities all over the country, from Seattle to St. Paul to St. Louis, remembered a conversation they had on a layover in 1991, while Cube and Da Lench Mob walked through Dulles airport in khaki suits. "It looks like we about to take some dope out of town," J-Dee remembered with a laugh. "Cube asked me, 'Why did you stop selling out of state?'" He explained that he'd met with too much resistance, and Shorty added details of his own. By the time the plane landed, Cube had the song written.

Said J-Dee: "I was like, Cube, you a fuckin' genius."

Moving Like the Military

Ice Cube toured regularly in the early nineties, and his shows from this era featured giant images of nooses, twirling electric chairs, and, at his Lollapalooza dates in 1992, pointed disses of then president George H. W. Bush. Members of the Nation of Islam's paramilitary arm, Fruit of Islam, were often on hand to keep order. Cube already had a robust security team—guys with names like Big Tom, Zulu Ed, and Big Cal—but he couldn't be too safe, considering that everyone from the federal govern-

ment to his former labelmates had it in for him. T-Bone and Shorty both
say their crew fielded death threats.

Tour stops would go something like this: Cube and his partners would
arrive in town, and then head over to the local mosque, where they were
treated like royalty. The city's Nation of Islam members would arrange for
them to get some food, either at a local restaurant or a nice home-cooked
meal at one of the sisters' homes.

A security detail would be organized, involving either plainclothes
bodyguards or Fruit of Islam members wearing suits and steel-toe boots,
or both. Starting at soundcheck the team would be on hand, and while the
concert was going on the plainclothes team might be spread out secretly
among the audience. "They would have the free run of the building," said
Sir Jinx. "They moved like the military—they were not playing."

Afterward, while the performers went from the venue to the tour bus,
the Fruit of Islam made a diamond shape around them; four men on each
diagonal slant, with Cube, Da Lench Mob, and their associates in the
middle. "That shit looked militant," said J-Dee. "You might have thought
they were escorting Farrakhan himself."

While on tour, Cube also functioned as something of a disciplinarian
and study group leader. During their free time he helmed sessions about
Nation-endorsed texts like Elijah Muhammad's *Message to the Blackman
in America* and Carter Woodson's *The Mis-Education of the Negro*, or listen to audio of Saviours' Day speeches given by Farrakhan. Cube also had
a strict rule: No drinking before shows, though afterward they might have
some St. Ides and talk about how to improve the next concert.

As for the Muslim prohibition on drinking alcohol? The devout Shorty had
a crisis of conscience after Da Lench Mob signed on for a St. Ides commercial,
for the rate of $30,000. He opted not to do the spot, but his colleagues cut him
in for $4,000 of the money anyway, which he gave to the Nation.

The idea of a corporation co-opting the cool new black art form to sell
swill to the inner cities upset more than a few people. On Public Enemy's 1991 song "1 Million Bottlebags" Chuck D rhymed: *Watch shorty*

get sicker / Year after year, while he's thinkin' it's beer / But it's not he got it in his gut. That same year Chuck D filed a lawsuit against McKenzie River, after a St. Ides ad sampled his voice from the group's song "Bring the Noise." (In response the company—claiming they hadn't realized Chuck D's voice was being used, since the commercial was produced independently—promptly pulled it.)

That same spot featured Cube's voice. He, more than anyone else, had become the face of the malt liquor; his character Doughboy gives it serious product placement in *Boyz n the Hood*, as well. As Cube told *The Source* in 1991, he spoke to Khalid Muhammad about the issue, who agreed that the whole enterprise was against their values. "But we gotta use them as a stepping-stone, we gotta use them to build our nation," Cube said they concluded. It helped that McKenzie River agreed to donate $100,000 to community projects of his choosing. "How else could the black community come up with $100,000 to help an organization?"

This thinking represents Cube in a nutshell: always doing bad in order to do good. He would probably despise the comparison, but he resembles an adroit politician in his ability to speak sincerely to groups with opposing interests. Even if you don't believe what he's saying, his charm carries the day.

Stacking Memories

Da Lench Mob's 1992 debut *Guerillas in tha Mist* took its title from Officer Laurence Powell's racist "*Gorillas in the Mist*" comment on the day of the Rodney King beating. Its concept was largely Cube's creation. "I wanted to do a gangsta rap album, like *Amerikkka's Most Wanted*, but Cube wanted to take it in the direction of the Nation stuff we were learning," said J-Dee.

Though J-Dee could spit, neither Shorty nor T-Bone were natural rappers. But as a rough-and-ready threesome they were formidable, and quickly mastered the approach Cube envisioned. *I wish I was in Dixie (AK! AK!) / And shit wouldn't have been bad in the sixties (No way! No*

Way!) the group sang on "Freedom Got an AK." "You and Your Heroes" made the case that Babe Ruth couldn't have hit Dwight Gooden, while "All on My Nut Sac" castigated black drug dealers for selling dope to other blacks. *Use your mind black man / I can tell that you're head strong*, rapped J-Dee, to which Cube, playing the dealer, responded: *So what should I do? Work for $3.22? "Welcome to McDonald's may I please help you?"* By the skit's end J-Dee has shot him down.

It was a pretty striking turnaround for J-Dee, a man who until fairly recently had been doing dirt himself. "We were called hypocrites," he said. "But at some point, aren't you allowed to wake up?" As a militant black power artwork, *Guerillas in tha Mist* didn't have much precedent in hip-hop, and helped pave the way for like-minded groups. As evidenced by its gold status, its appeal cut across race. My high school white friends and I didn't think Da Lench Mob was coming for us. We thought they were coming for the racist assholes, who, frankly, deserved it.

But the group suffered setbacks. Not long after J-Dee's 1993 arrest, his Lench Mob crewmate T-Bone was *also* charged with murder, following the shooting death of a man and wounding of a woman at a South Central bowling alley. T-Bone was exonerated, however, in a pretty clear case of mistaken identity. He had been at the bowling alley that night shortly before the murder, wearing a similar black hoodie as the perpetrator, who was never caught. T-Bone thought the sheriffs who came to his mother's house three weeks later to arrest him for murder were kidding. Cube immediately sprang to his defense, putting down $1.5 million in cash for his bail, in addition to around $100,000 in lawyers' fees.

J-Dee claimed that Cube didn't financially support him for his trial, the way he did for T-Bone. But T-Bone says that Cube did, in fact, pay for J-Dee's lawyer—and that T-Bone himself saw the carbon copy of Cube's check. (He adds that J-Dee's aunt, who was organizing his defense, told him that the lawyer said "the check got stuck in the mail.") Whatever the case, J-Dee was further enraged when, having recorded a few songs for the next Lench Mob album before being sent to prison, he was scrubbed from the work, replaced by rapper Maulkie, formerly of Ruthless duo Yomo &

Maulkie. Da Lench Mob's 1994 follow-up *Planet of da Apes* did not have the impact of their debut, and the group split thereafter, amid disputes over money.

Decades have healed most of the group's wounds. Today J-Dee, who was scheduled to come up for parole in 2016, maintains a vivid recollection of the years between 1990 and 1993, when he, Cube, and Da Lench Mob were on top. For every Ice Cube and Dr. Dre who made it out, there remain many, many others who weren't so lucky. "While others keep stacking memories, I stopped making memories when I got to prison," J-Dee says.

He remains glad Ice Cube took Da Lench Mob in the direction he did, making them into "street politicians" rather than just gangsta rappers. "Cube said, 'This is gonna go down in history,' and it did. That was the best thing that happened to me. I got ten to twenty thousand fan letters. I didn't realize I touched so many people."

CHAPTER TEN

LIKE WINNING THE LOTTERY

As Ice Cube found himself increasingly focused on study and self-reflection in the early 1990s, Eazy-E and Dr. Dre were enjoying the lifestyle that came with their celebrity.

Around the release of their *100 Miles and Runnin'* EP in 1990, N.W.A held its first of two "Wild 'N Wet" pool parties, which drew hundreds of guys in shorts and polo shirts and women in bikinis. The first bash, which featured open bars, DJs spinning N.W.A songs, and lots of twerking (before "twerking" was a word), was held at Eazy's Westlake house. Ren said they would have thrown the parties in Compton except the police would have broken them up, and he was probably right. MC Ren, DJ Yella, Eazy, and Dre lounged with women in their laps, and the wet T-shirt contest had a $500 prize. Before sunset the party devolved into a virtual sex show, with beer bottles turning into sex accessories. "I had a drink in one hand, and was smoking a blunt with the other," said rapper CPO Boss Hogg, who was signed to MC Ren's label for Capitol Records. Eazy and Dre also threw a "pajama party" at the ornate downtown Mayan Theater, with Eazy donning a turban and a Hugh Hefner–style robe. Go-go dancers gyrated on raised blocks above the packed dance floor, while women vied in the "freaky lingerie" contest.

"How has our lifestyle changed?" Dr. Dre asked, repeating an interviewer's question between swigs of 8 Ball in the studio while they worked on N.W.A's second full-length album, *Efil4zaggin*. "Eatin' a little bit more, a little bit fatter," he said, patting his belly.

"Only thing changed is our tax bracket," said DJ Yella.

Indeed, Dre had put on a few pounds. But they were also living much larger, at least Eazy, Heller, and Dre, who joined the other two by purchasing a French colonial mansion in their Calabasas gated community in 1991. Michel'le outfitted the house with marble tables, and special touches included a huge fish tank that could be viewed from both sides, as well as a recording studio. Dre liked to host barbecues by the pool, with deafening music, and even amateur boxing matches. Jonathan Gold, writing for *Rolling Stone*, asked if his neighbors ever complained. "They try to," he said, "but I slam the door in their face. I paid a mil-plus for this house, so I figure I can do whatever the fuck I want to do in it." He spent recklessly to keep the good times going. He said he bought between eight and ten cars, Ferraris, Mercedes, Corvettes, and bankrolled a nonstop soiree. "You could come over on Sunday morning and there's just people laying out on the floor asleep," he said.

Heller lived a couple of blocks away. His cars included a white BMW with the license plate "RTHLSS2," which Eazy bought for him. (The rapper's matching version, same make and model, had "RTHLSS1.") Eazy's pad, two doors down from Heller, boasted Graceland-levels of goofy grandeur. A neon sign in the marble foyer read "Eazy's Playhouse." The house included a pitch-black TV room complete with a LaserDisc player, fluorescent pillows, and mirrors all around. "He'd impress girls by bringing them there, a select few," said his assistant Charis Henry. Eazy also collected various monster movie mementos, including a life-sized version of *Hellraiser* villain Pinhead (with the nails in his skull), and a creepy Chucky doll, from the horror movie *Child's Play*.

Despite the fancy trappings, Eazy didn't actually spend much time at the Calabasas home, since it was so isolated in the Valley. He let friends and Ruthless artists live there, as well as at his main house in Norwalk.

Dr. Dre's first group World Class Wreckin' Cru combined rap and electro, and released two albums in the mid-'80s. It also featured DJ Yella, making it something of a precursor to N.W.A, although their glammed up outfits (notice Dre's purple doctor's suit) would be discarded in favor of a "gangsta" image. Left to right: Alonzo Williams, Dr. Dre, DJ Yella, and Cli-N-Tel. (Courtesy of Alonzo Williams)

Seen here at a mid-'80s Skateland Halloween party, Rodger Clayton was the leader of Uncle Jamm's Army, a popular mobile DJ crew that brought turntables and a massive sound system wherever there was a party. These were the kinder, gentler days of early L.A. hip-hop, which went by the wayside when N.W.A emerged in the late '80s. (Courtesy of Craig Schweisinger)

Before he got into music, Eazy-E dealt drugs at this Compton apartment building, referred to as "Atlantic Drive" because of its location. Its layout prevented most units from being seen from the street, obscuring potential police observation. Still, this area was a dangerous gang nexus where a number of Crip subsets' territory collided, each hoping to expand their drug-dealing sphere. (Author photo)

Left to right: Arabian Prince, Dr. Dre, Eazy-E. Taken in 1987 in an alley near Macola Records, this picture was shot the same day as the photo-shoot for the cover of N.W.A's unauthorized debut *N.W.A. and the Posse*. (Courtesy of Sir Jinx)

Left to right atop the Suzuki truck: Ice Cube, Arabian Prince, Dr. Dre, Eazy-E. Also taken the same day as the *N.W.A. and the Posse* shoot, this early group photo features the members wearing colors, before they began mostly adopting neutral black and white. (Courtesy of Sir Jinx)

This 1985 cassette was mixed by Dr. Dre, featured local hip-hop and electro artists signed to Don Macmillan's Macola Records, and was sold at outlets like the Roadium Swap Meet. Dr. Dre was fairly unknown at the time, but releases like these helped build his name. (Courtesy of Don Macmillan)

SPECIAL THANKS and appreciation to the guys who have allowed us to do this special mix and for their support of Macola Records.
—DON MACMILLAN

Producer: Dr. Dre
Special Mix: Dr. Dre
Design/Art Direction: Don MacMillan

MACOLA RECORD CO.
6209 Santa Monica Blvd., Hollywood, CA 90038
(213) 469-5821

©℗ 1985. WARNING: All Rights Reserved

Reborn from a ravaged bowling alley, Compton skating rink Skateland was home to some of L.A. hip-hop's most seminal early concerts, including N.W.A's first show, March 11, 1988. (Courtesy of Craig Schweisinger)

Skateland, which opened in 1984 and hosted its last show in 1988, was located in the heart of Bloods territory, which meant that attendees tended to wear red rather than blue. (Courtesy of Craig Schweisinger)

Top row left to right: DJ Train, MC J.B., Baby D, Lavetta Washington, Dr. Dre. Bottom row left to right: Joyce Bragg, Sassy C, Eazy-E. DJ Train was the DJ for J. J. Fad, a Ruthless group known for its hit "Supersonic" that included MC J.B., Baby D, and Sassy C. Lavetta Washington and Joyce Bragg were Dr. Dre and Eazy-E's girlfriends, respectively. (Courtesy of Juana Sperling)

Left to right: Dr. Dre, Eazy-E, MC J.B. of J. J. Fad, DJ Yella, taken in a hotel lobby during a 1989 tour that included N.W.A and J. J. Fad. (Courtesy of Juana Sperling)

Left to right: MC Ren, Baby D of J. J. Fad, Dr. Dre, taken around 1988 at Torrance, California studio Audio Achievements, where Ruthless acts like N.W.A and J. J. Fad recorded their albums. (Courtesy of Juana Sperling)

Left to right: Arabian Prince, Jerry Heller, Eazy-E, Dr. Dre, DJ Yella. Rock music industry veteran Jerry Heller reinvented himself by managing early L.A. hip-hop acts from Macola Records, and after meeting Eazy-E threw his lot in with Ruthless Records and managed N.W.A. (Courtesy of Juana Sperling)

UNCLE JAM'S ARMY
★★★ *LIVE IN CONCERT* ★★★

EAZY E
AND
N.W.A.

THIS FRI. MARCH 11
8 P.M.

SKATELAND U.S.A.

135th & CENTRAL

N.W.A's first concert was performed at Skateland on March 11, 1988. Eazy-E, already a solo star, was listed separately as was common in their early days. (Courtesy of Craig Schweisinger)

While other members of N.W.A were sowing their wild oats, Ice Cube began to settle down as a one-woman guy. He's pictured here in 1990 with his then-girlfriend Kim Woodruff. They married in 1992. (Courtesy of Sir Jinx)

Left to right: Sir Jinx, D.M.C. of Run-D.M.C., and Ice Cube in 1990 at Greene St. Recording studio in Manhattan, while working on Cube's debut album *Amerikkka's Most Wanted*. (Courtesy of Sir Jinx)

Before it was pared down to a three-man group that released its hit debut *Guerillas in tha Mist* in 1992, Da Lench Mob was a sprawling collective featuring both rappers and streetwise friends of Ice Cube, who backed him up after he left N.W.A. (Courtesy of J-Dee)

Tairrie B was the first white female rapper signed to a major record deal. After meeting Jerry Heller at an N.W.A concert, she auditioned for Eazy-E and he signed her on the spot. His subsidiary imprint Comptown Records released her debut *Power of a Woman* in 1990. (Courtesy of Tairrie B)

This promotional poster from 1990 features members of the Ruthless Records universe, from artists to security guards to rappers' children. (Courtesy of Juana Sperling)

Left to right: Treach from Naughty By Nature, Tupac Shakur, and Eazy-E at the Jack the Rapper convention in Atlanta, probably in 1992. At the time, Eazy was attempting to court Tupac to Ruthless Records. (Courtesy of Chariś Henry)

Initially a bodyguard for Ruthless Records rapper D.O.C., Suge Knight convinced Dr. Dre to leave Ruthless and start Death Row Records with him, where they created some of the most venerated albums in rap history. Suge went to prison after contributing to the attack on Tupac Shakur's alleged killer Orlando Anderson in 1996, and is pictured here with a fan at the BET Awards in 2002, about a year after his release. (Courtesy of Harris Rosen, author of *N.W.A – The Aftermath*)

The former Solar Records building, at 1635 North Cahuenga Blvd. in Hollywood. Owned by Dick Griffey, the building was home to the Galaxy Studios, where parts of *The Chronic* and other Death Row Records albums were recorded. (Author photo)

Can-Am Recorders in Tarzana, California, where Guns N' Roses recorded parts of *Appetite for Destruction*, became Death Row's headquarters in the mid-'90s. Tupac recorded there often, and Suge Knight sometimes slept in a room next to his office. Near one of the doors he had a wall of bulletproof glass installed. (Author photo)

Ruthless Records group Above the Law was led by Cold187um, a rapper and producer known for his G-funk sound, who brawled with Ice Cube and his crew shortly after Cube left the label. Cold187um is seen here in 2015. (Author photo)

Rhythm D, who produced Eazy-E's 1993 hit "Real Compton City G's," the rapper's comeback after his former N.W.A group mate Dr. Dre dissed him on "Dre Day." This picture was shot at Rhythm's Atlanta studio. (Author photo)

When rapper Steffon (seen here in 2015) signed with Ruthless Records, Eazy-E gave him a $7,500 advance and a grocery bag full of marijuana. (Author photo)

As an act called 213, Snoop Dogg, Nate Dogg, and Warren G recorded some of their earliest work at Long Beach landmark V. I.P. Records, after the store's owner Kelvin Anderson set up a studio there. Snoop's video for "What's My Name" was also filmed at V.I.P. The store was set to close its retail business at the end of 2015. (Author photo)

Snoop Dogg at a 2014 press event in Culver City, California for the Swedish company Happy Socks. Having watched violence take the life of his former colleague Tupac, he transformed himself into a pitchman and an advocate for peace in hip-hop. (Author photo)

Warren G at Red Bull Studios in Santa Monica, California in 2014. Trained as a DJ and producer by his older stepbrother Dr. Dre, Warren G never signed with Ruthless or Death Row, but created the song that was arguably G-funk's biggest hit, 1994's "Regulate," with Nate Dogg. (Author photo)

Macola Records founder Don Macmillan at his Palos Verdes Estates, California home in 2015. Macmillan founded Hollywood pressing plant and label Macola Records in 1983, distributing works from acts including Dr. Dre and Ice Cube's first groups, as well as N.W.A's first album. Without Macmillan's efforts, early L.A. hip-hop might not have taken off the way it did. (Author photo)

World Class Wreckin' Cru founder Alonzo Williams at his South Central Los Angeles home in 2014. Williams was a successful DJ from the disco era who went on to found World Class Wreckin' Cru, giving Dr. Dre and DJ Yella their starts. N.W.A and its members created some of their earliest music at Williams' home studio, and the group likely would not have succeeded without his mentorship. (Author photo)

MC Ren at the Hard Rock Hotel in Palm Springs, California in 2014. Though not as well known today as his former N.W.A groupmates Dr. Dre, Ice Cube, and Eazy-E, MC Ren was a critical member of the act, delivering brutal lyrics with a virtuosic flow. (Author photo)

Eazy also had a home in Woodland Hills, close to Ruthless's offices and in the shadow of the 101 freeway. "You wanna move in?" Eazy asked rapper Steffon, almost immediately after he signed with Ruthless in 1993. The Woodland Hills home's previous occupant, Eazy's girlfriend Tomica Woods, had moved into yet another of Eazy's homes, in Topanga. Steffon took him up on the offer. It was like winning the lottery.

The Republican Inner Circle

Despite the lavish living, Eazy kept his focus on business. As he pondered how to promote N.W.A's upcoming second album *Efil4zaggin*, an opportunity fell into his lap. He'd somehow ended up on a Republican Party mailing list. (It was likely owing to a charitable donation he'd made.) In early 1991 he accepted an invitation from Texas senator Phil Gramm to hear President George H. W. Bush speak to a group of campaign contributors called the "Republican Senatorial Inner Circle."

Somehow nobody put two and two together, and Eazy received a follow-up letter from Senate minority leader Bob Dole, which noted that Inner Circle members included Arnold Schwarzenegger, Sam Walton, and Estée Lauder. The cost? A mere $2,490 for two tickets (one for him and one for Heller) to an event called "Salute to the Commander-in-Chief" on March 18, 1991, two months before the new N.W.A album would drop. It would pay off in what Wright would characterize as "a million dollars worth of publicity."

Eazy arrived at D.C.'s National Airport, carrying his suit in a bag over his shoulder and signing autographs for fans. Ruthless had tipped off *CBS News,* and Bob Schieffer was there to report on the absurdity of the whole thing. Do you think the Republicans know who Eazy is? he asked Heller, who responded that he doubted it. "But as for us," the Ruthless manager went on, "we're happy to be here." The event was held at the Omni Shoreham Hotel (not the White House, as is claimed in the *Straight Outta Compton* film and often reported) and went off without a hitch. Eazy showed his ticket, went through the metal detector, and dined on roast beef and salmon.

Not everyone thought Eazy's cavorting with right-wingers was funny. Though before the luncheon Eazy's PR flack told the *Los Angeles Times* that Eazy was a "big fan" of Bush, Eazy afterward switched gears in an interview with *Spin*, complaining that many, including director Spike Lee, failed to get the joke. "I'm not a Republican or a Democrat. I don't give a fuck. I don't even vote."

The incident wasn't Eazy's only brush with political controversy. He enraged the hip-hop community by publicly supporting Theodore Briseno, one of the officers charged in the Rodney King trial. Eazy met Briseno through his lawyer, Harland W. Braun, who also did work for Ruthless, and the rapper attended the 1993 federal trial. At a time when most people believed all four cops to be guilty, Eazy put his reputation on the line by literally standing next to Briseno. The pair made the *Los Angeles Times* front page, prompting Geto Boys' rapper Willie D to call Eazy a "sellout." Eazy responded that he believed Briseno had attempted to stop the beating and that, despite the media's characterization of the four officers as white, Briseno was a Latino. (It is possible to be both white and Latino.)

Indeed, Briseno did not hit Rodney King with a baton, and broke ranks with the other officers at trial, saying their use of force was not justified. But he can clearly be seen in the video kicking King in the back of his head with his boot. "Sure, I've seen that little stomp Briseno does on the video, and I'm not saying it's justified, but we don't know what it was about, do we?" Eazy said. "It could have been him just trying to tell Rodney, 'Stay down, man, stay down.' Who's to know?" (Eazy sometimes didn't appear to be very sympathetic toward King. In a 1991 interview with *Spin* he said: "Rodney King's all fucked up, man! He going out with transvestites now. He don't know what the fuck's goin' on! He don't know his ass from a hole in the ground!") A rapper in Eazy's own camp named B.G. Knocc Out was so enraged about Eazy's support of Briseno that he wrote a diss song about him. Ruthless rapper Toker said Eazy later regretted standing by the officer.

Whatever the case, one can't help admire Eazy's chutzpah. He never did what anyone expected of him. This, along with the Bush fund-raiser, were vintage contrarian Eazy-E.

Temporary Insanity

In May 1991 *Efil4zaggin* ("Niggaz 4 Life" spelled backward) debuted at number two. Many reviews were not flattering, but it reached *Billboard*'s top slot the next week, displacing Paula Abdul's *Spellbound* and making it the first gangsta rap album to hit number one—buoyed by a new system implemented by SoundScan that determined rankings not based on dodgy figures supplied by record store employees, but tabulations of actual sales. It was a watershed event, the moment when rap began its decades-long dominance of mainstream music.

Efil4zaggin also marks a great leap forward in Dr. Dre's production skills. Whereas *Compton* was all over the place sonically, *Efil* is mostly unified in its doomsday grooves. "Always into Something" is a slow-building sonic masterpiece, kicking off with a spoken-word MC Ren introduction and a quick Dre verse before unveiling the alien-sounding, high-pitched Moog synthesizer sound, similar to the "funky worm" Dre had employed on "Dope Man." It would become a staple of Dre's solo work. Hoping to capture the magic of Parliament-Funkadelic member Bernie Worrell's eerie, melodic keyboard sounds, Dre had engineer Colin Wolfe go out and buy a Moog.

On *Efil4zaggin* Dre realized that less is more, that silence on a track can be just as important as sound. "Dre has a lot of space in his music. It's open, there's not always too much going on," said his future collaborator Dawaun Parker. The basslines are mostly played live in the studio—the funk of James Brown was also in his ears—and there's a real musicality. When you add in the taunts from Above the Law and Kokane, along with Dre's own much improved efforts as an MC, *Efil* delivers on its rebellious, R-rated promises. (Once again DJ Yella received a coproduction credit on the album, but his contributions weren't on the level of Dre's.)

Owing to Ice Cube's departure, there's not much political commentary, though "Niggaz 4 Life" addresses their use of the inflammatory word in the title: *Why do I call myself a nigga, you ask me?* MC Ren raps. *Because police always wanna harass me.* "*We* didn't give ourselves this name," Eazy elaborated around this time to a quasi-outraged *NBC News* reporter who asked why he used it so often. "People have been calling us 'niggas' for years, and so we carry that word." To promote the album, Eazy portrayed himself in the media less as a street soldier and more as a cartoonish psychotic, with duct tape over his mouth and glasses missing a lens. For *Arsenio* he donned a straightjacket and hockey mask. (He even began putting together, but eventually scrapped, an album called *Temporary Insanity*.)

Today, *Efil4zaggin* is not remembered as warmly as *Straight Outta Compton*. Ice Cube's voice is definitely missed. Whereas Cube's enemies were clearly defined—those who would suppress the black man—*Efil's* themes and antagonists aren't well drawn. *Efil4zaggin* features blowjob tutorials, stories about girls who won't give it up, and tales of violence against women that range from cartoonish to appallingly realistic, especially considering Dre's history of abuse. *'Cause if a bitch tries to diss me while I'm full of liquor / I smack the bitch up and shoot the nigga that's with her*, Dre raps on "Findum Fuckem & Flee." But mainly it seems shocking for the sake of being shocking. "We were trying to see how far we could push the envelope," Dre admitted. MC Ren perhaps found that limit on "She Swallowed It," in which his character preys on a preacher's fourteen-year-old daughter.

The bitch sucks dick like a specialized pro
She looked at me, I was surprised
But wasn't passin' up the chance of my dick gettin' baptized

"I'd Rather Fuck You," Eazy's lounge-style parody of Bootsy Collins's "I'd Rather Be With You," flips a straightforward love song into an Andrew Dice Clay–style seduction anthem. Singer Jewell, who'd recently done an impromptu audition for Dre in the corner of a club, sings on the chorus. ("I was thinking, 'Oh, my God, my mom is going to kill me'" for being on the song, she remembered.)

Owing to the album's sex and violence, reaction from social conservatives was swift. Libraries banned the album, British police confiscated thousands of copies, and Minnesota's attorney general Hubert "Skip"

Humphrey III—son of the former vice president—called its lyrics "nothing but filth" and threatened to prosecute Minneapolis-based record store chain Musicland Group if it sold *Efil4zaggin* to minors. Ultimately, the Minneapolis city attorney's office determined the work didn't violate Minnesota's statutes.

Despite receiving little radio airplay—they didn't bother recording a radio-friendly track without cursing—*Efil4zaggin* went platinum. "We ain't selling out. Fuck crossing over to them, let them cross over to us," MC Ren said at a live show in 1989. He had no idea how prophetic his words would be.

"Beating Up the Charts"

The nationally syndicated TV hip-hop show *Pump It Up!* launched in 1989, a counterpart to *Yo! MTV Raps* that mixed videos with artist interviews. The program was hosted by Dee Barnes, a petite, Afrocentric rapper from a duo called Body & Soul, who were signed to Delicious Vinyl and rapped on "We're All in the Same Gang." (They once recorded a demo in Alonzo Williams's house coproduced by Dr. Dre.)

Barnes's interviews, like her music, tended to be upbeat, though she didn't shy away from asking tough questions. She, along with her sometime cohost, Ruthless rapper Steffon, featured everyone from De La Soul to Biz Markie to N.W.A. Barnes began hanging out with Dre at one point, though it's unclear in exactly what capacity. When Dre was asked by *The Source* in 1992 if he and Barnes had been romantically involved he said, "so-so," though Barnes denied it.

In November 1990 *Pump It Up!* did another story on N.W.A, who were on the tail end of promoting the EP *100 Miles and Runnin'*. The interview went fine, but the editing of the piece angered the group. Following their segment was Barnes's interview with rapper Yo-Yo on the set of the *Boyz n the Hood* movie. Ice Cube crashed the interview. On camera, he disparaged his former group, and mocked the title of their EP. "I got all you suckers a hundred miles and runnin'," he said.

N.W.A had dissed Cube in the episode as well. But they hadn't been told Cube would have a chance to respond, and felt the editing made it look like he had the final word. Reportedly Barnes herself wasn't a fan of the final cut—chosen by a producer—but the group blamed her. "She tried to make us look stupid," MC Ren said. "Tried to play us in front of millions of people."

On January 27, 1991, at a West Hollywood nightclub called Po Na Na Souk, Def Jam hosted a record-release party for a group called BWP, or Bytches With Problems. Niggaz With Attitudes had opened the floodgates for tough girl groups with three-word names, including Ruthless acts H.W.A. (Hoez With Attitudes) and G.B.M. (Gangsta Bitch Mentality). At the Def Jam event the liquor was flowing freely, and Dre later admitted to *Spin* that he was "drunk." Doug Young, N.W.A's promoter, was talking to Dee Barnes when Dre and a bodyguard walked up to them. "[Dre] looked over to her, said, 'That was some fucked-up shit you did, bitch, on that show,'" Young recalled in an interview with me. Then Dre suddenly hit her in the face, Young said. "He just fired on her. BAM! I saw the punch, and I just saw her fall like a sack of potatoes."

"He grabbed me by my hair, picked me up and started slamming me into a brick wall," said Barnes, who is nearly a foot shorter than Dre and weighed about half as much. Dre's bodyguard held back the crowd, she added in a statement. According to eyewitness accounts, Dre began kicking her and tried to push her down a flight of stairs. She fled to a bathroom, but Dre followed her in and began beating her more. Doug Young said the room full of spectators watched and did nothing.

"I was thinking, 'He's trying to kill me,'" Barnes said. The police and ambulance were called, but Dre was hustled out without being arrested. Barnes suffered bruises on her face—and recorded episodes of *Pump It Up!* behind dark glasses. "Dre was like a big brother to me," she told *Rolling Stone* in August 1991. "I still get very emotional about it."

The day after the beating, Dre told *The Source*, Barnes called to say she wasn't going to press charges. She soon changed her tune, he went on, saying that if he wanted to avoid court he was going to have to produce some songs for her group, "without putting my name on it or anything like that and they would forget it." Dre said he agreed to the deal, but that Barnes later reneged and instead wanted "a million dollars." "I was like, 'What? Fuck you, take me to court,'" Dre said he responded. "Next thing I know, the shit is in every motherfuckin' newspaper there is and I'm in court."

The alleged Lisa Johnson, Michel'le, and Tairrie B beatings had never been reported in the media, but following Dee Barnes's attack the allegations against Dre were widely publicized. *Rolling Stone* entitled its first major story on N.W.A "Beating Up the Charts."

Barnes, fearing for her safety, hired a member of fearsome Samoan rap crew the Boo-Yaa T.R.I.B.E. to act as security. "She's going through a lot of emotional turmoil," said her mother Joan Barnes. "The first three months, we were both really paranoid. Now it's gone beyond fear. We're just trying to exist." Statements Dre made to reporters further fueled the situation ("[I]t ain't no big thing—I just threw her through a door," he told *Rolling Stone*) and Eazy and Ren callously defended him, bragging about the beating and offering further intimidations. Said Ren: "It's not over yet."

Barnes's mother speculated that the violence of N.W.A's songs was coming to life. "They started believing [what] they were writing," she said.

In August 1991 Dre pleaded no contest to battery charges. His sentence was a $2,400 fine, 240 hours of community service, and probation. He was also ordered to pay $1,000 to a victims' restitution fund, and to make an antiviolence public service announcement. Barnes also filed a $20 million civil lawsuit against him that was settled out of court, for six figures. "People think I was paid millions, when in reality, I didn't even get *a* million, and it wasn't until September of 1993. He and his lawyers dragged their feet the whole way," Barnes wrote.

For many years after the incident Dre never offered a formal public apology. Following the release of the *Straight Outta Compton* movie in 2015, his abuse allegations again became news. "Twenty-five years ago I was a young man drinking too much and in over my head with no real structure in my life," he told *The New York Times*. He continued: "I apologize to the women I've hurt. I deeply regret what I did and know that it has forever impacted all of our lives."

In his statement, Dre partly tied his abuse to alcoholism. But Johnson and others who knew him in the early and mid-eighties, including World Class Wreckin' Cru companions, told me he didn't have a drinking problem in this time. (His alleged abuse of Lisa Johnson occurred in 1984 and 1985.) Dre said he started "boozing" following the death of his brother Tyree in 1989. "I think that triggers it because he turns into somebody else," said Michel'le. Tairrie B also said Dre had been drinking before he hit her, which was seconded by her manager Linda Martinez.

Barnes says the incident with Dre cast a spell over her life. She was "blacklisted" from further television work, she wrote, because potential employers didn't want to threaten their relationships with Dre, and ended up working "a series of nine-to-five jobs" to live. "I suffer from horrific migraines that started only after the attack," she went on. "I love Dre's song 'Keep Their Heads Ringin'—it has a particularly deep meaning to me. When I get migraines, my head does ring and it hurts, exactly in the same spot every time where he smashed my head against the wall."

CHAPTER ELEVEN

THE ENFORCER

Marion Knight Jr. entered the Ruthless fold quietly. Nicknamed "Suge" by his dad—he was said to be sweet like a sugar bear—he was something of a mama's boy, regularly sending her roses. His father, who once sang in an R&B group, worked in UCLA's laundry and housekeeping departments and, later, as a truck driver. "No matter how hard he worked, he barely had enough money to buy himself an extra beer," Suge told *Esquire*. "I made up my mind that I wanted everything, and nothing would stop me."

Suge was raised in a Piru Bloods–controlled section of Compton. But he didn't join any gangs, and they left him alone because he was a football star at Lynwood High School. "His dad used to pay him for every sack," said Sharitha Golden, who began dating him in high school and later became his wife. He attended El Camino Community College on scholarship and later transferred to University of Nevada, Las Vegas, on scholarship, where he was a standout defensive end. "I used to go to football practice in college and see how many teammates I could hurt," he said. He may have been exaggerating; his coach Wayne Nunnely said Suge "wasn't a problem guy at all," and he "didn't really see that street roughness about him." He loved soul music—Sam Cooke, Donny Hathaway—as well as hip-hop, and on the weekends, he worked at clubs as a security guard.

In 1987 Suge was offered a contract with the San Francisco 49ers, but he lost it after being arrested following an altercation with a friend named Ricardo "Ricky" Crockett, with whom he had a dispute. Las Vegas police accused him of shooting Crockett and then taking his car on October 31 that year, and he was charged with attempted murder and grand theft auto, although in the end he pleaded guilty to misdemeanors, receiving three years' probation and a $1,000 fine. (In 1993, Crockett was accused of trafficking drugs between Las Vegas and L.A. The same federal probe also named Knight; Crockett was convicted on drug charges, but Knight was found guilty only of gun possession, receiving probation.)

Suge was devastated about losing his shot with the 49ers, but returned home and successfully tried out for the Los Angeles Rams, joining the team in 1987 for a pair of games when its regular players went on strike. But his NFL career was short-lived; his on-again, off-again girlfriend Sharitha Golden said he skipped out on Rams' training camp one day and showed up at her mother's house. He wasn't invited; they were in a rough patch. She nonetheless agreed to get into his car to talk. "All of the sudden he pulls my ponytail down. He reached back in the seat pocket of the car and he pulls out these scissors,'" she told filmmaker S. Leigh Savidge. "He cut my ponytail clean off." She filed a restraining order against him, but it didn't totally sour things, and by the end of the eighties they were married.

Over the years the soft-spoken Suge has portrayed himself as simultaneously innocent and sinister, a product of the streets where he grew up. "Sometimes you end up in the wrong place at the wrong time," he said. "But the way I was raised it was like this here: The only things you have are your word and your manhood. No matter what they say about you, before anything else, you got to be a man."

His football career finished, he worked security at the Forum, then home of the Lakers. He also became R&B singer Bobby Brown's bodyguard, but his big break would come from meeting D.O.C. through a mutual friend, Andre "L.A. Dre" Bolton, who played keyboards on a number of Ruthless Records albums. L.A. Dre and Suge would help D.O.C., fresh from Dallas and not yet legal drinking age, get into clubs,

D.O.C. said. The rapper was mesmerized by this new scene, populated by celebrities like Eddie Murphy and Prince, and older women who were hitting on him. "It was heaven," D.O.C. said.

Jerry Heller said Suge was employed by Ruthless as a seventy-dollar-per-day bodyguard, but D.O.C. denied this. He insisted Suge simply latched on to him, serving as his protector more or less because he enjoyed pounding people. "Suge got off on that shit, it was fun to him," D.O.C. said. "If I got drunk and slapped a girl's ass, and her guy got upset, Suge would beat the motherfucker up. And then we'd just leave." (When I sought comment from Suge in 2015, his lawyer said he was not available, owing to his imprisonment.) The pair grew especially close following D.O.C.'s crash, with Suge doting on him every day in the hospital. "Whatever I needed him to do, he handled," D.O.C. said. Suge also helped him set up autograph sessions and other revenue-generating appearances.

Suge mainly stayed out of the limelight, at least at first. N.W.A affiliate Krazy Dee had no idea who he was when he encountered him in April 1990 at the Celebrity Theatre in Anaheim (the same night Above the Law and Ice Cube got into it). Hanging out backstage, Krazy Dee approached D.O.C. "What's up, nigga?" he said. He hadn't meant anything by the comment; he was simply making conversation. But Suge, six foot two and topping out over three hundred pounds, seemed to think Krazy Dee was talking trash. Their conversation grew heated, and Krazy Dee threatened to call for reinforcements. At that point Suge knocked Krazy Dee "through a closed door," remembered eyewitness DJ Speed. Krazy Dee said Suge sucker punched him as hard as he could, right in the face. "He hit me really hard," he told me, adding that his face became swollen and his eye turned black. "Some of my teeth shifted."

Krazy Dee went home, and later discussed the situation with Eazy, who recommended suing. Dre intervened, inviting Krazy Dee to Solar Records in Hollywood, where he was recording. Upon arriving Krazy Dee was taken down a long dark hallway into a dark office. "I thought I was being set up," he said. Suge was inside, and invited him to sit down. They shook hands. "I didn't know who you were, and I just wanted to apologize to you," Suge said, according to Krazy Dee. "I thought you were trying to argue with D.O.C."

Suge's apparent philosophy was that it was easier to ask forgiveness than permission, though certainly not everyone got an apology. Cunning and ambitious, he let his fists cash his checks, and demand grew for his skills as an enforcer. Most famously, he pursued Vanilla Ice, the white rapper who dominated pop music at the beginning of the nineties with his blow-dried do, daffy rhymes, and quite suave dance moves. Vanilla Ice's debut album *To the Extreme* sold seven million copies, propelled by hit "Ice Ice Baby," which he claimed to have written when he was sixteen. However, a rapper named Mario Johnson, who went by Chocolate and was signed to Suge's management company, told Suge that while working with Vanilla Ice in Texas, he helped write many of the album's songs, but hadn't received just compensation.

Suge said he would handle the situation, and this is where the tale becomes tall. The oft-repeated story is that Suge shook down Vanilla Ice for his publishing by dangling him by his ankles over a hotel balcony. That never happened, according to Chocolate, Vanilla Ice, and Suge.

In reality, Suge first tried negotiating in good faith, producing as evidence Chocolate's original handwritten lyrics for songs including "Ice Ice Baby." (A girlfriend had also apparently witnessed him scribbling them down.) But Ice's record company didn't take Suge's claims seriously, telling him, "Look, we'll give you a couple of dollars if you'll let bygones be bygones," Suge told BET in 1996. "I wouldn't go for it." He ultimately decided to take his appeal to Vanilla Ice himself. The former defensive end and a group of large men interrupted the white rapper's meal at downtown L.A. steakhouse the Palm. "They were bigger than my bodyguards," Vanilla Ice said. "They pretty much grabbed my bodyguards, pulled them out, and sat down next to me right there and started talking to me."

The conversation didn't amount to much more than vague intimidations, but Suge's crew tracked them down again a few months later. "I'm thinking, 'Wow, this guy knows where I'm at, at all times!'" Vanilla Ice said, explaining how Suge showed up at his Beverly Hills hotel room one night with a half dozen armed men. "We knew where he was staying because I was supposed to be hearing some tracks he was doing," Chocolate said. "He wanted me to come by myself. But Suge said, 'I'm going with you.'"

Ice said Suge's entourage roughed up his security guys, and then took him out onto the balcony of the fifteenth-floor room. "He had me look over the edge, showing me how high I was up there. I needed to wear a diaper on that day," he said. Suge demanded he sign away points (a percentage of royalties) from the record, and Vanilla Ice consented, despite insisting that Chocolate "had nothing to do" with "Ice Ice Baby." He estimated that the points he gave up were worth $3 to 4 million.

Suge denied that his men were armed, or that Vanilla Ice had to be strong-armed. "He agreed to everything, it wasn't a problem," he countered. "He said the guy wrote the song." Chocolate said his side subsequently sued successfully for his royalties, through regular legal channels. It took more than a year before money started coming in, but then it came like a geyser. Rapper CPO recalled being later invited to Chocolate's stunning new house. When giving directions Chocolate told him: "Come up the hill. My house is the one with the two Porsches and the white Benz." Suge got his cut, too, and he and Sharitha got a home in Alta Loma.

The Smell of Leadership

Suge may have been a bully, but he was not a common thug. Around 1989 he started spending time with the Ruthless artists and closely observing what was going on behind the scenes. "I investigated and found out, 'Who do the writing and the music?' and, 'How do they get paid?'" he said.

Suge soon linked up with an agent named Tom Kline, who represented athletes and was trying to branch out into the music industry. The two of them, with D.O.C., planned to start a label called Funky Enough Records, named after the D.O.C. hit song. (At this point, D.O.C. believed his voice could still potentially be rehabilitated.) Suge began auditioning rappers out of Kline's Beverly Hills office, even recruiting up-and-coming rapper-producer DJ Quik for the label. But D.O.C. was getting cold feet about the venture. To succeed, he felt they needed something more. They needed Dre. So, Suge began strategizing how to get the producer on board. He quickly surmised that Dre was disgruntled with his contract—the same document that caused Ice Cube to walk.

By this point, Dre and Eazy had been tight for about five years. But Dre was growing increasingly irate about his earnings. He wasn't poor—he had his Calabasas mansion—but Dre felt he should be making top dollar, considering that the platinum and gold albums he'd produced for J. J. Fad, N.W.A, Eazy-E, D.O.C., and Michel'le had generated tens of millions of dollars in sales. (Remember, these were fifteen-dollar CDs and ten-dollar tapes, not $1.29 downloads.) It's unclear how much Dre was paid in total, but Heller told *Rolling Stone* Dre made about $86,000 from Ruthless in 1992, a figure that seems almost comically low. "[Eazy] took advantage of me not knowing the record business back in the day," Dre said. He also blamed Heller for the skewed contracts he signed.

Dre resented being paid as an employee, instead of as an owner. In his mind, he and Eazy had founded Ruthless together. Eazy denied this, and no one gave Dre's claim much credence, considering he didn't have any paperwork to back it up. But he may have been right; Eazy's close friend and artist Toker said Eazy later privately admitted as much. If Dre indeed cofounded Ruthless, he would have received a greater share of the proceeds—perhaps millions.

Around the time of Cube's departure, Dre gradually began confiding in Suge about his financial concerns. Suge eventually began managing Dre and Above the Law. Why would the well-established Dre suddenly get in cahoots with an undistinguished, shadowy newcomer? One explanation is Suge's personality. Alonzo Williams, who'd seen Dre jump ship with the World Class Wreckin' Cru during a different financial dispute, characterized Dre as easily swayed by the smell of strong leadership, by someone willing to handle financial details while he focused on making music. "He was an aggressive person that cleared the way for me to go in and do what I had to do," Dre said of Suge. "By any means necessary."

And so, when Dre asked him to take a look at his contract in early 1991, Suge simply showed up one day unannounced at Ruthless's lawyer's office, grabbed what he wanted and departed the premises. "We found out that Cube was right," Suge said. "Ruthless was taking Dre for a ride. And not just Dre, every other artist on the roster, too."

Was Dre really being taken for a ride? Legally, the answer is likely no. Dre never filed any lawsuit against Ruthless. More likely he'd simply signed an unfavorable deal, similar to decades' worth of artists before him. Legality aside, Ruthless probably should have done more to accommodate their franchise player. Doug Young, N.W.A's promoter, and a relatively neutral third-party observer, believed Eazy should have offered to renegotiate the contracts. Indeed, Heller tried to sweeten the pot for Dre in other ways. He attempted to create a sublabel for him through Warner that, he said, would have paid Dre a $2 million advance. But Warner was "clearly spooked" by the FBI's letter, Jerry noted, and balked.

Priority Records, Ruthless's distributor, however, did step up to the plate. Around this time they gave Dre a quarter of a million dollars, according to Dre's testimony in a 1991 deposition; $100,000 for a future album and $150,000 for back payments. (Priority could afford it; buoyed by gangsta rap, the label was later sold to EMI, in a deal rumored to exceed $100 million, and cofounders Bryan Turner and Mark Cerami bought homes worth millions.) But they kept Ruthless out of the loop, which infuriated Heller and further strained the relationship between Ruthless and Priority, the latter of which was now the label home of Ice Cube. "[Turner] was obviously trying to induce Dre to leave Ruthless like he did Ice Cube," Heller said. "There is no legal legitimate explanation why he offered him this money."

Eazy would later blame Priority for N.W.A's demise. But at the center of the dispute was the collapse of the relationship between Eazy and Dre themselves, with Heller's influence looming large. "I'm recording platinum records and getting two points as a producer," Dre said, referencing the relatively modest percentage of royalties he said he was receiving. "So I stepped to Eazy at this time and told him, 'Look man I'm not dealing with Jerry Heller anymore. I don't want him in my mixture.' I said, 'If I'm going to stay, he has to go. It's one of the two.'" According to Dre, Eazy thought about his ultimatum for a couple of days, and decided that he was going to stick with the veteran manager.

So that was that. But, complicating matters, Dre was still under contract with Eazy—barring him from recording with another label—and Eazy had no intention of letting him go quietly.

We Know Where Your Mother Lives

In the popular imagination Suge Knight is synonymous with rap world thuggery. Over the years, he's been accused of beating and murdering his adversaries, as well as financial crimes running from embezzlement to extortion. He punishes and humiliates others for the slightest offenses, some say, forcing them to disrobe in front of him or to drink urine from champagne flutes. Suge has done much to propagate this image, from his mob boss–style cigar habit to his blood-red Ford F-150 Raptor, with which in 2015 he allegedly ran over two men—killing one and then fleeing the scene.

And yet under Suge's watch Death Row Records released some of the most beloved and important albums in music history. With a traditional suit-wearing record label executive at the company's helm, it's highly unlikely these works would have been made or had the same impact. "The thing I like most about him, is that he don't ever let my shit get watered down. He keeps the music real," said Snoop Doggy Dogg. "He's got an ear to the street." To keep the music real, Suge twisted some arms. According to Eazy-E, he intimidated him into signing over Dr. Dre's contract. Eazy told the story numerous times, and even testified to it under oath. Though some details vary, and Dre denied any involvement, it goes roughly like this:

Late in the evening on April 23, 1991, Eazy received a call, or a page, from Dr. Dre, asking to meet up. He said he wanted to work out their differences, and so Eazy headed over to Solar, parking in the dark basement lot and heading upstairs to a studio known as Galaxy. Dre was not there, however. Instead, Suge Knight greeted him when he got off the elevator, along with two (or three) bulky men. They held oversized lead pipes, or Louisville Sluggers, and possibly had guns bulging from their pants. One thing was clear: Eazy was outmanned and under-weaponized. He was led to a dark, soundproof room.

"Where Dre at?" Eazy asked.

Suge ignored the question and instead levied an allegation: "I heard you was trying to get me killed, Blood." (Indeed, Heller has said Eazy batted around the idea of having Suge offed.) Suge then pulled out some documents, which were purportedly designed to let Dr. Dre, D.O.C., Michel'le, and Above the Law out of their Ruthless contracts. In one version of this story, the papers gave some concessions to Ruthless: Dre would finish the (yet-unreleased) N.W.A album *Efil4zaggin*, and Suge would negotiate better terms for Ruthless with Priority.

In all versions of the story, Eazy told him where he could stick the releases.

At this point Suge twisted the screws. We have Jerry Heller tied up in a van, he said, and we know where your mother lives. As proof he presented a scrap of paper with an address, or a picture of the house, depending on the account. Whatever the case, this threat was entirely credible, considering Eazy had openly stamped his home address on his earliest printings of records.

And so Eazy signed the papers. (He was not beat up by Suge's men, as depicted in *Straight Outta Compton*.) "He didn't want anything to happen to his mom, and he signed under duress," his girlfriend Tomica Woods said in the 2008 documentary *N.W.A: The World's Most Dangerous Group*. At first he wrote "Mickey Mouse," she added. But eventually he was forced to take the proceedings seriously. What else was he going to do?

Suge later denied all of this, taking the opportunity to belittle Eazy. "Do I need a bat to force him to do a few things?" he said at an August 1993 Death Row press conference. "If he walked between my legs, excuse my French, people would probably think he was my penis."

One thing was clear: These releases weren't worth the paper they were printed on; since Eazy signed under duress, the releases weren't binding. He sent letters to the major record companies warning them against signing Dre.

Eazy may have won the battle, but Suge would not be deterred. His stunt drove home the point that Dre was truly done with Ruthless Records. Who cared if he was still technically under contract? If he didn't put forth his best efforts, it made no difference.

Suge Knight kept showing up at the *Efil4zaggin* recording sessions, leading to a tense atmosphere. After that album—and Dr. Dre's producing an experimental work from multi-instrumentalist Jimmy Z called *Muzical Madness* that includes Ron Burgundy–style jazz flute—Dre was effectively done at the label.

D.O.C. gave me yet another version of these events. He said Dre left Ruthless at *his* behest, so they could start a label together. He, Dre, and Suge did, in fact, soon quietly launch a label called Futureshock, named for a Curtis Mayfield song. Their fourth partner in the venture was Dick Griffey, a veteran music industry player, founder of Solar Records, and cofounder of Soul Train Records. The name wouldn't stick. "Futureshock Records?" Suge said. "That sounds like some bullshit. It's gonna be called Death Row. Because once you get on this label, that's the end."

Eazy and Heller plotted their next move, emerging with a legal plan they hoped would drive Suge Knight back underground. On August 23, 1991, Ruthless lawyers filed suit against Suge, Dre, Death Row, Sony, Solar, and others, claiming they had violated the Racketeer Influenced and Corrupt Organizations (RICO) Act, a federal law generally used to take down the Mafia and other organized crime targets. The suit leveled charges of extortion, racketeering, and money laundering against the record companies and brass including top Sony executive Tommy Mottola.

Sony, Death Row, and Solar were guilty of conspiring to put Ruthless out of business, the lawsuit claimed. As Ruthless argued, Dre hadn't just left because Suge charmed him. He left because Sony Records secretly offered him a boatload of money. Those release forms Eazy signed under duress? Those had been drafted by one of Sony's attorneys, Ruthless insisted. Heller's lawyer Michael Bourbeau claimed that, immediately after Eazy signed the releases, Suge sent a fax to a pair of executives at Sony's Epic subsidiary, David Glew and Hank Caldwell. The fax said Dre was "available for all production work. And it asked for $125,000 in advance," Bourbeau said.

How much Dre received from Sony isn't clear, but in April 1992, Epic and Solar coreleased the soundtrack to the drug-world thriller *Deep Cover*. The title track was produced and performed by Dr. Dre, along with newcomer Snoop Doggy Dogg. To *The Source*, Eazy expressed incredulity that Sony thought they could get away with this, asserting the company knew full well Dre was still under contract.

Sony's lawyers argued that Dre's contract with Ruthless actually did permit him to make music for other labels. "Sony was very careful," said Wayne Smith, part of Sony's legal team. "They only signed Dre to the rights Ruthless didn't have."

Muscle and Tactics

While the two sides battled in court, a culture of fear set in at Ruthless. Following Suge's intimidations, Heller began taking a different route home each night. He stashed guns throughout his house and installed an expensive security system.

His fears were not unfounded. Suge and about "five carloads of dudes" suddenly showed up at Eazy's Norwalk house one day, said DJ Speed, who was living there at the time. Suge demanded the "reels"—the master recordings Dre had produced at Ruthless. Speed peered at them through protective bars shielding the house, he said, and told them they were out of luck. The men left.

Eazy had hoped to jettison the violence of his past. He had attempted to run a legitimate business, even moving into a fancy office building in the suburbs. But playing by the rules wasn't working. Suge was growing brazen, and their run-in made him look weak. His longtime collaborator was out the door. His empire was crumbling. Ruthless needed to increase its firepower.

Heller recruited as security director an Israeli named Mike Klein, whose job was to put the fear of God into their adversaries. Klein had a background in "Israeli security forces," Heller wrote, but was currently working in the garment business for a company out of Canoga Park, near Ruthless's first offices. Nobody seems to know the specifics of Klein's background. Wrote *Vibe*: "Before he moved to Los Angeles, says somebody who knows him, the Israeli-born Klein 'led a commando raid into southern Lebanon when they caught those guys who blew up the kibbutz kids on the school bus.'"

"That stuff I can't comment on," Klein responded to the magazine. (I was unable to contact him for an interview.)

Klein was lean with thinning hair, wore an expensive gold bracelet, and spoke in a deep voice with an accent. Ruthless producer Rhythm D said he was a dead ringer for the actor Peter Sormare, who played Karl Hungus in *The Big Lebowski*. "Nobody messed with him," Rhythm added. Indeed, by all accounts, he was an incredible badass, a martial arts expert who also took the Ruthless team to the gun range for target practice.

Klein offered "muscle and tactics when you talked to people," said Tomica Woods. Rhythm D found this to be true. He'd produced songs for rapper Paperboy, including his breakout 1993 hit "Ditty," but hadn't received his proper royalties for his work, he said, that is, until he linked up with Ruthless, and Heller set up a meeting with the owners of Paperboy's label. "He didn't have to do nothing but bring big Mike in the room," Rhythm said, "and we did the contracts."

Rapper Krayzie Bone, whose group Bone Thugs-N-Harmony later signed to Ruthless, recalled an occasion when the group complained about money they felt the label owed them. Eazy assigned Klein to take care of them, and so the Israeli took them to his home—which looked like something "out of a Mafia movie, like *The Godfather*" complete with an elevator, said Krayzie. Klein then produced a duffel bag full of cash totaling $20,000, which he handed to them. The guys took the money, but were stupefied. "We was like, 'Awww, shit,'" Krayzie said.

For further aid in their battle with Death Row, Klein and Heller enlisted the services of the Jewish Defense League, a New York–based organization that seeks to protect Jews against anti-Semitism, and which the FBI regards as a "right-wing extremist group" for its violent tactics. The JDL provided Ruthless with bodyguards. Before long there were "Israeli soldiers wielding Uzi machine guns at the office," wrote S. Leigh Savidge, a filmmaker who visited the Ruthless headquarters in this period. "It felt like a military zone. I wanted to get out of there as fast as I could."

In 1997 the FBI began a two-year investigation into the JDL, which they suspected was extorting rappers, including Eazy and Tupac Shakur. The alleged scam went like this: Someone would make death threats to the artists, and then someone else—with whom they were in cahoots— would offer to protect the artists, for $50,000 or so, at which time they'd be taken to a safe spot until a "deal" could be worked out with the perpetrators of the threat. The FBI closed the case without filing charges, and the JDL's spokesman Irv Rubin stated in a press release that "there was nothing but a close, tight relationship" between the organization and Eazy-E.

Eazy credited Klein with helping deflate the Suge menace for the time being, and later made him the company's director of business affairs. At a time when the label was strapped for cash, Klein invested his own money, making him a part-owner, and when Eazy decided it was time to part ways with Priority, Klein helped negotiate Ruthless's deal with a new distribution company, called Relativity.

In the middle of all of this Klein and Suge, the two baddest enforcers-cum-executives in West Coast hip-hop, helped negotiate Dre's release from Ruthless. The RICO lawsuit didn't go anywhere; a vast conspiracy was hard to prove, and a judge dismissed the case in 1993. But Klein helped salvage the situation for Ruthless; since Dre wasn't going to make music for Eazy and Heller, the most they could hope for was a cut of profits from music he made elsewhere.

With Klein, Heller, Eazy, and their attorneys on one side of the table, and Dre, Suge, Suge's lawyer David Kenner, and Jimmy Iovine of Interscope (the fledgling label that became Death Row's distributor in 1992) on the other, the terms of Dre's departure were hammered out. Ruthless would receive publishing rights from his new projects, whether as rapper or producer. According to Heller, Ruthless would get 10 percent of Dre's producing proceeds, and 15 percent from his own albums, as well as a "huge advance." Eazy said the terms were to last for six years. *The same records that you makin' is payin' me*, Eazy would later rap, and he wouldn't be lying.

Despite the settlement, Suge never ceased trying to get under Eazy's skin. At the 1992 Death Row Christmas party, he announced a new rapper at the label: Tracy Jernagin, the mother of one of Eazy's children. Even though he'd also been with other women their relationship had endured, but lately she and Eazy had been feuding, and she'd taken to spending more time with Suge, a platonic friend dating back to her pre-Eazy days. The word that she would be rapping for Death Row quickly got back to Eazy, who was incensed. "You embarrassed me!" he said. "How could you be over there with them?" She argued that he hadn't exactly been loyal to her, and they eventually made up. In truth, Jernagin wasn't particularly serious about her hip-hop career, which would stall out not long afterward. In retrospect, she suspects that, beyond just interest in her as an artist, Suge was also probably "messing with Eric and being funny and kind of taunting him."

The Villain in Black

Of all the people caught in the middle of the Death Row and Ruthless feud, it was perhaps most difficult for the remaining N.W.A members DJ Yella and MC Ren, who declined to throw barbs at either side and did their best to stay neutral. "[Dre] said, 'I'm leaving. You wanna come?'"

said DJ Yella. "I was like, 'Um, I'll let you know.'" He stayed with Ruthless, as did MC Ren, who released the platinum EP *Kizz My Black Azz* in 1992 and the full-length *Shock of the Hour* in 1993. The latter is something like two separate albums in one. Its first half is dominated by the gangsta invective he's known for: braggadocio, brutal sex, and gunfights. But the second half takes a hard left turn, influenced by Ren's real-life conversion to the Nation of Islam during the album's recording. Ice Cube's signee Kam appears on the title track, which describes an apocalyptic hellscape in which those who haven't recognized the Nation's teachings suffer the consequence. Ren raps:

> *Motherfucker shoulda listened when you got your final call*
> *Think you're doin' the brothers a favor by buyin' a paper*
> *Shoulda read your paper, it tells ya the devil raped ya*
> *Stripped ya of the scripture, blood ya then he crypt ya*

Ren raps best when he's fired up, when he has a cause, and *Shock of the Hour*'s second half presents him as a man on a mission. His wordplay is on point, his inferno vividly drawn. The album got good reviews (Jonathan Gold called it, in the *Los Angeles Times*, "a small, ugly masterpiece of gangsta rap"), but Ren's momentum nonetheless slowed, owing in part to his conflicts with Ruthless, who he also didn't believe was paying him properly. It's not that he didn't have other options. Dr. Dre took him to check out the scene at Death Row. But Ren didn't want any part of it. "My street smarts said, 'Fuck this. This is a worse situation,'" he said.

No Such Infrastructure

While Ren tried to make the most of things at Ruthless, Dre dove into his new life at Death Row. But once again, he didn't take much care when it came to financial details. "He didn't write checks, he didn't sign nothin'," wrote Bruce Williams, who became Dre's assistant shortly thereafter, in 1993. "He wouldn't do no paperwork."

D.O.C. said their original deal for the company that became Death Row gave 35 percent ownership to him, 35 percent to Dre, 15 percent to Suge, and 15 percent to Solar's Dick Griffey. Griffey was a key player in the deal because he had national distribution with CBS Records, and Death Row was to be brought into the fold under that partnership. Suge, Dre, and D.O.C. also pooled their money to buy the Galaxy Studios from Dick Griffey, in his Solar Records building in Hollywood. (Suge's wife Sharitha says she wrote out Suge's $25,000 check, and that Dre and D.O.C. paid the same amount.)

But things went off the rails from the start.

"When you think about a corporation, it's got stockholders, regular meetings, someone who keeps track of the books," industry analyst and former record executive David Kronemyer told me. "But Death Row had no such infrastructure. Money would come in, but then Suge would parcel it out to who was most insistent upon being paid. That's why you saw things that wouldn't be acceptable in larger organizations. It was more street-level stuff."

Suge's most notorious connection was Los Angeles drug dealer Michael Harris. Known as Harry O, the towering kingpin moved cocaine all over the country, and was sentenced in 1987 to twenty-eight years for trafficking and attempted murder. But before going to prison he parlayed his earnings into a number of legitimate businesses, and was a coproducer of a Broadway play called *Checkmates*, starring Denzel Washington. Even being locked up hadn't stifled Harry O's entrepreneurial ambitions, and he remained interested in the entertainment industry.

Suge began speaking with Lydia Harris, who was Harry O's wife and a singer herself. She became slated to be one of Death Row's first artists. In addition to performing, she facilitated her husband's prison dealings with Death Row, from the outside. In December 2015, *Vanity Fair* dubbed her the "real Cookie Lyon," after the flamboyant protagonist of the hit Fox drama *Empire*, about a hip-hop company. Lydia Harris was a Houston native who met Harry O through a connection to venerable Houston label Rap-A-Lot Records, home of the Geto Boys. Harry O's involvement with Rap-A-Lot is murky; he claimed he provided seed money for the label, but this claim was disputed by the label's owner J. Prince, and it did not hold up in court.

Introduced by a mutual acquaintance, Harry O and Suge began speaking over the phone, and discussed a potential Death Row partnership. Dr. Dre's involvement particularly piqued Harry O's interest; he hoped Dre would produce a song for his wife.

Harry O's lawyer was David Kenner, a former county prosecutor and criminal defense attorney drawn to headline-grabbing cases, who excelled at defending alleged drug kingpins. He "had a habit of getting very close to his clients and getting involved in their lives," said reporter Sam Gideon Anson. Kenner brought Suge to the prison where Harry O was incarcerated, and the men got down to brass tacks. "Suge told me we could be fifty-fifty partners for about $1.5 million," Harry O said. He claimed that he, his wife Lydia, and Suge hatched a plan for Death Row to be a division of Harry O's Godfather Entertainment company. (Another convicted drug trafficker, Ricky Crockett—whom Suge was accused of shooting in Las Vegas—was also at one point suspected by federal investigators to have provided money to launch Death Row, as was PCP kingpin Patrick Johnson, another incarcerated client of David Kenner, though neither claim was substantiated. Mark Friedman, a friend of Harry O and Lydia, also claimed, to the *Los Angeles Times*, to be an early Death Row investor owed $1 million for his efforts.)

The effects of Suge's partnership with Harry O could immediately be seen at the studio, according to its inhabitants. Carpet was installed, equipment was upgraded, and new furniture was brought in. And that wasn't all. "[Harry O] thought everybody should look good. He got Suge a Benz, a 500 series," said studio engineer John Payne. "Before that, Suge had a Suzuki Samurai." Payne said he was also given money to find apartments for the young rappers on the label.

When it came to the talent, his wife said, Harry O spoke frequently with Dre about what sort of music he thought would sell, based on the tastes of his fellow prisoners. "Because the guys listened to it all day in jail," Lydia Harris said. She also claimed credit for helping convince Death Row to put out the yet-unknown rapper Snoop Doggy Dogg.

Houston rapper Big Mike, who would later join the Geto Boys, said Lydia Harris called around this time and invited him and his group the Convicts to California to record for Death Row. Since he was still under contract with Rap-A-Lot, she contacted its owner, J. Prince. "I don't know what kind of deal they made down there, but I know I got a call one day and it was like: 'Y'all pack y'all bags; y'all going to California tomorrow,' " Big Mike said, "and it was on from there."

Harry O said that despite his $1.5 million investment he was cheated out of Death Row's profits when they started coming in. Interscope, Death Row's distributor, eventually agreed to pay him a six-figure settlement after he threatened to sue the two companies in 1996. But Lydia Harris, arguing for her own contributions to the label, nonetheless sued Suge in 2002 for her share of the company, and in 2005 a Los Angeles judge ordered Death Row to pay her $107 million; she agreed to give her husband half. Suge filed for bankruptcy and only $1 million of their money was paid. Along the way the Harrises divorced; Harry O remains incarcerated, while Lydia Harris owns a Houston catering company. She declined my interview request.

Flush with Capital

After being introduced to Suge, David Kenner became Death Row's lawyer, despite little experience in music industry law. Over the years he saved Suge from many a legal pickle; it's largely owing to his skills that Suge was able to avoid long-term prison sentences for many alleged crimes. Before long Kenner began exerting influence on the label's day-to-day operations. He was signatory to Death Row's accounts, Anson said, and employees used credit cards with his name on them. Meanwhile, he lived the flossy lifestyle of the hip-hop stars he represented. Rhythm D visited his mansion in the hills one time and was awed: "The house is ridiculous," he said.

Presenting a flashy image was part of Death Row's game plan. In

February 1992 they threw a lavish launch party at the swanky Chasen's restaurant in West Hollywood, to promote the label and its emergent artists, most notably Dr. Dre. The tuxedoed male attendees and women in expensive dresses included some of the industry's biggest names; the invitations they received looked like subpoenas. "'You are hereby ordered to appear before the honorable Dr. Dre and the offices of GF Entertainment as a guest of the court, witnessing the springing of Death Row Records,'" they read, according to Death Row publicist Norman Winter, who added: "We had it delivered by two large security gentlemen."

Industry expectations for Death Row were high, and it was indeed a great place to work, at least at first. Flush with financial and creative capital, Suge fostered his artists. His young rappers had access to first-rate equipment. With their room and board accounted for, they could focus on their craft.

Behind the scenes, however, Death Row was financially fraught at its inception. D.O.C. said his supposed 35 percent ownership stake in the label was not honored. The speed with which Suge had turned on D.O.C. is shocking in retrospect. The man who had been the D.O.C.'s biggest advocate only a few years before—who'd doted on him at his hospital bedside after his car accident—had cast him off.

Dick Griffey, also an original Death Row founder, later testified that Suge Knight "secretly incorporated" Death Row and "transferred into it all of the assets" from their original partnership. In 1997—with Suge behind bars—Griffey and D.O.C. successfully sued Death Row, alleging that they'd been cut out of the label's profits. D.O.C. said his cut was about $350,000, which amounts to a pittance.

D.O.C. said he was initially reluctant to pursue his Death Row ownership stake because he didn't want to mess with Suge. "I didn't want to be killed," he said.

CHAPTER TWELVE

L.A.'S ON FIRE

Today Tupac Shakur is remembered as perhaps the fiercest West Coast rapper of all. But his roots were firmly East Coast: He lived in Manhattan and the Bronx until he was fourteen, when his family moved to Baltimore. His dad was absent, and he had few male role models in his life. The closest thing to a father figure was his mother's boyfriend Kenneth "Legs" Sanders, an associate of Harlem drug kingpin Nicky Barnes, who eventually died from a crack-related heart attack. Hip-hop was the primary male influence in Tupac's life. "Ice Cube, Public Enemy, KRS-One, LL Cool J, Big Daddy Kane, all them niggas was my daddy, 'cause I ain't have none," he declared. "It's like you're paying ten dollars for a whole lifestyle of game."

His greatest influence, however, was his mother, who instilled his fighting, activist spirit. "My great-grandmother was a slave," she said. "My grandmother was a sharecropper. My mother was a factory worker, and I was a legal worker." Born in 1947 and raised Alice Williams in Lumberton, North Carolina, she said her father beat her mother, who brought Alice and her sister to the Bronx as children. Following the assassinations of Malcolm X in 1965 and Martin Luther King Jr. in 1968 Alice joined the Black Panther Party, and that year she also married a party activist and Muslim named Lumumba Abdul Shakur, changing her name to Afeni Shakur. (The surname was adopted by many in their circle to cast off their "slave" names.) He was already married; Afeni was his second wife—acceptable according to the Islamic law he followed. "He'd sleep with me sometimes. He'd sleep with her," Afeni said, referring to Lumumba's first wife, adding that she could have taken up with another man if she'd so chosen. "She took care of the kids and the house... And me and Lumumba did our thing with the party."

Afeni—as aggressive and strong-willed as any man in the organization—was ushered into the Black Panther leadership. She and Lumumba were jailed in 1969, along with nineteen other members of the group, who became known as the "Panther 21." They were charged with conspiring to bomb department stores, a police station, and railroad facilities, as well as murder police officers. Testimony was supplied by a trio of undercover officers who infiltrated the organization. The Panthers were under heavy scrutiny from law enforcement including the FBI's Counter Intelligence Program. J. Edgar Hoover, FBI director until his death in 1972, called them "the greatest threat to the internal security of the country."

For their trial the Panthers found support in high places. Bail, set at $100,000 for some of the arrested members, was seen as excessively high, and a group of wealthy New York liberals came to their defense. In 1970 conductor Leonard Bernstein, who had recently stepped down as music director from the New York Philharmonic, and his wife hosted a fund-raiser, inviting dozens of influential arts and media figures, including Barbara Walters, to their Park Avenue apartment. They raised the money, but the gathering was widely mocked, most famously in Tom Wolfe's *New York* magazine article "Radical Chic: That Party at Lenny's." Wolfe's piece portrayed the white guests as desperate to look edgy and cool, munching on "Roquefort cheese morsels rolled in crushed nuts" and gushing over a Black Panther named Don Cox, whose words they found, in Wolfe's description, "so, somehow... *black*... so *funky*... so metrical."

Afeni made bail before the others, and she set out to raise money on their behalf, including at Columbia University in Manhattan, where another *New York* magazine piece described her as "galvanically beautiful." "If you don't want a race war in this country, there's got to be a class war!" she told the students.

Along the way Afeni and her husband split up, and while out on bail she became pregnant by a Black Panther named William Garland. After her bail was revoked, owing to the absconsion of some of her codefendants, she returned to jail, where she remained until only about a month before Tupac's birth, June 16, 1971. "This child stayed in my womb through the worst possible conditions. I had to get a court order to get an egg to eat every day," she said. "I had to get a court order to get a glass of milk every day." Afeni represented herself at trial, and ultimately she and the other Black Panther members were acquitted. Afterward, Afeni was a civil rights star for a time, invited to speak at universities.

Tupac was born into this atmosphere of militant black activism confronting an overbearing judicial system, with a soupçon of glamour. Born Lesane Parish Crooks, his name was soon changed to Tupac Amaru Shakur, with his first and middle monikers taken from a martyred Incan emperor. "She always raised me to think I was the Black Prince of the revolution," he said. Afeni's associates—the first people Tupac knew—were a who's who of famous black revolutionaries from the era. Tupac's godmother Assata Shakur was found guilty of the 1973 murder of a New Jersey state trooper. But she broke out of prison and later fled to Cuba; her brother Mutulu Shakur was convicted of aiding her escape. Mutulu, a renowned acupuncturist known for developing drug-treatment programs, had an even closer relationship to Tupac. In 1975 he married Afeni, and they moved to a house in Harlem, where Tupac and Mutulu's son Maurice became close. Mutulu was accused of participating in a 1981 attempted robbery of an armored Brinks car containing $1.6 million in Rockland County, New York, which left two cops and a security guard dead. He became a fugitive and the FBI put him on their Ten Most Wanted list, before finally catching him and sending him away for the rest of Tupac's life. Tupac's godfather Geronimo Pratt also served a lengthy sentence for the murder of a teacher, though his conviction was overturned in 1997.

Assata Shakur remains in Cuba. In 2013 she was added to the FBI's list of Most Wanted Terrorists.

A Hippie

Afeni, Tupac, and his half-sister Sekyiwa (the daughter of Mutulu) moved constantly between Manhattan and the Bronx. Afeni raised her son to be an intellectual, punishing him by forcing him to read *The New York Times*. He wrote in his diary, composed poetry, and at age twelve performed in *A Raisin in the Sun* at the Apollo Theater, a fund-raiser for Jesse Jackson. In 1985, Afeni, who struggled to maintain employment, moved the family to Baltimore, where they received welfare. The lights were sometimes shut off, and Tupac slept on a mattress without sheets.

Tupac found inspiration at Baltimore School for the Arts, a free magnet secondary school, where he studied acting, read Shakespeare and Niccolò Machiavelli's *The Prince*, and took ballet. "He was always, like, 'peace, peace,' before people said peace," remembered his schoolmate Teresa Altoz, who described him as a "hippie."

He also became friends with Jada Pinkett, whose celebrity would rival his own. They weren't attracted to each other. "There was a time when I was like, 'Just kiss me! Let's just see how this goes,'" she said. "And when I tell you it had to be the most disgusting kiss for us both."

"He was just on all the time, with an incredibly contagious personality," said Donald Hicken, who taught Tupac at the School for the Arts. "He had charisma that was astounding." Considered by some a pretty boy, Tupac was defensive about his toughness. He continued writing poetry, but since poets were seen as "wimps," he said, he devoted more energy to hip-hop. Calling himself MC New York, his first rhyme, penned after a friend shot himself while playing with a firearm, advocated gun control, and he rapped at benefits for his mother's Black Panther affiliates.

Afeni was smoking crack by his high school years, and Tupac's studies suffered; he said he was forced to read by candlelight. Concerned for their safety after a neighborhood murder, Afeni sent her children across the country to live with one of her associates—Linda Pratt, the wife of imprisoned Black Panther leader Geronimo Pratt. Tupac wasn't quite seventeen when he arrived in Marin City, California, which was largely populated by poor African-Americans despite its location in wealthy Marin County across the Golden Gate Bridge from San Francisco. Tupac's mother soon followed her children out west, and the family moved to a housing project called the Jungle. Tupac didn't fit in. "I dressed like a hippie, they teased me all the time. I couldn't play basketball," he said, adding that he was jumped by street gangs. With a Gumby-style haircut and an earring in his right ear, he attended the diverse Tamalpais High School. With a friend named Ray Luv he began performing with a rap act called Strictly Dope. His rhymes featured Fresh Prince–style whimsy.

Tupac fought with his mother, who was in the throes of crack addiction. He dropped out of high school and bounced around, at one point moving in with the family of a twentysomething woman named Leila Steinberg, who ran a poetry and music workshop. "He was the sloppiest, messiest person I've ever lived with," said Steinberg. Once, when a cop showed up requesting they turn down their music, Tupac put on N.W.A's "Fuck tha Police" to taunt him. Steinberg was married with kids. Her husband was a successful DJ and promoter, and Tupac's presence in their home created stress in the marriage. But she couldn't help being drawn to the young rapper. She worked relentlessly to help him launch his hip-hop career, networking and helping to spread his music, but when he started gaining success she refused to accept much money from him, which she attributed to her "guilt for my privilege and my whiteness."

Before long Tupac moved to Oakland, where his stepbrother Maurice Shakur—the son of Mutulu Shakur, who became known as Mopreme—had settled after a stint in the army. Mopreme's rap career had been jump-started when he performed a verse on the hit 1990 Tony! Toni! Toné! song "Feels Good." In Oakland Tupac "learned the game," he said, moving through a world of street hustlers. He purchased an AK-47 for protection and briefly sold drugs. For him, dealing was a means to scrape by, but he also understood the perils drugs caused the black community—to see this, he didn't have to look any further than his own mother. And so he and Mopreme began to brainstorm a code of ethics for drug dealers to live by. "When you're going through poverty, everybody dibbles and dabbles," Mopreme said. "But let's try to be smart about what we're doing. Maybe we can save some lives."

Meanwhile, Steinberg introduced Tupac to Atron Gregory, who was N.W.A's road manager and also managed the rap group Digital Underground, who were based out of Berkeley and Oakland. Bay Area rap jumped off in the late eighties and achieved mass popularity by way of Oakland rappers MC Hammer and Too Short, the latter of whom released a long string of gold and platinum albums, and was known for his pioneering street rhymes and pimp stories. Heavily influenced by the funk, the Bay Area hardcore hip-hop scene was just as compelling as L.A.'s, and the early nineties saw the rise of acclaimed gangsta rappers like Mac Dre, Spice 1, and E-40, as well as more playful acts like Souls of Mischief. The constantly evolving Northern California underground scene churned out independently recorded and distributed music, its artists developing styles and slangs that influenced the culture nationwide.

Digital Underground, comical and socially conscious, were in a class all their own, and led by the sharp-witted rapper Shock G, who also rhymed as his alter ego Humpty Hump. Gregory arranged an audition, and Tupac performed a song called "Panther Power," wowing the group. It was extremely fortuitous timing; they were just about to release their breakout 1990 album *Sex Packets*, featuring enduring party-starter "The Humpty Dance." At first Tupac served as a lowly roadie, carrying the group's luggage and boxes of records when they traveled. He graduated to the role of backup dancer, performing an incredibly enthusiastic version of "The Humpty Dance" on *Arsenio*. But Tupac always had his sights on rapping, and finally got a chance when the group was featured in the soundtrack for the 1991 Dan Ackroyd–Chevy Chase movie *Nothing But Trouble*, performing a verse on "Same Song."

Now I clown around when I hang around with the Underground, he raps on his breezy debut, not an adjective normally applied to Tupac's music. His association with the group—suddenly among the most popular in the country, with *Sex Packets* going platinum—helped him gain connections in the industry, and he worked to launch a solo career. Atron Gregory agreed to manage him, and sent around his demo. Numerous labels passed, but Interscope A&R Tom Whalley—whose daughter loved Tupac's tape—agreed to have dinner with him. "He just had an aura. I left that first meeting with him incredibly excited. I knew he had something important to say and that he would create meaning with his art," said Whalley, whose admiration for Tupac was seconded by Interscope cofounder Ted Field.

Specializing in brutally honest, vivid stories of African-American tragedy and triumph, his strong songwriting informed his debut *2Pacalypse Now*, released on Interscope, Jive, and Tupac's label Amaru on November 12, 1991. Though its samples include N.W.A, Ice Cube, and Public Enemy, it's very much a Bay Area creation, recorded in Richmond, just north of Oakland, and mixed and mastered in San Francisco. Tupac, who had recently turned twenty, wrote the lyrics, and the beats were supplied by a mélange of producers, including his Digital Underground colleagues. The inset art features an outline of a handgun surrounding his artist name 2Pac.

Tupac conceived stand-out track "Brenda's Got a Baby" after reading about the abandoned newborn of a twelve-year-old Brooklyn mother, who was rescued from a trash compactor in the nick of time. "Brenda" shows sympathy for its protagonist, who has a junkie father, a scheming mother, and a boyfriend who's her cousin. *She didn't know what to throw away and what to keep*, Tupac raps, to heartbreaking effect. Brenda descends into crack and prostitution, and is ultimately found slain. It's a rare song from a male rapper told from the perspective of a woman. *2Pacalypse Now* went gold; not a giant hit, but it won him praise as a complex black artist addressing the causes of society's breakdown.

Even as Tupac forged ahead with his solo career, he and stepbrother Mopreme worked on another project: developing a young male rap group. This was the era of teenybopper rap acts like Another Bad Creation and Kris Kross, but they wanted their group to be streetwise. Tupac and Mopreme recruited kids from poor neighborhoods in Richmond and Oakland, and gave them names like The Have Nots and Young Thugs. The project didn't really get off the ground, but different rotations also included some of Tupac's younger East Coast friends from childhood, like E.D.I. Mean, Yaki Kadafi, and Tupac's cousin Kastro. Together, along with a rapper named Napoleon, they became known as Dramacydal, and would eventually become the core of Tupac's fearsome backing group, the Outlawz.

Anger for the Verdict

Tupac moved to L.A. in 1992 while filming *Poetic Justice*, for which he was recruited by director John Singleton, who admired his work in *Juice*. They shot some of it in the Simi Valley, where the Rodney King trial was held, and in his off hours Tupac also worked on his follow-up album, called *Strictly 4 My N.I.G.G.A.Z...* While recording at a studio in the L.A. neighborhood of Atwater Village on April 29, 1992, Tupac saw the Rodney King verdict announced on TV. In the next room at the studio, New York rapper Kool G Rap was in the middle of a session with Sir Jinx, Ice Cube's partner. The impact of the verdict didn't really set in until Jinx's friends arrived at the studio, carrying armfuls of beer and liquor and wearing obviously stolen hats, one on top of another.

"L.A.'s on fire," they announced.

The three hip-hop artists jumped into Jinx's Honda Accord, heading south. Passing flipped-over burning cars, Tupac took out his 9 mm as they approached Wilshire and fired repeatedly through the Accord's sunroof up into the sky. Inside the car the sound was deafening, and it terrified a group huddled at a nearby bus stop.

"Pac was expressing his sense of anger, for the verdict," said Kool G Rap.

Arriving in South Central, they found traffic on Crenshaw had come to a stop. Some cars were abandoned altogether. They parked in the middle of the street, near a record store called Tempo, where hundreds of people had gathered. "Everybody was looting," said Kool G Rap. "Some dudes was legitimately mad, and some dudes just took it as opportunity to do shit." Some looters who recognized Tupac grabbed copies of his CDs from the store for him to sign. He gamely played along. Upon realizing he was out of bullets, they drove to Jinx's friend's house for a refill. Tupac later bragged that the same day he'd been filming a Hollywood movie with Janet Jackson, that evening he was "shooting up motherfucking Chinese takeouts."

The riots would go on to last for the better part of a week; the Marines, National Guard, and U.S. Army were called in, and schools were closed.

All told, it was an even bigger calamity than the Watts riots. Neighborhoods across South Central, Mid-City, Koreatown, Pico-Union, and as far north as Hollywood suffered grave damage, with total destruction citywide estimated at a billion dollars. More than sixty people died, including ten who were killed by police officers, and those were only the official totals; many more died in incidents not directly tied to the riots. As depicted in Ryan Gattis's *All Involved*—a novel drawn from real-life accounts—some criminals took advantage of the chaos to make people disappear.

N.W.A affiliate Laylaw, a producer on *Strictly*, also spent time with Tupac during the riots. He said the two brutally beat a random man they encountered in Hollywood—for no good reason at all: "We don't even know what's going on," he said, "we just think it's everybody for theyself, we beat the hell out of this motherfucker." They next tried unsuccessfully to break into a music store—they faced armed resistance—before arriving at a liquor store near the heart of the riots, which was dark and on fire. "We just grabbed whatever we could," Laylaw said.

The riots experience encapsulated the mania and tragedy of Tupac that would manifest in his music—the anger, frustration, and joy—all at the same time. "I was feeling beautiful to see all the unity," he said. "But then again I was feeling nervous, because I knew that America was not going to let the riots go on long, and I knew we were going to lose a lot of people."

This Is for Rodney King

If at first the videotape of Rodney King's beating seemed certain to bring him justice, a mostly white jury in the Simi Valley had other ideas. Judge Stanley Weisberg chose the venue location—an hour's drive in traffic northwest of downtown—for its "convenience" to L.A. The demographics of Simi Valley, a conservative stronghold full of retired cops, would prove detrimental to the defense, however. In the end, all four officers were acquitted on the assault charge. On the excessive force charge the jury was deadlocked for Powell, while the other three were acquitted. (A year after the riots the officers again faced judgment in a federal trial, with Powell and Koon found guilty. They both served thirty months in prison.)

The videotape's initial release crippled police chief Daryl Gates. In July 1991 he announced his retirement, but didn't say when, specifically. This led his many would-be successors to scramble for advantage. "The early response to the riots was controlled by some of these same people, who really didn't mind if the LAPD looked bad, because it would make Chief Gates look bad," said LAPD detective Russell Poole. Gates himself left his post during the early, critical hours of the riot to attend a Brentwood fund-raiser.

The mayhem kicked off at a Korean-owned deli and liquor store called Pay-Less, at Dalton and Florence avenues. Around four p.m., five young black men grabbed bottles of 8 Ball and attempted to leave without paying, whereupon the owner's son blocked their path. One of the men hit him in the head with a bottle, while others threw theirs at the store's door, shattering its glass. One yelled out, "This is for Rodney King," and the men fled. Arriving officers were too late to catch them, but were quickly dispatched to a nearby scene, where they found a man swinging a baseball bat at a Cadillac containing two white men. Police captured him and took him to the station, but, quickly realizing the magnitude of the riots, headed back out without booking him. Mayor Bradley, meanwhile, voiced his frustration with the verdicts in a televised address. "We saw what we saw, and what we saw was a crime," he said, in part. "No, we will not tolerate the savage beating of our citizens by a few renegade cops." He believed his response was measured, but detractors accused him of further inciting the riots.

Not far from Pay-Less, at Florence and Normandie, police were showered with rocks; a crowd taunted them after they arrested a teenage boy. More than thirty cops had arrived, but they were overwhelmed. "Most of the policemen had no helmets. They had no bulletproof vests, no tear gas, no face shields," said the ranking officer Lieutenant Moulin. "I think we're going to have to use deadly force, we could have a massacre here. So

I ordered a pullout." Upon their withdrawal they failed to block off the streets, however, and rioters began yanking nonblack people out of their vehicles, including thirty-six-year-old truck driver Reginald Denny. He was pulled from his cab and smashed with a brick, a claw hammer, and an oxygen tank taken from another truck. Denny survived but was left with brain damage; footage of his assault was captured by videotape from a helicopter, and shown repeatedly on the news.

Meanwhile the Parker Center downtown—the LAPD's headquarters, named for Daryl Gates's mentor William H. Parker—was surrounded by protesters. They chanted "fuck the police," threw garbage cans at the doors, and ripped down a parking kiosk, before setting it on fire. Some fifty helmeted cops with batons lined up to hold back protesters. The nearby *Los Angeles Times* building was also besieged.

The spiritual counterpoint to the chaos was the First African Methodist Episcopal (FAME) Church, about four miles north of Florence and Normandie. There, Mayor Bradley helped launch Operation Cool Response, an effort to quell the outrage. Rodney King's mother spoke, asking for calm, while outside the crowd grew increasingly restless. "We got people in there right now that's sitting in there talking about peace," said a man in a Malcolm X T-shirt. "Every time somebody talk about peace we get a foot in our ass!"

Exploding and Ricocheting

During interviews, my final question to this book's principal players was usually the same: What were you doing during the riots? Most rappers I talked to participated, whether helping people out, documenting the proceedings, or looting themselves. Some just watched. But nearly everyone had a crazy story.

Following the verdict, hundreds of Los Angeles Nation of Islam members, anticipating chaos and an aggressive police response, spread out across South Central and preached a message of calm. "We said, 'Y'all need to chill out, because we don't want them to come in and kill our people wholesale,' " remembered Shorty from Da Lench Mob, a lieutenant in the Nation. He drove around in his Jeep Wagoneer urging everyone to get to safe locations and secure their families. His fear was not so much the rioters, he said, but the National Guard. "They locked everything down and was literally killing people," he said. "A lot of people were killed that wasn't reported on the news."

He said he saw a Hispanic man gunned down by the National Guard one night after curfew, across the street from a Nation temple in the Vermont Square neighborhood. "They pulled up on him, he had his hands up in the air, and you heard the bursts of machine guns," he said. "They sprayed him with an M16, took off his clothes, threw him in the Jeep, and sped off." (The *Los Angeles Times* reported that a twenty-seven-year-old man named Franklin Benavidez was killed by LAPD Metro Division officers on April 30 at the location described. Investigators said Benavidez tried to rob a gas station, and was shot after pointing a shotgun at officers and being told to drop it. Another suspect during the incident, nineteen-year-old Victor Munoz, was "struck in the stomach" by police, and soon hospitalized. Though he was believed to be armed, it turns out he was only carrying a beer can.)

Meanwhile, Shorty's Lench Mob crewmate T-Bone grabbed his video camera after the verdict, and, with some friends, piled into his Chevy Astro van. He piloted toward the South Central intersection of Florence and Normandie avenues—the flashpoint for the riots. Driving up Western, traffic moved slowly, smoke was everywhere, and businesses were being pillaged. "People were coming out of grocery stores with boxes of cereal, out of liquor stores with drinks, smiling and celebrating," he said. "I said, 'This shit ain't just here, it's spreading everywhere.' "

Ruthless producer Rhythm D was hanging out with friends including his girlfriend Tamla, the daughter of Smokey Robinson. When the verdict was announced they were shopping at the Fox Hills mall, in Culver City just west of South Central. Stores began closing, and so the crew piled into Tamla's BMW. They drove north to Pico Boulevard, which was quickly becoming another flashpoint for rioting. Rhythm helped pull the bars off an appliance store window. "We snatched a TV and one rim," he said. "We just wanted to get something and be a part of it."

As Molotov cocktails flew through the air, Rhythm said the police mostly let them rage—"All they were concerned about was [protecting] Beverly Hills," he said. That is, until a member of the group tossed a forty-ounce beer that nearly hit a cop car, and was promptly arrested. Eventually they departed for Smokey Robinson's house in Encino. "My dad wanted us out of the city," said Tamla Robinson. The group bunkered down at the gated pad for two weeks.

Snoop Dogg said as soon as he and his friends saw the looting on TV, they drove to South Central "and got ours." Some people recognized him and enlisted his labor: "Get the other end of this couch!"

Ice Cube stayed away on the riots' first day, but soon came back to check on his house. He found out a guy from the neighborhood had died, and attended the wake, which took place in the midst of the chaos. "It was kinda strange, surreal," he said.

Frightened white residents all over L.A. stockpiled weapons, worrying the riots would spread. Though many south L.A. gun stores closed immediately, some were broken into and stripped of their wares by gang members. Sir Jinx remembered driving past a Western Surplus store, looted of its guns. But bullets remained inside and now, with smoke pouring out of the building, they were catching fire, exploding and ricocheting around.

Truce

On the riots' second day, Sir Jinx visited parts of the city he couldn't normally access. Though not a gang member, he came from a Crips-controlled area, making Bloods strongholds usually off limits to him. But that day he explored an indoor swap meet in a Bloods-aligned area near Crenshaw, not far from the Jungles housing project. Upon arrival he found the place on fire, with water that went up to his ankles. But he was nonetheless swept up with emotion. "That was the most love I felt with my brothers, that second day," he said.

Jinx's mobility was enabled by a truce between the Bloods and the Crips, enacted, coincidentally, the day before the riots began. It was dramatic. Matthew McDaniel's documentary *Birth of a Nation 4x29x1992* features stunning footage of a gang member ripping off his red undershirt and leading a chant: "Africans unite!" Crips-aligned rapper Kurupt was similarly stunned when he was welcomed by rivals in the Jungles. "Bloods walked up to me and was like, 'What's up, Kurupt, blood? I fucks with your shit,'" he said. "I was shocked, like, 'Damn.'"

The cease-fire was born from a place where it was desperately needed: Watts. Following the 1965 riots the neighborhood, located in the southeast corner of South Central, saw its economic base greatly diminished. By 1992 unemployment, illiteracy, and dope dealing were rampant. Watts contains L.A.'s most infamous and well-known housing projects, which harbor thousands of people in sprawling, brightly painted clusters just blocks apart from each other. They're not towers like the stereotypical New York or Chicago projects, but rather one- or two-story buildings lacking fencing or privacy of any kind, labeled with their numbers ("BUILDING 142") on white signs. They're impersonal, to say the least.

In the early nineties heavily armed gangs dominated the projects; if you wanted to use the gym at Jordan Downs, you didn't call the building managers, you contacted the Grape Street Crips. Crossing into another's territory, even if you weren't a gang member, was taking your life in your hands. Which is what made the truce so astonishing. It was marshaled in part by former NFL star Jim Brown, who met with Bloods and Crips in locations including his Hollywood Hills home, in hopes of breaking the cycle of gang violence. World Class Wreckin' Cru member Cli-N-Tel attended some of the meetings, and remembered a flyer circulating, depicting the Bloods and the Crips as puppets being manipulated on strings by a hooded Ku Klux Klan member. Following the riots, representatives of the Watts gangs, including Grape Street Crips, PJ Watts Crips, Bounty Hunter Bloods, and Hacienda Village Bloods, met on one another's turfs. These were summits, raucous parties, and family picnics all in one.

Fights interrupted the proceedings, and a police helicopter descended upon the scene to break things up. But the meetings produced fruit; the involved parties agreed to abide by a twenty-six-point treaty, a code of ethics for the drug-dealing game to reduce violence and harm to the community at large. Its bullet points decried selling to the underage and pregnant, as well as protecting civilians and making the hood "safe for squares."

This was the code Tupac and his stepbrother Mopreme had dreamed up before the truce meetings took place. They called it Thug Life, and had received help from Mopreme's father, Mutulu Shakur, locked up at Lompoc federal prison upstate, who put it to paper. Mopreme said their thinking was: "If we could just put a governor on the greed and focus on survival, we might save a few lives." It's extraordinary that Tupac was able to facilitate this. He'd only recently arrived in California and didn't come from a gangbanging background. But suddenly the hardest gang-bangers were enlisting his counsel. Tupac's Black Panthers connections, with whom he'd stayed in touch even after moving away from his mother, helped connect him with these veteran Watts gang members, who loved his music and what he stood for. "I got people in the penitentiary, big-time OG criminals, calling me, telling me they want me to lead their movement," Tupac explained.

Tupac didn't attend the Watts truce negotiations, but his involvement was critical in facilitating it. And he did attend a treaty with similar goals in Brooklyn, where shot-calling drug dealers from all over New York City—the Bronx, Queens, Harlem, Brooklyn—discussed the Thug Life code and worked on resolving their differences. "They were running the streets on the East Coast back then," said Mopreme. "Different gangs, different groups, but they're all doing the same shit." There wasn't unanimous consensus, but simply getting everyone to the table was an example of Tupac's extraordinary diplomatic and community-building abilities, which he undertook with no fanfare in the midst of an exploding recording and film career. In a move reminiscent of Johnny Cash, Tupac even performed before inmates at Lompoc. Mutulu hosted the event, in which Tupac, Mopreme, and others rapped at the federal prison in 1993. (Mopreme noted that the boys behind bars were particularly glad to see the pulchritudinous female R&B group that accompanied them, called Y?N-Vee.)

Though the Watts truce eventually petered out, those involved believed it contributed to the dramatic drop in Los Angeles gang violence, which continues today. One profoundly affecting memento of the era was the song "Peace Treaty," from Watts native Kam, signed to Ice Cube's label. With Italian immigrant Simon Rodia's folk art monument Watts Towers in the background, the track's video reenacts blue and red coming together, lowriders bouncing, and steaks grilling in celebration: *It wasn't just the blacks / Everybody was lootin', and had each other's backs...Daryl Gates—that's where all the hate went.*

A pair of collaborative albums put out by a group calling itself Bloods & Crips also saw independent release. The oversized, bandana-clad, coed crew featured gang members of both sets, and their funk-infused debut *Bangin' on Wax* brims with raw talent. It was also probably wise to heed the warning on the CD: "Bootleg this at your own risk!"

One legacy of the riots was an overhaul of Los Angeles police practices. The Christopher Commission, set up in the riots' wake, demanded sweeping LAPD changes, which, combined with the exit of Daryl Gates, improved community relations. In the decades since, the murder rate has dropped precipitously. And while police departments across the country have faced protests for shootings of unarmed black men, LAPD is considered a model for reform.

That's not to say Los Angeles rappers are singing odes to the boys in blue. "LAPD only checked themselves when the people demanded it," said Ice-T.

A Good Day

Latino rapper Kid Frost's album *East Side Story* came out just days before the riots, and features "I Got Pulled Over," which captures both the fear and recklessness that police profiling can inspire. Shortly after the riots "Get the Fist" was released, an all-star collaborative song in the vein of

"We're All in the Same Gang," but with an anti-police-brutality message. Its lineup includes Ice Cube and his affiliates J-Dee, Kam, Yo-Yo, and Threat, as well as Cypress Hill's B-Real, King Tee, and Compton's Most Wanted's MC Eiht, with proceeds going toward the rebuilding effort. The riots even inspired the normally apolitical Dr. Dre. He was working on his solo debut *The Chronic* at his Calabasas home studio when the jury's verdict came down. Dre devoured news reports, and talked with protesters and looters; his track "The Day the Niggaz Took Over" is a show of solidarity. *Feeling that gotta-get-mine perspective / 'Cause what I just heard, broke me in half,* Dre raps, adding: *Bloods, Crips on the same squad / With the Eses' help and, nigga, it's time to rob and mob.*

As for Eazy-E? Perhaps not surprisingly, he had a slightly different perspective. "With every revolution, there's violence and murder, but it's not right to go out and destroy your own neighborhood," he said in a radio interview.

Los Angeles gangsta rap not only predicted the riots, but served as its soundtrack. N.W.A's "Fuck tha Police" blasted from cars, while Ice Cube's "Black Korea" proved more prescient than anyone could have imagined. *We'll burn your store, right down to a crisp.*

Cube had been speaking, very clearly, on his community's concerns for years. Like many, he called the riots an "uprising," and afterward emerged as something of an elder statesman—at only twenty-three. "Anything you wanted to know about the riots was in the records before the riots," Cube said, accurately, in a clip that was featured on his album *The Predator.* Released in November 1992, it features tracks like "Who Got the Camera," about a black motorist pulled over and beaten like Rodney King. The protagonist of album-closer "Say Hi to the Bad Guy" gets vengeance on a cop by luring him in with doughnuts and then murdering him. "Now I Gotta Wetcha" and "We Had to Tear This Motherfucker Up" threaten the King jurors, while the latter gives a ground-level narrative from the perspective of rioters: *Western Surplus got the heaters / Meet us, so we can get the 9s and the whatnots / Got the Mossberg with the double-eyed buckshot.*

The Predator became Ice Cube's first number-one album, and remains his most popular, having sold more than two million copies. It's not as revered as *Amerikkka's Most Wanted* or *Death Certificate*, perhaps because they feel so prophetic, while *The Predator* rips open barely healed wounds. (That, and the beats aren't as hot.)

But it does have "It Was a Good Day," which has become Ice Cube's most popular song. Produced by DJ Pooh, it lifts the slow, melancholy melody from the Isley Brothers' "Footsteps in the Dark." Cube said he was happy when he wrote it, and the song is a celebration, but what makes it so powerful is its twist on the traditional urban nightmare story. Instead of jackings and police persecution, it describes a brief moment when those things are absent, and how odd it all seems.

CHAPTER THIRTEEN

SILENCING THE MESSENGER

In 1993, Ice Cube released his fifth consecutive platinum release, *Lethal Injection*. "Cave Bitch" featured Nation of Islam firebrand Khalid Muhammad's invective against white women (*Miss six o'clock, subject to have the itch / Mutanoid, caucazoid, white cave bitch*) as well as three full verses of Cube decrying Caucasian ladies interested in bedding him. *You can't get mine, ho / I'd rather fuck an albino.* By his own admission, the album is not his strongest work.

Though music wasn't quite an afterthought, by this point he'd moved strongly in the direction of film. In 1992 he starred in *Trespass* with Ice-T (following the riots, it was renamed, from *Looters*), followed by *The Glass Shield*, *Higher Learning*, and, in April 1995, the beloved *Friday*. He and his manager Patricia Charbonnet each put up $25,000 for the work, which he cowrote with DJ Pooh and was filmed on the block where its director F. Gary Gray grew up. Their goal was to tell a different kind of hood story, a comedy that wasn't focused on tragedy and gunplay. Chris Tucker's stoner character Smokey gets Cube's character high after he's fired from his job, and they while away the day on the porch, attempting to stave off undesirables including the neighborhood bully, Deebo. It became a commercial success, and opened the door for Cube to assume a new role: Hollywood mogul.

*   *   *

Cube's ascension in film was just one sign that by 1993 gangsta rap and its stars were everywhere, though the headlines weren't always positive. In an interview that year Dr. Dre summed up a feeling among many L.A. rappers: "[W]ho came up with that term *gangsta rap* anyway?"

"You did," responded the interviewee, *Rolling Stone*'s Jonathan Gold.

"Oh, maybe so," Dre responded. "Never mind, then."

Gold nowadays can't recall the occasion when Dre initially used the term, but it first appeared in print on March 25, 1989, when *Los Angeles Times* pop music critic Robert Hilburn described an N.W.A concert in Anaheim. "Ice-T, who helped popularize the L.A. gangster rap image, was the evening's headliner and he is a more polished performer and writer than the members of N.W.A," he wrote.

Whatever the case, "gangster rap" had really come into vogue by 1991, inspiring Ice-T's album that year *O.G. Original Gangster*. "OG" was a then-local expression describing gang members who'd been there since the beginning. Ice-T obviously had the musical credentials, and in the early nineties he, N.W.A, and the Geto Boys constituted the genre's axis of evil. *Original Gangster*'s cover showed off his muscle-bound physique, while "New Jack Hustler" tells the story of a cold-blooded coke dealer who's destined to fall. *There'll be another one after me*, he raps.

O.G. Original Gangster also introduced his rock band Body Count. "A lot of people don't realize that rock and roll is truly black music," he explained on the song of the same name. "It was created by Chuck Berry, Little Richard, and black people like that." Ice had long been a rock fan—Boston and Blue Öyster Cult were among his favorites—and he was inspired to jam after touring with Public Enemy, whose high-energy tracks like "Welcome to the Terrordome" got European kids moshing. So he and his guitar-playing buddy Ernie C recruited some Crenshaw High School friends and became Body Count, named for the favored phrase of somber L.A. newscasters recounting murders.

Playing a metal–hardcore punk hybrid, the group really brought it, and Ice-T was a convincing frontman. In 1991 Perry Farrell invited him on his new traveling music festival, Lollapalooza, which featured progressive rock acts like Farrell's own Jane's Addiction, Living Colour, and Nine Inch Nails. At shows Ice-T performed some of his own hip-hop songs, and some Body Count numbers, which got fans headbanging. Body Count released its debut on Sire about six weeks before the riots; the imprint thought *Cop Killer* was too inflammatory for an album title, so they went with *Body Count*.

"Everything was good. Life was perfect," Ice-T said. "And then all of the sudden, the shit hit the fan."

The song "Cop Killer" was not an original concept. N.W.A lyrically killed cops on two different albums. Dr. Dre and Snoop's title track to the *Deep Cover* soundtrack was about killing cops. There's a band out of Austin called MDC (Millions of Dead Cops). "I Shot the Sheriff" has been a radio staple for decades.

"Cop Killer" wanted to shock, but also had a righteous streak. Kicking off with a spoken-word message decrying LAPD brutality, it launches into a bracing assault of guitars and drums. Sings Ice-T:

> *I got my twelve-gauge sawed off*
> *I got my headlights turned off*
> *I'm 'bout to bust some shots off*
> *I'm 'bout to dust some cops off!*

Ice-T channeled the rage of millions evoked by the Rodney King beatings. "If you've never been out on the streets and had to deal with the cops firsthand," Ice-T said, "you're not capable of understanding how corrupt they can be." But despite the track's fury, no one could have predicted the backlash; it managed to work the government up into even more of a lather than "Fuck tha Police."

In June 1992, months after the album's release, Ice-T was at home playing the Nintendo game Tecmo Bowl when he learned Vice President Dan Quayle was talking about the song on TV. Speaking shortly after two Texas police unions called for a boycott of Sire's parent company Time Warner, Quayle said, "Here is a very influential corporation, supporting and making money off a record that suggests it's OK to kill cops. I find that outrageous."

Critiquing entertainers had become a theme of the 1992 presidential race. The oft-bumbling former Indiana senator also found it outrageous that *Murphy Brown*'s title character was having a baby out of wedlock. Even Bush's opponent Bill Clinton got outraged, denouncing rapper Sister Souljah after she told *The Washington Post*, following the riots: "If black people kill black people every day, why not have a week and kill white people?"

But following Quayle's comments, Ice-T said he was audited by the IRS repeatedly, and that his junior high–age daughter was pulled out of school (presumably by law enforcement officials) and asked if her father was "connected to paramilitary organizations." In June, President George H. W. Bush piled on as well, not referencing "Cop Killer" by name but insisting: "[I] stand against those who use films, or records, or television, or video games to glorify killing law-enforcement officers. It is sick." Oliver North soon weighed in, and in July, movie star and future NRA president Charlton Heston gave his opinion at a Time Warner stockholders meeting in Beverly Hills; he owned a couple hundred shares of their stock, and was thus entitled to speak. He read the lyrics to "Cop Killer" aloud to a crowd of about a thousand. He also read the lyrics from another Body Count song called "KKK Bitch," which has a supposedly humorous but rather nonsensical plot involving the seduction of KKK members and "Tipper Gore's two twelve-year-old nieces." A pair of officers who had been shot in the face addressed the board to denounce "Cop Killer" as well.

"I was learning that freedom of speech is just a concept," Ice-T said.

Though Heston would basically take credit for torpedoing the rapper's relationship with Time Warner, it didn't really go down that way. Ice-T met cordially with Time Warner executives in New York, and company co-CEO Gerald Levin wrote an op-ed for *The Wall Street Journal* defending the song, saying it didn't "incite or glorify violence" but was rather a "fictionalized attempt to get inside a character's head." The fifty-three-year-old white executive suggested that instead of "finding ways to silence the messenger," it would be best to heed "the anguished cry contained in his message." Nonetheless, some music chains stopped carrying the record, and in Greensboro, North Carolina, police told a retail store's management that if they continued selling the album, they wouldn't respond to emergency calls there. All the controversy spurred *Body Count*'s sales; after a dip, it once again began climbing the *Billboard* charts.

Nonetheless, Time Warner faced attacks on other fronts, including boycotts of its amusement parks, and threatened mass divestitures of stock. Still, Ice-T says the company's leadership never demanded he act. They did, however, call him in for a meeting and present him with a visual metaphor: The table in front of them represented Time Warner and the quarter placed upon it represented the music division. He himself was simply a spot on the quarter. The problem was, the tiny spot was threatening the existence of the entire table. In a gesture of solidarity, and as a way to put this whole, scary episode behind him—his label had received a bomb threat—he pulled "Cop Killer" from future printings of his album, opting instead to give away free copies at his concerts.

He remained signed to Sire. But that changed when, later in 1992, he turned in his solo follow-up album *Home Invasion*, which contained more material about killing cops. Worried it would stoke further outrage, Ice-T and the label agreed to part ways, and he took the album to Priority Records, controversial lyrics and all. In the end, *Home Invasion* went gold, but Ice-T's name faded from headlines. His commercial relevance as a rapper began to decline, and he focused more on acting, becoming widely known as Detective Fin Tutuola on *Law & Order: SVU*.

Ice-T felt the "Cop Killer" fallout in hip-hop circles, too. Some thought he had caved. "It fucked with my credibility, because the streets didn't understand it. They looked like I backed up," he said. Really, it's hard to imagine the kind of pressure he faced. Most who say they'd fight for free speech even if it risked their family's safety likely haven't had to make that choice. Ice-T remains proud of the song, which was undoubtedly heard thousands of times more than it would have been without the controversy.

"If you feel injustice, make a record about it," he said. "That's what art's about."

Insane in the Membrane

"Cop Killer" aside, the major record labels by the early nineties considered hard-edged hip-hop commercially viable, and gangsta groups became ascendant. Particularly popular, and enormously influential, was trio Cypress Hill. The first Latino rap group to break big, their name comes from a street they hung out on in the South L.A. suburb of South Gate. Featuring the nasal, sinister rhymes of frontman B-Real and rapper Sen Dog over the sample-heavy production of DJ Muggs, their sound is laid-back—yet fraught with tension. Their 1991 self-titled debut layers nostalgic clips like Gene Chandler's 1962 doo-wop hit "Duke of Earl" beneath threatening lyrics. *Sawed-off shotgun, hand on the pump / Left hand on a forty, puffin' on a blunt.* It scared the bejesus out of me when I was in ninth grade.

N.W.A may have kicked down the door for them, but elements of Cypress Hill's style were later adopted by both Ice Cube and Dr. Dre. The Cypress Hill sound is all over *The Predator*, and the group's marijuana-obsessed rhymes undoubtedly helped inspire Dre to go all in on *The Chronic*. Today, being a pro-marijuana rapper is about as controversial as being a pro-life Republican. But back then Cypress Hill were on the vanguard. As absurd as their message of legalization sounded at the time, it quickly gathered steam, and in 1996 a California voter referendum permitted medical cannabis. DJ Muggs would also produce one of the most-enduring rap singles in history, "Jump Around," for the group House of Pain, who portrayed themselves as Irish hooligans.

Houston's Geto Boys told street truths, but also employed a southern gothic, over-the-top horrorcore style. *Some say I'm insane*, member Bushwick Bill, a dwarf who came up in Brooklyn, raps on 1991's "Chuckie." *You give me some gin, and I might eat a dog's brain.* During a confrontation that year with his girlfriend, Bill was shot in the eye, and the cover for the group's album *We Can't Be Stopped* features a photo of him not long afterward, on a hospital gurney, a bandage removed to reveal his eye socket. Geto Boys' lead MC Scarface became the godfather of psychological hip-hop, probing his own tortured upbringing, including a stint in a mental ward, to produce some of the most literary and complex rap albums in history.

Closer to home, harder-than-you-think Compton rapper Coolio emerged in the group WC and the Maad Circle, and then broke big with hits like "Fantastic Voyage," inspired by the Lakeside funk hit of the same name. Compton's Most Wanted combined gangsta tropes with a mellower, East Coast–influenced sound. Their 1990 debut *It's a Compton Thang!* marked the emergence of the group's leader MC Eiht. "He and I wanted to be a West Coast EPMD," said one of the group's producers, DJ Slip, referencing the golden era Long Island duo. Compton's Most Wanted's "Growin' Up in the Hood" was on the *Boyz n the Hood* soundtrack, and MC Eiht would star in *Menace II Society*. He's also remembered for his rivalry with Compton legend DJ Quik. Quik, the first rapper from the Bloods gang, gained fame as a prodigiously talented rhymer and studio technician, and his production style would also influence Dr. Dre. His 1991 debut *Quik Is the Name* remains an oft-referenced classic, as is his classic Eiht diss from the song "Dollaz + Sense":

> *Givin' your set a bad name with your misspelled name*
> *E-I-H-T, now should I continue?*
> *Yeah, you left out the "g" 'cause the G ain't in you.*

Hurricanes Like Kool-Aid

While those acts were heating up the movement he helped ignite, Dr. Dre was staying largely under the radar, mostly because of his murky contract situation with Ruthless. "We went to damn near every record company there is and nobody wanted to fuck with us," Dre said. Sure, he made a couple of songs for the *Deep Cover* soundtrack, but even those were contested. And so, Dre sat on the sidelines. Meanwhile, his bills mounted.

Perhaps it was his financial frustration that fueled his 1992 downward spiral. Maybe he was drinking too much. Maybe Suge Knight was a bad influence. Whatever the case, he was in near-constant trouble with the law. Dee Barnes's civil case and Ruthless's racketeering lawsuits hadn't yet been adjudicated, but Dre added some fresh cases to his docket. In early May 1992 he broke the jaw of a producer named Damon Thomas. According to the L.A. city attorney's office, Dre punched his lights out—leaving him unconscious—outside of the Woodland Hills apartment of one of Dre's girlfriends.

Less than three weeks after the Thomas incident, Dre, D.O.C., and others were in New Orleans for a convention put on by *Black Radio Exclusive* magazine. They were there to support the performance of trio Po' Broke & Lonely?, which featured Dre collaborator Chris "The Glove" Taylor, and is an outstanding handle. "We had just been hanging out that day, drinking hurricanes like Kool-Aid," D.O.C. said. At the downtown Sheraton Hotel they got into a dispute. Dre said he and others were drunkenly quoting from the movie *Harlem Nights* when a group of locals confronted them. A shoving match ensued, and a member of Dre's camp threw a punch. "And all this shit broke out. They start comin' at us—Boom! We got in a little tussle and I start headin' for the front door," Dre said. The riot police showed up, and the confrontation escalated into a full-blown melee. D.O.C. ran across the room and "dove" into a cop, drunkenly convinced the man was harming Dre. "The police socked me, and it was a free for all," D.O.C. said. He added that formidable Death Row rapper The Lady of Rage was there as well, "duking up, giving those boys the business."

By the time it was over two people had been stabbed and more than eighty police officers had arrived on the scene—some riding horses directly into the hotel's lobby. Four policemen were injured, and Dre and D.O.C. were taken to jail. Dre asserted he was unfairly arrested, and said he had no idea how the stabbings transpired. He pleaded guilty to roughing up a police officer, and also pleaded no contest to a battery charge in the Damon Thomas case. Because the incidents violated his probation from the Dee Barnes criminal case, he received five months house arrest. He was also forced to wear an ankle bracelet alerting police of his whereabouts, and though he could leave home to work, he faced a strict nine p.m. curfew, with which he sometimes had difficulty complying. "We literally rode a flat tire down to the rim and broke the thing in half while racing down the Ventura Freeway and running over a raised road divider," wrote his former assistant Bruce Williams, describing a frenzied mad dash to make the deadline.

House arrest at his Calabasas mansion wasn't the end of the world. Except that around this time it suffered a major fire following a barbecue. Dre's stepbrother Warren G took some hot coals and put them in a trashcan that was leaning against the home. The sparks flew up a vent pipe leading to the attic, engulfing one side of the house. But the partygoers were initially too drunk to realize what was going on. "One of the neighbors came over and said, 'Yo, the side of your house is on fire,'" Dre remembered. "We went over there and put it out. And the next thing I know, it was on the roof."

"We was like, 'Fuuuuuuuuck! The house!'" said Michel'le.

"Dre was surprisingly upbeat," D.O.C. said. "We were eating hot dogs, watching the roof burn, and he was telling jokes."

But it wasn't funny; two firefighters suffered heat exhaustion after spending the better part of an hour putting out the blaze, according to a *Los Angeles Times* account. Damage was estimated at $125,000.

As if all of this weren't enough, in July 1992, media outlets reported Dre had been shot in the leg outside of a hotel party. "We was talking 'bout this girl that came up for one of my homeboys and she was all fucked up...uglier than shit," Dre said. "So we came downstairs to talk about her, right? Shots rung out, we ran back into the hotel. I don't even know where they came from."

He added: "That's a pain you never want to experience."

In December of that year, Dre admitted, "1992 was not my year." But things were about to get a lot better.

CHAPTER FOURTEEN

THE FUNK

Today Snoop Dogg is as mainstream American as baseball or apple pie. He's ubiquitous on television and social media. Even those unfamiliar with his music are vaguely aware that in his younger days he was, perhaps, dangerous. But somewhere along the way he transformed into a friendly stoner, a laid-back figure who wouldn't seem out of place at a suburban potluck, and would make the party more fun.

His edgy-but-nonthreatening cool has become catnip to advertisers. Some of his endorsements are no-brainers (video games, porn, rolling papers), but he's often trotted out with an ironic wink, plugging Toyota minivans and Norton Antivirus software. Snoop Dogg shilling pistachios? How *random*! More often than a rap stanza, his appearances today usually involve a punch line. He's got natural comic timing, seemingly as in his element roasting Justin Bieber for Comedy Central or playing golf with Lee Iacocca as he is on stage performing his songs. No longer obsessed with saying things like "Fo shizzle my nizzle," he speaks fluent corporate-ese these days. Snoop, Inc., he notes, can help companies expand their brand's reach.

When not recording he's bringing his street edge to ventures that might otherwise seem soft. At a 2014 press event in Culver City, Snoop promotes a whimsical Swedish designer called Happy Socks. They have three Snoop-inspired sock designs, a blue paisley "gin and juice" pair, a

Rasta-themed Snoop Lion pair, and one imprecisely themed "art," featuring a paint can. Snoop's tagline? "Stay G'ed up from the feet up."

At the event Snoop sits on a small throne at the front of the room, clad in a burgundy sweater vest and skinny jeans. No one thinks this is the slightest bit strange. He chats for a bit before a publicist plays a video. In it, Snoop gets high and then, dreads flailing, paints, using aerosol cans and brushes, adopting a street-art style, before summoning his inner Jackson Pollock and flinging paint at the wall.

How exactly all of this is supposed to sell socks is unclear, but Snoop isn't sweating it much. He offers insight into his marketing machine. He won't just endorse anyone who pays him, he notes. "I gotta fuck with you, first of all," he says. In the case of Happy Socks he'd already been hipped to them—having a stylish socks game is quite hip-hop, believe it or not—and then began posting pictures of them to his ten million Instagram followers.

But Snoop's not all about the marketing. In 2013 I meet with him and L.A. groovemaster Dâm-Funk—Snoop's collaborator on an under-the-radar album called *7 Days of Funk*—at Snoop's Inglewood compound, an unmarked former industrial building near the airport. Part studio, part crash pad, and part sports park, the facility boasts a basketball court, and, in the parking lot, Cadillac lowriders and a school bus decorated with the Steelers logo, which transports kids in his peewee football league. We speak in a disco ball–lit upstairs room with old R&B records on the wall. Wearing a giant yellow T-shirt and gray Dickies, Snoop smokes a thin blunt, sips Coke with ice, and plays me some of his beloved throwback jams, including Smokey Robinson's smooth 1982 track "Tell Me Tomorrow."

"My mama used to *bang* this shit," he says.

He prefers the funk and soul of his childhood to what's on the radio today, and his own new music reflects this. He no longer cares if it's popular, he says. "You get to the point in your career where it's not about doing it for a contract—or to be seen or to be heard—it's about the feeling that it gives you and that it gives other people." His collaboration with Dâm-Funk, a middle-aged contemporary, evokes a time before gangsta sounds ruled the radio, a childhood of simple pleasures. "This is some-body who woke up the same time I woke up," he says, "watched the same shit, *Great Space Coaster*, *Tom and Jerry*, and ate the same [Apple] Jacks."

Rhymin' with a Singing Jingle

From the beginning, Snoop had many identities. Born Calvin Cordozar Broadus, after his stepfather Calvin Broadus, he went by Cordozar, except that nobody could pronounce it. So, owing to his *Peanuts* fanaticism (which continues) and because he was a hairy-headed baby who resembled a pup, they called him Snoopy. "To this day, my mama never called me by my real name, she always call me Snoopy," Snoop said.

He and his mother had a strong bond. She would buy them bottles of Schlitz malt liquor and they'd listen to R&B records together on Saturday nights, doing the bump. Like many other hip-hop stars, he developed his musicality in church, joining the choir at Long Beach's Golgotha Trinity Baptist, housed in a beautiful yellow Spanish colonial building on East Fourteenth Street. He played piano and even taught Sunday school classes. Though for a time as a teenager he bagged groceries and did other low-wage work, he fell in with the Crips and began dealing drugs. His mother dis-owned him, and at age sixteen Snoop moved out and surfed couches, still managing to graduate high school. Though recruited to play college bas-ketball, the streets beckoned, and he was soon arrested for drugs.

Music was an escape. Snoop's voice is a miraculous instrument, warm, textured, and a bit menacing. He often raps slowly, almost behind the beat, and sings as well, in a way that combines old and new, the fresh and the classic. He enjoyed the early L.A. electro style and the new street sound, and sought to combine them. His storytelling was rich with humor, influ-enced by eyepatch-wearing Bronx legend Slick Rick, and his ear for melody came from his love of old-school R&B. He told *The Source* that he was try-ing to revive the "rhymin'-with-a-singing-jingle," with a gangsta inflection.

Originally known as Snoop Doggy Dogg, the then twenty-year-old talent wasn't exactly television ready, often unwilling to look directly into the camera. He skipped at least one early interview because he was too high. There was something undeniably hard about him. Tall and gangly with a thin mustache, he hadn't fully grown into his body, which made him seem slightly combustible. In his cornrows, blue bandana, and plaid Pendleton shirt, he loudly proclaimed his Crips allegiance. He had a code, and a plan: to express himself as he was, damn all comers.

When Dr. Dre came calling, it was a no-brainer. He'd always wanted to be a member of N.W.A, and had been a huge Eazy-E fan. In fact, Snoop was originally discovered by Above the Law's Cold 187um, who was grooming him to sign with Ruthless. But when Dre left the label he brought Snoop with him. With Ice Cube gone and D.O.C.'s voice shattered, Snoop was someone he could rebuild his empire around, a young rapper with the rare combination of street smarts and professional dedication. "He was just, like, raw talent," Dr. Dre said. "An unpolished diamond."

And so Dr. Dre bet the farm on him. If he was going to mount a comeback, it would be on the back of Snoop, seven years his junior. The pair began to work on *The Chronic*, Dre's debut solo album, but in the meantime Snoop's debut came on "Deep Cover," the title song from the 1992 Laurence Fishburne and Jeff Goldblum film. It was conceived during a single evening at Dre's Calabasas home, built around a bass line played live by collaborator Colin Wolfe. "We did the song in a couple of hours. From nothing. Out of *air*. No samples, none of that," Dre said. Snoop said Dre gave him the song's opening lyrics—*Tonight's the night I get in some shit / Deep cover on the incognito tip*—and then he crafted the rest. Since he hadn't yet seen the movie, he drew from his own experiences. "I got caught for sellin' to an undercover cop," he noted. "Crooked cops gave me a grip of time."

The track's plot diverges from that of the movie: Dre plays an undercover policeman hoping to infiltrate a drug ring. He offers syndicate member Snoop a deal if he'll snitch on his boss, to which Snoop's character responds by gunning him down. It's best remembered for its chorus:

Dr. Dre: *And you don't stop*
Snoop: *'Cause it's 1-8-7 on an undercover cop*

"Tomorrow, I'm gonna be famous," Snoop told Chris "The Glove" Taylor right before the song dropped. The Glove agreed. The song took hold on both sides of the Atlantic, thanks largely to the efforts of promoter Doug Young, and Snoop's refrain—which references the California penal code for murder—became a chilling catchphrase, a rallying cry for gangstas, authentic and wannabe.

" 'Deep Cover' was the soundtrack to our lives at that moment," said Dâm-Funk, a Pasadena native. Dre and Snoop "moved like us and spoke like us," unlike East Coast rappers.

Eazy-E had popularized a West Coast–centric lyrical and sartorial style, but musically, L.A. was still indebted to its New York influences. "Deep Cover" was perhaps the watershed moment when Los Angeles cast off its predecessors and began to assert itself. "From then on," Snoop said, "there was more funk."

A Different Skill Set

The Chronic features a cornucopia of rap talent. Assembling the collaborators was a monumental task for Dre and Suge, requiring talent scouting, familial connections, and some luck. R&B singer Jewell, who scandalized her mother by appearing on N.W.A's "I'd Rather Fuck You," was the first offered a slot, and became known as the "First Lady" of Death Row. Warren G and his Long Beach friend Nate Dogg were recruited for the work as well.

For the rapper Kurupt, however, entree was more complicated. A rail-thin Philadelphia native transplanted to South Central, he was, like Snoop, a hot-tempered Crip affiliate, who also happened to love canines. (He and his buddies would dress their pups in blue rags.) But the pair didn't meet until one night outside the famous Roxy Theatre on Sunset Boulevard. Snoop was fresh from jail, and neither was yet known. But they nonetheless held themselves in high regard, and their duel that night would fuel their trajectories. Inside the Roxy, rappers battled, with Long Beach MC Domino taking home the prize. But the real action took place outside in the parking lot afterward.

As popularized in the 2002 Eminem movie *8 Mile*, battle rapping features two opponents facing each other down and spitting stanzas for supremacy. The particulars vary; there might be a backing beat or it might be a cappella. Sometimes there are formal judges, sometimes not. Some battles are freestyle, while some MCs come armed with memorized verses. Whatever the format, battles can get quite personal. When an imposing rapper is spitting in your face about doing unconscionable things to your personage, you must, instead of becoming irate, come up with a hilarious insult to save the day. It's an entirely different skill set than rapping on record. In the studio, crisp pronunciation and pacing are important skills. Battle rapping rewards impassioned outbursts and inspired digressions.

While waiting for their cars outside the Roxy that night, Snoop's Long Beach crew and Kurupt's South Central crew got to talking, and then battling. As Snoop looked on, Kurupt quickly slayed his opponents. "This nigga was serving all my homies, like a Chinese karate movie," Snoop remembered. Eventually Snoop and Kurupt went at it, and their epic battle lasted for maybe forty-five minutes. They fought to a draw, and vowed to stay in touch.

Kurupt still had to pass muster with the big boss, whom he soon met at Dre's Calabasas house. "I heard you was tight," Suge told Kurupt. "If you're whack, we'll throw your ass in the pool. If you're tight, we'll give you a record deal." Shrugging off the pressure, Kurupt gave an impromptu performance, freestyling a tribute to a kid in attendance having a birthday. Suge gave him a record deal on the spot. (As it turned out, Kurupt had already signed promotional contracts with brothers Lamont and Kenneth Brumfield, and the pair later sued Death Row, winning some $5 million in punitive damages.)

Nearly every rap crew worth its salt had a strong female MC, and Death Row landed the toughest of all. The Lady of Rage was a thick rapper in Timberland boots—*175 pounds of beef / Beatin' yo ass down to the concrete*, in her own estimation. A Virginia native, she may have inspired Queen Latifah comparisons, but was a vicious, self-proclaimed "lyrical murderer" with a penchant for stealing the scene. When Dre first heard her recordings with a production team called L.A. Posse, she was quasi-homeless, sleeping on a couch in Manhattan studio Chung King. He got her on the phone, and before long Death Row sent her a ticket to fly to Los Angeles.

Also in the mix for *The Chronic* was a pair of Snoop's cousins, one on his dad's side, a rapper and producer named Dat Nigga Daz—Daz for short—who partnered up with Kurupt for the Snoop-allied group Tha Dogg Pound. Daz was also affiliated with Long Beach Crips, and the act was sometimes called Dogg Pound Gangsta Crips. Snoop's cousin on his mother's side, RBX, was a former football teammate of Suge's at the University of Nevada, a towering defensive end who came back to Los Angeles on the weekends to battle with the Freestyle Fellowship at the Good Life Café, hoping to win rent money. He boasted a heavy, thick flow. "The first time I heard RBX rap I was high on mushrooms," D.O.C. said. "[I]t was like havin' your eyes closed and havin' muthafuckas hit you with rocks from all different directions."

RBX, whose name stands for "Reality Born Unknown," saw his life changed forever one day when Snoop came by the shoe store where he was working and hit him up for a ride to Dre's house. When they later arrived there, the producer noticed RBX's deep, resounding baritone, hoping he might be able to rap as distinctively as he sounded. Later that night RBX showed him he could. "You can't leave," Dre told him.

Suge wanted everyone to know that Death Row had the toughest, realest crew in all the West, particularly the people who mattered to him most—the guys on the block. To impress them, his MCs needed to be more than just studio rappers. They needed to be courageous, street smart, and quick on their feet. They needed to be battle rappers.

Suge put the word out: Anyone who thought they could beat Death Row artists would have a chance to prove it. Suge began sending his label's artists to small amphitheaters or housing projects like Watts's Nickerson Gardens to battle total strangers, performing on mics hooked up to sound systems. Snoop—who despite his laid-back flow is also a freestyle beast, quickly concocting hard-edged poetry and humorous punch lines—was often the first to battle. He would be followed by Kurupt, who specialized in taking down particularly lyrical opponents with wicked freestyles. Next, the Lady of Rage battled any female rappers. "Rage would start eating these niggas alive," Kurupt said. RBX was the last line of defense.

Suge sought to make it worth the competitors' whiles: "If you can serve Kurupt, I'll give you a record deal," he told them. No one got a record deal. "Kurupt's still the best freestyler alive," said Chris "The Glove" Taylor.

A group of legendary Houston rappers were in the mix as well. In a video from this era filmed at a Beverly Center club, Snoop performs in a freestyle cypher before passing the mic to Scarface, of the Geto Boys. 'Face's groupmates Bushwick Bill and Big Mike participate in the cypher as well, and were involved in early Death Row projects. Unfortunately, owing to a combination of factors—Death Row's financing from Interscope hadn't yet come through, for one thing—they soon headed back to Texas.

In any case, these freestyle sessions bonded the Death Row crew and pushed them creatively. Their efforts would shine through on *The Chronic* tracks like "Stranded on Death Row," which evokes the East Coast cypher tradition with its dense verses. West Coast gangsta rappers are sometimes accused of having more bark than lyrical bite, but the team assembled for *The Chronic* could go toe-to-toe with anyone.

Comically Broke

Though signed to Death Row, this cohort was living modestly as they worked on *The Chronic*. Suge paid the new artists a modest retainer (Snoop said he got a thousand dollars a month), with promises of big paydays at some future point. They often congregated at Snoop's one-bedroom Hollywood apartment, which he rented for $500 a month. The peach stucco complex on La Mirada with a great view of the Hollywood sign was only a ten-minute walk from Solar's studios. Hollywood itself was rough then—crack dealers plied their trade on nearby Santa Monica—but Snoop loved the space, sometimes piling a half dozen people into the apartment's sole bedroom and nurturing a pet roach he called "Gooch." Daz, Kurupt, RBX, Nate Dogg, and Warren G were regulars. The apartment stayed unfurnished, save for some chairs and a table to play dominoes, and the fridge was usually bare, too, except maybe for some Seagram's and a bottle of juice. They were almost comically broke. When *The Source* scribe Ronin Ro stopped by in 1992, Snoop hit him up for five dollars to buy weed. The Lady of Rage and Jewell shared an apartment in the same building, and they sometimes cooked up spaghetti or tacos for the fellas. "We was like a family," Kurupt said.

No one had a reliable car, and the money situation was sketchy. But they could walk to work and had most everything they needed. Many would look back on this time as the happiest of their careers. "The best records came out when we were starving," Nate Dogg said. After all, until recently, some of them had been homeless, locked up, or dealing drugs, but they were now recording at a real-deal studio. In addition to sometimes paying Snoop's rent, Dick Griffey would descend from his garish top-floor office and give the rapper tours of the Solar building, where hit groups like Shalamar, Lakeside, and the Whispers recorded. "We would see reels with the old records and old songs," Snoop said. "To have a young kid in that environment, it's like if you were a basketball player and Michael Jordan let you use the facilities where he practiced. How wouldn't you become LeBron James or Kobe Bryant?"

The squabbles about percentages and royalties could wait until later. For the time being, they spent their hours rhyming, eating Popeye's chicken, watching TV, or just goofing around. Mainly, they wrote, working on their fledgling song sketches, bouncing ideas off one another.

The Chronic wasn't just the name of the album they were working on, it was their inspiration. "Chronic" is slang for particularly potent weed, sticky, vibrantly colored buds that are much stronger than the stems-and-sticks, dull brown herb most potheads were smoking. For decades California has been known for superior marijuana, much of it originating in the so-called Emerald Triangle in the wooded northern part of the state—Humboldt, Mendocino, and Trinity counties—where ex-hippies fostered colossal farms. "When it comes to cannabis, there's a history, a set of traditions and a depth of knowledge in those communities that's just unparalleled," said former *High Times* editor David Bienenstock.

"That's why we made *The Chronic*, because we *had* the chronic," Snoop said.

Dr. Dre had never been much of a weed smoker. Snoop hipped him to the chronic, and convinced him it should be the album's name. Though Dre never became a gung-ho enthusiast like his protégé, he certainly got into the spirit of the thing at the time. *Snoop Dogg came to visit / And was like "What up, cuz? Let me show you what this chronic like,"* Dre rapped on his 2015 song "It's All on Me." *Couldn't help myself, just had to dip into that chronic life.*

The Signature Sound

The young spitters were fired up. They had their verses written, and if those ran out they could freestyle off the top of their heads. But it was Dre's job to make sense of the madness. Though only twenty-seven at the time, when it came to making hit records, he was by now a savvy veteran.

He recorded the first half of *The Chronic* at his Calabasas house, in a bedroom he'd converted into a studio. After the fire there, the rest was made at Solar's Galaxy studios, where he made use of a state-of-the-art SSL console, a huge, futuristic mixing board with preprogrammable "flying faders," capable of automatically adjusting itself to your preferred settings. "It was like the Starship *Enterprise*," Rhythm D said.

Yet it was still the predigital era, and so they edited on analog tapes, literally cutting them by hand. "You would mark the tape with a grease pencil, and then use a razor blade," remembered Chris "The Glove" Taylor, an engineer and musician on the album.

More than ever, Dre was finding inspiration in Parliament-Funkadelic. He, too, employed the Moog synthesizer, creating both a chunky bass sound and, using different settings, the "funky worm" squeal. It's that enchanting, high-pitched whine, originally borrowed from the Ohio Players, which is the signature sound of *The Chronic*. It's melodic, it's somewhat terrifying, it instantly makes your ears prick up.

On the album Dre sampled or interpolated a half dozen songs from either Parliament or Funkadelic, sister groups that were both led by George Clinton. Dre's genius was realizing how well they'd combine with rap lyrics. Part of the connection was emotional. P-Funk's psychedelic rock was cutting edge, but to those who grew up in the seventies it was also warm and nostalgic, the soundtrack to backyard parties and civil rights rallies. Combining it with the rough-and-tumble lyrics of gangsta rap merged the hard and the soft, the light and the dark. The sound was called G-funk—gangsta funk—and it would come to dominate hip-hop for years.

Snoop's present-day collaborator, the aforementioned Dâm-Funk, is a keytar-toting funk revivalist who loves the genre in the deepest fibers of his body. He told me that, for many who grew up on Parliament-Funkadelic, the sound came to symbolize a halcyon time before crack cocaine came along and decimated the inner city. Dâm-Funk cites Funkadelic's 1979 song "Not Just (Knee Deep)"—which Dre would later sample for a Tupac track—as "almost like the end credits rolling on a certain era.

"Because, before that, there wasn't crack," he went on. "And then that era came, and a lot of people got lost after that. You can almost feel it in the music that something was on the horizon.... It symbolizes happiness *and* sadness. That's what the funk is."

Who Invented G-funk?

Who invented G-funk? Though Dr. Dre is its most famous purveyor, the question is a matter of some debate.

DJ Quik, who emerged in the early nineties, has long been injecting serious funk into his hip-hop, and was undoubtedly influential on Dre's sound. But it was Ruthless group Above the Law that would directly claim credit for the G-funk sound, offering as evidence their early 1993 sophomore album *Black Mafia Life*. That work wasn't a massive hit like

The Chronic, but the albums bear some clear similarities: "Nuthin' But a 'G' Thang" echoes Above the Law's "Never Missin' a Beat," for example, while their "Pimp Clinic" and Dre's "Let Me Ride" both borrow from Parliament-Funkadelic's take on the spiritual "Swing Low, Sweet Chariot." *Swing down, sweet chariot, stop, and, let me ride.*

Black Mafia Life was released about two months after *The Chronic*, but, according to many accounts, was finished beforehand. "G-funk was our style of music," said Above the Law collaborator Kokane, adding that group producers Cold 187um and KMG the Illustrator forged the sound.

During Dre's final months at Ruthless, he worked on N.W.A's *Efil-4zaggin* while Cold 187um was simultaneously working on *Black Mafia Life*, and the pair often sounded each other out. It was during this period that he fashioned the G-funk sound, Cold 187um told me. "You're highly influenced by people that are around you. The only thing I can say is that G-funk was my theory," he said. Dre "utilized it and made lots of money and commercialized it, and I never got credit for it. All I wanted was my credit. I don't think he was being malicious. I think he heard a hot sound and then he used it."

Many agree with this version of events, including Eazy-E. "Dre stole that style," he told Phyllis Pollack. "Dre stole stuff from Above the Law, *Black Mafia Life*'s 'Never Missing a Beat.'" N.W.A promoter Doug Young agreed that Above the Law had the sound first. But Dre, he added, deserves credit for turning G-funk into the powerhouse it became. "When you listen to that stuff to this day, it still holds up because of the sonics of the production," he said.

The dispute caused tension between Ruthless and Death Row, following *The Chronic*'s release. In February 1993, at an industry event called the Urban Network Power Jam held at the Marriott Hotel near LAX, Cold 187um angrily approached Warren G, who had worked closely with Dr. Dre on *The Chronic*. Warren had also previously stayed, for a time, at Cold 187um's crash pad in Colton, California, along with members of Above the Law. The pair had previously been friendly, but now there was tension in the air.

"That's fucked up how motherfuckers just integrated our style into they shit and created *The Chronic*," Cold 187um said to Warren G, in the former's recollection.

"I ain't got nothing to do with that, that's between you and Dre," Warren responded.

"Wait a minute man, I let you stay at my house, I let you be a part of my family, and you treat me like this?" said Cold 187um. "If you ain't got nothing to do with that, you ain't got nothing to do with me no more."

Warren was accompanied by fellow Death Row affiliates Snoop Dogg, Lil' ½ Dead, and others. Cold 187um was backed by artists including Eazy-E and an artist Eazy was recruiting at the time—Tupac Shakur. (They'd been linked up through Atron Gregory, who managed Tupac and was N.W.A's road manager.) The camps got to barking at each other, and before long everyone reached for their guns.

"There were fifteen of them, and about twenty-five to thirty of us," remembered Charis Henry, Eazy-E's assistant. "It was a standoff. It was the most nerve-racking thing imaginable."

No one pulled the trigger. A bodyguard named Hollywood—who'd worked with both camps—interceded. "I need you, Death Row, to turn around, drop your guns, and walk out the door," he said, in Henry's recollection. "Eric, I need you to wait for fifteen minutes, and then take yourself home." Both sides complied, and the situation resolved peacefully.

"It shows you how intense things were back then," said Cold 187um. "Easily things got out of hand."

Gangsta-ism

The Chronic may have been named for, and to some extent created under the influence of, marijuana. But its central theme is gangsta-ism. Lead single "Nuthin' But a 'G' Thing"—that is, a "gangsta" thing—became the biggest hit of Dr. Dre's career. Throughout much of the album he and Snoop portray themselves as nihilistic, lawless street villains bent on defending their honor at all cost.

Dre was never a gangbanger. He and World Class Wreckin' Cru mocked the culture on their song "Gang Bang You're Dead" (*You dress so tacky 'til you look like a slob / And you wonder why you can't get a job?*) while on "We're All in the Same Gang" Dre warns of its dangers without explicitly denouncing gang life (*Bullets flyin', mothers cryin', brothers dyin'*). In the N.W.A years he became ever more comfortable portraying a tough guy, with his persona even cooking up dope in their "Appetite for Destruction" video. Now at Death Row, he was surrounded by gang members of both stripes. Suge's people were Bloods, Snoop and his crew were Crips. But when asked point-blank by MTV in early 1993 if he considered himself a gangsta, Dre said no. "I'm here to make money, and that's all I'm in this for," he said.

On *The Chronic* Dre walks a fine line. He never affiliates himself with any specific gang, but instead promotes gangsta-ism as almost a state of mind. Being a G is about standing up for yourself, not taking shit, and representing your city. "Nuthin' But a 'G' Thang" expresses this vision, and in its video Dre wears neutral black, drives a '64 Impala, and makes vague threats. Snoop raps: *Compton and Long Beach together, now you know you got trouble*, before Dre asserts: *I'ma continue to put the rap down, put the mack down / And if you bitches talk shit, I'll have to put the smack down.*

The track and its video would solidify Dre's image as a steely street cat. But it never really explains what a G thing *is*. N.W.A's "Gangsta Gangsta" was much more specific: Cube was drinking straight out the eight-bottle and takin' people out with a flurry of buckshot. But for Dre gangsta-ism was, literally, a posture; with his slight slouch and mean stare at the barbecue in the video, you don't doubt his resolve. It was D.O.C.—the Dallas native who knew nothing whatsoever of L.A. gang culture—who penned Dre's verses. The listener was left to connect the dots in his or her own mind. And that's what likely spurred "Nuthin' But a 'G' Thang" to widespread appeal. Suburban kids couldn't really imagine themselves as a Crip or a Blood, but anyone could be a G. The word "gangsta" was gradually stripped of its meaning, and nowadays in popular culture is synonymous with "badass."

Dre recorded the initial version of "Nuthin' But a 'G' Thang" over a

Boz Scaggs track—he can't remember which one. Snoop was in jail at the time on a drug charge, but Dre was in a rush to get the demo done. "So he called in, and I taped the receiver of the phone to the mic. You can hear jail sounds in the back and everything," Dre said. Subsequently, however, when Dre was at his mother's house going through her records, he happened upon Leon Haywood's "I Want'a Do Something Freaky to You," which he swapped in as the backing track. When Snoop emerged from jail they rerecorded the vocals. Colin Wolfe played live bass, Dre overlaid an 808 drum machine for emphasis, and he knew it was a hit when people at a party kept asking him to rewind it.

For all the ambiguity of "Nuthin' But a 'G' Thing," *The Chronic*'s next single "Fuck wit Dre Day (And Everybody's Celebratin')" was cruelly specific. Most of the venom was directed at Eazy-E, starting with a skit preceding the video, in which Eazy is portrayed by comedian A. J. Johnson as a locs-clad, Jheri-curled Uncle Tom being sold a load of BS from Jerry Heller, played by portly Interscope executive Steve Berman.

"You trust me, don't you?" the Heller character asks.

"Yeah, boss."

"Oh, no no, I work for you. I work for *Sleazy-E*."

Eazy soon scampers out the door in search of new talent, to Heller's demeaning encouragement: "Go, boy!"

It was a low-budget humiliation straight out of Eazy's own playbook, reminiscent of the video in which N.W.A mocked Ice Cube by bribing him with a suitcase full of activator. But now Dre was on the offensive, and over the bass-rattling, slow funk track, he took direct aim at Eazy: *Used to be my homie, used to be my ace / Now I want to slap the taste out your mouth / Make you bow down to the Row / Fuckin' me, now I'm fuckin' you, little ho*. Eazy was no longer respected by his own people, he went on, and should watch his back because he might get "smoked."

Snoop, who grew up idolizing Eazy and later said he only echoed Dre's disses because he was a "rider," reserved most of his venom on the song for Tim Dog, the Bronx rapper who had ruffled feathers with his 1991 track "Fuck Compton," which took shots against Dre and others.

Also in their crosshairs was Luke Campbell of the 2 Live Crew. He'd pissed them off with his song "Fakin' Like Gangsters," and followed up with "Cowards in Compton," which seems to have precipitated a melee between the two camps at the 1993 Atlanta industry event Jack the Rapper. "A free-for-all broke out in the lobby on the escalators. Guys even threw a [Coca-Cola vending] machine off one of the lobby balconies trying to hit Luke's crew," said Wendy Day, who helped run the event.

Then there was Ice Cube. Along with Da Lench Mob, he received a few thinly veiled disses on *The Chronic*. But it turns out he and Dre were already in the process of reconciling, and Cube ended up appearing in the "Let Me Ride" video.

The majority of Dre's scorn on *The Chronic* was directed at Eazy, which by all accounts stunned his former partner. But the beef brought out the best in Dre, artistically. His production skills had reached their apex, and he was rapping more deftly than ever, his delivery filled with confidence, his verses unraveling smoothly. The work has real dramatic tension. Even if you found it horrifying that a prominent black artist was threatening real-sounding violence against another, the album was musically groundbreaking.

The accolades, however, were still in the future. By the time *The Chronic* was nearly finished in 1992 Dre still didn't have a suitable distributor willing to work with Death Row, owing to his contractual problems. A number of potential partnerships fizzled out before an upstart imprint—in need of a hit itself—decided to take a chance.

CHAPTER FIFTEEN

THE HEIR AND THE JANITOR

One day in April 1992, a troubled nineteen-year-old was pulled over on a routine traffic stop on a southeastern Texas highway. The African-American driver, Ronald Ray Howard, had grown up in poverty and said he was beaten by his dad; that day, he was driving a stolen vehicle and blasting Tupac's *2Pacalypse Now* from the cassette deck. "The music was up as loud as it could go with gunshots and siren noises on it and my heart was pounding hard," Howard said. As he watched a forty-something white state trooper named Bill Davidson approach his car, he grew agitated. "I was so hyped up, I just snapped. I jacked a bullet in the chamber and when he was close enough, I turned around and bam! I shot him."

Howard was tried for murder, but his lawyer attempted to pin the blame on rap, arguing that Howard's favorite artists, including Tupac, N.W.A, and the Geto Boys, had unduly influenced him. Davidson's widow agreed. "There isn't a doubt in my mind that my husband would still be alive if Tupac hadn't written these violent, antipolice songs and the companies involved hadn't published and put them out on the street," she said. Vice President Dan Quayle jumped into the fray, criticizing *2Pacalypse Now*—which features songs like "Soulja's Story" and "Trapped," in which characters murder police—and calling for Interscope to withdraw it from stores. "There is absolutely no reason for a record like this to be published by a responsible corporation," Quayle said.

"They ain't even judged the dude that shot the cop yet," Tupac complained, "and they judged *me!*"

In the end, the jury agreed that Howard's love for violent hip-hop had influenced him, but he was nonetheless convicted and given the death penalty, and was executed in 2005.

Quayle, of course, had also denounced Ice-T's "Cop Killer," and during the eighties and nineties politicians frequently took shots at popular musicians. But while some record companies did not stand by their artists, Tupac's label Interscope—which would go on to sign controversial performers like Nine Inch Nails and Marilyn Manson—was different. "[Interscope's] owners believed in the artist being able to say whatever they wanted," said journalist Jeffrey Jolson-Colburn. "And the more controversial, the better."

"A lot of this [criticism of rap] is just plain old racism," said Interscope cofounder Ted Field in 1993. "You can tell the people who want to stop us from releasing controversial rap music one thing: Kiss my ass."

Field was a Chicago-born heir to a department store and media company fortune. He dabbled in the family businesses and became a successful racecar driver, before mashing his left hand in a 1975 accident. He reinvented himself as a Hollywood power player, producing hit movies like *Revenge of the Nerds* and *Bill & Ted's Excellent Adventure*. In 1989 he dove into the music industry, cofounding Interscope Records with Jimmy Iovine.

If Field was born with a silver spoon, Iovine was self-made. He prided himself on his hardscrabble upbringing. Raised in a working-class Italian family in Downtown Brooklyn, his father was a union longshoreman and drove a bread truck. Jimmy dropped out of criminal justice college and diligently worked his way into the music business. He got his first industry job as a teenager, sweeping studio floors. He eventually became known as a guy who could make hit records, even with prickly personalities. He navigated the coked-up major label rock world of the seventies and eighties, coaxing top-sellers out of artists like Stevie Nicks and Meatloaf. He worked as an engineer on Bruce Springsteen's *Born to Run* and John Lennon's *Walls and Bridges*, and produced Patti Smith's *Easter*. Like Dre, he was known for his tenacity and perfectionism.

"He's a heat-seeking missile," said Bono about Iovine, who produced the 1983 U2 live album, *Under a Blood Red Sky.* "Jimmy wants everything cut like a diamond that can be seen from a long distance. And he's not subtle about how he tells you."

But studio wizardry was one thing; with Interscope Iovine sought to be a mogul. The label launched in 1990 as a joint venture with Atlantic Records. Field contributed some of his inheritance—he received millions when his father Marshall Field IV died—and Iovine contributed his expertise.

There were questionable early decisions, like signing Gerardo, a Latino Vanilla Ice of sorts responsible for the gimmicky hit "Rico Suave." Their roster also included Marky Mark and the Funky Bunch, also rather vanilla, though "Good Vibrations" remains the jam.

When Dr. Dre met Iovine, the latter knew little about hip-hop. Iovine prided himself on being a man who could smell a hit in almost any genre. It's just that he found the product sonically lackluster; there was no *oomph*. But when Dre came to his office and played him "Nuthin' But a 'G' Thang," it sounded so crisp and right that Iovine could barely believe it.

"Who produced this?"

"I did," said Dre.

"Who's the engineer?"

"I am."

Urged on by a whipsmart A&R named John McClain, Interscope set their sights on securing the rights to *The Chronic*. But they knew it wouldn't be easy. Just about everyone in the industry was steering clear of Dre, owing both to his legal issues—the contract dispute with Ruthless—and bad publicity surrounding his arrests and lawsuits. Even Sony Records, which put out the *Deep Cover* soundtrack, had been scared off.

Iovine didn't believe everything he read in the news. "If this was a white artist, I believe that these court cases would be a footnote in the story," he said. He set about untangling the strands of Dre's legal situation. He helped negotiate a deal with Ruthless, which would see a cut. Then Iovine worked on Dre's deal with Priority, which also had him under contract. Iovine was able to do legally what Suge had allegedly attempted with baseball bats.

Dre reportedly received a million-dollar advance from his new deal, as part of a complicated food chain: Dre recorded for Death Row, which had a distribution deal with Interscope, which in turn was partly owned by Atlantic, a Time Warner company.

"[N]obody wanted to take a chance on me because of all that legal shit," said Dre. "Jimmy made it happen." They became attached at the hip. Dre was grateful for an ally, someone who truly understood his brilliance. Sure, Eazy-E and Jerry Heller appreciated his hit-making abilities, but they seemed to treat him like a commodity. Iovine, a producer himself, knew he was a *treasure*.

Iovine allowed Dre to expand his role as well, tapping him to direct the video for "Let Me Ride" in 1993. Once, as he watched Dre ease into a lowrider, hitting switches to bounce the car up and down like a shark devouring its prey, something dawned on Iovine: Snoop and Dre were the new Mick Jagger and Keith Richards. Brilliant musicians and cultural spokesmen alike, they'd soon be dictating what kids listened to, how they moved through the world, and what they wore. Indeed, baseball caps, hoodies, bulky sports jackets, and baggy pants remain classic youth garb to this day.

This wasn't a British invasion, this was a West Coast invasion. The lingua franca of the new youth movement would be the language of the inner city.

The Hole Is Still There

For the most part, Suge left his artists alone to do their thing in Hollywood. "He might come in, nod his head a bit," said The Glove. "Dre was the decision maker." Suge spent more time across town in Westwood. Death Row had moved into an office adjacent to Interscope, in a red brick and glass tower on a corporate stretch of Wilshire Boulevard. Cultures clashed from the jump. Suge's label lacked a formal reception area, and tough characters would mill about the lobby. Those who'd arrived on legitimate business might find a gang member in their face: "Who are you, Blood?"

Interscope staff quickly began realizing what they'd been signed up for. Since Death Row was accessed directly from the elevator, cautious Interscope employees might take the stairs rather than potentially face Suge associates. One morning, a promotions department worker saw some Death Row affiliates appropriating furniture from his boss's office. "Don't start no problems," he claims to have been told, "and there won't be none."

In July 1992, a pair of brothers named George and Lynwood Stanley arrived at Solar. The rap duo was there at Dre's invitation, and he'd given them permission to make a phone call on Death Row's line, they said. "I don't give a fuck what Dre says, Dre ain't payin' no bills," said Suge. They began arguing and then, according to the Stanleys' complaint filed in L.A. Superior Court, Knight proceeded to beat them, threatened to shoot them, and fired off a warning round. He ordered them to take off their pants, took Lynwood's money, and then said he'd kill their families if they mentioned the incident, the complaint continued. "He shot through the wall to scare 'em," added Dick Griffey. "The hole is still there."

Suge was often accused of this sort of intimidation. Many alleged victims declined to press charges, citing a fear of retaliation. This case played out differently. Under a plea bargain, Knight pleaded no contest to two counts of assault, receiving a nine-year prison sentence that would be suspended so long as he completed five years of probation. According to the Stanley brothers, Deputy District Attorney Lawrence Longo had urged them to accept a subpar deal. It turned out that Knight rented Longo's Malibu home in 1996, for $19,000 per month plus a hefty commission. And that wasn't all: A few months earlier, Longo's eighteen-year-old daughter Gina signed a recording contract with Death Row, reportedly for $50,000. Longo was fired from the DA's office in 1997 and disciplined by the state Bar.

The case gave insight into Suge's MO. Using the three main incentives at his disposal—brute force, money, and access to the entertainment industry—he became a master manipulator. "Suge is the kind of dude to piss on your leg and laugh because he's 350 pounds and he knows you ain't really fittin' to do shit," said D.O.C. "He got sort of a kick out of that kind of shit. So the more power he got, the more outrageous he got."

Westward Swing

Despite Suge's shenanigans—or perhaps because of them—the stars had begun to align for Death Row, Inc., by late 1992. They only had one product to sell, but that product was exquisite. *The Chronic* became a massive hit upon its December release. Videos for "Nuthin' But a 'G' Thang," "Dre Day," and "Let Me Ride" soon dominated MTV, and the first two tracks cracked *Billboard*'s Top 10. The album sold over three million copies, and is largely credited with doing in pop rappers like Vanilla Ice and MC Hammer, under whose feet the ground suddenly shifted.

Despite Interscope's confidence, *The Chronic*'s pop breakout was unexpected. N.W.A never had much chart success with their singles, because most radio programmers refused to play them. The smart money had the same fate befalling first single "Nuthin' But a 'G' Thang," which similarly had trouble getting into rotation—at first.

"We can't get it played on the radio," Jimmy Iovine said the radio guys told him.

"It's 'Satisfaction,'" he retorted.

"Radio doesn't think so. They think it's a bunch of black guys cursing who want to kill everybody."

Iovine decided to create a minute-long commercial, consisting of nothing but the song. "Don't say who it is, and buy it on fifty stations, drive time. I want the program directors to hear it in their cars."

It wasn't program directors who were swayed. It was the listeners themselves, kids who called in requesting the song in droves. This populist wellspring set the music industry hype machine in motion. Before long, Dr. Dre was being promoted on the same stations as Aerosmith, Whitney Houston, and U2. He and Snoop got the September 30, 1993, *Rolling Stone* cover. Soon they didn't seem out of place among other popular acts of the day. "It's my business to know these things," said Interscope's promotion director Marc Benesch, "and there's no difference between the people that are going out and buying the Dre album and the people that are buying Guns N' Roses."

Guns N' Roses, N.W.A's rock counterparts had with great fanfare in 1991, released a pair of albums, *Use Your Illusion I* and *II*, their melo-dramatic follow-ups to the lean and mean *Appetite for Destruction*. The group's core lineup would soon split apart, and rock's mainstream dominance was beginning to unravel. Though Seattle grunge, led by Nirvana and Pearl Jam, was briefly ascendant in the early nineties, it wouldn't survive the fallout of Kurt Cobain's suicide in 1994, which inspired an industry identity crisis spawning forgettable subgenres like post-grunge, mainstream alternative, and nu-metal.

Hip-hop, meanwhile, was birthing one classic after another. The genre's golden age had kicked off in the late eighties: De La Soul's progressive, brainy musings had mass appeal, while the Beastie Boys traveled to Los Angeles and recast themselves as sonic innovators on their sophomore album *Paul's Boutique*. In the early nineties A Tribe Called Quest changed the game with their jazz-fueled meditations, while Wu-Tang Clan caused mayhem with their grimy, brutal lyricism on *Enter the Wu-Tang (36 Chambers)*. On the West Coast, the Pharcyde's *Bizarre Ride II the Pharcyde* was emotionally honest and hilarious, while Oakland's Souls of Mischief offered warm, acrobatic poetry on *'93 'til Infinity*.

The Chronic came to be considered one of the very best albums in rap history. Notorious B.I.G.'s *Ready to Die* also gets some votes, and the most frequently mentioned for the top spot is Nas's *Illmatic*, a dark, gritty reflection on urban dangers wrought by poverty. That came out in 1994. Two years before, *The Chronic* swung hip-hop's center of gravity dramatically westward, finally establishing Los Angeles's dominance after years as rap's redheaded stepchild. When I started writing about hip-hop in the mid-2000s, virtually every rapper-producer duo I talked to, from all parts of the country, expressed their desires to be the next Snoop and Dre.

"Fire" in a Crowded Theater

In summer 1993, the Death Row artists toured with acts including the Geto Boys and Run-D.M.C., performing on an elaborate set that included a live band and an actual '64 Chevy Impala. But with *The Chronic*'s success came controversy, which still continues today. It inspired a rash of imitators, and gangsta tropes began to choke out almost everything else.

"The gangsta element is 2 to 3 percent of our culture, but it's portrayed in the media as 98 percent," said Ben Caldwell, an outspoken critic of the subgenre who ran the I Fresh rap workshop in Leimert Park in the eighties. "It would be better if they could rap about something other than shooting someone in the head. We need to think about feeding and clothing our children, but this takes us back to the very beginning."

Though he called gangsta rap simply an "extension" of an already violent culture, Jesse Jackson called for a boycott of the record companies selling it. "It is not a question of censorship," said Al Sharpton. "You have the right of free speech in this country, but you don't have the right to yell 'fire' in a crowded theater. And that is what some of these records are doing. They are yelling 'shoot' in a community that is crowded with guns."

Some hip-hop voices of conscience lamented the rise of gangsta rap. "Before, we had people that was teaching, in New York," Afrika Bambaataa told a Columbia University audience in October 1993. "You had X-Clan, you had Public Enemy, you had KRS, and they was [painting] pictures that was waking up people. Then this whole thing came from the West Coast, which, I'm sorry to say, was negativity. Those are still my brothers, but they was teaching negativity."

"Gangsta rap was highly financed and endorsed more than Afrocentric rap," said Chuck D. "I never got mad at my peers. I just got angry at the puppeteers."

The gangsta rap spawned by *The Chronic*—which often embraces a nihilistic, "get mine" philosophy and continues to dominate today— barely resembles the righteous hardcore of Chuck D's heyday. The political messages of Boogie Down Productions, Public Enemy, and *Straight Outta Compton* were largely stripped as gangsta rap matured, leaving a hollow shell of macho tropes performed by bulletproof vest–clad rebels without a cause. One could argue that Dr. Dre led the genre in that direction. *No medallions, dreadlocks, or black fists*, he rapped on "Let Me Ride." Though *Chronic* tracks "The Day the Niggaz Took Over" and "Lil' Ghetto Boy" (a poignant update of Donny Hathaway's 1972 song of the same name) show solidarity with the oppressed, Dre was more concerned with his bank account than his message. He removed an anticop song called "Mr. Officer" from *The Chronic*, explaining: "Making money is more important to me than talking about killing police."

CHAPTER SIXTEEN

IT'S ON

When Eazy-E first heard *The Chronic*, he tried to convince himself it wasn't any good. Listening to each song briefly and then skipping to the next one, he flippantly assessed them to MC Ren.

"That shit's whack," he said. "That shit's whack, too."

Ren shook his head. It was hot. *Anyone* could tell. If Eazy faced facts, he was too hurt to honestly assess the work. He and Dre had been friends for years, after all. They'd built an empire together. Sure, they'd fallen out over money, but their bond had been stronger than music industry bullshit. Hadn't it?

The success of *The Chronic* compounded Eazy-E's humiliation. Sure, he was getting paid a percentage of its sales, which was nice, but the general public didn't know that. And anyone who knew Dre knew that he wasn't actually gunning for Eazy's life. But the fact was, this *looked* bad. Eazy had carefully cultivated an image as the hardest gangsta on the block. And now he was a laughingstock. It wasn't just the attacks on the album, it was the "Dre Day" video and Snoop's jokes, like his comparison of Heller and Eazy to Mr. Roarke and Tattoo, that is, *Fantasy Island*'s overlord and his diminutive sidekick.

Like any self-respecting street boss, Eazy's first instinct was to come back twice as hard: to craft a diss record scathing enough to send Dre scurrying under a rock. But his timing was bad. In this pre-YouTube era, rap beef moved at the speed of molasses. In fact, Eazy had released a solo EP, *5150: Home 4 tha Sick*, just a few days *before The Chronic* dropped. (5150 is the California code authorizing involuntary confinement of someone with a mental disorder.) Though it kicks off with a taunt in the vague direction of his former collaborator—*You thought I couldn't do it without ya!*—*5150* doesn't address Dre by name. The work is largely forgettable, save for a fun appearance by Rudy Ray Moore—aka Dolemite, Eazy-E's comedic godfather. The album went gold, with more than 500,000 copies sold, a flop considering Eazy's previous platinum sales history. Nowadays, it's hardly remembered.

In late 1992 Ruthless Records was at a creative nadir. Eazy's world-beating producer and his game-changing ghostwriters were gone. But some new talent was brewing. *5150* featured the debut of an eighteen-year-old rapper named Will 1X. He, like Dresta, Dirty Red, Dismost, and others, was recruited as a ghostwriter, and he was part of a jazzy, conscious group called Atban Klann, which stood for "A Tribe Beyond a Nation."

From the start, Will was a multi-hyphenate talent, a writer, rapper, producer, and even video director; Heller was impressed with his group's promotional film for their song "Puddles of H2O," shot for a tiny budget. But Will 1X's brief appearance on *5150*'s holiday-themed "Merry Muthafuckin' XMas" is bizarre, including lines like:

> *A Jew will eat some matzoh ball soup, but a nigga will eat some*
> *Chicken and chitlins, watermelon, corn bread and some Fruit Loops*

Will 1X would later be known as will.i.am, and Atban Klann would morph into the Black Eyed Peas, later adding hit-making singer Fergie. It was an inauspicious start for the man who became one of the most successful rappers and producers of his era. "He would tell me, 'Your songs don't match the energy of your freestyles,'" will.i.am said. "Years later we would sell out stadiums, sell millions of albums, and travel the fucking planet. [Eazy] saw that before we even figured that out."

Apart from a few pockets of ingenuity at Ruthless, no one seemed particularly motivated. Producer Rhythm D smelled the stench of defeat when he walked into Eazy-E's Norwalk home around this time. Morale was low. Bodyguards were lying around on couches, while Ruthless affiliates watched LaserDiscs from Eazy's library or were out driving his luxury cars. The house boasted a top-of-the-line studio, armed with equipment like a brand-new E-mu SP-1200 drum machine and sampler. But nobody was using it.

Rhythm D had come over to play Eazy his beats. It was something of an audition for the tall, light-skinned South Central producer, whose career was on the rise thanks to his hit track for Los Angeles rapper Paperboy, "Ditty." During a dalliance with Death Row, Rhythm D also made a song for the *Deep Cover* soundtrack called "Down with My Nigga," featuring rapper Paradise. But he was broke, and anxious for his next payday. To Eazy's house he brought with him a green tackle box. Rather than fishing lures, it held a floppy disk of his beats.

While Rhythm cued up his songs, Eazy ducked into the shower. He seemed to have only half his mind on the proceedings. Undaunted, Rhythm plugged in his speakers and played a beat. It featured him and producer Battlecat going back and forth, trying to outdo each other with samples. The track had a wild energy about it, which Eazy felt immediately. He jumped out of the shower, hair all crazy, throwing on a towel and running into the room.

"You rollin' with Ruthless," he exclaimed, signing Rhythm to one of his famous, impromptu record deals. After hearing the rest of his beats (and putting on his clothes) he paid Rhythm $5,000 cash, which he produced from inside his socks.

Rhythm immediately moved into the house and got to work. The job description: Ruthless's newest in-house producer.

Here Comes My Left Blow

Rhythm quickly realized he would have to do more than just make songs. He was going to have to shake Eazy out of his creative coma. He wasn't himself lately. The conflicts with Suge and Dre had taken a toll. It probably didn't help that, not long ago, Eazy had taken to smoking weed.

None of the guys really got high while they were in N.W.A. Once Eazy started, however, he went all the way. Not long after *The Chronic* came out he smoked weed constantly, with his artists, friends like *Friday* actor Faizon Love, or by himself. He favored joints, rolled with brown Rizla papers coated with licorice. "He would say, 'Burn a brown one,'" said rapper Steffon.

Eazy even started selling again. During downtime at his Calabasas kitchen table, he bagged up dime bags and eighths.

"Why do you do that? You're a millionaire," his assistant Charis Henry asked him.

"It makes me feel like I'm still in the street," he said.

He wasn't running a giant operation; he handed out weed to struggling rappers or old Compton buddies more as a favor, to help them put money in their pockets. For his artists he used it as a creative lubricant, giving them as much free dope as they wanted. When he signed the introspective MC Steffon (a former dancer who'd cohosted *Pump It Up!* with Dee Barnes), he presented him with an entire grocery bag's worth of bud, a signing bonus of sorts to go along with his $7,500 advance. Steffon was grateful enough not to complain that it smelled like insecticide.

Did the weed make him foggy? How had the man who'd made gangsta rap into a multimillion-dollar business lost sight of which way the hip-hop winds were blowing? He'd been putting his head together with the members of Naughty By Nature. Sure, they were an undoubtedly hot group—their early nineties hits included "O.P.P.," "Everything's Gonna Be Alright," and "Hip Hop Hooray"—but they were from New Jersey, and their sound was more "of the moment" than "of the future." Their contributions to *5150: Home 4 tha Sick* (some production and ghostwriting) hadn't saved it.

Rhythm had sat in on *The Chronic* recording sessions, and had a strong feeling that G-funk was about to take over. After much arguing he convinced Eazy that their "Dre Day" response should include the haunting new gangsta sound. But what about the song's message? How could they hit Dre back where it hurt?

Rhythm lit up a fat one and got to thinking. Sure, Dre was the hotshot producer of the gangsta sound. But there was a big difference between *sounding* like a gangsta and *being* a gangsta. To the guys in the streets this was not incidental.

They needed to convince these guys that Dre was phony, an opportunist. After all, not long ago, while Eazy was out hustling and getting into trouble, Dre was dancing on stage and wearing makeup and fitted suits in the World Class Wreckin' Cru. Eazy was *authentic*. He was *real*. It was time to drive that point home. Rhythm stayed up all night one night in 1993, fashioning the template for the song that would become "Real Muthaphuckkin G's," or, on the radio, "Real Compton City G's."

Mirroring the tempo of "Dre Day," the track also features a high-pitched Moog squeal. But it sounds even more intimidating, owing largely to Eazy's performance. Eazy hadn't been regarded as a deft rapper in his early days, but by now he'd come into his own. No one had to "punch him in" line for line anymore, like Dre had during the recording of "The Boyz-N-the Hood." The pace of "Real Compton City G's" suited him, and his own eerie instrument—a "demonic, gnome type of voice," Rhythm D called it—fit the track's tone. And so, in the studio, Eazy launched into a series of disses and rebuttals.

> *All of the sudden Dr. Dre is the "G" thang*
> *But on his old album covers he was a she-thang*

The song took aim at Snoop (*Tell me where the fuck you found an anorexic rapper*) and the tense situation at Death Row (*I hear you're getting treated like boot camp*). It featured Eazy-E's newest, toughest recruits: Dresta, who had recently emerged from prison for assault, and who wrote the hook and Eazy's verses, and Dresta's younger brother B.G. Knocc Out. Both of them were Nutty Blocc Crips whom Eazy met through a connection from Watts's Jordan Downs projects. As was often the case in the gangsta rap nineties, when choosing a rapping partner, it helped to have someone who could also back you up in a fight. The brothers disputed that Dre was even *from* Compton, but mostly focused on his lack of gangsta credibility.

The song's accompanying EP *It's On (Dr. Dre) 187um Killa* contained a photo of Dre in his snug-fitting doctor's outfit from his World Class Wreckin' Cru photo shoot, with arrows pointing out his "eye shadow," "eyeliner," "lipstick," and "sequins." In an era before Google, the mere existence of this photo probably came as a surprise to many Dre fans.

The disses were disingenuous at times. Sure, Dre hadn't lived his whole childhood in Compton, but he'd spent much of it there, including in a house not far from Eazy himself. As for getting glammed up, that was overstated, and besides Eazy knew about all of that when he signed on with Dre for N.W.A, and it didn't bother him back then.

The particulars aside, one thing was clear: Eazy was back on message. On Arsenio Hall's show he called Dre a "studio gangsta." Hall asked him to define the term for Middle America. "Somebody that's not real. They go in the studio and all of the sudden become hard, when they used to do dance music."

Arsenio was not impressed. "Why don't y'all just make up?"

"He already made up," Eazy quipped. "You ain't never seen him with the lipstick?"

It's On (Dr. Dre) 187um Killa contained more serious invective. The producer's name on the cover is crossed out, similar to gang-style graffiti threatening someone's death. As *The Chronic* did for Dre, the album clearly reinvigorated Eazy creatively, and also featured his trademarked bawdy humor. ("Gimme That Nutt," somehow, has become a classic.) The EP sold over two million copies.

Eazy was soon making more big plans. In 1993 he and MC Ren talked to Fab Five Freddy at a screening of *CB4*, the Tamra Davis–directed mockumentary featuring an N.W.A-like group. The film's star Chris Rock was on the scene as well, asking half nervously if the pair planned to kick his ass. Eazy said no, but that his girl group Gangsta Bitch Mentality would.

Ultimately the male rappers declared the movie "cool," and Eazy also took the opportunity during the Fab Five Freddy interview to announce that N.W.A was getting back together. It would be him, Ren, DJ Yella, and even Ice Cube—but without Dre, because they were "staying sucka free in '93." Yella, Cold 187um, and other producers were to handle the music, and it's possible Eazy still controlled some Dre productions that could be used for an N.W.A album—even without his consent. But this sounded like a bad idea to Ren. "I told him an N.W.A album is not gonna work without Dre doing the beats," he said. This disagreement drove a wedge between Eazy and Ren, and the pair didn't talk for more than a year, Ren said.

Yella hoped these conflicts wouldn't last.

"He only did ['Real Muthaphuckkin G's'] because Dre came at him first," Yella said, adding that Eazy was hurt when Dre left.

Eazy had his swagger back, but Compton's police chief still denied him a permit to film the "Real Muthaphuckkin G's" video in town. When Eazy tried to get the decision overturned, mayor Omar Bradley responded with a lecture. "[W]hen the mayor of Compton goes to New York, he's a joke. He's a joke because they think the city is full of animals," Bradley said to the video's white director, Marty Thomas. To Eazy, he added: "And you don't even have the courtesy to hire black people to direct or orchestrate this film."

Then for good measure he threw in some anti-Semitism. "I won't name the specific racial group that's using you, brother, but they are destroying us and having a lunch and a bar mitzvah at the same time," Bradley shouted. "And we know from history that the minute they get finished making money off of you, you'll be sitting beside Mike Tyson [in prison]."

In the end, Bradley allowed the video shoot. He even showed up at an auto body strip mall on the chilly day of the filming, clad in a Malcolm X hat and a scarf, as did droves of Compton gangbangers, to serve as extras. Eazy wore his Raiders cap, baggy Pendleton over a bulletproof vest, and fingerless black gloves. The resulting work is a pretty intimidating little piece of cinema. The brawny Dresta carries a softball bat, and Eazy swings his arms viciously at the camera while he raps. As for the Eazy-E impersonator from "Dre Day"? In an inspired move, they enlisted actor A. J. Johnson to reprise his role—a bumbling, caricatured version of Eazy. Only this time, the character is chased out of town.

So, who won this showdown, Eazy or Dre? You could say they both did, as it reignited both of their careers. But one could argue that hip-hop ultimately lost, as their dispute had far-reaching consequences. Beef wasn't anything new in hip-hop. It went back at least as far as 1981, when the party-starting MC Busy Bee declared his supremacy at a New York rap contest, only to be one-upped by Treacherous Three rapper Kool Moe Dee, who came back with a venomous freestyle that changed the whole tenor of the genre. But they were friends before, during, and after this exchange.

Previously, rap confrontations had been about who was superior on the microphone. The emerging Ruthless–Death Row battle was about who was the toughest in real life. "That was the first time I began to think, man. This is going in a different direction now," said journalist Kevin Powell.

Hellraiser

For all these diss songs' jokes and barbs, neither side considered the dispute a laughing matter. They prepared their squads. Rhythm D was matched up with a bodyguard brought in by Mike Klein, named Big Animal, and was told not to go anywhere besides the house and the studio.

Eazy had his own hulking bodyguards, including Big Ron and a pair of three-hundred-pound, goateed Samoan brothers named Jacob and John, aka the Twins. He was glad to have them. He was often stressed out and waking up at absurdly early hours. He turned to acupuncture in hopes of relieving tension, having needles stuck into his head that made him look like the *Hellraiser* figure he had at his house.

Ruthless launched a Saturday night radio show on local station 92.3

The Beat, featuring friend of the label DJ Julio G at the controls. He asked Eazy if he could play tracks from *The Chronic*. Eazy said yes—since he was getting paid off it, after all—but Suge Knight was not amused, making threats that inspired the station to heighten security. When Eazy heard about this he laughed, Julio G said, and told him to play *even more* Death Row music.

The Death Row and Ruthless camps encountered each other in person following the 1994 Billboard Music Awards at Universal Amphitheater. Death Row artists had assembled to support Snoop, who won the prize for top male music artist. After the ceremony they and their entourages spilled out onto Universal CityWalk, an outdoor shopping tourist trap.

Death Row were "like three hundred deep," B.G. Knocc Out said. "Real Compton City G's" had been nominated for an award as well, but the Ruthless camp was smaller, mainly just B.G., Dresta, Eazy, and a few bodyguards. Like something out of the old West, the groups stared each other down, and approached slowly. From the front of the pack, Suge made his way over to Eazy, putting his arm around his shoulders in what seemed like an effort to intimidate him. The foot soldiers got to barking at each other as well. But before things could get too heated, Michael Concepcion—the Crips OG and "We're All in the Same Gang" orchestrator—intervened. "It's not gonna go down like that," he said. "Not the time or place."

Death Row backed off, but the Ruthless crew worried they hadn't seen the last of them. And so, B.G. said, they sent one of their associates back home, who quickly returned with an armory's worth of firearms. "We all got a pistol, stepped outside, and pushed up on Suge and them, like, 'What y'all want to do?'" B.G. continued. They backed off. "We went our way, they went their own way."

Kurupt said his camp had indeed been ready to jump into action if they received the word. "We were waiting for Suge to say, 'It's that time,'" he remembered.

Violence between the labels actually did break out at an even more unlikely setting, an L.A. area golf course. The occasion was the 1995 filming of Def Jam artist Montell Jordan's video "Somethin' 4 da Honeyz," the latest single from the South Central new jack swing crooner, known for his smash, "This Is How We Do It." A multitude of rap celebrities were present, including Redman and Wu-Tang Clan's Method Man. Another Def Jam artist, Warren G, brought with him his Long Beach associates Snoop and Nate, the brothers Dogg.

Dresta and B.G. Knocc Out, who, in addition to recording with Eazy were also signed to Def Jam, watched warily as Nate Dogg approached. He rode up in a golf cart with comedian Ricky Harris, and began yelling out his gang affiliations, B.G. said. The parties disagreed about who initiated the dispute, but B.G. said Nate promptly crushed his foot with the cart. "I had on brand-new shoes for one, and then he ran over my big toe," B.G. said. The pair exchanged heated words. "So I bombed on him. Bam!"

It's unclear what happened next. A blurry online video appears to show Nate Dogg swinging a golf club at an unarmed Dresta, making contact with a terrifying *crack* near the back of his neck. In the next frame some blond girls scamper quickly out of frame, while B.G. and Dresta grab clubs themselves—short-range irons, it looks like. Eventually security intervenes, and Dresta tosses his club away.

Though the golf course incident appears almost goofy on the video, the lines between on-record beefs and real-life disputes had begun to blur, a dangerous precedent that set the tone for hip-hop's dark times ahead.

CHAPTER SEVENTEEN

WHAT'S MY NAME?

Long Beach, California, once tried to sell itself as a balmy paradise, and was known during the mid-twentieth century as "Iowa by the sea" for its influx of Midwesterners fleeing winter. To give you a sense of how things changed: I was born in Iowa, but never knew of the Southern California city until I heard the line: *Compton and Long Beach together, now you know you got trouble.*

Today Long Beach—also known as the LBC—possesses haves and have-nots in seemingly equal measure. The city, the second biggest in Los Angeles County, is known both for gang-ridden neighborhoods and touristy waterfront spots like the Queen Mary, the majestic former ocean liner now permanently docked and doubling as a hotel. The Virginia Country Club neighborhood, site of the *Ferris Bueller* house, isn't far from the storied Carmelitos Housing Project, where a postal worker once refused to deliver mail unaccompanied in 1989.

The city has reinvented itself frequently over the years. In the 1920s it boasted one of the world's top oil fields. A naval shipyard opened during World War II, while a vast aerospace industry churned out military planes. Oil production slowed, and the shipyard downsized before closing for good in 1995. Boeing shut down its massive C-17 plant in 2015. During Snoop Dogg's childhood downtown was listless, until investments in business and tourism infrastructure during the Reagan years began reviving it. Today a booming cultural scene encompasses everything from craft breweries to art galleries.

Downtown Long Beach now gleams, and harbor resorts, parks, and a popular aquarium line the surrounding Queensway Bay and Los Angeles River. Nearby, the forebodingly named Terminal Island houses the Los Angeles and Long Beach ports, the largest of their kind in the country. The ports are a city unto themselves, a maze of roads, overpasses, and railways accommodating giant tractor-trailers, trains, and cargo ships. Sprawling bureaucracy and cutting-edge technology coexist side by side, and the landscape is dotted with towering cranes and multicolored shipping containers. (There's a federal prison there, too.)

The contrast between rich and poor feels more stark here than in Los Angeles, forty minutes north but a world apart. Plenty of Long Beach residents commute there, but the city of nearly half a million is its own center of gravity. It's tremendously diverse. LBC hometown music luminaries include Latin pop icon Jenni Rivera, stoner punk heroes Sublime, indie psychedelic rockers Crystal Antlers, and hip-hop melody makers the Dove Shack. Cameron Diaz and Snoop went to high school together in Long Beach, where she said she was "pretty sure" she bought weed from him. The city has a strong southern black influence and boasts many Baptist churches, as well as long-entrenched Cambodian, Samoan, and Chicano immigrant populations. Each of these ethnic groups has its own street gangs, like the famous Mexican set East Side Longos. Acclaimed local rapper Vince Staples represents the Crips; still, he said his Compton-native parents moved him to adjacent Long Beach for a safer upbringing. "Long Beach is like the next step to getting out of the ghetto," he said.

Snoop attended the well-regarded Long Beach Polytechnic High School, also known as Poly, where you can even take Japanese. For his first video, 1993's "What's My Name?," a huge crowd of kids getting out of school came across the street to VIP Records, and waved their hands like they just didn't care. Ensconced in a strip mall, VIP was the city's quintessential hip-hop landmark; you probably recognize its roof, which Snoop raps on top of in "What's My Name?" next to its towering sign with a man with his hands in his pockets. (The store, its demise long predicted, was slated to shut for good in late 2015, with plans to go online.)

This is the east side of Long Beach, repped by Snoop and his colleagues, including Snoop's group, Tha Eastsidaz. He spent some of his childhood in North Long Beach, near the intersection of East Sixty-First Street and Linden Avenue, a neighborhood with multifamily buildings and handsomely built homes that have fallen into disrepair. Snoop's upbringing wasn't all bleak. He played football in the Pop Warner youth league, and at Poly excelled on the basketball court. But gang culture and the easy money of the drug trade beckoned. Snoop's gang was the Rollin' 20s Crips, so named both for their territory (areas surrounding East Twentieth Street) and because of their original preferred transportation mode—mopeds. Dating back to the late seventies and early eighties, the Rollin' 20s originally considered themselves "hustlers," making money however they could, which is another reason for their name—their pockets were fat with twenties. Their local rivals the Insane Crips, meanwhile, were the more violent "enforcers." "We were insane, and we were going to live up to the name, period," said Long Beach rapper Tray Dee, a longtime Insane Crips member.

The Crip subsets are also differentiated by their preferred NFL teams. Snoop and the Rollin' 20s favor the Pittsburgh Steelers—hence his bus I saw parked outside of his Inglewood compound. "I grew up watching them in the seventies. Mean Joe Greene, Terry Bradshaw, those guys," he told me. When the Rollin' 20s are not wearing blue, they sport black and gold, while the Insane Crips prefer Raiders colors, black and silver. Along the way the two sets got to beefing with each other. The rivalry is serious, but not all consuming. Snoop's cousin and *Doggystyle* cover artist, Joe Cool, for example, has been a member of the Insanes, as has Tray Dee, from Snoop's trio Tha Eastsidaz.

Snoop maintained that joining a gang was hardly a choice, after his childhood friends were swallowed up. "When the other set come by to rock, they're not going to say, 'OK we know he don't bang, we going to just shoot them two,'" he said. "They're going to ride on everybody. So you're a victim of society regardless."

You Drink Whiskey, I Drink Wine

Nate Dogg and Warren G were caught up in similar circumstances. Born Nathaniel Hale, Nate joined the Marines following his graduation from Poly, and upon his return he, like Snoop, came to loggerheads with his mother. "I didn't want to be no damn police, so my mom was like, 'You grown, you got to leave,'" he said. He and Snoop lived in hotels together, hustled, and put whatever money they could save into their songs. Nate started out rapping but, having trained in the choir, gravitated toward singing his rhymes instead.

Warren G was Snoop's longtime friend from summer youth sports programs. He'd acquired his love of music from his father, Warren Griffin Sr., who married Dr. Dre's mother and loved jazz. He would put on a record and walk around the house watering the plants, or maybe light up some incense. "He would dip off in the other room—I knew what he was doing. He'd act like I didn't know, but I knew," said Warren G.

After high school Warren scraped by working at El Pollo Loco, Burger King, and, for a time, as a shipyards fire watchman. He and Snoop had already joined forces as hip-hop group Voltron Crew, along with others including Dewayne and Deon Williams, later known as Warren G's rap duo Twinz. Warren's rapping skills weren't too hot in those days, and so, to impress his friends, he'd steal his stepbrother Dr. Dre's lyrics from World Class Wreckin' Cru songs. "They used to think I was hard as shit," he said, laughing.

Snoop was more advanced. Inspired by the Sugarhill Gang, he'd begun rapping at the dawn of the eighties, before he'd even made it to junior high. He credits Warren with helping train him to freestyle. He'd point to, say, Snoop's shoes, and Snoop would rattle off a verse about them. With Nate they formed a group called 213, named for their Long Beach area code. (They were inspired by Oakland act 415; nobody shows hometown pride better than rappers.) Their white friend Money B made some beats for them, and 213 recorded their first song, "Long Beach Is a Motherfucker," at his house. Nate Dogg sang, Snoop rapped, and the aspiring DJ Warren G scratched.

The tape gained popularity locally, and the trio caught a break when Rodger Clayton of Uncle Jamm's Army began hosting them at a downtown club he promoted called the Toe Jam. Warren G kicked off sets by leading the crowd in a chant: *You drink whiskey, I drink wine. Come on everybody it's gangster time!* Before long they began recording at the back of VIP Records. The store's owner Kelvin Anderson set up a little studio and even bought a drum machine.

Snoop kept getting busted for coke and thrown in jail. He wasn't always gone for very long—maybe eight months or so—but it wore on the other members. Even fellow inmates implored him to get his act together; he was wasting his talents. Finally, during a stretch at the Pitchess Detention Center, known as Wayside, Warren G made a plea: Music may not get them rich, like slanging, but they should do it anyway. "Let's just be broke and work hard at what we want to do, music," he said. (He later recalled the conversation in his song "Do You See.") When Snoop emerged he'd sprouted like a weed, owing to a late growth spurt, and was full of determination.

There was still the matter of a record deal. VIP's Anderson had no luck shopping their demo to labels (213 would only release a proper album years later, after its members were already famous). Their most obvious connection—Dr. Dre—wasn't giving them the time of day. "Warren was coming at me in a crazy way about his group 213, but it was a 'big brother, little brother' kind of thing going on," Dre said. "Like, 'Yeah yeah, OK, I'll listen to it when I get a chance.'" But the group's fortunes turned at a 1991 bachelor party Dre put on for a friend. During a lull in the music, Warren retrieved his 213 tape, popped it in the stereo, and Dre—caught off guard—heard it with fresh ears.

"What *is* this?" he asked.

"That's Snoop, that's who I've been telling you about!"

Dre immediately set up a studio session. Snoop couldn't believe his luck. "Stop lying," he said when told Dre wanted to speak to him. Snoop was about to have his big break, though Warren would remain overlooked.

Tha Shiznit

In these halcyon early days, Suge Knight stressed that the Death Row members were a team. Rather than hoarding songs for themselves, everyone was to contribute their best efforts to the label's upcoming releases. Following *The Chronic*, next up was Snoop's solo album *Doggystyle*, to be followed by Kurupt and Daz (as Tha Dogg Pound). Eventually, Suge promised, all the supporting players—Lady of Rage, Nate Dogg, *everyone*—would get a chance to shine.

In the meantime, it was easy to get caught up in the excitement. With *The Chronic*'s success, even a loose affiliation with Death Row gained you access to the hottest clubs and parties. In his memoir, Dre's assistant Bruce Williams describes private soirees thrown by an associate named Party Man (seriously), which featured gambling and a VIP room with women "in G-strings servin' drinks" and others "who'd [perform fellatio]."

It's amazing any work got done at all, and it almost didn't. Whereas *The Chronic* was recorded fairly expeditiously, *Doggystyle* dragged, partly because the group kept getting booted from production spaces. "'Cause we were having a bunch of fun," Dr. Dre said. "A lot of the people that worked at these studios didn't understand our type of fun."

They may have been partying, and they may have been cocky, but most everyone in this cohort was performing at the height of their talents. D.O.C. mentored Snoop closely and helped him write. "We would stay up to two or three in the morning at his house, playing video games and drinking beer," Snoop said. "Then we'd go off and write rhymes and record them on cassette and deliver them to Dre the next day." Dre recruited a crack crew of new session musicians to tighten the sound, and success seemed inevitable.

Some critics pegged *Doggystyle* as a sequel to *The Chronic*, and indeed it features the same rappers and singers, as well as Moog and P-Funk samples galore. George Clinton himself was on hand to keep the proceedings funky. On "Who Am I (What's My Name)?" the chorus from Clinton's 1982 track "Atomic Dog"—*A-tom-ic doooooggg*—was retrofitted to introduce our hero—*Snoop Doggy Dooooooggg*. "Atomic Dog" is, in fact, one of the most borrowed-from songs in history. It's been sampled (or mimicked) in over two hundred different songs, with its "bow wow wow yippie yo yippie yay" refrain particularly ubiquitous, heard on tracks including "Fuck Wit Dre Day." Yet "Who Am I (What's My Name)?" brings a driving energy all its own, along with crunching bass, robotic talk box, and Snoop's inimitable singsong.

The album's enduring second single "Gin and Juice" remains the quintessential G-funk party anthem. Whether or not you believe Tanqueray and chronic are appropriate elixirs for driving, the track's breezy tempo and high-pitched whistle are practically Pavlovian in the way they inspire head bobs. "Ain't No Fun," the album's wildly misogynistic tribute to group sex, is an unlikely dance floor staple. *It ain't no fun, if the homies can't have none*, Nate Dogg sings on the chorus, making the whole thing sound perfectly normal. It also has Kurupt's most famous line: *If Kurupt gave a fuck about a bitch, I'd always be broke / I'd never have no motherfucking indo to smoke*. Never mind the false dilemma of pitting one's women against one's weed; Kurupt insists he was showing off his softer side. "Snoop was like, 'You can't kill everybody, you have to make records people can relate to,'" he said. "Sometimes you have to talk about reality."

Was "Ain't No Fun" reality? Absolutely, said Warren G, who is also featured on the song. "We had a lot of women and they was with it, too. Shit. We was having fun—it was protected. They'd have a bunch of their friends and we'd have a bunch of our guys and we'd just...*fuck*!"

As a performer, Snoop met and then promptly exceeded everyone's expectations. The world is full of rappity-rap-rappers, but he offered up his sui generis melodic stamp throughout, riding (rather than wrangling) the beat and letting it take him where it would. "Tha Shiznit" was entirely freestyled, while "Lodi Dodi" remade "La Di Da Di," the 1985 Doug E. Fresh and Slick Rick classic, Snoopifying it through details like the part where he throws on his brand-new doggy underwear.

Doggystyle features *Chronic*-style gangsta themes as well, on tracks like "For All My Niggaz and Bitches" and "Serial Killa." *I got the machine that cracks your fuckin' chest plates* raps RBX on the latter. On "Who Am

I (What's My Name)?" Snoop threatens: "I kill dem blood clots," which angered some L.A. Bloods.

Nothing could stop it. Dre's track record and Snoop's buzz made *Doggystyle* one of the most anticipated, hyped albums in history. Owing to production problems, its release was delayed. At one point, eager to get the album to the pressing plant, Suge and Jimmy Iovine began breathing down Chris "The Glove" Taylor's neck while he edited a final track. "They told me that it would cost them $42,000 for every hour that it went over. They had trucks lined up, and they were waiting to ship it," The Glove said.

Doggystyle's extravagant record release party was held on November 22, 1993, on a yacht embarking from beachside suburb Marina del Rey. Coolio, Queen Latifah, and other celebrities boarded the 165-foot vessel, called *Lord Hornblower*, but it quickly reached capacity and did not complete its pleasure cruise as planned. Brawls broke out both on land—when dozens of people were refused entry—and on board. "A fight broke out on the main deck, in a dance floor area," said The Glove. "It became a riot." Snoop broke up a squabble, but the ship's captain called the sheriff's department, and seventy deputies quickly arrived. Soon police and TV helicopters were circling overhead.

The LAPD sought to question partygoers as they left the boat, but the Nation of Islam, who was providing security, intervened. The Glove said about fifty bow tie–wearing male members (known as Fruit of Islam) lined up shoulder to shoulder in the parking lot, to prevent cops from arresting the disembarking passengers. Before long the boys in blue were clashing with the Muslims. "It was one of the weirdest things that ever happened to me in my life," said The Glove. Somehow, amid all of this, there were no reported injuries

Doggystyle sold more than 800,000 copies in its first week, at the time the most ever for a debut. The work eventually went four times platinum, besting any N.W.A album and even *The Chronic*. While the latter work was a high-water mark for many critics, others counter that *Doggystyle* is actually superior. My former *L.A. Weekly* colleague Jeff Weiss feels that way, as does gangsta rap aficionado Chris Rock. "*The Chronic* is sonically incredible, but it's hard to drive around singing songs about, 'Eazy-E can eat a big fat dick,'" Rock wrote on his website. "But I got a feeling I'll be singing 'Gin and Juice' when I'm ninety."

Snoop was quickly becoming a household name. In March 1994, he was scheduled as the musical guest on *Saturday Night Live*—hosted by Helen Hunt—but he missed his first plane because Daz's weed man arrived late with the hookup. In the end Snoop caught another flight and made the taping.

CHAPTER EIGHTEEN

NEGATIVE RAP

Philip Woldemariam came to the U.S. from Ethiopia with his family. Before fleeing in 1979, they lived a middle-class life in the region of Eritrea, which was then engaged in a war for independence and later became its own country. The family moved to Idaho both to escape the violence and to help find better medical care for young Philip, who was diabetic, as insulin was growing increasingly difficult to find in their homeland. After Idaho they moved to the Palms neighborhood in Los Angeles, a working-class area bordered by the 405 and 10 freeways that, even today, has largely resisted gentrification. They hoped to start over in their new country. Instead, Woldemariam's life fell apart.

He received superior medical care and developed a love for basketball. But he had a difficult time growing up. He dropped out of high school, spent time in foster homes, and was jailed for gunplay. According to police, he joined a Palms-area gang called By Yerself Hustlers. Though his family moved to Long Beach, Woldemariam returned to Palms often, and at one point encountered a new resident in the neighborhood: Snoop Dogg. It's unclear how exactly they knew each other, but their crews were at odds. On August 25, 1993, they confronted each other. Woldemariam had just turned twenty, Snoop was twenty-one, and *Doggystyle* was three months away.

Woldemariam and two gang friends were on their way to Palms' Woodbine Park when he began arguing with a Snoop associate named Shawn

Abrams, in front of Snoop's apartment. They separated, and reports vary about what happened next. Within an hour, Snoop's bodyguard McKinley "Malik" Lee, Abrams, and Snoop were headed to a recording studio in the latter's SUV when they confronted Woldemariam's party, now at the park. Snoop was behind the wheel and Lee was armed. They later claimed they were attempting to resolve the situation when Woldemariam jumped out of the bushes and pulled up his shirt, revealing a .380 automatic handgun. "Either he was going to die or I was going to die," Lee said. He shot Woldemariam and Snoop peeled out. The Ethiopian immigrant stumbled into an alley before collapsing, and died soon after. Woldemariam's defenders contended that Lee was the aggressor, noting as evidence that the victim was shot in the back and the buttocks.

Though Lee said they promptly called 911, he and Snoop failed to turn themselves in. Snoop was out on bail for weapons charges (they would eventually be dismissed), and Lee said they weren't going to surrender without Death Row's attorney, David Kenner, who was then out of town. They went on the lam, and Snoop stayed in hiding for a full week, inspiring a dramatic manhunt that brought the LAPD and sheriff's department to the 1993 MTV Video Music Awards, held at Universal Amphitheater. Detectives were tipped off that Snoop would present an award, and indeed he did, for best R&B video, alongside Dre and George Clinton. The cops somehow still couldn't snag him, but following the show he turned himself in. He and Lee were charged with murder—1-8-7—and Death Row quickly posted his million-dollar bail.

The criminal case would stretch on for almost two and a half years, with Woldemariam's family accusing Snoop of using the murder charge against him for commercial gain. At the 1994 MTV Video Music Awards Snoop capitalized on his legal trouble, performing his new, fictionalized song "Murder Was the Case," whose lyrics begin with his character getting shot and falling into a coma. Wheeled on stage in a wheelchair, Snoop was accompanied by a full choir, before a giant cross hanging from the ceiling and a prop casket, which emitted a spotlight up toward the heavens. *It's going to take a miracle they say for me to walk again*, he rapped, before springing out of the chair. As the song finished Snoop proclaimed his innocence, and soon after released a short film of the same name. Again, its plot departs from real-life events, such as the scene where a pair of bumbling ambulance drivers, carting Snoop's dead body and smoking weed, engage in an epic gun battle, before crashing the ambulance and exploding.

The soundtrack featured "Natural Born Killaz," Ice Cube and Dr. Dre's first post-N.W.A collaboration, and went double platinum. But Snoop took little joy. Despite the cocksure posture he displayed in his videos, behind the scenes he desperately feared that everything he'd worked toward, his very freedom, was in jeopardy. "It was probably the worst two and a half years of my life," Snoop said.

Painted by the prosecution as a ruthless gangbanger, Snoop faced trial in the court of public opinion as well. The mainstream media had been poking nervously at gangsta rap for a number of years, but Snoop's charge, alongside his burgeoning popularity, sparked blanket coverage. Wearing a knit cap and looking surly he appeared on a November 1993 *Newsweek* cover alongside the headline "when is rap 2 violent?" "You may never have heard of some of these stars, but your kids have," warned Tom Brokaw, introducing a lengthy *NBC Nightly News* piece on the subject. Mentioned in the same breath as Snoop were Flavor Flav of Public Enemy, charged with attempted murder, and Tupac Shakur, who, with two associates, was alleged to have sexually abused and sodomized a woman in a New York hotel. This was shortly after Tupac was picked up for shooting two off-duty policemen in Atlanta.

In early 1994, the U.S. House and Senate held hearings about the effects of hardcore hip-hop, following the lead of Tipper Gore's Parents Music Resource Center from the previous decade. The hearings were led by a pair of female black elected officials from Illinois, Senator Carol Moseley Braun and Representative Cardiss Collins, but accomplished little, and gangsta rap found a vocal ally in another black, female U.S. representative, Maxine Waters, whose district included much of South Central. "These are our children and they've invented a new art form to describe their pains, fears, and frustrations with us as adults," she said at one of the hearings. Other black leaders were not so sympathetic. Reverend Calvin O. Butts, from Harlem's Abyssinian Baptist Church, found wide support for his condemnations of "negative rap." Outside of his church in June 1993 he fired up a steamroller but, at the last moment, declined to destroy boxes of CDs and tapes brought in for the purpose, saying he'd meet with the offending rappers instead.

Apparently he didn't have Snoop's number. "We could have sat down and solved this, like black men," he complained on *The Arsenio Hall Show*. "He's a powerful leader, a preacher, he's supposed to school me. Don't patronize me, putting me in the media, crushing my CDs, 'cause you making me money. You bought that CD, then you ran it over." Arsenio's audience applauded emphatically.

Snoop and his crew maintained that they were describing inner-city reality, shining a light on places the mainstream media tended to ignore. Further, their music allowed them to prosper *legally*, not to mention to employ others from their neighborhoods who might also get into trouble otherwise. "If I was a real gangsta I wouldn't be telling you what was going on, I'd just be *doing* it," Sticky Fingaz of Onyx told MTV. But Snoop's trial undermined this message, and it became easy for the mainstream media to portray hip-hop as a place where lyrical violence and real-life violence were one and the same.

These conversations could quickly get complicated, what with all the different socioeconomic, cultural, political, and historical threads. Part of what made them difficult was that they often pitted two repressed groups against each other, women and African-Americans. Even if you supported rappers reporting on inner-city troubles, you might want them to do so without calling women "bitches" and "hoes." But someone else who bristled at those words might not believe we needed to continue attacking the black men saying them. "[A] central motivation for highlighting gangsta rap continues to be the sensationalist drama of demonizing black youth culture in general and the contributions of young black men in particular," wrote black feminist scholar bell hooks.

In the end, gangsta rap won. Though conservative commentators and politicians still trot out a hip-hop boogeyman every now and then, hard-core hip-hop has assimilated into our culture. Lyrics that sounded shocking in N.W.A's time—the derogatory terms for women, the violent taunts—are now the norm. Despite their long and documented histories of condoning lawlessness in various forms, rappers including Snoop, Ice Cube, Eminem, Jay-Z, and many others are highly paid corporate spokesmen for mainstream brands. There aren't even all that many serious music critics anymore who disavow hard-edged hip-hop, despite that it remains rife with violent, misogynist story lines. Ultimately, American society has more or less come to accept the music as legitimate protest art—or at least as legitimate entertainment.

By the fall of 1995, facing attacks from all corners, and on trial for his life, Snoop was spooked. "My heart was beating like I was smoking crack in the courtroom every day," he said. He even gave occasional signs now and then that, just maybe, his critics might have a point. "I probably will become more of a positive image," he told Arsenio Hall. "But that's way down the line."

He was buoyed by reuniting with both of his parents. His mother Beverly, from whom Snoop had been estranged for years, stood by him during his trial, which began on November 27, 1995. Snoop's long-absent father, Vernall Varnado, a Detroit postal carrier, took early retirement and returned to L.A. to support his son. Snoop was also boosted when key evidence in police custody mysteriously disappeared. Celebrity attorney Johnnie Cochran was brought on as well; he had recently helped clear O. J. Simpson in his own murder case, and echoed that famous closing argument when referring to the missing evidence, critical shell casings and Woldemariam's bloody clothes. "If it doesn't fit," he told reporters, "you must acquit."

Jurors agreed, and after six days of deliberation, on February 20, 1996, Snoop and McKinley Lee were acquitted of murder charges. When the verdict was announced, Snoop's head dropped into his chest and he put his hands together in prayer. To celebrate, Death Row splurged on four new Rolls-Royces.

Snoop would have other legal trouble. In August he settled a civil suit filed by Woldemariam's family for an undisclosed amount. (They had originally sought $25 million.) Meanwhile, he quietly handled suits from musician David Ruffin Jr. (who cowrote "Gin and Juice") and actor Michael Todd Jones, who alleged they were battered during the filming of two Snoop music videos.

Shortly after his acquittal, Snoop married his longtime girlfriend, Shante Taylor. The pair had begun dating in high school. Behind the scenes, the man who'd lived a wild, sometimes-criminal lifestyle was changing his outlook. "It put everything in the right perspective, as far as my life, as far as not wanting to bring no harm to nobody or betray myself like that anymore," he said. "From that day on, I seen myself turning into a different person, creating myself into a man."

Stepbrothers

Despite fronting Snoop's considerable legal fees, Death Row not only survived during this time but prospered, generating well over $100 million in sales from its first releases. But while his close associates were realizing their music industry dreams, Warren G was suffering in silence. Unlike Snoop and Nate Dogg he was not offered a record deal by Death Row, and he sunk into despair.

It doesn't make much sense. Considering Warren's talents, his ties to Snoop, and the fact that his stepbrother was the lynchpin of a rap empire, he should have been in the thick of things. But he's barely on *Doggystyle* and was underutilized on *The Chronic* as well; the only time you hear him is on the humorous intro to "Deez Nuts," a telephone conversation. ("Did what's-her-name done get at you yesterday?" "Who?" "Deeeeez nuts!")

Warren received no royalties from *The Chronic*, he said, and is not credited for his technical contributions to the work, although they were sizable. Mining Blaxploitation soundtracks and other records, he said he brought Dre the samples used for "Let Me Ride," "Nuthin' But a 'G' Thang," "Lil Ghetto Boy," "Stranded on Death Row," and "Rat-Tat-Tat-Tat." Though others have whispered that Dre didn't give his stepbrother his proper due, Warren himself doesn't complain. "I'd do the little bitty shit and then he'd take it and make that motherfucker big," he said.

When Warren G's father married Dre's mother, their families merged, and Warren worshipped his older stepbrothers Tyree and Andre. They romped at the park, helped with Verna's fashion shows, and took karate. Dre and Tyree were always thick as thieves, but Warren's relationship with the budding super-producer was more complicated. Dre sometimes generously supported his kid brother, sometimes kept him at arm's length.

Dre has never embraced nepotism. Back in the eighties when his younger cousin Sir Jinx begged him to check out his group Stereo Crew, Dre at first resisted. Much later, two of Dre's children would attempt to break into the industry as rappers. Dre first met his eldest son Curtis when the latter was twenty (a paternity test confirmed the relationship), and he rapped as both Curtis Young and Hood Surgeon. Dre's daughter La'Toya Young, meanwhile, has rapped under the name Manaj. She complained loudly that her father was not involved in her career in her 2008, self-made documentary, *Daddy's Shadow*, in which she tried unsuccessfully to confront him at his Sherman Oaks studio, and bemoaned that he hadn't signed her or funded a label of her own. The viewer is left feeling sympathy for both perspectives; Manaj is a strong rapper, but Dre's desire to see his daughter chart a more stable career path is understandable.

When it came to Warren's musical aspirations, Dre was initially a fantastic coach. At their Compton home, he showed him DJ tricks like how to blend and how to switch back and forth between two turntables. He eventually taught Warren production techniques, too, such as how to sample and how to incorporate live instruments into his tracks. When Warren requested help with the MPC60 drum machine, Dre said he could *have* his drum machine. "He showed me everything," Warren said. In the spirit of Dre and DJ Quik—G-funk producers who also rapped on their own tracks—Warren began rhyming and excelled at that, too.

It's not clear how strongly Dre advocated for Warren at Death Row. It may have been a lost cause, considering the long line of artists in front of him, and Suge Knight also may have been a fly in Warren's ointment. In his book *LAbyrinth*, author Randall Sullivan writes that, following a *Source* article in which Warren appeared to take credit for Death Row's success, a rumor went around the label that gun-bearing Bloods visited him late at night and warned him to be more careful with his words. "Someone quoted me saying that I built Death Row," Warren said. "I didn't build it, but I definitely brought all my people there."

Whatever the case, it quickly became clear that Death Row was not his home. He also didn't have a home, *period*, though Cold 187um sometimes let him crash at his place. He tried to keep his spirits up. "I said, 'I know I got dope music.' I ain't gonna let nobody break me down and tell me my shit ain't dope," he said. It helped that his pal Nate Dogg kept pushing him. Warren began pursuing new channels, landing a production credit on MC Breed's 1993 song "Gotta Get Mine," featuring Tupac. He earned a four-figure cash payment, which got him a burgundy Regal. Even better, the track put him on Tupac's radar, who invited him to a studio session. Warren found him a sample for "Definition of a Thug Nigga," which appeared on the *Poetic Justice* soundtrack, released in June 1993. But they weren't finished that day; before long, Tupac's collaborators from his group Thug Life showed up, informing him that a mutual friend named Kato had been murdered, over little more than a set of expensive car wheel rims. Warren put on another beat, and Tupac quickly composed "How Long Will They Mourn Me?," which featured Nate Dogg and was released on Thug Life's 1994 debut.

Warren and Nate Dogg also landed another *Poetic Justice* soundtrack song, "Indo Smoke," headlined by West Covina rapper Mista Grimm. Extolling the virtues of a marijuana haze, the mellow hit served as great publicity for Warren, whom Grimm shouts out by name. "Indo Smoke" got the attention of Def Jam label executives Lyor Cohen and Chris Lighty, who hadn't even realized Warren's affiliation with Snoop or Dre. The pioneering New York label had largely missed out on the exploding L.A. scene, and righted things by signing Warren.

Regulate

By now Warren had his own Long Beach apartment, and set to work crafting tracks in a makeshift studio there, using the closet for vocals. He kept coming back to Michael McDonald's yacht-rock-era track "I Keep Forgettin'," which his parents played when he was young. "I had the sample and was, like, 'It would be so different to do a hip-hop song over this,'" he thought. And so, again enlisting his always-ready-for-action comrade Nate Dogg, they went about replacing McDonald's smooth falsetto with back-and-forth verses, the way Dre and Snoop had done on "Nuthin' But a 'G' Thang."

The plot of "Regulate," vividly detailed, involves a dice game gone bad, with gats-toting bad guys attempting to separate Warren from his wealth. But they have messed with the wrong east side Long Beach denizen, and Nate Dogg quickly comes to his rescue. Following a shootout, the men retire to the East Side Motel with some ladies who, for some reason, just can't seem to get their car started.

As for the song's title? "We used to always say 'regulate'—we need to 'regulate' the crowd, we need to 'regulate' them over there," Warren said. "Then when I heard it in a movie, oh my God, I lost it." Said flick was 1988 youthful-studs-in-the-old-West drama *Young Guns*, and the quote in question came from ranch enforcer Charley Bowdre, played by Casey Siemaszko. He advises would-be posse member Billy the Kid, played by Emilio Estevez: "We regulate any stealin' of his property. We're damn good, too. But you can't be any geek off the street. You gotta be handy with the steel, if you know what I mean. Earn your keep."

"Regulate" was, arguably, G-funk's biggest hit. You won't find many people born in the seventies or eighties who won't whistle along. There's really nothing like it; the song lacks a chorus, but Warren's crisp raps and Nate's buttery-smooth verses obliterate the need for one.

The biggest question surrounding the song was which label would get it. After an A&R representative played it for Jimmy Iovine, he insisted on it for the Death Row–produced *Above the Rim* soundtrack, citing Nate Dogg's involvement. But Def Jam wanted it for Warren's debut, and so a compromise was brokered, and the song appeared on both albums. Released in March 1994, *Above the Rim*, also boasting the Lady of Rage's signature anthem "Afro Puffs," became Death Row's fourth consecutive multi-platinum release. An even bigger seller was Warren G's album *Regulate... G Funk Era*, which followed three months later. Though Warren said Suge wouldn't let Snoop appear on it, the album succeeded, going much deeper than "Regulate." Particularly poignant is "Do You See," cowritten with Kurupt. It is an autobiographical tale of 213's ascent, and sympathetic to those driven to a life of crime.

> *Now who's the real victim, can you answer that?*
> *The brother that's jacking or the fool getting jacked?*

The song's spoken intro—*Why should the blues be so at home here? Well, America provided the atmosphere*—came courtesy of proto-rap poet Gil Scott-Heron, whose work Warren discovered by chance one day while digging through vinyl at Hollywood shop As the Record Turns. He told me that he was also turned on by black activist collectives Watts Prophets and Last Poets, particularly the latter, whom he discovered after Dre sampled their tracks like "Die Nigga!!!" on *Efil4zaggin*.

Regulate... G Funk Era sold over three million copies, and is credited with almost single-handedly propping up Def Jam at a time when its fortunes were flagging. All considering, Dre and Suge's resistance may have been just the thing for Warren to find the fire in his belly. As for the debate about who invented G-funk? Warren argues that he deserves credit. "I started it," he said in 2011. "[T]aking some gangsta shit and putting a melody to it and having a guy—which was Nate Dogg—sing some soulful gangsta shit about how he felt. That was G-Funk."

Smoke Weed Every Day

Nate Dogg died in 2011 at the age of forty-one. His career was bigger than the sum of its parts. He never had a solo song or album in the Top

10, but yet during his twenty years singing hooks on hard-edged hip-hop songs, he helped trace the genre's evolution. His self-assured, pitch-perfect choruses provided gangsta rap's foundation. He would have prospered in any genre; born decades earlier, he might have sang the soul blues or jazz. Countless rappers came and went, but Nate Dogg was always there. As Ice Cube put it on his group Westside Connection's 2003 track "Gangsta Nation": *It must be a single, with Nate Dogg singin' on it.*

His influence was so vast, his voice such a critical part of the canon, it's hard now to remember a pre–Nate Dogg rap world. Before he put hip-hop's mentality to melody, R&B singers mostly did their own things while rappers did theirs. "Nate was different," Snoop said. "He was the first R&B singer to say what all the R&B singers wanted to say."

These things were, of course, largely about loose women and sticky herbs. But like Snoop, Nate started in the church, performing with his brother and sister in a gospel trio called the Hale Family Singers, which took them as far away as Mississippi. "My family don't listen to R&B— never have, never will," he said in 2004. "They only listen to gospel. That's where I get my voice from." In high school he moved in with his grand-mother, and got into secular singers like Stevie Wonder, Marvin Gaye, and New Edition. His first self-penned track went: *Baby darling darling girl / I really love your Jheri curl.*

He didn't have much formal training, but knew what sounded right. After all, as he told *Vibe*, he could sing before he could talk. Still, early producers and engineers often didn't know what to do with him, exactly. His voice is too low in the mix on tracks like "Lil' Ghetto Boy," "Indo Smoke," and "How Long Will They Mourn Me?" But his talents rose to the surface, despite the fact that Nate wasn't much of an entertainment industry hustler. Wearing a thin goatee and a perpetually sleepy expression, he didn't bother with hobnobbing. Before Auto-Tune made everyone sound like they had chops, Nate did it naturally. "He had a special voice, the way his voice layered on top of itself, and how he knew how to stay in pocket," said producer Mike Dean.

He had a temper—don't forget the golf course incident—and he also faced domestic violence and gun allegations. But Nate Dogg's legacy is great music. He stood next to bigger-name MCs who got their tracks' top billings, even if Nate's contributions won out. Would we still remember Ludacris's "Area Codes" without Nate's hilariously earnest chorus? *I've got hoes (I've got hoes) / In different area codes (Area codes).* He elevates 50 Cent's otherwise cliché-packed "21 Questions" and saves Snoop's "Ain't No Fun" and Tupac's "It's All About You" from sounding too nasty. And with all due respect to Mos Def and Pharoahe Monch, the ultimate takeaway from their 2000 song "Oh No" is Nate's part:

Oh no!
Look at who they let in the back door
From Long Beach to Brooklyn, they know
We rock from the east to west coast

He wasn't a one-trick pony, though, demolishing tracks on his own as well. The song "One More Day" from *Murder Was the Case*, for example, maintains the weight of a spiritual. *If I live to see tomorrow*, he sings, *Thank you for one more day.* But he never quite fit into the Death Row game plan, and his first solo album wasn't released until 1998. As a trio 213 lost momentum, and their proper debut *The Hard Way* felt anticlimactic when it came out in 2004.

Nate excelled as a gun for hire, the man you enlisted if you needed a surefire hit. When Dr. Dre finally figured out how to properly deploy him he usually stole the show, on tracks like "The Next Episode," which features his signature line: *Smoke weed every day.*

Suffering strokes in 2007 and 2008, Nate lost the ability to talk, though he could "blink and spell out messages using his eyes and an alphabet board." But music was always with him. Even as his health declined he put together a choir, called Innate Praise, which featured Jacob Lusk, a singer known from his *American Idol* appearances. "He was getting into gospel music and there wasn't going to be no more 'I got hoes,'" said Warren G.

CHAPTER NINETEEN

THE ONE BY HIS SIDE

By his late twenties, Eazy-E had achieved his dreams. He'd created one of history's most successful independent music labels. In the early nineties he maintained a coterie of talented artists, loving women, and adoring children. His girlfriend Tracy Jernagin drove a new Acura with the license plate "LUV 4 E."

He indulged hobbies like skateboarding and built his collection of monster dolls. He amassed lowriders. At Christmas, he drove around in one while wearing a pom-pom Santa hat. At restaurants he'd order one of everything, just because he could. He came and went as he pleased between his various houses and mansions, where his friends and artists lived in the extra rooms, rent-free. His social circle stretched all over the L.A. metro area, from Cal State, Northridge, students to old Compton friends. He'd even created a film company, planning to release a thriller he'd helped write and would star in, called *Smilin' Facez.*

Most everyone who knew Eazy remembers him fondly. "He treated us like princesses, from the moment we met him," said J. J. Fad's MC J.B. "He was like, 'Do you need anything? Do you need any money?'" As his success mushroomed, he became increasingly generous. His bodyguard Joe Fierro recalled Eazy covering fancy dinners and medical bills for the birth of two of his children. His former crack-dealing partner Mark Rucker had gone on to get a straight job as a welder, but when they reunited Eazy insisted he quit, and gave him a job with Ruthless.

Eazy bailed people out of jail and tipped waitresses lavishly. He gave to charity, too. He was particularly devoted to a mentoring and education organization called Athletes & Entertainers for Kids, not just writing checks, but helping plan their trips to amusement parks in painstaking detail, down to the goodie bags and the T-shirt design. "He was fully engaged. I cannot say enough about Eric as a human being," said Elise Kim, the organization's founder. His friend Jada Pinkett attended some of these events with him, sporting head-to-toe denim. Kim believes they were dating. "They were like college kids," she said. (Charis Henry, Eazy's assistant, remembers Eazy having a crush on Pinkett—"she was short, little, and light-skinned, and that's what he likes"—and that she was an aspiring rapper with a demo tape who hoped, unsuccessfully, to sign to Ruthless. Pinkett did not respond to a request for comment.)

With his own children—by 1994 he had nine—Eazy was usually generous, and with their mothers as well. "Christmases were ridiculous," said Henry, recalling how he would fill trucks with bikes, toys, and clothes for his kids.

He was also involved in numerous child-support cases. In 1993 he was ordered to pay $58,000 annually to the mother of his two-year-old, Nebraska-raised daughter, in what a prosecutor called "the largest child-support order handled by the Los Angeles district attorney's office." Having shot ahead in his "baby race" with his friend Mark Rucker, he now had a new goal. "He would say, 'I want a football team,'" said Charis Henry.

Jerry Heller helped handle Eazy's child-support payments and scheduled paternity tests. "He always had so many girls around him," said Rebekka Armstrong, a former Playboy Playmate who appeared on the cover of Ruthless act Penthouse Players Clique's album *Paid the Cost*. "It didn't seem he had any preference. All sorts of different colors, races." (Armstrong said she resisted Eazy's advances.)

From time to time, Eazy found himself in legal hot water, usually for traffic incidents—reckless driving, driving with a suspended license—but sometimes for more serious charges. In 1993 he pleaded no contest to charges of battery and theft (the details are unclear) and as punishment was ordered to make a fire safety public service video, which you can see on YouTube. Pacing in front of a fire engine as a rescue is dramatized, Eazy preaches the importance of preparedness, warning: "Toys could be replaced, your kids can't."

Though Henry said she never saw him lose his cool, his knuckles were scarred from fights. Ruthless assistant general manager Gary Ballen said he saw Eazy knock out a three-hundred-pound man "cold with one punch."

Eazy had a violent streak, which extended to women. Tracy Jernagin, whom Eazy once shot in the head with a BB gun, demurred when I asked her directly whether he ever hit her. "We had a really volatile relationship," she said. "When you keep going through all this craziness, and two people can't stay away from each other, it's just some kind of strong love." Lisa Johnson, the mother of three of Dr. Dre's children, who said Eazy beat her in Compton and sent her to the hospital before a planned trip to Magic Mountain, surprisingly didn't have much bad to say about the Ruthless Records founder. "He was a sweetheart," she concluded.

Reaching New Audiences

Eazy's pagers and cell phones were always going off, and he never got much sleep. He ate out constantly, junk food usually, or maybe a plate of fettuccine alfredo. It's impossible to imagine living in this world, one with seemingly everything you ever wanted, but also constant stress. As a young hustler he didn't drink or smoke weed, because he wanted to stay sharp. But in the years following N.W.A's breakup he gave himself over to these indulgences, shooting Jack Daniel's and getting high constantly. He dropped big cash at strip clubs and hung out with porn stars. According to Jerry Heller's memoir, he encouraged his female group H.W.A. (Hoes with Attitude) to "Sharon Stone" record executives, referencing the famous *Basic Instinct* legs-uncrossing scene.

For all his largesse, Eazy was unsettled. He had trouble on his mind. The Suge Knight menace wasn't going away, and he soon learned of another enemy: heavily armed Southern California white supremacists. In July 1993, the *Los Angeles Times* reported that the FBI was investigating a group of skinheads who wanted to start a race war and had amassed a giant cache of machine guns, sawed-off shotguns, and pipe bombs. Their purported targets included Rodney King, Al Sharpton, and Eazy. Eazy and some of the others were never warned they were in danger. He couldn't help but see this as further payback for "Fuck tha Police." "Again, the FBI has shown their true feelings," read a statement he released. The FBI contended Eazy's "safety was not endangered."

But more than external threats, Eazy was being eaten up from within. Since Cube and Dre left N.W.A—and became even bigger stars—he'd had a chip on his shoulder. Henry believes this is why he began smoking weed after *The Chronic* came out: "I'm thinking he was trying to mask how he was feeling deserted and embarrassed." He was anxious to prove he could win without them. He sat on Arsenio Hall's and Howard Stern's couches and complained that Dr. Dre was a fraud, a "studio gangster." Before he took up with Eazy, Dre had been wearing biker shorts, and wasn't even repping Compton, he went on, but the public didn't care. *The Chronic* was the bomb. Dre's music spoke for itself, and his youthful indiscretions, if that's what you want to call them, didn't change that.

Eazy's jealousy began affecting his business dealings. MC Ren complained that his recording budgets kept getting slashed—not because he wasn't selling, but because he wouldn't come out swinging against Dre. Another reason Ren may have gotten the short shrift was because Ruthless was on an insane hiring spree, looking for the next big act to make everyone forget Cube and Dre. Early on, Ruthless had signed very few artists and hit with nearly every release. Now Eazy signed dozens of different acts. In 1994 alone Ruthless released albums from nine different artists, including little-remembered acts like Nashville rapper Pistol and female duo Menajahtwa, pronounced "ménage à trois." Eazy didn't want Ruthless to be known for just gangsta rap. He toyed with the ideas of a sublabel dedicated to children's music, and even made a song himself with Guns N' Roses, though it never saw the light of day.

Curiosity was one of his defining traits. Eazy was fascinated by Judaism, for one; he'd stuck with Jerry Heller despite countless anti-Semitic insults, and at his nephew Terry Heller's grandfather's funeral, Eazy wore a yarmulke. Tracy Jernagin was Jewish, and said the faith was "very prevalent" in her relationship with Eazy. He even signed a group called Blood of Abraham, a pair of early-twenty-something Jewish kids from the Valley. Though major labels expressed interest, Eazy promised them freedom to express their political messages, on songs like "Niggaz and Jewz (Some Say Kikes)." "He said, 'You guys are on a militant tip,'" said group member Benyad. "'You can talk whatever shit you fuckin' want.'"

Eazy was also fond of Mexican-American culture, which he called the "sleeping giant." Convinced Latino rap was the future, he signed Kid Frost, who'd come up in the electro scene and broke out with his 1990 Chicano pride anthem "La Raza," from his album *Hispanic Causing Panic*. Eazy bought him out of his Virgin contract.

Kid Frost was already a legend, but Eazy also befriended a South Central gangbanger named Gilbert Izquierdo, known as Toker. He and his friends weren't impressed with early Latino rappers, and, as the group Brownside, made hardcore rhymes describing their real lives in their neighborhoods. They even self-financed with street money, following Eazy's template.

One 1994 afternoon the whole crew arrived at the Ruthless offices. They were a dozen or more, rappers and neighborhood associates alike, with names like Danger and Trigga, in hairnets and Pendletons buttoned at the top. They rolled up in Chevy lowriders, hardtops, and convertibles, even a station wagon. Eazy couldn't believe the fleet. "Whose cars are those outside?" Eazy said, by way of "hello."

"That's our shit," said Toker.

"Those motherfuckers are nice," Eazy continued. "You want to sell them?"

Toker declined, but let him hit the switches on his '61 Impala hardtop; he made it hop like a pro. "Damn, fool!" Toker said.

They began chatting. Eazy knew their neighborhood in South Central; he was involved with a woman from the Twenties streets, he said, adding that she'd even talked up their affiliated gang, East Side Trece.

Nothing could have endeared him more to the crew, and meanwhile Eazy was impressed with their video for their song "Gang Related." He offered to sign them but Toker eventually convinced him to give them a distribution deal. Brownside recorded their own version of "The Boyz-N-the Hood" called "Vatos 'n the Barrio," and Eazy and Toker became close. When Eazy recorded his fire safety PSA, Toker recorded a Spanish-language version.

Eazy liked Toker for his generosity, and because he helped him feel close to the streets. The Brownside crew, indeed, remained in the thick of things. Danger was later murdered, and not long after linking with Ruthless, Toker fought a murder charge himself. He was found guilty and agreed to be sent back to Mexico, where he hadn't lived since childhood. But his sentence was overturned on appeal, and he and Brownside today continue to make music in Los Angeles.

Of all the new Ruthless acts, one was poised for a huge break-out: Bone Thugs-N-Harmony, a wholly original quintet that included a pair of brothers and a cousin, whose members came out of desperate circumstances. As he later explained on the show *America's Most Wanted*, Bizzy Bone was abducted as a child, and worked at a dope house during his teen years. They exquisitely layered their parts and varied their tempos, switching back and forth between singing and lightning-fast rapping, a style learned because they spent so much time together that they all memorized each other's parts, creating an unprecedented new sound. "It just started to sound like we were harmonizing," Krayzie Bone told me. "And people started telling us, 'Y'all sound like the rapping Temptations.'" Originally called Bone Enterprise, and then just Bone, they came out to L.A. on something of a whim; group member Flesh-n-Bone was attending school in the area, and convinced the others it was crawling with celebrities and opportunity. Longtime N.W.A fans and intent on signing with Eazy, they took a Greyhound to Los Angeles, where they began to call Ruthless, leaving persistent messages. Eazy finally called them back and Krayzie Bone rapped for him over the phone. Eazy said he'd be performing in Cleveland in a couple weeks, where Eazy finally met them backstage.

"Were you the dudes rapping on the phone?" he asked them, to which they responded affirmatively. "I wanna work with y'all," Eazy went on. "When are you trying to leave?"

"Immediately," they responded.

Bone Thugs single-handedly reinvigorated Ruthless Records. They gave Eazy nostalgic pangs of himself and his group when they were younger. Krayzie Bone said that when one of the group members got up to use the bathroom, the other four followed. "Man, if N.W.A would have been as tight as y'all nobody would have never came between us," Eazy told them.

As with Brownside, Eazy felt he understood them because they came from the streets. But they were incredibly raw; upon arriving in the Valley to record their 1994 debut EP, *Creepin On Ah Come Up*, they partied their young brains out and were kicked out of countless hotels. The guys could spit fast and tell street stories, but Eazy and their producer DJ U-Neek crafted them into something slower and darker, bordering on horrorcore, combining creepy voices and chanting with lyrics about dark spirituality and Ouija boards. (Based on their early song "Thugs and Harmony," it was Eazy's idea to add the "Thugs-N-Harmony" to their name.)

Their brash, madcap personalities were captured on the debut, which produced a huge single, "Thuggish Ruggish Bone," and sold four million copies.

Tomica and Jerry

Tomica Woods met Eazy-E at an L.A. club in 1990. She wasn't an adoring fan; in fact, he had to talk her into a date. "Just based off of image, I thought he would be kinda disrespectful," she said. But he impressed her with his manners and interesting conversation, and soon won her over.

Like Eazy, she hadn't had much handed to her in life, reportedly shuttling between parents and living for a time in a foster home. She raised a child as a single mother and, at a young age when she was broke, posed nude for a magazine. "I've had a Vanessa Williams experience," she said. But she worked to lift herself, attending a pair of L.A. community colleges, and in 1989 landed a job as secretary for Tabu Records' Clarence Avant. A music industry luminary who has worked closely with Quincy Jones and Jimmy Jam and Terry Lewis, Avant took over as Motown Records chairman in 1993 and Woods went with him. "She's beautiful and she's ruthless and she's bright," said Avant.

Woods and Eazy vacationed in Hawaii, and had a baby boy together. Eazy moved her first into his Woodland Hills house, and then into a Topanga home, not far from Calabasas. Short and light skinned, wearing ponytails and toting Gucci purses, she was smart and serious, known to give as good as she got it. She laughed at him because he was afraid to open his sunroof on their first date. She wasn't his only woman, but, perhaps owing to her music industry background, Woods seemed to have had his ear to an extent when it came to business matters. (I could not reach Woods for comment for this book.) "I was indirectly doing things for Eric at the company," she said.

Eazy's ghostwriter Dirty Red, who was close to him in this period, downplayed Woods's influence. "[Eazy] never told me, 'Me and Tomica are thinking about doing this,' or 'Me and Tomica are thinking about doing that,'" though he admitted: "I don't know what their deal was behind closed doors."

Some speculate it was she who helped drive a wedge between Eazy and Jerry Heller, whose relationship began to disintegrate in late 1994. The N.W.A biopic *Straight Outta Compton*, for which she is credited as a producer alongside Dre and Cube and others, portrays her going through company books and looking for evidence of Jerry's malfeasance.

"I think that toward the end of 1994, a lot of people were in [Eazy's] ear. 'Jerry's doing this,' and 'Jerry's doing that.' 'He's charging you too much and he's making more than you are,'" Heller said.

Rapper Steffon said things were very awkward during this time, and that when Heller left the premises, Eazy would scamper into his office and close the door. "Jerry would be like, 'What's up with your little buddy?' And I was just like, 'I don't know.'"

Heller's role at Ruthless was more than just that of a traditional artist manager. He'd also been an investor in the company, putting up his own money to get it running. While Heller has never been found liable for any financial improprieties at Ruthless, some people who were close to the situation came to believe he was stealing, alleging there existed a bank account he shared with Eazy, and he was excessively drawing from it. "What I was told from Eazy—from his mouth—is that Jerry Heller put him $2 million into debt, and that's why he was done," said Dirty Red. B.G. Knocc Out recalled a time when Eazy showed him company documents. "He had records from where money was missing from the label—millions of dollars that he said Jerry was stealing from him. And Jerry was sending him idle threats—faxes and stuff like that." Krayzie Bone also said Eazy claimed Jerry was robbing him.

Other insiders defend Heller. "He never told me Jerry was stealing from him. He always told me he know where his money was," said Eazy's assistant Charis Henry.

"Jerry was always Eazy-E's protector," Toker told me, adding that Eazy nonetheless blamed Jerry in part for Cube's and Dre's departures.

Heller insists he didn't steal a dime. "It's the most ridiculous allegation I've ever heard," he said.

Around this time, Eazy took on a new lawyer, named Ron Sweeney, who was an acquaintance of Woods. Tracy Jernagin believes he and Woods worked to turn Eazy against Jerry. Others point to the influence of Mike Klein, who'd been brought on to run security at Ruthless after Suge Knight's intimidations, and was later promoted to director of business affairs. "The way I saw it, Klein was wedging Jerry out of the picture and Tomica was wedging Jerry out of the picture," Gary Ballen said. (Sweeney did not respond to a request for comment, and multiple attempts to reach Klein for this book were unsuccessful.)

Whatever the case, in early 1995 after nearly eight years of partnership,

Eazy and Heller parted ways; the latter said he received a letter ending their relationship that February but doesn't believe Eazy was in his right mind when he wrote it.

A Bad Cough

One person in particular was happy to hear this news: Ice Cube.

In late 1994 he and Eazy, who'd already reconciled, ran into each other at the New York nightclub the Tunnel. Eazy was in town promoting Bone Thugs-N-Harmony, who appeared on *Yo! MTV Raps*. It was a cold night, and though he'd just bought the group members black leather jackets, he opted not to wear his own. "We told him, 'Man, you going to freeze to death out here.' Plus his Jheri curl was wet," Krayzie Bone said. Cube arrived with upstart label owner Puff Daddy and his emergent artist Notorious B.I.G.; that meeting would lead to the latter's collaboration with Bone Thugs, called "Notorious Thugs."

Cube got a booth in the club, and Eazy joined him. The conversation turned to reuniting N.W.A. Eazy noted that Jerry was out of the picture. "I told Eazy I was down," Cube said. "He was in his feud with Dre at the time. I told him if he could work that out, call me."

A year earlier Dre said in an interview that the group couldn't reunite unless it was on Death Row, which, considering Eazy's animosity toward Suge, was never going to happen. But Dre said he and Eazy spoke on the phone in early 1995 about "maybe putting N.W.A back together." It seems likely that their icy relations were beginning to thaw, to the benefit of a reunited N.W.A. "It was definitely going to happen," Krayzie Bone said. He added that, though Eazy still didn't acknowledge Dre's critical role in starting Ruthless, he was focused on "fixing" the damage he'd done between them, with the hope of getting the band back together.

That night at the Tunnel, Eazy and Cube spoke for hours. When the club closed, Eazy was ill prepared for the chilly New York weather. He couldn't catch a cab, so he simply walked off toward his hotel, shivering. Eazy returned to Los Angeles with a bad cough.

*   *   *

Eazy was very sick. He didn't let on, but there were signs that he had begun to realize something was seriously wrong with him. In December 1994, after returning from New York, he recorded a track called "Tha Muthaphukkin Real," featuring MC Ren and produced by DJ Yella, in which he speaks on his fate and legacy.

> *When I die, niggas bury me*
> *Make sure my shit reads, "Eazy Muthaphukkin' E"*
> *And it's a fact, to be exact, my tombstone should read*
> *"He put Compton on that map"*

"All I remember is him coughing a lot," MC Ren said, concerning the song's recording. "I just thought he had a cold." Eazy started to act like someone whose days were numbered. He hurriedly signed on publicist Phyllis Pollack to help promote the yet-unrealized N.W.A project. And he got back in touch with Tairrie B, the white female rapper who'd released her debut on Ruthless in 1990.

After seeing Ice-T perform with Body Count, Tairrie had felt the call of rock music, and started a band called Manhole. But Eazy wasn't with it, and her rock dreams remained in limbo, since she was still bound by the terms of her Ruthless deal. That is, until early 1995, when Eazy called her out of the blue, asking to meet up at the Del Amo Fashion Center in Torrance. He announced he was letting her out of her contract. "That day was life changing for me, because it allowed me to go on with my life," she said. It was almost like Eazy was attempting to make amends.

One important relationship, however, had hit a snag: Tomica Woods. Eazy "threw her out" of the Topanga house, said Vince Caruso, Ruthless's college radio promoter. Rapper Steffon was in the midst of this squabble, he said, talking with Eazy there about Steffon's album, *Trippin Wit No Luggage*. They were going upstairs when they ran into Woods, coming down. "Tomica's carrying her shit out, huffing and puffing. So I say, 'Hey, Tomica.' She don't say shit to me. He say, 'Never mind her, 'cause she leaving.'"

One day in mid-February, Eazy began coughing violently and experiencing chest pains. He thought it might be an asthma attack, although he wasn't known to be asthmatic. His hulking bodyguards, the Twins, phoned Mike Klein, who told them to take Eazy to the hospital. They brought him to Norwalk Community Hospital's emergency room, where doctors elected to keep him overnight. A test determined that he had bronchitis, and Eazy was sent home. None of this seemed unreasonable. "Bronchitis runs in our family," said Eazy's sister Patricia Wright.

Eazy soon returned to the studio, where he was to record a verse for his song with B.G. Knocc Out and Dresta, called "D.P.G. Killa." Eazy hadn't yet recorded his part when he got to chatting with other people, thereby putting off an increasingly impatient B.G. Eventually he found Eazy in a hallway, "by himself sittin' on the floor wheezing, like terribly. And I was like, 'You all right?'" B.G. said. He added that Eazy was using some new, "huge-ass" inhalers in an attempt to control his breathing.

Eazy wasn't all right. He went to the Topanga house to recover; at some point Woods returned. But so did his symptoms, as bad as before, and on February 24 he was taken to Cedars-Sinai. Registered under an assumed name, he received a battery of tests, yielding a shocking result: Eazy was HIV positive.

"He was on the phone crying and couldn't talk, and then the doctor got on the phone and asked me, was I was sitting down," Woods said. She, too, cried her eyes out, but was forced to quickly compose herself. She would need to come in and be tested as well.

Woods was scared, and not just for Eazy and herself. She was pregnant again, with their second child.

CHAPTER TWENTY

TIME TO TESTIFY

These were dark days for HIV/AIDS treatment, which was causing devastation at an increasingly alarming rate. The side-effect-heavy AZT was the only antiviral drug available in much of the world. Within days of his diagnosis, Eazy's condition was downgraded to full-blown AIDS. Doctors gave him antibiotics to treat a lung infection, but his energy level quickly deteriorated. Woods monitored him around the clock, staying on a cot next to his bed. Word got out before long about his condition; his assistant Charis Henry came as quickly as she could, as did the mothers of many of Eazy's children. "Even the ones who used to fight each other, they were holding hands, crying, praying," Henry said.

Wearing long underwear and hospital gowns, Eazy watched television and tried to keep his spirits up, whistling when Halle Berry came on the tube. But he could barely get out of bed, and soon required an oxygen mask. His girlfriend Carmen braided his hair and put lotion on him. His mother brought him fresh fruit. His childhood friend Bigg A gave him a card signed by all the homies.

But Henry had a sinking feeling, and not just about his health. She was concerned that he was speaking with Ron Sweeney about creating a will. "I don't trust your baby mama's lawyer doing your will," Henry told him.

As Eazy's health faded, a power struggle commenced. Different parties positioned themselves as defenders of his interests, and it wasn't clear who was in charge. Heller still thought of himself as Eazy's primary ally, but could do nothing as Woods and Sweeney took over many of Eazy's affairs. "Ron Sweeney presented us with our first royalty checks, and we had never seen him a day in our life," Krayzie Bone said, adding that they hadn't spoken with Eazy for weeks. "Our whole thing at that point was, like, 'Where's Eazy at?'"

Meanwhile, a Nation of Islam detail arrived at the hospital, and began a twenty-four-hour security watch. They were there "to keep everybody from rushing in on him," said Shaheed Muhammad, a Nation of Islam captain who was part of the security detail, adding that they came at the behest of Mike Klein, Ruthless's director of business affairs. "It was Mike Klein who got them the detail, and paid them," he said, adding that, later, Ron Sweeney began making the payments.

This wasn't particularly strange; the Nation has a history of guarding black celebrities, including Michael Jackson, Jesse Jackson, Tupac Shakur, Ice Cube, and Johnnie Cochran. Eazy's detail included up to four security-focused Fruit of Islam members at a time, Cedars-Sinai spokeswoman Paula Correia told the *Los Angeles Times*, adding that it wasn't unusual for famous patients to hire private security. Heller claimed the guards blocked him from seeing Eazy in the hospital. "The baby mamas couldn't get up to see him, the babies couldn't get up to see him, we couldn't get up to see him," said Gary Ballen. Tracy Jernagin said Tomica Woods instructed the Nation to keep out practically *everyone*—including Eazy's children, and his children's mothers. Shaheed Muhammad, who was part of the detail, said that keeping the mothers and children away from Eazy was indeed part of the detail's stated objective. (Though, remember, Muhammad said he was initially hired by Klein, rather than Woods.)

Meanwhile, rapper Steffon arrived to the Woodland Hills home where he was living—Eazy's house—only to find himself barred from entering. A phalanx of Nation guards were standing in front of the door. He said his belongings were put onto a moving truck and he was told they were taken to storage, though he was never able to retrieve them. Vince Caruso, the Ruthless college radio promoter also living in the house, seconds Steffon's account, but adds that he had better luck permeating the security. He recruited Toker to come with him, and upon sizing up the South Central gangbanger they "parted like the Red Sea and let me in to retrieve all of my things," Caruso said.

But the Nation of Islam wasn't just interested in protecting Eazy and his belongings. They were interested in *curing* him. Rumors began circulating that the black nationalist group had a remedy for AIDS. "I heard that they were saying they had the cure," Steffon said.

In 1990 an experimental AIDS drug called Kemron came to market in Kenya. The Kenya Medical Research Institute reported that Kemron helped most patients gain weight, and alleviated their symptoms. The drug was unveiled with "fanfare and nationalistic triumph" reported *The New York Times* on October 3, 1990, with patients coming from as far away as the U.S. for treatment.

Other researchers urged caution about the tablet, which was also known as a low-dose alpha interferon, a natural chemical that's produced in response to infection. A World Health Organization study in Uganda in 1992 and 1993 concluded the drug to be no more effective than a placebo.

Nonetheless, some continued to believe its merits, and a Washington clinic run by the alternative medicine–focused Abundant Life Foundation received a $213,000 federal contract to treat AIDS patients. The foundation's director, Dr. Abdul Alim Muhammad, was a Nation of Islam member and former Louis Farrakhan spokesman. He didn't claim that low-dose alpha interferon cured AIDS, only that studies he contributed to showed it resulted in "weight gain, increased appetite and energy levels." Still, this hadn't stopped the Nation of Islam newspaper *The Final Call* from calling it a cure for AIDS.

Dr. Abdul Alim Muhammad personally procured Kemron for Eazy, Shaheed Muhammad said. "Dr. Alim shipped it from D.C. on a plane, having made sure it was fresh and potent, so it would go right into his system," Shaheed said, adding that he helped administer it to the rapper and it seemed, for a time, to make him feel better.

Ceremony

Eazy and Tomica Woods decided to marry. They wed on March 14, the day before his scheduled surgery to drain fluid from his lungs. "We got married at the hospital because he wasn't sure if he was going to make it through," Woods said.

In the presence of a pastor, the short ceremony took place that evening, well past dark, with Eazy in the bed but fully conscious. The proceedings were held before a small group that included Eazy's sister, brother, and parents. Almost immediately, Eazy's will was written to make Woods and Sweeney coexecutors of Eazy's estate.

The surgery, planned for the next day, was canceled, as Eazy's health was deemed too fragile. As for the Kemron, the "cure for AIDS"? According to Shaheed Muhammad, it had temporarily perked Eazy up. "His vitals picked up again and he really got better," he said, though he added that before long his pain returned. "We were all so hopeful," Tracy Jernagin said. But though many close to Eazy were in favor of him continuing the alternative medicine, Woods was against it. She didn't know what they were giving him, she reasoned. Perhaps it could kill him. Shaheed Muhammad said she called it a "miracle potion" that wasn't going to work, and that she and Ron Sweeney promptly removed him from the security detail. He was also told to cease administering the Kemron.

Woods's opposition to an unproven drug can hardly be faulted. But to Eazy's desperate supporters it seemed like throwing in the towel. "That's when everybody starts saying, 'They got the cure, and she won't even let them give him the cure,'" Steffon said.

"When I started asking Tomica questions, she started saying, 'There's nothing else that can be done,'" said Henry. "She'd given up."

The morning after Eazy was married, he was taken to the intensive care unit.

"He always said he was going to marry Tomica," Eazy's sister Patricia Wright told me. We met at a party held on September 7, 2014, to commemorate what would have been Eazy's fiftieth birthday. Wright wore short, dyed green hair, a lip ring, and smart-looking glasses. Her voice sounds uncannily like Eric's.

Some dispute Patricia's claim that Eazy had long intended to wed Woods—or anyone for that matter. "Eric was not a person to get married to anybody. He was not one to marry Tomica," said Bigg A. Mike Klein also maintained that Eazy had expressed no interest in getting hitched, and in a lawsuit he soon filed, he claimed Eazy signed his will "while in a debilitated state and under medication." (Sweeney and Woods denied the claims.) Even if he did say he was going to marry her, Tracy Jernagin argued, that didn't mean much: He'd told Tracy the same thing, she said. (For his part, Jerry Heller called Jernagin and her daughter with Eazy, named E.B., "the longtime true loves" of Eazy's life.)

Was Eazy a one-woman guy? Of course not. But did he believe it was in his best interest, and the best interest of his company, to sign it over to the woman now known as Tomica Woods-Wright? It seems quite possible. Putting aside the question of true love—which we can't really know— Eazy may have wanted to marry her at least in part because she was a sensible candidate to run Ruthless. She had a half decade's experience in the music business, after all, training under the great Clarence Avant. (Heller, though, complained that she was simply Avant's "secretary"—though she later took the title of executive assistant.) "In fact, I had already given Clarence notice that I was leaving to join Ruthless as general manager when Eric went into the hospital," Woods-Wright said.

According to numerous Ruthless employees and contractors, Woods-Wright quickly parted ways with much of the staff. Bodyguard Joe Fierro said he was abruptly fired and not given severance. Gary Ballen said he was fired by Woods-Wright "a week or two weeks after Eazy passed away." Above the Law left Ruthless because their contract was finished. Toker said Brownside also left the label voluntarily, believing it wouldn't be the same without Eazy, even though Woods-Wright said she'd honor their deal. Bone Thugs and some of the label's top acts were spared.

Tracy Jernagin told *Vibe* she encountered Woods-Wright in the hospital while the latter was working on paperwork. "She sat there with Ruthless checks on her lap. Making out checks, like, 'He won't be here anymore. *You'll* see who's running things now.'"

"Yeah, I had paperwork there," Woods-Wright responded in the *Vibe* story, "but for me to say something like that, to be that cruel—anybody who would say that about me is just being malicious."

Before It's Too Late

Not many people outside of Eazy's inner circle knew about his condition. But on March 16, while he lay in the ICU, Eazy's camp released a statement on his behalf. At a Hollywood news conference attorney Ron Sweeney read the message aloud, revealing to the wider world for the first time that Eazy had AIDS.

I may not seem like a guy that you'd pick to preach a sermon, but I feel it's now time to "testify" because I do have folks that care about me hearing all kinds of stories about what's up.

Yeah, I was a brother on the streets of Compton doing a lot of things most people look down on, but it did pay off. Then, we started rapping about real stuff that shook up the LAPD and the FBI, but we got our message across big time and everyone in America started paying attention to the boyz in the hood. Soon, our anger and hopes got everyone riled up.

There were great rewards for me personally like fancy cars, gorgeous women and good livin'. Like real nonstop excitement. I'm not religious but wrong or right, that's me. I'm not saying this because I'm looking for a soft cushion wherever I'm heading, I just feel that I've got thousands and thousands of young fans that have to learn about what's real when it comes to AIDS. Like something good that will reach out to all my homeboys and their kin because I want to save their asses before it's too late. I'm not looking to blame anyone except myself. I've learned in the last week that this thing is real and it doesn't discriminate. It affects everyone.

My girl, Tomica, and I have been together for four years, and we recently got married. She's good, she's kind and a wonderful mother. We have a little boy who's a year old. Before Tomica, I had other women. I have seven children by six different mothers. Maybe success was too good to me. I love all my kids. And I always took care of them.

Now, I'm in the biggest fight of my life and it ain't easy. But I want to say much love to those who have been down with me and thanks for all your support. Just remember: It's *your* real time and *your* real life.

Woods-Wright stood nearby, sobbing.

Heller and others close to Eazy believe he had little, if anything, to do with the statement's composition. Indeed, at the time of its release he couldn't breathe without the help of a machine. The statement also miscounts the number of Eazy's children. He sired ten in total, by eight different mothers, although one with Woods-Wright hadn't yet been born, and it seems likely that he didn't know about two of them at the time. (Woods-Wright said the statement was written with his involvement when he was still lucid, around the time of his AIDS diagnosis.)

Eazy's assistant Charis Henry said that before he was put on life support she told him it was his responsibility to let others know he was sick, if only for the sake of the women he'd slept with.

"What would everybody think?" Henry recalls Eazy asking.

"When would have you ever cared what anyone else thinks?" she responded. "They'll think you're a good person, a man of character." He agreed, and she soon after asked Woods-Wright to craft the statement, Henry said.

Even if he didn't write it, the *spirit* of the note feels like Eazy. He may have portrayed a nihilistic gangster, but his fans were important to him, particularly the young ones. While the prominent black athletes Magic

Johnson and Arthur Ashe had previously revealed HIV diagnoses, Eazy was the first urban music star to announce an infection, and he knew his followers would pay attention.

The question remained: How did Eazy *contract* HIV? The statement, alluding to "other women" and "nonstop excitement," seemed to hint that promiscuity might have taken him down. Some people close to him said he liked to use lambskin condoms, which can prevent pregnancy, but aren't recommended in preventing HIV. Others, including Dre and Cube, said he went bareback. Eazy seemed to confirm this in a 1992 interview with Howard Stern and his sidekick Robin Quivers on Stern's radio show. "You heard about AIDS?" asked Quivers.

"Yeah, but the people I mess with—" Eazy began to respond.

"They're clean," Stern said.

"Yeah."

"How do you know?" asked Quivers.

"Because I would have had it myself, if they would have had it."

Eazy told his doctor, William Young, that he did not use intravenous drugs or have homosexual sex. Therefore he, "must have contracted AIDS through heterosexual contact," Young said. But was it that simple? Isn't it very difficult for men to get HIV from women through heterosexual sex?

To help separate fact from fiction I consulted Gabriel Rotello, the author of *Sexual Ecology*, a book about the epidemiology of AIDS. He said long-term studies give the odds of a male "insertive" partner contracting the virus through unprotected sex with a woman to be about 1 in 10,000. That said, a number of factors can greatly increase those odds, he went on, like if the woman has only recently contracted the disease, or if the man is uncircumcised. (Eazy, however, was circumcised.) Since HIV—the infection that attacks the immune system and leads to AIDS, a condition of seriously degraded health—is transmitted through blood, the odds also go up if the man has an "opening" on his penis, like a scratch, a cut, or an untreated venereal sore.

Rotello added that, across African-American and other disadvantaged communities, needle sharing is often largely responsible for fueling the virus's spread. In fact, he said, heterosexual sex between minority women and minority men who have gotten the virus by sharing needles is "the primary thing that keeps the epidemic going among women of color."

So, how did Eazy contract HIV? The answer may simply be that Eazy didn't know, and no one else knows either.

Whatever the cause, the news that Eazy-E had AIDS shocked even those who knew him best. "[I]t was like a wake-up call, not just for his fans and people who don't know him, but even for me," Dr. Dre told the *Los Angeles Times*. Distressed fans began calling Cedars-Sinai at an unprecedented rate. "There's been an incredible outpouring of sympathy and we're not equipped to handle it," said hospital spokeswoman Paula Correia. She said they were receiving some 2,500 calls per day—even more than Lucille Ball when she was admitted there shortly before her 1989 death. More than any celebrity, for that matter.

Eazy's condition quickly deteriorated and he was moved to the intensive care unit. "We told him we loved him," said Jacob T., one of Eazy's bodyguards known as the Twins. "But he couldn't talk. Then we said, 'If you can hear us, just squeeze our hand.' He did."

"He said, 'Come over here tomorrow with the homies,'" remembered Toker. "'I want to leave the hospital in the lowriders.'"

Dr. Dre also got one last chance to visit. With trepidation he entered the room, shocked to see his friend-turned-rival unconscious, unable to breathe without a machine. "I felt real bad," he said. "The couple years we spent mad at each other, was nothing compared to the time we spent together and had happy times. I felt bad that we didn't get to kick it and have more fun, before he passed away."

His immune system devastated, Eazy was ravaged by a type of pneumonia common in AIDS patients called *Pneumocystis carinii*. A collapsed lung led to heart issues. The situation began to look helpless, and Eazy was taken off the ventilator. A Christian minister, brought in by his family, read him his last rites.

"It was one of the saddest days. It was like losing a family member," said DJ Yella.

Questions

Some members of Eazy's inner circle believe his life could have been saved. A number of my sources for this book insisted he'd been treated by a bogus, unqualified doctor. I did some checking into Eazy's attending physician, William Young, who died in 2004. According to his *Los Angeles Times* obituary, he was a longtime pulmonary and critical care specialist at Cedars-Sinai. A prominent doctor in the black community, his patients included politicians and celebrities, and he founded a nonprofit dedicated to helping low-income people live healthier lifestyles. His record had one notable blemish: In 2002 he was disciplined in writing by the Medical Board of California for "repeated negligence in prescribing for a patient while failing to provide proper documentation, and renewing the prescription for years without evaluating the patient." Apart from this—what amounted to a slap on the wrist—he seemed well qualified to treat Eazy.

Still, speculation that something fishy occurred in the lead-up to Eazy's death has persisted. His sister, many Ruthless artists, and some of his friends do not accept that Eazy died of AIDS. They note that none of his children, and none of the mothers of his children, have come forward saying they have the virus themselves. But this, said author Gabriel Rotello, isn't all that strange. He said people with the virus often don't spread it to their sexual partners, or even to their offspring. "HIV is the hardest to transmit, of all sexually transmitted diseases," he added.

Others note suspiciously that while Eazy moved quickly from HIV positive to full-blown AIDS and died right away, others have been able to live long lives with the disease, like Magic Johnson, who was diagnosed with HIV in 1991. Johnson's wealth and prominence, of course, afforded him access to treatments that were then rare, drug cocktails that have since turned HIV into a "chronic" condition, like diabetes, rather than an automatic death sentence. But Eazy was rich, too. (In the *Straight Outta Compton* film he's portrayed as running low on money near the end of his life, but everyone I consulted said this was not true.)

Eazy may have been living with HIV for a long time without realizing it, which is common; many people with the virus have no symptoms and appear healthy. In 2015 the Centers for Disease Control and Prevention reported that more than 150,000 Americans didn't know they had HIV, about 13 percent of the total. It's possible that Eazy's transition from HIV to AIDS only *seemed* fast. The average "latency" period for untreated HIV—when the individual is infected, but isn't showing symptoms—is about ten years, which means Eazy could have been infected well before he was famous. For those whose HIV progresses into AIDS, they can expect to survive an average of three years in the absence of treatment.

Eazy's sister Patricia Wright doubts he had AIDS, because he "would always go get checked, every six weeks," she said. Jerry Heller said Eazy had a physical with a Beverly Hills doctor in July 1994, and was given a clean bill of health. Indeed, if Eazy got tested regularly for STDs, something should have come up. But HIV screening wasn't then a common component of physicals.

Eazy's son Eric Wright Jr. posited a wild theory in an Instagram post in 2015, not long after the *Straight Outta Compton* film's release. Wright indicated in the post that, if his father died of AIDS, it may have been the result of a purposeful injection. "Eazy did not get sick until after the studio incident with Suge," he posited. He also pointed to the infamous 2003 Suge Knight interview on *Jimmy Kimmel Live*, where Suge discussed a "new" murder tactic, in which the assailant gets "blood from somebody with AIDS and they [inject] you with it." Suge called it the "Eazy-E thing." It's an intriguing theory, that Suge might have injected Eazy with AIDS, some four years before he died, but raises many questions. Where would Suge have gotten the tainted blood? Why would he choose this murder method, instead of another? And even if he had injected Eazy, would Eazy have remained silent about it? It all seems extremely unlikely.

Ice Cube didn't accuse Suge, but when I interviewed him he was unwilling to discount conspiracy theories about his friend's death. "I can't say they're crazy, because I don't know for sure. I don't know for sure how he contracted that," he said.

As a journalist, I thrive on this sort of intrigue. Reporters often build their careers on dispelling accepted narratives. But none of these theories add up. I've talked to numerous doctors and experts about the chain of events leading to Eazy's death on March 26, 1995, and none thinks them especially out of the ordinary.

Eazy was buried in a Whittier cemetery in his Compton hat, Pendleton, and jeans, lowered in a golden coffin. DJ Yella, the only N.W.A member who'd never fallen out with Eazy, and the only one to attend the funeral, served as pallbearer. The memorial service featured a giant photo of Eazy in his locs. People drove great distances to pay their respects, and thousands of mourners lined up for blocks to watch his coffin pass. Compton mayor Omar Bradley, who'd once dressed down Eazy for his lyrics, declared "Eazy-E Day" in Compton. One female attendee's shirt read, "AIDS is Ruthless. So take it Eazy."

In the parking lot, Bone Thugs member Wish Bone was apoplectic. "My nigga ain't dead!" he sobbed. "And if anybody says he is, we fighting!"

Though Eazy's gravestone, and most obituaries, list his birth year as 1963, that is likely not accurate. The funeral program gave his birth year as 1964, as do most official court documents. That would make him only thirty at his death, rather than thirty-one as was widely reported.

Total Chaos

Ruthless was valued at around $30 million at the time of Eazy's passing, and even before he breathed his last, the machinations to gain control of the company had begun.

Mike Klein gave notice to Eazy's lawyer Ron Sweeney that he was "fired" on March 24, two days before Eazy's death. When Sweeney nonetheless showed up to the Woodland Hills office three days later, guards blocked him from entering; owing to Eazy's incapacitation, a superior court judge had ordered the office closed and the locks changed. Mothers of his children stopped receiving child-support payments, label artists ceased receiving paychecks, and employees were told to go home.

Having already gotten their first royalty checks, some members of Bone Thugs had returned to Cleveland to buy houses. No one bothered telling them what was happening with Eazy; Krayzie Bone learned about his death from *MTV News*.

On March 27, the day after Eazy died, a trust company became administrator of his estate. Music industry veteran Ernie Singleton—who'd worked at Ruthless since the previous summer—was appointed to run the label on an interim basis. Singleton's tenure lasted about a year, during which time he released the massive Bone Thugs album and brought Woods-Wright into the fold.

Everyone under the sun insisted Eazy owed them money, and their claims were slowly sorted in probate court. D.O.C. and other artists claimed unpaid earnings, while car dealers including Mercedes and Jeep said he owed hundreds of thousands. Realty companies, credit card companies, a video game company, a funeral home, and lawyers all sought sums of varying sizes. Heller said he was owed more than a million, while Woods-Wright countersued, accusing him of misusing Ruthless funds.

An alleged former lover claimed Eazy had given her AIDS, and another wanted posthumous paternity testing. (The child was found not to be his.) Meanwhile, many of the mothers of Eazy's children pursued a claim to Eazy's estate, contesting the validity of his will and his marriage. In a settlement, trusts were established for each child, valued at $75,000 each, Jernagin said. Eazy's widow also settled with Heller. The terms were not disclosed, but their drawn-out negotiations finally wrapped in 1999, and included a mutual nondisparagement clause.

Mike Klein, meanwhile, filed suit against Woods-Wright and others, claiming they'd unlawfully seized control of the label and taken funds for their own use. He further asserted to own 50 percent of the label. "Klein thought he was going to be the person who stepped up and took Jerry Heller's place and be the confidant, the person getting the percentage," Woods-Wright told *Vibe*. "He basically underestimated my relationship with Eric and underestimated me. I wasn't just another woman who laid on her back and fucked Eric. I did have business knowledge." This suit was settled for around $1.5 million, according to an FBI file.

Just about everything surrounding Eazy's label was filled with chaos. According to an FBI report, footage intended to be used for Ruthless videos was stolen from Eazy's Norwalk house. The most shocking allegation, however, concerned missing recordings. Ruthless was hoping to profit off Eazy's unreleased music. But some of it was gone. Soon after his death the FBI investigated the theft of two titanium suitcases containing recordings—sixteen-inch reels or maybe digital audiocassettes—apparently taken from the trunk of his leased Mercedes. They were likely worth millions. Much of the FBI's declassified report is blacked out, so some details are murky. The man who turned out to be in possession of the music claimed Eazy gave it to him before he died. He fled to Ontario, Canada, where he attempted to set up a Ruthless "satellite" office. Someone purporting to represent Ruthless paid him $12,500 to do this. It's unclear who. But this Canadian office seemed like an attempt to circumvent Ernie Singleton and Tomica Woods-Wright's control. Someone even went so far as to rerecord the outgoing message on Ruthless's Woodland Hills office's answering machine. The new message said the label's number had been changed, and told callers to phone a different, Canadian number.

The FBI tracked down the man with the tapes, who said he was afraid to return to L.A. In the end, the agency closed the case without charging anyone, and the tapes were never recovered. It's possible unreleased Eazy-E music is still out there.

Ultimately the probate court found Eazy's marriage and his will to be legal, solidifying Woods-Wright's leadership at Ruthless. Despite the purported theft, Eazy had yet more unreleased tracks in the vault, and late 1995 saw the release of his modestly received, gold-selling *Str8 off tha Streetz of Muthaphukkin Compton.*

Though Ruthless signed a new distribution deal with Epic in 1997, the label gradually relinquished its heavyweight status. An announced comedy album from Chris Tucker never materialized. The new release schedule slowed to a drip, mainly from its shrinking list of marquee artists like MC Ren, Kid Frost, and Bone Thugs. The latter became increasingly disgruntled, and squared off in court with Ruthless a number of times. "Everything has basically changed since Eazy passed away. It just ain't the same. Basically, we like slaves now," Krayzie Bone told *Vibe* in 1998, laying the blame on Woods-Wright. "She a cool person, but I don't feel she know how to run a record company," said MC Ren.

The label moved offices, released a compilation album, and put out another posthumous Eazy-E album in 2002. It nowadays subsists primarily on its back catalog, sales from which were greatly invigorated by the *Straight Outta Compton* film.

Hell and Back

Tomica Woods-Wright has been accused of shrouding the events of Eazy's final weeks in secrecy. One cannot, for instance, obtain a copy of their marriage certificate. A courthouse employee told me it had been made "private," which is uncommon. "There is no autopsy on this man," Tracy Jernagin said. "The marriage certificate is a secret. The medical records are a secret. Who could go in there and see him was secret."

The ensuing decades have also been contentious. When I talked to Eric Wright Jr. in 2014 during the film's preproduction, he said Woods-Wright had excluded him and his siblings from the spoils of the movie deal. Wright admits, however, that his stepmother has helped out the family a bit over the years, including paying some bills, paying for a wedding, and giving him an administrative job at Ruthless, though he says it didn't pay well.

After her brother's death, Patricia got his Norwalk house, and lived there for nearly twenty years, before losing it to foreclosure. "It's nobody's fault but my own," she said.

Elise Kim, founder of Eazy's favorite charity, Athletes & Entertainers for Kids, said that Woods-Wright has been generous to her organization, continuing to send out Christmas gifts for their annual gala.

It's impossible to know if Woods-Wright has done, with his estate, what Eazy would have wanted her to. Wright wishes the company had been passed to Heller. "As a Jew, as a white man, he would have handled business," he said.

One thing is clear: Woods-Wright's life since his death has been no fairy tale. "That woman has been to hell and back," said S. Leigh Savidge, a filmmaker who said she broke down in front of him during a 2006 interview.

I'm inclined to give Woods-Wright the benefit of the doubt. Only twenty-six when Eazy died, it's unimaginable how much stress she's experienced, starting from the moment Eazy told her he had HIV. (Ultimately, she and her two children with Eazy tested negative.) She became responsible not just for his care, but for the label and handling the media and dealing with everyone who wanted a piece of him. Such duties would try anyone.

"I was not the cause of his death," she told *Vibe* in 1998. "I did not kill him. I was the one by his side, and I am the one trying to keep his dream alive. As far as anybody else who might be saying stuff, I could give a damn."

Through little more than instincts and hard work, Eazy, the onetime drug dealer, launched the most enduring movement hip-hop has ever seen. The popularity of gangsta rap was further solidified by the success of Bone Thugs-N-Harmony's four million–selling magnum opus *E. 1999 Eternal*, released just four months after Eazy's death. Their enduring, Grammy-winning ballad "Tha Crossroads" is dedicated to him, and the album has Eazy's stamp all over it. As with Bone Thugs, he gave voice to people who were born with little, but who weren't going to be pushed around. Anyone defining themselves on their own terms, who couldn't care less about convention and expectation, harbor a little bit of Eazy's renegade spirit.

POLITICAL PROPHET

Slight of stature, with a shaved head, crooked teeth, and a diamond on his nose, Tupac's most striking physical features were surely his beautiful, expressive brown eyes. Though he wasn't much for sports, he had an athlete's body and a seductive, liquid way of moving. He forever churned with ideas and spoke with great intensity on whatever subject, the veins in his head popping when he really got on a roll. During his short life, he wanted to experience everyone, feel the deepest emotions, and speak the greatest truths. He detested sobriety and smoked weed like cigarettes, although he smoked cigarettes, too.

He impatiently recorded his songs immediately after writing them. As a rapper, he wasn't the master of cadence and wordplay like his rival Biggie Smalls, though he was no slouch. What he did was reach more people than any other MC. In America he's a staple of classic rap radio, and in South America you can find his fans in the most desperate shantytowns. Democratic Republic of the Congo soldiers and Ivory Coast rebels have worn gear adorned with Tupac images, as did a Sierra Leone rebel army, who conquered villages to the tune of "California Love." Houston tattooist Dennis Coelho gave Tupac the giant cross on his back, with the words "Exodus 1831"—referencing the year of Nat Turner's slave rebellion. Coelho said the shop has since done "thousands and thousands" of Tupac-inspired tattoos. "We do the Tupac cross almost daily," he said.

Eminem has sold more albums than any other rapper, narrowly edging out Tupac. It's not quite apples to apples, considering Tupac's heyday was before digital downloading cut into record sales. Then again, Eminem has been making music for decades longer than Tupac. They share a movie star aura and R-rated pinup appeal, and have both shaped popular culture. But only Tupac transcended music to become something of a political prophet. Admirers pore over his lyrics, letters, and interviews like those of famous revolutionaries.

In terms of influence, I'd say his closest musical equivalent is Bob Dylan. Like Dylan, he may not be the best technically at his craft, but there's something *true* about him, something that hits you right *there*. Tupac brought to life the experience of being desperate, black, and poor. He didn't judge criminals, gangbangers, or anyone doing what they needed to do. He spoke out against the U.S. Congress's 1994 crime bill, signed by Bill Clinton, now seen by many as a fear-driven mistake that drove us to historically high incarceration rates. When asked by *Vibe*'s Kevin Powell why so many young African-Americans identified with him, Tupac said, "'Cause we all soldiers, unfortunately. Everybody's at war with different things. With ourselves. Some are at war with the establishment. Some of us are at war with our own communities."

He was as passionate and vulnerable as he was provincial and vindictive. Tupac rapped about fighting back, extending the ethos of Ice-T and N.W.A. But he was even brasher. He battled with cops who did him dirty. Drawing more bad press than nearly anyone this side of O. J. Simpson, he came out on top through charisma and brutal honesty. "'I love it when they fear me,' he said," wrote *Vibe*'s Danyel Smith. "But more truly, he loved not fearing them. He was free when he didn't give a fuck about anything, including continuing his own life, when he felt like the world—for a change—was his."

Though he used "ho" in his songs and was convicted of sexually abusing a nineteen-year-old woman, he penned three of the most elegant songs ever dedicated to black women, "Brenda's Got a Baby," "Keep Ya Head Up," and "Dear Mama." Long before the Black Lives Matter movement,

Tupac pondered aloud why African-American murders were often seen as no big deal. He mused about building an underground bunker, where he and his armed comrades could go if things went south.

And go south they did.

Tupac's distrust of police dated back to the very beginning of his life, when his pregnant mother was falsely imprisoned. He sometimes carried a video camera so he could document interactions with cops. Though his debut *2Pacalypse Now* featured stories about characters taking them out, Tupac said that he'd personally never had a run-in with police. That changed in October 1991, shortly after the album's release, when he was stopped by Oakland officers for jaywalking and asked for ID. The police "sweated me about my name" he said, and an argument ensued. "Next thing I know I was in a choke hold passing out with cuffs on, headed for jail for resisting arrest." It was life imitating his song "Trapped," in which his character is brutally manhandled by cops.

Tupac filed suit against the department and received a $42,000 settlement. Even more astonishingly, two years later he somehow got away with *shooting* a pair of off-duty cops. In late 1993 two suburban Atlanta officers, brothers named Mark and Scott Whitwell, were arguing with a motorist when Tupac, in town to perform a local show, came upon the scene. He didn't know the car's African-American driver and didn't realize the Whitwells were police, as they were dressed in civilian attire. Believing the brothers were harassing the driver, Tupac jumped into the fray. Bullets began flying and Tupac hit both cops, at least one in the behind. The motorist, named Kendall Hunter, later credited Tupac with saving his life, but Tupac was nonetheless jailed and charged with aggravated assault. To many reporters, this was a clear case of him acting out a revenge fantasy from one of his songs. News accounts were peppered with *2Pacalypse Now* lyrics like *Drop them or let 'em drop you? / I chose droppin' the cop.* But Mark Whitwell was also charged with firing at Tupac's car and giving false statements to police, and in the end charges against both parties were dropped when it was revealed that the Whitwells had been drinking. Further, a prosecution witness testified that a gun from one of the officers had been illegally seized from an evidence locker.

It was one thing to say "fuck the police" but something else to battle them so brazenly, in the South no less. The incident "sealed him as not only a rapper but a person who was true to the game," said his stepfather, Mutulu Shakur.

Poetic Justice

Tupac's breakout film role in 1992's *Juice* was serendipity. He had tagged along with Digital Underground's Money B to the audition, and, without any prior preparation, he competed for the part against Treach from Naughty By Nature. Drawing upon his real-life hurt and anger, Tupac's audition made him the obvious choice for the role of Bishop.

The film, directed by Ernest R. Dickerson, came on the heels of John Singleton's *Boyz n the Hood*, and has some similar themes, though it's set in Harlem. A group of high school friends attempt a robbery, urged on by Bishop, but the situation unravels as he becomes increasingly unhinged. Tupac comes alive in the film's second half with his manic intensity. Featuring a score by Hank Shocklee and the Bomb Squad, the film was a success, and Tupac was singled out for praise. Having studied at Baltimore School for the Arts, Tupac was familiar with Method acting. As he explained, "The camera just happen to catch real emotions."

Singleton picked Tupac for his *Boyz* follow-up, 1993's *Poetic Justice*. Strong admirers of each other's work, the pair envisioned a collaborative partnership like Martin Scorsese and Robert De Niro. Still, *Poetic Justice* was a difficult shoot, and Tupac clashed with his costar Janet Jackson; he said he was asked by members of the crew, presumably at her request, to take an AIDS test before a romantic scene, and he refused. Poet Maya Angelou, meanwhile, deplored his on-set cursing and talked him down after he almost got into a fight. "Do you know that we stood on slave ship decks, and stood on auction blocks, and were hosed down like dogs, for you, so you could live?" she asked him. He began crying and she put her arm around him, wiping his tears with her hands.

The film was partly shot in Oakland, often in the depths of night. Tupac was taunted by community members who'd known him as a semi-transient only years before. They hung out on the periphery of the set, trying to get his attention or provoke a fight. "Don't pretend that you don't know me, nigga!" they yelled. "Nigga's a movie star and can't speak to nobody." Tupac, somehow, took all of this graciously. "They're sitting there knowing they used to give me money to go to the store, and now I've got their whole family taking pictures with me," he said. "That's an animosity that nothing I can do can kill, because that's poverty shit and I can understand."

Tupac had diverse taste in music beyond hip-hop, running from Kate Bush to the *Les Misérables* soundtrack, which he'd listen to at night to calm his nerves. During the day he'd get high in his trailer and storm around set. Once he was told he'd have a day off, only to have producers inform him that he'd instead have to shoot publicity photos. "I can't take this shit. Y'all treat a nigga like a slave," he groused, and then proceeded to punch out a window in his trailer.

Filming also took place in L.A., and Tupac moved there for the first time, living in a house on a tranquil street in the San Fernando Valley with his mother, with whom he had reconciled. He journeyed all over L.A. and its southern perimeter, to Watts and Compton, learning the neighborhoods and the gangs, determining whom he could and couldn't trust. He warned Singleton when specific gangbangers planned to come to the set. But it wasn't just the guys on the corners. Tupac got to know everyone under the Southern California sun, the "alcoholics," "pimps," "robbers," "burglars," "nerds," "homosexuals," and "prophets," he said, anyone who could teach him how to survive in the big city.

Also in 1993 he released his second album, *Strictly For My N.I.G.G.A.Z...*, another hit. Though its most popular track, "I Get Around," is a boilerplate warning to ladies who'd tie him down, the work is otherwise populated with heartbreaking stories about the struggles of black folks. The title, according to his stepbrother Mopreme, references the fact that, "no matter what we do, we still gonna be niggas to certain people." *I'm sick of being tired*, Tupac raps on "The Streetz R Deathrow," a song unrelated to the label. *Sick of the sirens, body bags, and the gun firing / Tell Bush, "Push the button!" 'cause I'm fed / Tired of hearin' these voices in my head. Strictly* shows a maturity in his songwriting. "Papa'z Song" is not a standard "fuck you, Dad" lament; rather, after a son admonishes his father for being gone during his childhood, Papa gives his side of the story. Having heard the Five Stairsteps' "O-o-h Child" (*O-o-h child, things are gonna get easier*) in *Boyz n the Hood,* Tupac employed a sample of it on "Keep Ya Head Up." *Some say the blacker the berry, the sweeter the juice / I say the darker the flesh then the deeper the roots,* begins the song, which would later inspire rapper Kendrick Lamar. It's dedicated in part to Latasha Harlins, the fifteen-year-old killed in 1991 by a South Central store owner who believed she was shoplifting.

Like *2Pacalypse Now, Strictly for My N.I.G.G.A.Z...* documents the tribulations of—and provides a balm for—those making their way through a racist society. These aren't really gangsta rap albums, since "gangsta" implies characters enriching themselves through criminal enterprise and violence. That wasn't Tupac, at least not yet.

Tupac's activism was largely lost on white critics. It probably didn't help he was constantly going to jail. Slated to perform a homecoming show at a 1992 Marin City festival, he was confronted by a group of people angry over negative interview comments he'd made in the press about his former town. "It was a combination of jealousy and anger," said Mopreme, who was with him that day. "'Pac was becoming successful, there was a lot of haters." A tussle broke out, shots were fired, and a six-year-old boy riding a bicycle nearby was accidentally killed. Though Tupac didn't fire the gun, a .380 Colt automatic, it was registered to him; a sheriff's sergeant accused Mopreme of pulling the trigger. "I'm not talking about who did what, I'm not a snitch," Mopreme told me when I interviewed him in 2016. "It was just unfortunate and sad, and we didn't start it." Tupac and Mopreme were arrested and then released, owing to a lack of evidence. But the boy's parents filed a civil suit, which was settled for a six-figure sum, paid by Tupac's record label.

Tupac was dogged by legal trouble for much of his adult life. In 1993 he allegedly assaulted a limo driver outside of an *In Living Color* taping, after the man complained the rapper was smoking weed. (The charges were dropped.) Shortly thereafter at a show in Lansing, Michigan, Tupac brandished a baseball bat against another rapper and did a short jail stint. (He said he and his road manager were provoked.) "I beat up the director of *Menace II Society*," he bragged on *Yo! MTV Raps* that same year, referencing the film directed by Allen and Albert Hughes, in which he'd been slated to appear. "They fired me, but did it in a roundabout, punk, snitch way, so I caught 'em on the streets and beat their behind." Allen Hughes tells the story differently. Before he was canned, Tupac was disruptive on set in front of a cast that included Jada Pinkett, Hughes said. For the sake of the movie Tupac needed to go, he added, saying the firing was straightforward. But Tupac lost his $300,000 payday, and not long afterward at a video shoot confronted Hughes with a posse of Crips in tow. Tupac "threw a sucker punch," Hughes threw him "on top of a truck," and then the Crips beat Hughes badly. After bragging about the incident to *Yo! MTV Raps*, Tupac got fifteen days in jail.

The Hughes brothers had worked with Tupac before, initially finding him funny and charming. But something changed around the time of *Juice*'s release in early 1992, Allen said, claiming that after Tupac saw a screening of the film "he was never the same." He said Tupac subsequently began rolling heavy with gang members, "switching sets a lot...whether with the Rollin' 60s, or the Bloods, or some gang in Houston, whichever fit where he was at the time." Indeed, Tupac was photographed in both red and blue bandanas, though he doesn't appear to have joined any gang in particular.

He also got increasingly tatted up. Though common today, heavily inked rappers were then rare. Tupac's work included his now-iconic "THUG LIFE" tattoo across his abs, which stood for "The Hate U Give Little Infants Fucks Everyone." Thug Life was Tupac's mantra; it was a code that informed the Watts peace treaty he helped craft, and it was the name of one of his rap groups. "It was really supposed to be about saving thugs' lives," said Mopreme, a Thug Life member. "A lot of people got the message, but a whole lot didn't."

"I'm thugging against society. I'm thugging against the system that made me," Tupac said. Even Tupac's mother Afeni didn't initially understand it, finding the word "thug" hard to reconcile with the Black Panther ideals on which her son was raised. On the 1992 day when she found out he was going to get his "Thug Life" tattoo, she begged his friend Charis Henry to drive over to the Sunset Strip tattoo parlor to stop it. Henry arrived too late.

A Terror Since the Public School Era

Voletta Wallace equated bulk with health, and she fed her son Christopher well. An immigrant, Voletta arrived in the U.S. from Jamaica at age seventeen in the late sixties. She became involved with a much older Jamaican man named Selwyn Letore. After Christopher was born, Letore fell out of the picture. As it turned out, he had a whole other family in London.

Raised in the Bedford-Stuyvesant neighborhood of Brooklyn, Christopher was an intelligent student who was good at drawing, and worked for a time as a grocery bag boy. He began drug dealing when he was about twelve, he said, buying polo shirts and fancy shoes with his earnings, and stashing them on the roof to retrieve them in the morning before he went to school, so his mother wouldn't suspect. Eventually Voletta, who was working two jobs and obtained a master's degree in education, kicked him out. He traveled to North Carolina to sell rocks, and was arrested on a drug charge when he was seventeen, he said, spending about nine months behind bars. With a girlfriend named Jan Jackson he had a daughter, named T'yanna, in 1993. Along the way he managed to impress some well-connected people with his blossoming rap skills. Big Daddy Kane's DJ, Mister Cee, heard his tape, and encouraged him to send it to *The Source* magazine, who selected him for their influential Unsigned Hype column.

Wallace, whose weight would swell to well over three hundred pounds, rapped under the name Biggie Smalls. But after a dispute with those involved with the film from which the handle came—the Sidney Poitier–Bill Cosby 1975 movie *Let's Do It Again*—he went officially by Notorious B.I.G.

A *Source* editor named Matteo "Matty C" Capoluongo played Biggie's tape for Sean "Puffy" Combs, who worked as an A&R for a hip-hop and R&B label called Uptown Records. Puffy's rise was like something out of a movie: His father, before being gunned down, was an associate of famed Harlem drug kingpin Frank Lucas. Like Tupac, Puffy started as a backing dancer, for acts including Heavy D & the Boyz. But his career was almost derailed before it began. In 1991, nine people were killed at an event he organized called the Heavy D and Puff Daddy Celebrity Charity Basketball Game. Held at City College, it was wildly oversold. Fans tore doors off hinges, and gate-crashers were crushed up against ticket holders inside a stairwell. A subsequent investigation questioned whether the AIDS education outreach program flyers claimed the game would benefit actually existed.

Puffy rebounded from the tragedy, as well as his 1993 firing from Uptown Records. (He was headstrong, and growing increasingly interested in gangsta rap, which was outside Uptown's scope.) He took Biggie to his own imprint, called Bad Boy, which was funded with the help of a partnership with Arista Records, founded by Clive Davis. Bad Boy was largely inspired by the styles and tropes of Death Row and *The Chronic*. New York hip-hop wasn't used to following other cities' trends, but it was hard to deny the appeal of funky, hard-edged rhymes.

Notorious B.I.G.'s first appearance was on a remix of Uptown artist Mary J. Blige's 1992 hit "Real Love," followed by his own "Party and Bullshit" a year later, from the *Who's the Man?* soundtrack. The latter track is a small miracle of pacing, style, and assonance, with Biggie rapping expeditiously about being *a terror since the public school era*, when he was wielding *bathroom passes, cutting classes, squeezing asses*. He hadn't quite found his tempo, but his potential seemed unlimited.

Biggie himself had an undeniable West Coast influence, listening to Ice Cube's *Amerikkka's Most Wanted* before recording his own debut *Ready to Die*. One of Biggie's favorite rappers was Compton's King Tee; he adopted a similar cadence, and a love for weed rhymes. "Biggie came out here and studied under King Tee," said Chris "The Glove" Taylor. "When he came out here he sounded one way, and when he went back he sounded like King Tee."

Having absorbed the West Coast influence, Biggie emerged with his own dense, melodic style, and 1994's well-reviewed, game-changing *Ready to Die* sold six million copies. From a technique perspective, he was untouchable, his rhymes platonic ideals. With extraordinary timing and breath control, each line inspired the next, like a high-speed train effortlessly pushing through mountains. The album birthed his most famous track, "Juicy," a nostalgic, nothing-to-something story that makes everyone who hears it fall for him. *Fifty-inch screen, money green, leather sofa / Got two rides, a limousine with a chauffeur.*

In the summer of 1994, Biggie married R&B singer and fellow Bad Boy artist Faith Evans, barely a week after their meeting. "When I first saw her, she was killing me with those eyes," Biggie said. "I rolled up to her and said, 'You're the type of girl I would marry.' She said, 'Why don't you?' So I was like, 'Fuck it, it's on.'"

Tupac's Lieutenant

Tupac and Biggie first encountered each other in 1993. The latter had a pair of extracurricular goals on his business trip to L.A.: to find weed, and to meet Tupac. A local dealer got ahold of Tupac, who invited Biggie and his party to his house, where he shared with them a "big freezer bag of the greenest vegetables I'd ever seen," according to Uptown Records intern Dan Smalls, who was part of the group. Tupac got them high and pulled out a "green army bag" filled with handguns and machine guns. "So now, here we are, in this backyard running around with guns, just playing," continued Dan Smalls in *The Fader*. "Luckily they were all unloaded.

While we were running around, 'Pac walks into the kitchen and starts cooking for us. He's in the kitchen cooking some steaks. We were drinking and smoking and all of a sudden 'Pac was like, 'Yo, come get it.' And we go into the kitchen and he had steaks, and French fries, and bread, and Kool-Aid and we just sittin' there eating and drinking and laughing. And you know, that's truly where Big and 'Pac's friendship started."

"We all thought he was a dope rapper," said Tupac's longtime friend E.D.I. Mean, a member of Tupac's affiliated group the Outlawz. Tupac gifted Biggie a bottle of Hennessy. Biggie slept on Tupac's couch when he was in California, and when Tupac was in town he came by Biggie's neighborhood, picking him up in a white limousine and throwing dice with the locals. The pair freestyled back to back at a concert called Budweiser Superfest at Madison Square Garden in 1993, with Biggie wowing the crowds with lines like *Oh my God I'm dropping shit like a pigeon / I hope you're listenin' / Smackin' babies at their christenin'.*

Despite the Garden cameo, Biggie still wasn't much known outside of Brooklyn. Tupac, by then a platinum-selling movie star, acted as a mentor. Biggie and other young rappers assembled in record studios or hotel rooms to hear Tupac lecture about how to make it in the game. "'Pac could get up and get to teaching," said E.D.I. Mean. "Everyone was transfixed on this dynamic individual, and soaking up all the information we could soak up." But Tupac devoted special attention to Biggie, grooming him and letting him perform at his concerts. Biggie even told him he'd like to be a part of his Thug Life group. "I trained the nigga, he used to be under me like my lieutenant," Tupac said.

Tupac claimed to have directly influenced Biggie's style. "I used to tell the nigga, 'If you want to make your money you have to rap for the bitches. Do *not* rap for the niggas,'" he said. "The bitches will buy your records, and the niggas want what the bitches want." As proof that Biggie had heeded his advice, Tupac cited the difference between the aggressive "Party and Bullshit" and softer *Ready to Die* hits tracks "Big Poppa," which appealed more to the ladies. *Soon as he buy that wine, I just creep up from behind / And ask what your interests are, who you be with?*

But before *Ready to Die* came out, Biggie worried he could miss his shot, considering the uncertainty surrounding Puffy's new label. Things weren't happening for him quickly enough, he complained to Tupac. He asked Tupac to take over as his manager, in hopes Tupac could advance his music and film career as rapidly as he'd done his own. "Biggie looked like he was wearing the same pair of Timberlands for a year [while] 'Pac was staying at the Waldorf-Astoria and buying Rolexes and dating Madonna," E.D.I. Mean said.

But Tupac declined the offer. "Nah, stay with Puff," he told Biggie. "He will make you a star."

Character

Biggie had moved weight as a drug dealer, but exaggerated his experiences for the sake of his songs. His true love was hip-hop, and as his star rose he had little energy for dirty business. Tupac was far more interested in passing as a real-life gangsta. "It irked him when they said, 'Fake gangsta rapper,'" said his stepbrother Mopreme.

In New York to shoot the 1994 film *Above the Rim*, Tupac became enmeshed with a group of notorious Queens toughs. He was modeling his character Birdie—a gangster involved in youth basketball programs—on a Haiti-born high roller called Jacques "Haitian Jack" Agnant. A feared and influential music promoter, Haitian Jack also had a hustle resembling the character Omar from the seminal TV series *The Wire*. "My thing is robbing drug dealers," he told Derrick Parker, the retired NYPD "hip-hop cop" who ran a special unit focused on rap-related crimes. "The drug dealer, see, he isn't going to call the police."

Tupac had noticed Haitian Jack at a Manhattan club, surrounded by women and champagne, and asked for an introduction. They also spent time at a Queens bar, where Jack would bring through celebrities including Madonna, Shabba Ranks, and Jamaican musician Buju Banton. (Tupac briefly dated Madonna, after Rosie Perez introduced them at the 1993 Soul Train Awards in L.A.) Biggie warned Tupac to keep his distance from Haitian Jack, to no avail. Tupac liked Jack's swagger. He introduced the rapper to high-end jewelry and Versace duds, as well as the local gangstas who called the shots. "[H]e loved the respect and recognition I got in New York and I think he wanted that same respect," Haitian Jack said.

The two were partying at a downtown Manhattan club called Nell's in November 1993, where Tupac met a nineteen-year-old woman named Ayanna Jackson. They got close on the dance floor (Tupac says she gave him a blowjob in a corner at the club) and went back to his suite at the Le Parker Meridien hotel. Four days later she met up with him at the hotel again, only to encounter not just Tupac, but Haitian Jack, Tupac's road manager Charles "Man Man" Fuller, and another man who was not identified. There, she alleged, the group gang-raped her and forced her to perform oral sex. Tupac claimed he left the bedroom when the other men entered and fell asleep. She called the police, and Tupac, Haitian Jack, and Fuller were arrested. The police also found guns, which Tupac later claimed belonged to Biggie.

The prosecution alleged Tupac, charged with sexual abuse, sodomy, and illegal weapons possession, had offered up Jackson "as a reward for his boys." Tupac denied this, but after the trial told *Vibe* he blamed himself for "doing nothing" to protect Jackson from the other men. Before the trial began, Tupac's and Fuller's cases were severed from Haitian Jack's; in a deal that Tupac and his lawyer deemed too good to be true, Jack pleaded guilty to two misdemeanors and avoided jail time. Believing Haitian Jack was a snitch, Tupac told a New York *Daily News* reporter that Jack had set him up. (Ayanna Jackson and Haitian Jack have denied this.)

Calling out a reputed gangster in the press is not sensible. But, ironically, after spending so much time with Jack and his ilk, Tupac had begun to feel invincible. He went wherever he wanted, wearing flashy jewelry worth thousands of dollars. Secure in his street credentials, he was convinced that nobody would mess with him.

Supporting his extended family and paying lawyers for his interminable string of court cases, Tupac's bank accounts withered. In late 1994 he agreed to record a guest verse for a rapper named Little Shawn, who was close with Puffy and Biggie. The invitation came from Shawn's manager, Jimmy "Henchman" Rosemond, whom Tupac had met through Haitian Jack, and Tupac was to be paid $7,000.

On November 30, 1994, Tupac arrived stoned to Quad Recording Studios in Times Square, the spot where he recorded much of his next album, *Me Against the World*. Arriving with three associates, none of whom were bodyguards, he encountered three other men he didn't know, wearing army fatigues. This was Brooklyn fashion, so Tupac assumed they were with Biggie. He felt better about the situation when Biggie's affiliated rapper Lil' Cease yelled down to him that Biggie was upstairs recording. Puffy was there, too.

But before Tupac's crew could get on the elevator, the men in army fatigues drew 9 mm guns and ordered them to the floor. Instead, Tupac reached for his own gun. He was shot, beaten, and robbed of his jewelry. He played dead and the assailants left, at which time he staggered into the elevator and rode it upstairs. When the doors opened he saw a group including Puffy, Biggie, and Haitian Jack's associate Henchman. Tupac said the crew looked surprised and guilty, but Puffy claimed they showed him "nothing but love and concern."

Tupac believed the incident was more than a random heist. "It was like they were mad at me," he said. He claimed to have taken five bullets, including shots to the head and through his scrotum. Forensic evidence, however, seemed to indicate he shot himself. "In the haste of getting his gun out of his waistband, I believe he pulled the trigger," said former LAPD investigator Greg Kading, who has reviewed the investigative material. "I think the wounds to his head were superficial lacerations from being pistol whipped. If they went there to execute him, they could have certainly done that."

Bill Courtney, a retired NYPD cop who also worked hip-hop cases, believed the stick-up was a response to Tupac's *Daily News* comments against Haitian Jack. "A message was being sent to him not to name-drop," he said.

"Nobody came to rob you," Henchman told *Vibe* in 2005. "They came to discipline you."

Tupac believed Henchman himself orchestrated the crime, which was also the conclusion of a bombshell 2008 *Los Angeles Times* story. That piece, by Pulitzer Prize–winning reporter Chuck Philips, asserted that both Puffy and Biggie knew about the setup in advance, although they were allegedly told it would only involve a beating, and no shooting. The story was later retracted after it was found to have been informed by falsified documents, and Philips was soon laid off. That wasn't the end of the story, however. In 2011 one of Henchman's former associates, named Dexter Isaac, claimed in an interview he was one of the men in army fatigues, and that he'd been hired by Henchman. "He gave me $2,500, plus all the jewelry I took, except for one ring, which he took for himself," Isaac said. Not long afterward, Henchman himself confessed to his involvement. (Philips demanded, but did not receive, an apology from the *Los Angeles Times*.)

Puffy and Biggie denied their involvement in the crime, or any prior knowledge of it. Haitian Jack also claimed he wasn't involved, and following a separate conviction was deported to Haiti in 2007. One of Tupac's associates who came with him to Quad studios that day, Randy "Stretch" Walker, was murdered in Queens exactly a year later. Police suspected a connection between the two events, but were unable to prove it.

Penalized

Tupac was taken to Manhattan's Bellevue Hospital, but didn't remain there long. He feared for his life, and though the Fruit of Islam provided security, they weren't carrying guns. He left Bellevue and was admitted to Metropolitan Hospital under an assumed name, but said he still received an anonymous, threatening phone call from someone saying, "You ain't dead yet?" Shortly after surgery he checked himself out—against doctor's orders—and went to the home of his friend, actress Jasmine Guy. (They'd worked together on the sitcom *A Different World*; he played Jada Pinkett's thugged-out ex-boyfriend Piccolo.)

Tupac's father Bill Garland visited him while he recovered, and they stoked the fire of their long-lost relationship, even smoking pot together at Guy's place. "I was *fucked* up," Garland said. He also said he exchanged pleasantries with Biggie, who came to visit Tupac in the hospital; Garland remains convinced Biggie didn't know about the shooting in advance, and at this point Tupac hadn't accused him either.

On December 1, 1994, Tupac arrived to a New York City courtroom wearing bandages and confined to a wheelchair, and was pronounced guilty of sexual abuse in the Ayanna Jackson case, though acquitted on the sodomy and weapons charges. Sentenced to a minimum of a year and a half in prison, pending appeal, his bail was set at $3 million. To some observers, the case against Tupac was weak, the punishment and bail harsh. Was it payback for his anticop lyrics? An in-depth *New Yorker* article by Connie Bruck concluded that Tupac "was penalized more for who he was—a charismatic gangsta rapper with a political background—than for what he had done."

Unable to raise bail, Tupac served most of his time at Clinton Correctional Facility, a maximum security prison in upstate New York. (The same prison where two men escaped in 2015, inspiring a dramatic manhunt where one was killed and the other recaptured.) Guards sought to humiliate him, Tupac's lawyer said. A rumor surfaced that he was raped, which he denied. Meanwhile, his paranoia and anger intensified. He called Haitian Jack and Henchman "the walking dead."

Prison wasn't entirely a hardship, however. Tupac dried out. He wrote a screenplay and read *The Art of War*. Al Sharpton visited. He got mail from Jim Carrey and Tony Danza, the latter of whom urged him to stay strong. ("He is the bomb forever," Tupac told MTV, of Danza.) Maya Angelou came to visit at his request, and he immediately besieged her with questions about James Baldwin and Tolstoy. He signed autographs for fellow prisoners, including a white supremacist who wanted one "for his little cousins."

While inside Tupac married a woman he'd been seeing named Keisha Morris, a criminal justice student who was something of a straight arrow. They'd met at a party thrown by Puffy; she was not impressed by his advances, which only made him try harder. On their first date, in summer 1994, they saw *Forrest Gump*; at dinner afterward he mentioned that he'd read for the part of Bubba. But their relationship was difficult from the start. Morris lived in Harlem while Tupac, drawn by cheaper real estate, resided primarily in Atlanta, along with his mother and members of his group the Outlawz. Morris supported him during his trial, and moved close to the prison to better assist him. But following his release the marriage collapsed; she said she felt "used," but didn't harbor animosity.

Me Against the World, Tupac's third album, was released soon after his prison sentence began. Its tone was a departure from his first two albums. Whereas "Brenda's Got a Baby" came from headlines, now his *own* stories were news, and the album begins with reporters running down his trials and tribulations. He'd never been particularly optimistic, but *World* descends into full-blown paranoia and anguish, as evidenced by song titles like "If I Die 2Nite" and "Fuck the World." *Stugglin' and strivin', my destiny's to die*, he raps on "Death Around the Corner." (His album with Thug Life the year previous also reflected his transition from would-be revolutionary to presumably doomed street soldier, on songs like "Bury Me a G.") But *Me Against the World* also has buoyant tracks like "Old School," an homage to New York rappers who laid the foundation of the genre, and "Young Niggaz," a cautionary tale to would-be baby gangstas.

"Dear Mama" would become one of the most beloved songs in hip-hop history. The album came out a year before Bill Clinton signed his notorious welfare reform law, and the track portrayed its African-American female protagonist as a hero. The song's most famous line—*Even as a crack fiend, Mama / You always was a black queen, Mama*—harbors nuance rare in popular music. Despite little promotion, *Me Against the World* went double platinum and became his bestselling album yet.

Tupac considered making it his swan song; he was tired of all of the music industry drama. But his passion reignited after a disturbing rumor began to sink in, one that came from people he trusted: that Biggie knew in advance about the Quad studios shooting.

"He owed me more than to turn his head and act like he didn't know niggas was about to blow my fucking head off," he said later. And even if Biggie hadn't set him up, he should at least have been able to *find out* who did it. "You don't know who shot me in your hometown, these niggas from your neighborhood?"

This probably wasn't entirely fair. According to sources I interviewed for this book, even if Biggie knew about the setup in advance (which is far from certain), he may have been helpless to stop it or warn Tupac, without risking violence upon himself.

The way Tupac saw it, the whole thing was fucked. Someone tried to harm him, and when they couldn't do that, the justice system got him for a crime he didn't commit. And now it turned out that his own *friend* had betrayed him? A friend whom Tupac had helped to acquire fame and fortune?

Angry and seeking revenge, Tupac decided he was ready to start recording again, to pay back his enemies.

"Selling My Soul"

Before he went to prison, both Ruthless Records and Death Row were vying for Tupac's services. Tupac rolled with Eazy to industry events, they shared meals, and some Ruthless camp members took to wearing Thug Life caps. "Tupac was around us every day," said Cold 187um, from Ruthless group Above the Law. Mopreme said Eazy had talked with Tupac about signing Thug Life to Ruthless. Eazy's assistant Charis Henry believes that, if Eazy were still alive when Tupac got out of prison, he would have signed with the label.

Meanwhile, Tupac appeared on the Death Row–orchestrated *Above the Rim* soundtrack, and was paid well to record a song for the *Murder Was the Case* soundtrack—which wasn't even used. (Suge did him the favor to support him during his legal wranglings, Tupac said.) Tupac began to see Suge as a well-funded, well-armed potential ally. While in prison he asked his wife Keisha Morris to relay a message to Suge: He was broke and needed help. On top of the lawyers' fees and everything else, his mother was losing her house.

"Suge sent $15,000 and put it on his books," said Reggie Wright Jr., Death Row's head of security. Tupac was jubilant, and sent Suge another message, that he'd like to see him.

Few places in the U.S. were farther away from Los Angeles than Dannemora, New York, where Tupac was incarcerated, but Suge began coming out to see him. Further, Death Row offered him something no one else seemed to be able to deliver: release. Death Row's lawyer David Kenner pledged to help Tupac with his case, and began working to spring him on an appeal bond.

Suge didn't just try to recruit Tupac to his label, he offered him a place in his family, the most powerful and out-of-control family in hip-hop.

Death Row was under the umbrella of Interscope, the label where Tupac released his first three albums. Relinquishing Tupac to Death Row amounted to little more than shuffling paperwork, at least from a corporate perspective. Suge's courtship of Tupac came with Jimmy Iovine and Interscope's blessing; according to many accounts, Iovine seemed anxious to get rid of Tupac, stressed out about the chaos surrounding his every move. From a musical perspective, pairing Tupac with Dre—a producer the rapper had long admired—was smart. In real life, the consequences of putting Suge and Tupac together would be nuclear, and some have blamed Iovine for not anticipating the fallout. (Iovine declined comment on this issue.)

Although many close to him advised him against it, Tupac decided to jump to Death Row. "I know I'm selling my soul to the devil," he said. Tupac's manager Atron Gregory, who'd worked tirelessly for Tupac's release, grudgingly stepped aside. On September 16, 1995, Kenner presented Tupac with a three-page, handwritten "memo"—standing in for a contract—appointing Suge as his manager and binding him to Death Row for three albums, promising him an advance of at least $1 million per work, as well as $500,000 in expenses, including $125,000 for a car and $250,000 for his legal fund. Less than a month later Interscope and Atlantic Records put up the $1.4 million bond, and he was out. Though Tupac always thanked Suge for bailing him out, he didn't actually supply the money. Suge's role seems to have had more to do with greasing the wheels; and the $1.4 million was actually an advance on Tupac's future royalties.

"It wasn't a legal contract," said Charles Ogletree Jr., a lawyer who would later represent Tupac. "It was absurd that anyone with an opportunity to reflect would agree to those terms. It was only because he was in prison that he signed it." Suge Knight's dual role as Tupac's manager and his label representation was a conflict of interest. But the deal came with front-end benefits, including a house for Afeni, and material spoils galore for Tupac—vehicles, jewelry, vacations. Outside the prison's doors, a white limousine took him to a private plane, and he was off.

MY .44 MAKE SURE Y'ALL KIDS DON'T GROW

The first black female secretary of state for Pennsylvania, C. DeLores Tucker is best known for her antirap activism. She called the genre "pornographic filth" and protested the NAACP's 1994 nomination of Tupac for an Image award. That year, largely owing to her efforts, Congress held hearings on the negative effects of hip-hop. Not much came of them, and Tucker was portrayed by critics as a narrow-minded school marm, or worse. In "How Do U Want It," Tupac rapped:

> *C. Delores Tucker, you's a motherfucker*
> *Instead of trying to help a nigga you destroy a brother*

Tucker was nonetheless a force to be reckoned with. She purchased Time Warner stock so she could rail against its gangsta rap offerings at shareholder meetings. With conservative former education secretary William J. Bennett she took out an ad accusing Time Warner of promoting music celebrating the "rape, torture, and murder of women." The company had already been under fire for Ice-T's "Cop Killer," and Connecticut senator Joe Lieberman and senate leader Bob Dole also joined the chorus. Dole accused Time Warner of the "marketing of evil."

Time Warner felt the heat. Its Interscope-run sublabels Death Row and Nothing Records, home to Marilyn Manson and Nine Inch Nails, weren't exactly helping matters. In 1995 Time Warner sold its interest in Interscope back to the company, reportedly for $120 million. (Critics pointed out that Time Warner still maintained its share of, and continued profiting off, the publishing rights to the music.) Tucker and singer Dionne Warwick talked with Suge about cleaning up his label's lyrics. In a bizarre twist, Tucker was accused by Death Row of unsuccessfully offering to bring the label to a new division of Time Warner, and attempting to profit off such a deal. By early 1996 Jimmy Iovine and company had sold Time Warner's share of Interscope to Universal, making a nine-figure profit.

None of this slowed Death Row's roll. The label continued churning out monster hit after monster hit, bringing in tens of millions annually. Suge moved the label's operations to a studio in a sleepy spot in the San Fernando Valley, only a ten-minute drive from Ruthless headquarters. Called Can-Am Recorders, the facility was ensconced in an anonymous industrial park in suburban Tarzana—named for the character Tarzan created by Edgar Rice Burroughs, who once lived on a ranch there. It's long been a renowned studio, used by Harry Belafonte, Michael Jackson, and Phish over the years; *Appetite for Destruction* was partly recorded there.

Can-Am still operates. When I visited in 2014, the receptionist showed me where Suge had installed a floor-to-ceiling wall of bulletproof glass. In the Death Row era Can-Am resembled a hip-hop frat house, a testosterone-heavy, smoke-filled boys club. Suge virtually resided there, sleeping in a room next to his office, which was decorated in blood red, from the furniture to the walls. The Death Row logo on the carpet featured a shackled man in an electric chair with a hood over his head. (One was advised not to step on it.) Suge monitored the security cameras, lifted weights in the on-site gym, fed rats to the piranhas in his tank, and threatened to do the same to journalists who asked the wrong questions. His vicious German shepherd Damu (Swahili for "blood") terrified visitors. He also maintained a pair of expensive Belgian Malinoises trained to attack, one named P-Funk.

The studio's neighbors were horrified by the steady stream of gang members coming and going. But the police didn't do much, likely in part because Death Row's security *was* the police, featuring numerous LAPD, Compton, Long Beach, and sheriff's department officers. The label's security arm Wrightway Protective Services was run by former Compton cop Reggie Wright Jr., Suge's friend and Compton schoolmate. Like Suge, Reggie played football growing up, and followed in his father's footsteps to become a cop. He began working for Suge in late 1994 and before long formed Wrightway; the majority of the company's work was for Death Row, including staffing Suge's Las Vegas music venue, called Club 662. (The numbers spell "M-O-B" on a phone pad.) For about a year, Wright's police work overlapped with his Death Row work, and many of his guards were similarly moonlighting. Using off-duty and retired police was his company's major selling point. If you're going to have guards "putting hands on people or using guns" they should have proper police training, he explained. Further, police were more likely to be considered credible witnesses if cases went to trial. Wright blamed Snoop's civil liabilities in his murder case to the fact that he'd used an untrained "homeboy" as security.

According to guard Frank Alexander, Suge called "all the shots" for Wrightway.

Extreme Loyalty

Beyond Death Row's formal security, Suge was surrounded by a group of tough associates, many known from his youth, and many with Bloods affiliation. They had names like Heron, Neckbone, Buntry, Hen Dog, and Big Jake, and Suge put them on the Death Row payroll for doing artwork, managing artists, or running the studio. They were intimidating, but they weren't necessarily bad guys. Frank Alexander described them as "hardworking, intelligent people who showed an extreme loyalty to Suge. Many of them had never had a job in their lives before Suge offered them one."

"You remember Turtle in *Entourage*?" Reggie Wright Jr. asked me. "That would be a good example of most of them." But not everybody hanging around the studio wore red. About half of the crew, including Snoop's affiliates, were Crips. Suge bragged to *Rolling Stone* that Death Row was a place where gang members of differing stripes could coexist.

Suge ran the company by instinct, making promises before changing his mind and switching everything around. "Every day our phones were busy with irate, frustrated artists trying to get in touch with Suge. They had been told *their* album, or *their* video was next…what was happening?" wrote Nina Bhadreshwar, a white Englishwoman who worked for the label in the mid-nineties. But the complaints died down when the money really started coming in. Suge bought Lexuses, Land Rovers, and custom-designed jewelry for his artists, and for himself a Las Vegas home near Mike Tyson's, the house of Robert De Niro's character in the movie *Casino*.

It's easy to paint Suge as a villain, but tales abound of his charitable largesse. He opened a lowrider shop called Let Me Ride Hydraulics with the goal of employing people from the neighborhood. He contributed to get-out-the-vote efforts, gave away Thanksgiving turkeys and Christmas gifts, donated school supplies, gave away his old shoes, bailed people out of jail, and threw lavish Mother's Day parties at the Beverly Wilshire for urban moms. The parties were legendary; hundreds attended, and performers ranged from the Isley Brothers to Tupac, who rapped "Dear Mama" with his own mother in attendance. The first year, mothers left with party favors including miniature Death Row gold chains.

"He would go to a children's hospital, with two trucks filled with toys, and hand out toys to sick kids," said Death Row publicist Jonathan Wolfson. A *New York Times Magazine* profile describes a scene where a young girl with a puppy strolls up to Suge's Compton home and asks to water his lawn; he consents, and pays her fifty dollars. While incarcerated outside of Sacramento in 2000, he heard about a burned-down Head Start program playground, and promptly had a $21,000 check cut to replace it.

The Source Awards

In the mid-nineties, Death Row was in expansion mode. Suge approached hugely popular R&B artists Mary J. Blige and Jodeci about management deals, promising to free them from what he perceived to be unfavorable contracts from their label Uptown Records, where Puffy got his start. Rumors swirled that Suge intimidated Uptown chief Andre Harrell. Suge's courtship of Jodeci's DeVante Swing included a Lamborghini Diablo worth a quarter million dollars, and Jodeci member JoJo said Suge gave his mother a $37,000 ring for no particular reason. (Jodeci members recorded for Death Row, and Blige was initially receptive to Suge's overtures, but their partnership didn't come to much.)

Suge also enlisted outside-the-box talents, including pop rapper MC Hammer. His popularity had already peaked, but Suge hoped he could help Death Row's crossover appeal. Suge also brought DJ Quik into the fold, and signed a bespectacled, Chicago-raised singer with big pipes named Danny Boy, who he thought could be the next Michael Jackson. Suge met him at age fifteen; his mother was deathly ill, and Suge legally adopted him so he could work in the state of California.

The pair became inseparable. Danny Boy even accompanied Suge on stage during a seismic moment in rap history, 1995's The Source Awards, held on August 3 at Madison Square Garden's Paramount Theater. The event was hosted by the influential eponymous rap magazine, sprung from Harvard in 1988 by a pair of Jewish hip-hop enthusiasts named David Mays and Jonathan Shecter. By the nineties it was hip-hop's most important magazine. Hip-hop award shows weren't common then, and Death Row spent some $100,000 on their opening-act stage show, which included life-sized jail cell replicas. Ascendant Atlanta duo Outkast were booed by the New York crowd when they won for best new artist—which illustrated the parochial bias on display. "The South got something to say," Outkast's André 3000 famously responded while accepting the award.

With his chest puffed out, Suge took the stage with Danny Boy to accept his label's award for best soundtrack, for *Above the Rim*. Giving a stink eye to the audience he digressed, alluding to Puffy's tendency to insert himself in his performers' works: "Any artist out there wanna be an artist, and wanna stay a star, and don't have to worry about the executive producer trying to be all in the videos, all on the records, dancing—come to Death Row."

The venue erupted in boos. "Why would you do that?" Nate Dogg thought to himself. Snoop made things worse when he joined Dr. Dre to accept the latter's award for producer of the year. Every other producer nominated hailed from New York, and the crowd was nonplussed. Snoop, blue bandana around his neck, grabbed the mic away from Dre and went off, letting loose a string of epithets with his eyes blazing. "The East Coast ain't got no love for Dr. Dre and Snoop Dogg and Death Row?"

Snoop was loyal to his label, but what inspired Suge's bizarre attack? After all, he and Puffy had been cool with each other until fairly recently. They'd discussed how to keep the feds from tracking them, and, around early 1995, Suge had even invited Notorious B.I.G. to perform at his Club 662 in Las Vegas. The show never went off, but this didn't sour their relationship.

What soured it was Tupac.

Suge had flown straight to The Source Awards from upstate New York, where he'd visited Tupac in prison. That's where they'd not only decided to join forces, but where Tupac told Suge about his anger at Biggie. "I need you to ride with me because I'm going to destroy Bad Boy Records. I believe they had something to do with me getting shot," Tupac told Suge, according to Reggie Wright Jr. Suge pledged his loyalty. Tupac's enemies would be his enemies. Battle lines had been drawn, and The Source Awards were the first shots.

Security Issues

In mid-August 1995, Biggie was scheduled to perform at radio-station sponsored festivals in California. Puffy faced a dilemma. The prospect of coming out to Suge's territory was daunting. But he had a business to run; he couldn't stay away forever.

Puffy took a calculated risk, enlisting the support of the Compton set known as the Southside Crips as protection. Though he denied it, it had a certain logic, considering the Southside Crips and Suge's affiliated gang the Mob Pirus were reputed enemies; perhaps teaming up with them was Puffy's best hope for protecting his crew in Southern California. "Puffy was in a very precarious situation and I don't know that a lot of people would've done anything different if their own lives were in danger," former LAPD investigator Greg Kading, who worked this case, told *L.A. Weekly.* "You can't go to the cops and say, 'Please help protect me from Suge Knight.' From Puffy's perspective, the cops were working for Suge Knight. It was a preemptive situation."

As a general rule, nationally known rap artists from out of town aren't permitted to simply waltz into Los Angeles to perform. They're required to get permission from the reigning gang authorities and pay for protection—a practice that persists even today. An affidavit from homicide detective sergeant Richard Biddle in a 2015 case against Suge Knight illustrated this. Biddle reported that a "business manager for a well-known rapper" said his artist refused to perform in Los Angeles because he "did not want to pay the $30,000 tax every time he came." The money was required by Suge and a Crips counterpart who were "working together to extort money from rappers and artists."

Puffy was accused of worse than just having protection on his mind. On the 1995 Southern California trip, in an Anaheim hotel suite, he told a roomful of Crips he'd "give us anything for them dudes' heads," referring to Tupac and Suge, a Southside Crip named Keffe D told investigators. Keffe D further maintained that, later at Greenblatt's Deli in West Hollywood, Puffy clarified his offer: $1 million to murder Tupac and Suge. "We'll wipe their ass out quick, man. It's nothing," Keffe said he told Puffy.

Puffy has denied making this offer or having any involvement in Tupac's death. Since the alleged conversation was one-on-one, it can't be otherwise substantiated.

Even today many hip-hop insiders believe the East Coast–West Coast rivalry was a media creation. I don't entirely agree with that, but at the very least it's a misnomer. Really, the problem was mainly between two labels, one based in L.A., and one based in New York. Certainly nobody in Charleston, South Carolina, was much involved.

Peripheral players abounded. Tim Dog's "Fuck Compton" seemed to come from out of nowhere, as did the mixtape line *To you West Coast haters, we will bust your shit*, from A Tribe Called Quest's Q-Tip, around 1995. At one point rapper King Sun jumped into the fray, as did Ras Kass. Bay Area legend E-40 took issue with rookie Washington Bullets forward Rasheed Wallace and East Coast rapper AZ on his song "Record Haters" (he felt both had dissed him).

E-40 also had something of an issue with Biggie, who, while rating rappers in an interview on a one to ten scale, judged E-40 a "zero." Not long afterward, Biggie was performing in Sacramento—E-40's general neck of the woods—and a partisan loyal to E-40 offered to kill him. E-40 declined. "Just being upset 'cause somebody said they ain't fuckin' with your music, that ain't enough to try to do somebody in," E-40 said. "That's not cool."

There were other incidents not mentioned here. But the back-and-forths were primarily between Bad Boy and Death Row, and they were mostly initiated by the latter. "We were in defense mode; there was definitely no aggression on this side," said Biggie's manager Mark Pitts. "We weren't going after them."

"I was more in the mind frame of, 'Keep your mouth shut, Big,'" Biggie said. "If you feed into it, it's going to do nothing but escalate."

That said, they certainly engaged in innuendo. Biggie's song "Who Shot Ya?" was widely seen as baiting Tupac, with the line *You rewind this, Bad Boy's behind this* seeming to reference the Quad studios shooting. According to everyone involved, it had been recorded months before the shooting. That said, it's hard to imagine Bad Boy didn't realize the timing of its release—in early 1995, just months after Quad studios—would provoke him.

Biggie later recorded what is perceived a more overt Tupac diss, "Long Kiss Goodnight," featuring the line: *When my men bust you move with such stamina / Slug missed ya, I ain't mad at cha.* This seems to reference the shooting and Tupac's song "I Ain't Mad at Cha." *Heard through the grapevine you got fucked four times* seems to allude to the Tupac prison rape rumors. But "Long Kiss Goodnight" wasn't released until after Tupac's death.

It's possible Biggie wasn't trying to antagonize Tupac, that he was simply trying to save face. He wanted to be seen as tough, without exacerbating the situation; he even tried to defuse tensions on his song "Going Back to Cali."

As for Puffy, despite Suge's taunts, he remained mostly diplomatic at The Source Awards, complimenting Death Row and decrying East–West animosity. He even gave Snoop a hug. But Puffy is a complex figure. Today, the producer-rapper-actor–vodka pitchman is largely considered a mainstream pop culture creature, throwing parties in the Hamptons, running a marathon for charity, and even substitute cohosting *Live! with Regis & Kelly*. But there's nothing soft about him. From his early days he's associated with underworld and criminal characters, and he was well prepared for battle when Death Row went on the offensive. He faced trial on gun and bribery charges following a 1999 shooting at a Manhattan nightclub party, which he attended with then-girlfriend Jennifer Lopez. He was acquitted, though his rapper Shyne was found guilty of attempted murder and served almost nine years in prison.

According to a claim made by Suge, Puffy played a role in the murder of his close friend, Death Row employee "Big" Jake Robles. Both the Bad Boy and Death Row entourages found themselves at the same September 1995 after-party at an Atlanta club, following producer Jermaine Dupri's birthday party. They began arguing, and Robles was shot outside the club, dying not long afterward. Suge immediately blamed Puffy. "[H]e was, like, 'I think you had something to do with this,'" Puffy said. "I'm like, 'What are you talking about? I was standing right here with you!'"

An eyewitness accused Puffy's bodyguard Anthony "Wolf" Jones of the murder, though he denied this. The case remains unsolved. In an interesting side note, an off-duty sheriff's deputy identified Orlando Anderson on the scene; he's the Southside Crip who would later be accused of murdering Tupac.

Following the Robles murder, with Puffy's blessing, Louis Farrakhan's son Mustapha requested a meeting with Suge, in an effort to quell tensions. Suge turned him down.

New York, New York

One major figure resisted much involvement in the rivalry. By 1995 Dr. Dre had largely withdrawn from the Death Row fold. Sharitha Knight, Suge's wife and Snoop's manager, said that, for a tour with Snoop, "Dre only agreed to go if Suge wasn't involved," she told filmmaker S. Leigh Savidge. "I tried to let Suge know, 'Your friend is about to leave you.' "

Into this production void stepped Daz. He was a member of Tha Dogg Pound, along with his blue Pendleton–clad counterpart Kurupt. While Kurupt is wiry and high energy, Daz has a perpetually stoned look on his doughy face. He doesn't get as much shine as many of his colleagues, but he produced and wrote numerous tracks on successful albums like Tupac's *All Eyez on Me* and Snoop's sophomore album *Tha Doggfather*.

Daz also did the bulk of the production on *Dogg Food*, Tha Dogg Pound's debut, which hit number one upon its October 1995 release and went double platinum. The work is probably best remembered today for "New York, New York," which fueled coastal animosities. Still, Kurupt, who lived in Philadelphia until he was a teenager, swears the song was not intended as a Big Apple diss, but rather a tribute. Its chorus, sung by Snoop, is an interpolation of Melle Mel's hook on Grandmaster Flash and the Furious Five's song of the same name. Kurupt's jumble of brags, similes, and metaphors reflect on a particularly epic battle he'd had one night with New York MCs at the club the Tunnel.

The track is not blatantly antagonistic; one issue was simply that the Death Row artists were discussing New York *at all* during this time. Another problem was the song's beat, produced by DJ Pooh. While spearheading production of the St. Ides malt liquor commercials, Pooh gave the beat to Biggie, who used it in his spot. Then, for reasons unclear, Pooh also gave the beat to Tha Dogg Pound, who used it for "New York, New York." This led to a bizarre situation in which Biggie was rapping over the same beat that some thought was dissing his city. When Tha Dogg Pound came to town in December 1995 to film the video for "New York, New York," all hell broke loose.

Dressed in black peacoats and winter caps, Daz, Kurupt, and Snoop shot frosted-over footage in Times Square, to the great chagrin of Biggie, who called a local radio station to complain. (He apparently thought Tupac was part of their party. Snoop, meanwhile, was supposed to appear that night on the same station, but the interview was mysteriously canceled.) The next day the Golden State contingency traveled across the river to shoot a scene in Red Hook, Brooklyn. They were getting high that night when, suddenly, shots were fired at their trailer from across the street. A rumor circulated that Snoop was the intended target, but no one was hurt; the assailant fled.

The Death Row artists quickly shuttled out of town on a Lear jet. "We were just mad, 'cause we ain't know who, where or what," Kurupt said. But they were now angry. Though the video hadn't originally been intended to be disrespectful, all that was thrown out the window. The final cut contains green-screened shots of the rappers stomping through New York, Godzilla-style, knocking over skyscrapers and crushing cars.

A group of Queens rappers, Capone-N-Noreaga, Tragedy Khadafi, and Mobb Deep, shot back with their own diss track and video, "L.A., L.A." But the damage was done. Once again, Death Row had gotten away with a loud, proactive statement—this time right on Bad Boy's home turf. As Jay-Z rapped in 1998: *It's like New York's been soft ever since Snoop came through and crushed the buildings.*

Mad Cool

After his release from prison in October 1995, Tupac flew into Burbank and stayed at the five-star Peninsula Hotel in Beverly Hills. He shopped at the nearby Beverly Center, loading up on clothes, jewelry, designer bags, and cologne. While incarcerated, he'd longingly sampled the scented advertisements in magazines, and now he could have everything he wanted. "I walked into his suite the day he came home, and I couldn't even move, there were bags everywhere," said his friend Charis Henry. He ordered room service, smoked blunts, and drove his new convertible down Sunset Boulevard. He'd soon move into a six-bedroom Woodland Hills house rented for him by Death Row.

Shortly after his release Tupac met Faith Evans, Biggie's wife, who was in L.A. writing for an R&B group. They clicked, recording a song together called "Wonda Why They Call U Bitch," Tupac's attempt to explain to C. DeLores Tucker why he used the word. Evans didn't think Biggie would be upset; after all, their dispute hadn't yet gone public. "He was mad cool," Evans said. "I saw him at a couple of parties, and we was chillin', havin' drinks, him and my friends." She denied sleeping with Tupac, although he would claim otherwise.

Tupac was soon back in the studio, commencing at Can-Am one of the most frenzied, productive recording runs in history. Chain-smoking marijuana and cigarettes, sipping on Hennessy, he'd start in the late afternoon and work for twelve hours at a stretch, making three or four songs a day, quitting only when the engineers fell asleep at their posts.

Many of his new songs reflected Tupac's prison mentality. He was "dealing with my own anger," he said, and no longer aspired to write uplifting songs like "Dear Mama"—which he felt went underappreciated anyway. He considered titling his album *NC-17*, because he didn't think kids should hear it. He sat in on Snoop's murder trial and they commiserated about their encounters with the justice system, recording "2 of Amerikaz Most Wanted" while Snoop served house arrest. (Along with the Outlawz and Tha Dogg Pound, they even planned a collaborative album together as a group called Thug Pound.)

But these weren't songs he'd written in prison. Most of the tracks on the double album *All Eyez on Me* were written on the spot. Tupac was completely spontaneous, making adjustments on the fly. When former Death

Row rapper CPO, who'd just been laid off from his job at a hospital, called up the studio and told Tupac he'd love to work with him at some point, Tupac responded: "Nigga, I'm here now." CPO came by and they immediately recorded the classic "Picture Me Rollin'."

To give his vocals extra oomph he doubled them, layering them on top of each other. This required recording two nearly identical takes, and Tupac grew impatient when his collaborators couldn't keep up. "He wouldn't just say 'Do your vocals,'" said Natasha Walker from Y?N-Vee. "He would basically say, 'This is what I want you to do,' and he would do the note and he would stay there and produce you."

At another spot, called Echo Sound, Tupac recorded in one studio while a producer prepared a different song for him in another, and he'd hop back and forth. "Really, they couldn't keep up with him," said session musician and writer Stan "the Guitar Man" Jones. "He was moving faster than the producers." Tupac had an insatiable appetite for beats, and he didn't care who made them. At Can-Am, a stable of young Death Row producers composed songs in a room. When Tupac was ready he would abruptly call one of them over. "Play some shit," he'd tell them. "What you got?"

Almost half of *All Eyez on Me*'s tracks were produced by Johnny "J" Jackson, who was born in Mexico, raised in South Central, and had coproduced the 1990 Candyman hit "Knockin' Boots." "Whatever 'Pac requested, Johnny could do it," said Mopreme Shakur. "If 'Pac said, 'I want a slow, sad beat with strings, bass and guitar strings,' Johnny could hook something up. It was a perfect fit."

Johnny J's go-with-the-flow style was the opposite of Dr. Dre's. Though he'd been extraordinarily prolific in his early days (crafting *Straight Outta Compton* in six weeks), Dre's productivity had slowed to a trickle by 1995. He wasn't feeling the gangland vibe at Can-Am, and produced only two of *All Eyez on Me*'s more than two dozen songs. Still, those two are doozies. "Can't C Me" served as a perfect sonic encapsulation of Tupac's newfound fury, with fiery synth, crashing bass, and George Clinton's warning of "the blind stares of a million pairs of eyes." The song paints a scene where

Tupac, hiding in plain sight, prepares to dismantle Biggie and other enemies when they slip up. *I catch 'em while they coked up and weeded / Open fire, now them niggas bleeding.*

A less obvious taunt, but a declaration of coastal allegiance nonetheless, is "California Love," which became Tupac's most popular song. It kicks off with an interpolation of Joe Cocker's "Woman to Woman" intro, before segueing into funk mastermind Roger Troutman's talkbox refrain—*California knows how to party*—borrowed from Ronnie Hudson and the Street People's 1982 song "West Coast Poplock." Dre had been planning to use the beat for his next album, but, capitulating to Suge Knight's "team" mentality, agreed to use it for Tupac's first postprison single in late 1995. It was a wise choice. Millions of thirty- and fortysomething Americans, black, white, and otherwise, still know Tupac's verse by heart: *Out on bail, fresh out of jail, California dreamin' / When I step on the scene I'm hearing hoochies screamin'.* Its *Mad Max Beyond Thunderdome*–inspired video is a delightfully absurd postapocalyptic spectacle of chain metal and pyrotechnics, featuring a fleet of Jeeps, dune buggies, and motorcycles kicking up dust at high speed.

A Match to Gasoline

Some of Tupac's associates didn't gel with Suge's associates. During a stay in the New York City area for a February 17, 1996, *Saturday Night Live* appearance, Suge decided to mess with Tupac's assistants. According to Reggie Wright Jr., Suge and his "homeboys" told Tupac's guys to "run out in the snow, take their clothes off—I think they were in their boxers— and throw up snowballs in the air." When they did as ordered, Suge said it confirmed they were "weak and could be easily gotten to" and therefore should be replaced, according to Wright, adding that they were subsequently no longer part of the camp.

For reasons such as these, some have argued that Suge changed Tupac. Did he give the formerly conscious rapper a taste for blood? The reverse may be closer to the truth: Tupac changed Suge. Sure, Suge had long been a bully, but Tupac brought out something more frightening in him. "He was enabling Suge to think he was invincible," wrote Stormey Ramdhan, who has two children with Suge, in her memoir. "Everyone started to notice this new Suge; he was more direct, a bit colder, harder to get a hold of, and less about his business."

"Suge did not make 'Pac more aggressive," said E.D.I. Mean. "But the two of them together was like lighting the match to a can of gasoline."

Not everyone heeded the battle call. When Tupac asked the Lady of Rage to diss female New York rappers Lil' Kim and Foxy Brown, she declined. Even Snoop, despite stomping on skyscrapers in the Dogg Pound video, failed to get on board with Tupac's war. In a New York radio station interview in September 1996, he declared his love for Puffy and Biggie, angering Tupac. On their flight home, Snoop said he worried for his life, since he was surrounded by Tupac and people loyal to him. "Suge didn't let none of my security ride with me," he told the journalist Sway in 2013, adding that he slept nervously under a blanket at the back of the private plane, clutching a knife and fork in case he was attacked.

Tupac found willing allies in the Outlawz, a group of New York and New Jersey teenagers and early twentysomethings. Their ranks included one of Tupac's cousins, his stepbrother Mopreme, as well as fearsome, street-certified childhood friends (and friends of friends) whom he considered family. "We always kept guns on us, every single fucking day," Outlawz member Young Noble told me, adding that they were ready to defend Tupac at any cost. "We was some young warriors." To drive home the point, Tupac named many of them for famous dictators—Kadafi, Hussein Fatal, Kastro, Napoleon.

Most Outlawz members weren't established rappers, but following Tupac's release from prison, they switched coasts and moved into his home, driving around a soccer mom–style Dodge Caravan harboring the camp's weed and guns, which they called the "Murder Van." They trailed Tupac's Rolls-Royce from one spot to the next, giving him cover in case he was pulled over. They rolled his blunts, they rapped on his songs, they got "Outlaw" tattoos. They were ready to follow him to the gates of hell.

*   *   *

At the March 1996 Soul Train Awards, held at the Shrine Auditorium near the University of Southern California, Biggie's "One More Chance" won for best R&B or rap song. He took the stage with his entourage, and the scattered boos grew louder when he shouted out "Brooklyn."

Bad Boy enlisted Crips for protection that night. After the show, their party awaited their car outside when a black Hummer pulled up. Tupac rolled down his window, and he and Biggie came face-to-face for the first time since the Quad studios shooting. "West Side! Fuck y'all!" yelled Tupac, flanked by Suge and Death Row Bloods, one of whom yelled "Let's settle this now!"

Guns were drawn on both sides.

"That was the first time I really looked into his face. I looked into his eyes and I was like, 'Yo, this nigga is really buggin' the fuck out,'" Biggie said.

Nation of Islam members quickly stepped in, acting as human shields between the two camps. No one was harmed. But Biggie couldn't help but observe that his former friend Tupac had taken on the persona of his *Juice* character. "I was like, 'That's Bishop!'"

Death Row Style

Upon its early 1996 release, *All Eyez on Me* was a sensation. Fueled by "California Love," Tupac's omnipotence in the news, and Death Row's secret sauce, the album was a juggernaut, becoming one of only a handful of diamond platinum albums (ten million sold) in rap history. "Tupac was on Interscope the whole time," Suge Knight bragged. "They couldn't make him a superstar. But the minute I got 'Pac out of prison..."

Basking in the success, Tupac felt momentum in his battle against Biggie. "Nigga shot me five times," he said while performing at the House of Blues. "I fucked his bitch and sold five million, that's Death Row style."

He soon recorded the most searing and bombastic diss song of all time, "Hit 'Em Up," a track that knocked anyone who heard it back on their heels. Produced by Johnny J, its bouncy, jubilant beat betrays the venom within; it samples Biggie and his affiliated group Junior M.A.F.I.A.'s "Get Money," while its chorus—*Grab your Glocks when you see Tupac*—echoes another Junior M.A.F.I.A. and Biggie song, "Player's Anthem" (which goes, *Grab your dick if you love hip-hop*). Lyrically, Tupac's goal was to make the track as *personal* as possible, and at the song's onset he immediately goes for the jugular: *That's why I fucked your bitch, you fat motherfucker.* He quickly expands the scope of his wrath beyond Biggie to Lil' Kim and anyone at all who identifies with Bad Boy. Tupac's Outlawz crewmembers Hussein Fatal, Kadafi, and E.D.I. Mean take shots at Junior M.A.F.I.A.; in the song's video the crew gesticulates shirtless and peers imposingly down into the camera. E.D.I. Mean said they sought to top classic diss tracks like "The Bridge Is Over" and "No Vaseline"—and indeed, the song eclipses them both in its pure molten bellicosity. As the track fades out, Tupac all but loses it: *Fuck you, die slow motherfucker! My .44 make sure y'all kids don't grow!*

The message was heard. "The day this song dropped, New York was quiet, like we had got punched in our collective chests," said longtime New York hip-hop insider Combat Jack. "Plain and simple, the record was hot, and the rage that jumped from off the track was very disconcerting."

Biggie said he didn't believe his wife had cheated; if she had, Tupac never would have talked about her that way. "If honey was to give you that pussy, why would you disrespect her like that?" he said. He even made light of the situation on "Brooklyn's Finest," his duet with his protégé Jay-Z: *If Fay has twins, she'll probably have two 'Pacs.* (In October 1996 Faith gave birth to a healthy boy, Christopher Jordan Wallace.)

Publicly, the Bad Boy contingent put on a brave face, again trying both not to escalate things, and also not appear weak. "What it's been right now is a lot of moviemaking and a lot of entertainment drama," Puffy said. "Bad boys move in silence. If somebody wants to get your ass, you're gonna wake up in heaven. There ain't no record gonna be made about it."

Bow Down

In its early days, many New York rap fans saw Los Angeles hip-hop as a corny knockoff. For their part, L.A. artists often felt shut out by New York radio station programmers, record shop owners, and disc jockeys who wouldn't traffic their music. KDAY DJ Russ Parr, who performed as his satirical alter ego Bobby Jimmy, said he got the cold shoulder in 1986 when he performed in the Big Apple. "I made the mistake of saying I was from L.A. To them, no one west of the Hudson River had the right to rap. In unison, they all turned their backs on me. It was like it was planned."

This was perhaps understandable before acts like N.W.A kicked things into gear. But by the mid-nineties the West Coast was dominant. After *Straight Outta Compton, Amerikkka's Most Wanted, The Chronic,* and *Black Sunday*, doubting the potency of L.A.'s movement was laughable. Even Def Jam—perhaps rap's most iconic label—chased trends on the other side of the country in the early nineties with its Def Jam West subimprint.

Still, some L.A. rappers felt disrespected. None more so than Ice Cube, who for this reason decided to insert himself into the East Coast–West Coast beef. "I threw myself in the middle of it," he admitted.

It was an odd turn of events, considering that at the dawn of the nineties, owing to his collaborations with Public Enemy and the Bomb Squad, Cube was perhaps the West's biggest emissary to the East Coast scene. That soon changed. "I wanted to let them know, that they couldn't just treat us any kind of way," he said.

Westside Connection formed in the mid-nineties. The group included Cube, his South Central childhood friend WC, and Inglewood rapper Mack 10—"The gangsta, the killa, and the dope dealer," as they put it. Their 1996 first single, "Bow Down," serves as an anthem of regional pride. *If you live on the West side of your town, make them other fools bow down*, Cube says on the outro. Other tracks on Westside Connection's debut album *Bow Down* were even more inflammatory. On "Gangstas Make the World Go Round" Cube raps: *I got enough guns to fill the Empire*

State Building full of ones. "All the Critics in New York" reflected the group's opinion that West Coast hip-hop wasn't given its due respect by rap writers.

Cube wasn't the only one who felt the hip-hop media gave them short shrift, even though the editors of *The Source*—the reigning title— strenuously denied this. "I was selling millions of records, Cube was selling millions of records, and the rappers who were selling hundreds of thousands were on the front cover," complained Oakland rapper Too $hort. But "All the Critics in New York" went *way* over the top in its invective. *I hope blood ain't got to spill / I kill*, Cube raps. "It was a little heavy-handed," Cube admitted.

Cube had other beefs around this time, including with Chicago rapper Common Sense, now known as Common. The thoughtful, introspective MC's 1994 album *Resurrection* contains one of hip-hop's most cherished songs, "I Used to Love H.E.R.," with "H.E.R." standing for "hearing every rhyme." It's a metaphor for falling out of love with hip-hop as it becomes increasingly commercialized, and the song reserves criticism for Los Angeles gangsta rap styles:

> *Now she's a gangsta rolling with gangsta bitches*
> *Always smoking blunts and getting drunk*
> *Telling me sad stories, now she only fucks with the funk*

It's a powerful song, one that summarized many hip-hop fans' concerns about the genre's increasingly aggressive tenor. No one doubted that N.W.A helped establish this tone, and that its offshoot solo acts were, to varying degrees, perpetuating it. And so, even though on the track Common noted that he *wasn't salty she was with the Boyz in the Hood*, Cube took offense. On 1995's "Westside Slaughterhouse," Mack 10, Cube, and WC busted back, dissing Common and claiming *Hip-hop started in the West*. But it didn't amount to much; in the opinion of rap critics, Cube was bodied by Common's response song, "The Bitch in Yoo," which took aim at Cube's ideological inconsistencies. *Slangin' bean pies and St. Ides in the same sentence*, Common rapped.

This was, at root, a lyrical, ideologically driven back-and-forth. It seemed unlikely that real-life bloodshed might arise from it, considering Common's peace-and-good-vibes reputation. And Cube, of course, has always been a much better public citizen than he's let on.

Still, at the height of hip-hop's most violent era, anything seemed possible.

POTENTIAL LEADS

I'm way off my diet right now," Dr. Dre says, grabbing a flaky pastry with custard in the middle. It's May 2013, and I'm talking to him at a Santa Monica press conference announcing his and Jimmy Iovine's giant donation to the University of Southern California. The $70 million gift created the Jimmy Iovine and Andre Young Academy for Arts, Technology, and the Business of Innovation, basically a multidisciplinary major designed to create tech wunderkinds with music industry cool and engineering smarts.

I've wanted to meet Dre since I was in high school, and I'm shaking when we sit down for our interview. Oddly, he seems nervous, too—polite, but timid, his hands lodged in his pockets. After three decades in the business, you'd think he'd be accustomed to this sort of thing. He's not the Dre I expected—not the Incredible Hulk figure of his recent press photos, not the cocky hitmaker of Death Row outfitted in diamond-studded Rolexes, and certainly not the mercurial figure with a history of violence. Approaching fifty, he looks his age, trim, close-cropped hair, almost no jewelry. There's a gentleness about him. Or maybe it's just, as I'll learn later, his social anxiety. Rather than feeding off the energy of crowds and publicity, Dre generally prefers to stay in his studio, or in his mansion. "I don't like being in the spotlight, so I made a fucking weird career choice," he told *Rolling Stone* in 2015.

He's in a particularly weird place right now. Following *The Chronic*, Dr. Dre put out *Chronic 2001*, which was an even bigger hit. (The latter album has an odd title, considering its late 1999 release. Dre originally planned to call it *Chronic 2000*, but the ever-wily Suge beat him to the punch and released a Death Row compilation album with that name, forcing Dre to call his work *2001*.) He then didn't put out an album for a decade and a half before, in 2015, releasing the *Straight Outta Compton* movie and a surprise album called *Compton*. (It features all original music and isn't really a proper soundtrack to the film, but was rather "inspired" by it.)

During the fruitless period everyone was asking him about *Detox*, a long-rumored, near-mythical album that he finally announced in 2015 he was scrapping. Somewhere along the way it occurred to him that *Detox* wasn't going to work. Why? Was Dre tired of playing a gangsta?

This conflict has, in many ways, become the defining struggle of Dre's life. Born into tough circumstances, he avoided gangs as a kid, and his first group World Class Wreckin' Cru mocked them. But he found his artistic niche making music about street life, and he did it so well that it trapped him. "It felt funny going in the studio talking about 'this bitch' and 'this ho' and how 'I fucked this girl' with a wife at home," Dre said.

Dre's tried to retire his bad-boy character before, without success. He clearly wants a legacy of standing for something honorable. In addition to the USC gift announced today, he's done a lot for the city of Compton, including donating football uniforms and headphones, and pledging his royalties from his album *Compton* toward a performing arts center there.

Much of his financial success owes to his partnership with Iovine, the man who helped extradite him from the Death Row situation, and with whom, a year after the USC press conference, Dre would sell their headphone business Beats to Apple for $3 billion. It's obvious Dre made a series of brilliant business decisions. To get there—to realize just how fucked up things had gotten under Suge's watch—Dre had to hit rock bottom himself.

Night had turned to day in early January 1994, when Dre led police on a high-speed chase through Beverly Hills and Westwood. He was behind the wheel of his white Ferrari Testarossa, a classic 1987 model popularized by Don Johnson's character in *Miami Vice*, famous for the side intakes that look like cheese graters.

He was also drunk, reaching speeds of ninety miles per hour, according to the cops. "Next thing I know I'm surrounded," Dre said, miming police officers pointing their guns at him. "'Show me your hands! Get out! Get out! Show me your hands!' Like, 'All right, I'm caught.'" His blood-alcohol level was twice the legal limit. Having violated his probation from punching producer Damon Thomas in 1992, Dre pleaded no contest to DUI. He served about six months, beginning in January 1995, although he was allowed to leave the jail during the day to work.

It was the culmination of five years of self-abuse. After the death of his brother Tyree in 1989, Dre began to drink heavily. He got into fights and was arrested numerous times. With top lawyers at his disposal, Dre was able to minimize the repercussions. But now, with an extended jail stay for the first time in his life, Dre took the time to look in the mirror.

While Dre was locked up, it was business as usual at Death Row. The label was spending heavily, including numerous expensive pieces of jewelry. In 1995 downtown jeweler B. L. Diamonds received orders including: eighteen-karat gold Rolex ($35,000), "MOB" rings ($970 each), four-carat diamond ring ($35,000), men's diamond bracelet ($10,700), "fourteen-karat yellow gold four-prong, screw-back settings" diamond earrings ($18,000), gold-plated Dupont lighter ($440), eighteen-karat yellow gold "heart necklace" for "Suge's mother" ($7,600), and more than one thousand gold pendants for a Mother's Day brunch ($145,000).

The orders were facilitated by a Death Row accountant named Steve Cantrock, but eventually the funds ran out. Jeweler Brian Lemberger filed suit in 1997 against Death Row, Cantrock, and his accounting firm. Cantrock told police that Suge assaulted him and forced him to sign a hand-drafted confession saying he'd stolen the $4.5 million owed to Death Row's creditors. Suge and Death Row lawyer David Kenner denied the charges, instead blaming Cantrock and his firm for the company's financial woes; Cantrock's firm forced him to resign, and his family went into hiding.

Violence, too, continued to surround Death Row. At an after-party for the March 1995 Soul Train Awards at the El Rey Theatre, a twenty-eight-year-old construction worker named Kelly Jamerson was beaten to death. The party was promoted by Death Row, and many of its artists and affiliates were in attendance. Jamerson, reportedly a Rollin' 60s Crip, and his cohorts appear to have fought adversaries from the Bloods, who outnumbered them. Despite countless eyewitnesses, criminal charges were never filed. Jamerson's family and its lawyer speculated this was because of Suge's ties to law enforcement.

Death Row even began to turn on its own. Rapper and producer Sam Sneed was once considered one of the label's brightest stars; his successful 1994 single "U Better Recognize" featured Dr. Dre and was on the *Murder Was the Case* soundtrack, and he was a featured performer at the 1995 Source Awards. But some at Death Row weren't fans of the "U Better Recognize" video. They felt Sneed, who came from the Pittsburgh area, featured too many East Coast artists, without enough representation from Death Row members. Since Dre was on his way out, Tupac and others openly questioned Sneed's loyalty: "Are you with us, or are you with Dre?"

The day Snoop's murder acquittal was announced, Suge called a meeting at Can-Am. They screened Sneed's video, and Tupac grew incensed. "[E]ach time we see a East Coast muthafucka we gonna knock you in your muthafuckin' head," he said. By some accounts, a vicious beating of Sneed followed, though Reggie Wright Jr. insisted it mainly consisted of "slapping." Later, Suge and others went out to Monty's Steakhouse to celebrate Snoop's verdict.

Sneed had been pulled into the coastal animosity unwittingly, as was a New York promoter named Mark Anthony Bell, an associate of Puffy's. Bell told police he was intimidated at Death Row's 1995 Christmas party in the Hollywood Hills. According to Bell, Suge demanded the address of Puffy and Puffy's mother, and questioned him about the killing of Jake Robles. "They sat the dude down in the chair and just started punchin' him in the grill," wrote Bruce Williams, Dre's assistant, who said he witnessed the beating.

"This is for Jake," one of Suge's men said, according to the account Bell gave to police. "We're going to kill you." He said Suge then went to the bathroom and returned with a champagne flute with urine, and asked him to drink. Bell said he refused, tried unsuccessfully to escape off a balcony, and was then beaten more, and robbed. Again, the district attorney's office declined to press charges, though Bell reportedly received $600,000 in a settlement with Death Row, and moved to Jamaica. (Suge denied the allegations against him.)

Dre, now out of jail, and Tupac were both in attendance that night. Bell said Tupac was whispering in Suge's ear, while Williams said he and his boss Dre felt they had "walked in on some shit we didn't need to be around." The incident reflected divergent feelings about Death Row's direction; Dre had little patience for this kind of nonsense, while Tupac was consumed by it.

Moreover, Tupac took it personally that Dre was distancing himself from Death Row and its ethos. "I'm out here in the streets, whooping niggers' asses, starting wars and shit, putting it down, dropping albums, doing my shit and this nigger's taking three years to do one song," Tupac complained to journalist Rob Marriott. Tupac castigated Dre for not standing by Snoop at his trial, and even began loudly questioning Dre's sexuality, despite a lack of evidence to support such claims.

Tupac's antipathy for Dre was a major turn of events. The opportunity to work with Dre had been a major incentive for Tupac to come to Death Row in the first place. But, in the end, the pair—the greatest West Coast producer and the greatest West Coast rapper—barely collaborated. "Tupac never knew me," Dre said. "Tupac had never been to my house before. He doesn't even know where I live. We never even been in the same car together."

Princess in a Castle

During his jail sentence, Dre had begun to reassess his priorities. "When I got sentenced, my mom told me that jail was going to turn out to be a blessing in disguise—and she was right," Dre said. "It made me realize the value of my life and just how many things I needed to change." In early 1996, not long after his sentence was completed, Dre stunned the rap world by announcing he'd left Death Row. "[I]t turned into a fucking Don Corleone thing," Dre said. "I got tired of seeing engineers get they ass beat for rewinding a tape too far."

Reggie Wright Jr. told me that Suge wanted Dre to stay at Death Row—despite, like Tupac, having loudly criticized him to other label members for not attending Snoop's murder trial. But Suge insisted publicly that he was glad to see Dre go. It helped that Dre gifted his portion of the company away to Suge. His share was worth millions, but Dre walked away from it in favor of something far more valuable to him. "You can't put a price on a peaceful state of mind," he said.

The divorce was nonetheless contested in other ways. Just as he'd allegedly done at Eazy-E's house, Suge reportedly showed up at Dre's Calabasas home, demanding master tapes from Dre that Suge said he needed for a Death Row greatest hits album. According to Suge, Dre cowered inside while an "off-duty cop" answered the door. In Dre's version Suge was only let past the guards after claiming to be Jimmy Iovine, and had "eight or nine motherfuckers" with him. Dre put him off by telling him the tapes were being copied, but it helped perpetuate a feud between the two men that would continue for decades, despite the fact that, only five years before, they'd joined forces to found Death Row.

Director S. Leigh Savidge, who made the documentary *Welcome to Death Row*, compares the saga surrounding Suge and Dre to *Othello*. "There was Iago, who was in the trenches as a soldier with Othello, and at some point sees the need to usurp him," he said. "I always looked at Suge as Iago, and Dre as Othello. They were soldiers in arms during that critical period."

*   *   *

Perhaps the oddest part about Dre and Suge's relationship is that they have children with the same woman, former Ruthless Records hitmaker Michel'le. She and Dre began dating in 1987, and were together, on and off, until around 1995, after which time she linked up with Suge. She wasn't aware of Dre and Suge's feud until after she became involved with the latter, she said, although, according to Reggie Wright Jr., her coupling with Suge contributed to Dre's decision to leave Death Row.

As she tells it, Dre's infidelities practically drove her into Suge's arms. "I felt like you treat people like you want to be treated," Michel'le told me in 2015. She added that she was initially scared of Suge, but he won her over by standing up for her. After Dre would cheat on her and Suge encountered the offending woman at, say, a club or a video shoot, he'd expunge her from the premises, she said.

There were hiccups. He and Michel'le planned to wed, but he neglected to mention he was still married to Sharitha Golden, then known as Sharitha Knight. (Michel'le said he told her he was divorced and even showed her preliminary paperwork, but in fact the divorce had not yet gone through.) He was incarcerated for much of the time they were together, and their daughter was born when he was still behind bars.

Michel'le had very little independence. "I was a princess in a castle who didn't get to come out that often." She said that Suge's control caused her to give up singing for many years, and that she attempted suicide around 2013.

When Marcel, her son with Dre, was young, she feared he would get caught up in the feud between Dre and Suge. And so to prevent this from happening, she said, she abdicated his care to her mother and her grandmother. "I didn't connect to my son again honestly until he was about fourteen or fifteen," she told me.

In 2002, Michel'le and Suge had a daughter named Bailei. The two kids get along great. "People think they should be the Hatfields and McCoys," she said. "No, my kids love each other." She has long insisted that Suge and Dre are responsible, caring dads. "They are great fathers and they are there for them. It's not always monetary. It's about being there."

When we meet up in the lobby of a Koreatown hotel in July 2015, I don't immediately recognize Michel'le. I expected an entourage but she's alone, and, at forty-four, extraordinarily beautiful. Her manager said our interview would have to be in person, because, though she sounds normal on record, her impossibly high, squeaky speaking voice wouldn't translate over the phone. Indeed, she has the register of Betty Boop.

We talk about her childhood. Her parents weren't alcoholics or drug addicts, and didn't abuse her, she says. But they were never together as a couple—and never told her they loved her. Truth is, she can't remember much about her early days. "I don't know where we lived and what we did because there's no history. My mother just isn't that type of person." Her memory comes into focus for her in her teen years. At fifteen she began dating a local, big-shot drug dealer, though he never took her on dates. He'd come over around eleven p.m., they'd watch *The Tonight Show Starring Johnny Carson*, and then he'd leave. "But he would give me all this jewelry...necklaces, rings. I had rings on every finger," she said. Eventually she realized she wasn't his main girl. It was all part of a pattern. If someone paid lip service to caring about her, she'd tolerate most anything else, she told me. The attraction to Dre and Suge was that they told her they loved her, "even after they beat you, or whatever they do."

In the N.W.A saga, countless women have come and gone. Michel'le's story is different, and not simply because of her relationships with Dre and Suge. She remembers her early days with Ruthless as some of the best of her life. She's a survivor, and in many ways, she won. She can still sing her ass off; she released her second album in 1998 on Death Row, called *Hung Jury*, and her show business career took on a new life in her forties, starring since 2013 on the reality show *R&B Divas: Los Angeles*. At the time I interview her, she's arguably as famous as she's ever been.

Aftermath

The year 1996 was the major turning-point year in Andre Young's life. He married his girlfriend Nicole Threatt, the ex-wife of Sedale Threatt, a Lakers star who was then winding down a career with five NBA teams. Nicole and Sedale had a boy named Tyler together, whom Dre helped raise as his own. He and Nicole had two more children as well.

They married in a small ceremony in front of the ocean at the Four Seasons in Maui. Dre's assistant Bruce Williams was shocked to be asked to be Dre's best man, assuming Dre's longtime friend D.O.C. would get the nod. But they were on the outs, and D.O.C. didn't even attend. "He had grown up, and I hadn't," D.O.C. explained to me.

That same year, 1996, Dre announced the formation of his new label, a subsidiary of Interscope called Aftermath. This kicked off his great bromance with Jimmy Iovine, one of the most lucrative in music history. The pair wouldn't seem, on paper, to have much in common, but Iovine had also transcended his hardscrabble background to a life of wealth and glamour. (His ex-wife is a *Playboy* Playmate.) If Dre is the god of hip-hop beats, Iovine is the god of the record industry. When, in 2014, Iovine left the merged company known as Interscope Geffen A&M, its roster included Eminem, Madonna, U2, Lady Gaga, and Maroon 5. *Billboard* called him "the most successful head of a major label for the last twenty-five years." He wasn't just signing artists, he was helping reshape the music industry. Long before Apple's acquisition of Beats, Iovine had worked with Steve Jobs to help convince the major labels to sell their music on iTunes. Though not everyone agrees that "unbundling" the album to sell tracks à la carte was a good idea, it brought a level of stability to the industry following the Wild West years of the Napster file-sharing era.

Initially success eluded Dre at Aftermath. The label's first release, a compilation album that came out on November 26, 1996, called *Dr. Dre Presents: The Aftermath*, offered evidence of Dre's evolving worldview. The track "Been There, Done That" featured Dre decrying not just black-on-black violence but gangsta posturing generally: *A million motherfuckers on the planet Earth / Talk that hard bullshit 'cause that's all they worth.* "East Coast/West Coast Killas" enlisted a bipartisan group of MCs including KRS-One, Nas, and Cypress Hill's B-Real in an attempt to tamp down coastal animosities.

To Dre's chagrin, most of the team he'd assembled at Death Row was off limits, and so he worked to build his roster back up. Though the album sold a million copies, it was considered a misfire. "People were expecting 7UP and they got water," Dre later said, adding that his wife Nicole encouraged him to "get back on that hardcore shit."

Aftermath's next project was a letdown, too. Supergroup the Firm included New York stalwarts Nas, Foxy Brown, AZ, and Nature, and their 1997 debut work *The Album* features production and rapping from Dr. Dre. In retrospect it's not such a bad album, but sales were sluggish and the group shortly disbanded. Aftermath's future seemed in jeopardy, but it was boosted by Detroit white rapper Marshall Mathers, who would soon be known to the world as Eminem.

With an innovative flow, Eminem rhymed as an unhinged psychopathic maniac, mixing pop culture jokes with elaborate stories about killing his daughter's mother. His demo *Slim Shady* EP found its way to Iovine, who shared it with Dre. "When Jimmy played this, I said, 'Find him. Now,'" Dre recalled in a *Rolling Stone* interview. The two began working together and Eminem would become one of the bestselling pop artists in history. "Dre showed me how to do things with my voice that I didn't know I could do," said Eminem.

By 1999, which saw the multi-platinum releases of Eminem's *The Slim Shady* LP and Dre's own *Chronic 2001*, the success of Aftermath was assured.

Thriller

If Dre was taking some concerted steps to reshape his life in the first part of 1996, Tupac's was spinning in every direction at once. Much of the public knew him mainly from his problems with the law. And, indeed, following his release from prison he at times seemed to be growing more sinister. He had the word "MOB" tattooed on his right triceps, for example, though he claimed it stood for "Money, Organization, and Business." But he also took steps to repair his image. He sought to unify hip-hop through a project called One Nation, featuring rappers from every part of the country, including Outkast, E-40, and members of Brooklyn crew Boot Camp Clik.

Tupac's mainstream celebrity was developing as well. He made three movies: *Bullet*, with his friend Mickey Rourke, *Gang Related*, playing a vice detective, and *Gridlock'd*, with Tim Roth from *Pulp Fiction*, on which Tupac was also slated to act as music supervisor for the Death Row–released soundtrack. He planned to include alternative acts including Alanis Morissette, and, along with Suge and Snoop, even talked about opening a restaurant with her. But these projects were just the tip of the iceberg: He was starting a film company, helping organize a youth center, and supporting sports leagues. He even took a girl named Tushana Howard to her prom at John Muir High School.

There were changes in his personal life, too. He began a Hollywood-style romance with Kidada Jones, the daughter of music industry royalty Quincy Jones, who produced *Thriller*. Pursuing her required chutzpah, considering that in 1993 he'd dissed Quincy in unbelievably derogatory fashion. "All he does is stick his dick in white bitches and make fucked-up kids," he told *The Source*, in a diatribe about interracial couples. Quincy was furious, and another of his daughters, Rashida—now a famous actress who starred in the TV series *Parks and Recreation*—wrote an angry letter in reply. Kidada was nonetheless swept off her feet by Tupac, and managed to keep the relationship secret for a time. Then one night, as the pair were dining at an L.A. spot called Jerry's Deli, "two hands slammed down on Tupac's shoulders from behind, and there was Dad standing there," Kidada recalled. As he did with everyone, Tupac won him over. He and Kidada soon moved in together, and he told his mother they would be married.

Monogamy, however, wasn't in the cards. Women threw themselves at him in Milan, where he visited for Men's Fashion Week in 1996; he walked a runway and was feted by top designers. (Though he wasn't too thrilled to receive a European-style kiss from Gianni Versace.) In any case, he bedded numerous women, wrote his bodyguard Frank Alexander, somehow working around the fact that he was sharing a hotel room with Kidada.

Suge said he and Tupac had an inseparable bond until the end. But some contend the rapper was growing disillusioned with his label. "We thought he was trying to get off of Death Row. That's why he did those albums so fast," said Nate Dogg, referencing Tupac's recording spree that continued into 1996, and which informed his voluminous posthumous output.

Tupac plotted his own imprint, Makaveli Records, whose artists would have included the Outlawz and female rapper Storm. It's unclear if he intended it to be a Death Row subsidiary. "'Pac was a loyal dude. Even if he was planning on getting off Death Row, I'm sure they would still be doing some business together," said Outlawz rapper Young Noble, adding that Tupac remained grateful to Suge for his prison rescue.

Suge was blunt on the matter to MTV: "If you'd asked Tupac that question—'Was he planning on leaving Death Row?'—he definitely would have cussed you out."

Tupac was upset with lawyer David Kenner, however, who had abandoned most of the rest of his practice to focus on Death Row. Kenner's role went much further than that of a traditional lawyer; according to the memoir written by Suge's girlfriend Stormey Ramdhan, Kenner was responsible for everything from paternity issues to hiring nannies. (Kenner did not respond to a request for comment.)

Tupac enlisted an additional lawyer, named Charles Ogletree, who later told *The New Yorker* that Death Row had stymied his client's attempts to negotiate a more formal contract to replace the "memo" Tupac signed in prison. Eventually, according to Ogletree, Tupac began to plan his escape: "He had a strategy—the idea was to maintain a friendly relationship with Suge but to separate his business." In the summer of 1996 Tupac took the drastic step of firing Kenner, which shocked those at Death Row who learned about it.

Tupac's behavior was similarly brazen when it came to his ongoing feuds with New York rappers. Following the MTV Video Music Awards in Manhattan on September 4, 1996, he talked up plans for Death Row East and dubiously bragged that "we already run the streets out here." He trash-talked Queens rapper Nas, who he believed appropriated his style (though the pair reconciled shortly thereafter). When an MTV interviewer asked him about Biggie and Puffy, also in attendance at the awards, Tupac went on a gleeful, passive-aggressive rant, mocking Bad Boy's album sales and noting that though his camp were "businessmen" not looking for trouble, "if they see us and they want drama, we're definitely going to bring it like only Death Row can bring it."

Still, he finished with a plea that MTV exercise "restraint" in playing up the East Coast–West Coast beef, and gave himself the same responsibility.

Mob Style

Mike Tyson didn't know Tupac when they met outside a nightclub in the early nineties, but when the fledgling rapper was stopped at the door— even though he was scheduled to perform—the champion boxer intervened. A friendship developed, but they didn't get much opportunity to hang out, considering they both spent so much time in prison. (Tyson's biggest regret was that he declined Tupac's offer to get him high.)

Following Tyson's release in early 1995, after serving three years for the rape of Desiree Washington, he undertook a series of comeback fights. He won the first three easily, and was the favorite going into his bout against heavyweight titleholder Bruce Seldon at the MGM Grand in Las Vegas on September 7, 1996. Promoted by Don King, the fight drew a large pay-per-view audience and a frenzied crowd, who heard Tupac's new song "Let's Get It On" at full volume over the speakers as Tyson was led into the ring. Rappers have a long history of providing motivational tracks for their favored boxers, and Tupac's track touted Tyson's ferociousness and laid out the plans for the evening: *This ain't gonna last long / Y'all know how Tyson do it / We gon' watch him beat this boy silly / And then we gone all go party at 6-6-deuce, mob style.*

From the front row Tupac and Suge saw Tyson wallop Seldon in under two minutes. Tyson gave them a hug, and they said goodbye in his dressing room, planning to meet up later. Adrenalized, Tupac threw shadow punches as they exited the event. "Fifty blows! I counted them," he told his bodyguard Frank Alexander. Outside the arena, in the MGM, they met some of Suge's guys, including a Blood named Travon "Tray" Lane, who had some troubling news: He'd just spotted a guy in the hotel who'd snatched his Death Row chain, during a recent altercation at the Lakewood Mall, not far from Compton. The guy in question was Orlando Anderson. Not only was he a Southside Crip, but, according to a sheriff's deputy, he was on the scene in Atlanta when Suge's bodyguard Jake Robles was murdered there a year prior.

At Tray's news, Tupac took off running. He quickly caught up with Anderson. "You from the South?" he asked. Before Anderson could respond, Tupac punched him. The Death Row crew piled on. Suge and his associates kicked and stomped Anderson as MGM security cameras rolled. Security intervened, and the Death Row contingent hustled toward the doors. As they wound their way through the casino toward the exit, people began to recognize Tupac, streaming out from behind slot machines and trailing behind him en masse, like the pied piper.

As they departed the scene Tupac boasted of his fighting skills. "I took him out faster than Tyson!" he said, according to his bodyguard Frank Alexander. For Alexander, a genial former bodybuilder, the Death Row detail was growing increasingly stressful. For starters, they were shorthanded on this trip; they were missing three bodyguards, including Tupac's other main security, Kevin Hackie. Further, Alexander had neither his phone nor his gun; he'd left his firearm behind, he said, because he believed Death Row hadn't gotten the proper clearance from local authorities in advance. (Death Row's head of security Reggie Wright Jr. disputed this in an interview with me, however. "He could have, and should have [had his gun]," Wright said.)

Tupac made it back to his hotel, the Luxor, where he changed clothes and chatted with Kidada. The plan was to head over to Knight's Club 662, where Run-D.M.C. and Craig Mack were scheduled to perform; Tupac and company were hoping to use the opportunity to recruit Run-D.M.C. to Death Row East. Tupac decided Kidada shouldn't attend, however. "I'm not taking you," he said. "There's been a fight with a Crip and it's not safe. So you stay here."

Their caravan to the club included about a half a dozen vehicles, filled with a formidable lineup of security guards, Outlawz members, and Bloods enforcers. But Tupac opted to ride alone with Suge in the latter's new BMW 750iL. As they drove, they blasted music from the new album Tupac was working on, called *The Don Killuminati: The 7 Day Theory*. The BMW was stopped by a police officer who gave Suge a warning for not properly displaying plates, but they were quickly back on their way and the celebratory mood continued. With the BMW's windows open, a car of female Tupac fans recognized him and began screaming—he encouraged them to join the caravan.

As the BMW approached the intersection of Flamingo and Koval, in front of the Maxim Hotel, a white Cadillac going in the opposite direction did a U-turn and pulled up next to them. An arm holding a .40 caliber Glock extended out the window and began firing into the BMW. Tupac attempted to scramble out of the way and into the backseat. "I grabbed him and said, 'Get down!' and covered him," Suge said. A dozen shots or so were fired, and Tupac was hit four times. One of the bullets ricocheted off his hip bone, deflecting into his lung. Suge was grazed—likely from a bullet fragment or piece of flying debris from the shot-up car.

"He said, 'I'm hit,'" Suge recalled in an interview with BET's Stephanie Frederic. "So I'm driving like a madman to the hospital. And he said, laughingly, jokingly, loudly, 'I need a hospital? You're the one that's been shot in the head.'"

A car containing Suge's enforcers chased after the white Cadillac, exchanging gunfire, but the shooter managed to escape. Driving off wildly, Suge's car didn't make it to the hospital, instead colliding with a curb and blowing out its tires. The cops seized Suge, who was bleeding from his head, putting him spread eagle on the ground. Other members of the party were splayed onto the concrete, shotguns pointed at their heads, including E.D.I. Mean, who said cops asked for their gang affiliations and the meanings of their tattoos. An ambulance arrived to take Tupac, bloody but still conscious, to University Medical Center hospital.

Waiting for his return at her Luxor suite, Kidada Jones was lying down to sleep when she received the call that Tupac had been shot. She rushed to the hospital. "When I got to the hospital they handed me a bag of bloody clothes and jewelry and told me, 'He had no blood pressure when he came in,'" she wrote. "He's had two blood transfusions and is in the ICU hanging by a string." He fought for six days, undergoing surgeries, including the removal of his right lung.

Police and Fruit of Islam guards stood alert at the trauma unit doors. "Motherfuckers was calling the hospital, making threats," said Young Noble. He and fellow Outlawz member Napoleon had stayed behind in L.A., but after learning Tupac was shot soon arrived in Vegas, pistols in tow. Tupac's allies organized their own security detail, and the crew, which included members of the Outlawz, took shifts standing watch, armed and prepared for anything. "We was pretty much all ready to die at that point," said Young Noble.

News cameras crowded entryways and fans drove by blasting Tupac music. Jasmine Guy, Hammer, and Jesse Jackson visited, while Danny Boy sat at his bedside and sang him one of his favorite songs, Sam Cooke's "A Change Is Gonna Come." On September 13, Tupac's mother Afeni told doctors not to continue their efforts to resuscitate him. "Tupac would not have wanted to live as an invalid," she told *The New Yorker*.

"It was like a spaceship had beamed down, snatched him, and took him away," wrote Frank Alexander, "it was that fast."

Smoke My Ashes

Tupac's body was cremated. His family held a private service in Las Vegas the day after his death, and thousands of fans flocked to public memorials for him in New York and Atlanta. (A planned Death Row service for Tupac in L.A. was canceled, fueling conspiracy theories that he's still alive. Even Suge, in 2014, insisted to TMZ that the rapper was "smoking a Cuban cigar on an island somewhere.") Meanwhile, having taken over Tupac's estate, Afeni faced court battles on many fronts. She fought off a claim to half of the estate from Tupac's father, and she sued Death Row for $50 million in unpaid royalties. Tupac had very little to his name when he died, as some of his cars and his apartment were in Death Row's name. The label claimed Tupac owed *them* money—$7.1 million for advances and loans. The suit was ultimately settled for undisclosed terms. Then there was activist C. DeLores Tucker, who sued the estate for $10 million, alleging in part that Tupac lyrics caused her emotional distress, and thus her husband was left without "companionship and consortium."

The twin burden of mourning her son while battling in court took its toll on Afeni, who died herself in May 2016. She was most moved to hear "Dear Mama." "Can I listen to it without crying?" she said in a 1997 *People* interview. "No. It gets worse every time. It gets harder, it really does. That song gets deeper and deeper."

Some of Tupac's ashes were spread in the ocean. The Outlawz bonded with his spirit in their own ways, taking his lyric from his posthumous song "Black Jesuz" at its word: *Cremated, last wishes? Niggas smoke my ashes.* "We twist up some of that great granddaddy Cali kush, sprinkle some of the big homie in there, and guess what?" Young Noble said. "He's in our system for eternity." Afeni sprinkled another portion of her son's ashes in her Stone Mountain, Georgia, home's garden, making her eggplants and tomatoes "go crazy."

Owing to his participation in the beating of Orlando Anderson at the MGM, Suge Knight was cited for a parole violation, and sentenced to nine years in prison. Death Row continued in his absence, led by figureheads including Reggie Wright Jr. Still, "Suge was always kind of running the show," said their freelance publicist Jonathan Wolfson. Though temporarily buoyed by posthumous Tupac albums, the label's fortunes diminished in the years that followed. A federal racketeering probe against Death Row spurred misdemeanor tax charges against the label and David Kenner; Death Row and Knight filed for bankruptcy in 2006, with items like the label's iconic electric chair eventually sold at auction.

Though difficult to feel much sympathy for Suge, it's nonetheless dispiriting to consider Death Row's fall, and how its spoils were ultimately divided up. The white cofounders of Interscope, Jimmy Iovine and Ted Field, made countless millions. Tupac was left dead, and Suge and Dre came away with virtually nothing. Death Row's other two initial founders—Dick Griffey and D.O.C.—"had to sue to get [their] pennies," noted Griffey.

Tupac's first posthumous album *The Don Killuminati: The 7 Day Theory* came out less than two months after his death, and was released under his alter ego Makaveli, a shout-out to Renaissance-era Florentine politician Niccolò Machiavelli, best known for his book *The Prince*, which offers advice on power and leadership. "Machiavellian" may be shorthand for cynical manipulation for personal gain, but Tupac had found inspiration from the writer. "Machiavelli," according to Tupac, "said if you live your life how you should live your life—instead of excelling—then you're not living your life at all. You're a fool."

Said to have been recorded in seven days, the album doesn't feature leftovers from his previous work, but rather was intended as a stand-alone release. It captures magic from his frenzied, postprison recording sessions, like on the classic "To Live and Die in L.A." And his songcraft was clearly still developing, as evidenced by his layered wordplay on this and later posthumous albums, though the production and engineering on those works is hit-or-miss. But often the Makaveli album is a buzzkill, with shots levied against Haitian Jack, Jimmy Henchman, Mobb Deep, Biggie, Puffy, and even Nas, though they'd settled their beef before Tupac died. It's music to rage and spar by, when it was time to grieve and reconcile.

"I knew Tupac the human being, who wrote *2Pacalypse Now* and *Me Against the World*, not the tortured broken beast who wrote *Makaveli*," said Shock G from Digital Underground. "I don't recognize my friend Tupac Shakur on *Makaveli*, that's someone else."

Mutual Distrust

Tupac's murder should have been a slam-dunk case; he was a huge celebrity shot down on a crowded street with eyewitnesses galore. So why hasn't it been solved, twenty years later?

Some blame the Las Vegas Police Department. Their investigation was characterized as sloppy and indifferent, or worse. Former LAPD investigator Russell Poole had a chance to examine their clues, and concluded that they hadn't sufficiently followed up important leads. Department members, however, blamed the witnesses's code of silence. "It amazes me that when we have professional bodyguards as part of this entourage, that they can't even give us an accurate description of the vehicle," lead Las Vegas police investigator Sergeant Kevin Manning told gathered reporters. Suge Knight himself adhered to the no-snitching rule, famously saying he wouldn't reveal Tupac's killer even if he knew, because "I don't get paid to solve homicides," he told reporter Brian Ross.

But a number of Death Row affiliates did talk. "We all told the police that a white Cadillac came up and an arm reached out the window and started shooting," E.D.I. Mean said, who was in the car behind Tupac's. "It happened so fast that no one could get an accurate description or a license plate or anything like that." E.D.I. claimed another reason they didn't help police much is because investigators didn't seem particularly interested in what they had to say.

I believe neither the police nor the Death Row affiliates tried hard enough to bridge the gap between them. This atmosphere of mutual distrust began fermenting immediately after the shooting, when police threw Suge, E.D.I., and others on the ground, assuming them to be the perpetrators. The police were doing what they thought they had to do in that moment of chaos—but in the process fatally harmed their investigation. "I think they went through the motions, and that they would have liked to have solved it," said former LAPD investigator Greg Kading, of LVPD. "[But] you've got this built-in dynamic that leads itself to alienation and separation, as opposed to groups coming together to solve the crime."

Suge emerged as a prime suspect. Tupac was planning to leave Death Row, goes this line of thinking, and murder was his punishment—that or a way to capitalize on the believed hundreds of unreleased tracks he might have taken to another label, had he lived. Kevin Hackie, who worked as Death Row security, fingered Suge in the Nick Broomfield documentary *Biggie & Tupac*. Another bodyguard, Frank Alexander, also believed Suge was involved with the murder, citing all the hurdles thrown in his path when it came to guarding Tupac in Vegas (no phone, no reinforcements). Detective Russell Poole suspected Suge facilitated the Orlando Anderson stomping at the MGM to make it look like Tupac's killing was simple retaliation.

These theories sound far-fetched to me. It's counterintuitive that Suge would have put himself directly in the line of fire—twelve or so bullets came into the car, after all.

It's possible that Suge later intimidated Orlando Anderson. At the Death Row leader's parole hearing, Anderson reversed his previously stated assault allegations against Suge, insisting that Suge had actually been trying to *help* him during the MGM Grand stomping. (Anderson's attorney said he changed his testimony out of fear of Suge; Anderson later received a settlement from Tupac's estate, owing to Tupac's part in the assault.) But the stomping seemed to happen so spontaneously; it's hard to imagine something so chaotic and brutal, in a public place, could have been orchestrated. Finally, if Suge wanted Tupac dead, he could have found much cleaner and less risky ways to do it.

I also take issue with another theory, later championed by Russell Poole. It involves Suge's wife Sharitha and Death Row security head Reggie Wright Jr., who supposedly wanted Suge dead to take over his assets. They, the theory goes, enlisted a group of three men including Long Beach rapper Little ½ Dead, a Death Row affiliate. His motivation for supposedly killing Tupac? He'd actually recorded "Brenda's Got a Baby" first, and Tupac stole it from him. While Poole was a committed detective, this theory is excessively complicated and implausible. (The accused deny their involvement.)

Death Row bodyguard Kevin Hackie further claimed FBI agents were in the Death Row Las Vegas caravan that night and saw Tupac's murder. This added fuel to the belief that the government was involved in the death, a claim made explicit by addiction and mental health counselor and author John Potash in his book *The FBI War on Tupac and Black Leaders*. (The FBI, after all, long had it in for the Black Panthers and their affiliates.) I also don't believe this explanation holds up to scrutiny.

Bargaining

There is, however, a theory that may have legs. Though Tupac harbored a long list of enemies, two parties in particular had major, pressing beefs with him: Orlando Anderson and Bad Boy Records. Detective Greg Kading has implicated them both.

An LAPD homicide and gang investigator who'd previously worked in South Central, Kading in 2006 was assigned to a case that would lead him to Tupac, and he later led a task force looking into Tupac's murder that teamed up with the FBI and DEA. (Tupac's slaying was allegedly solicited in L.A., which gave Kading's team jurisdiction.) Eventually, their work led them to a Southside Crip named Duane Keith "Keffe D" Davis, a Compton-based PCP dealer and the uncle of Orlando Anderson.

Keffe D, who was in Vegas with his nephew at the time of Tupac's murder, gave a statement to the FBI in 1997. In the statement he said he and Anderson were uninvolved with the killing, and suggested Suge was responsible for Tupac's murder.

More than a decade later, in interviews with Kading's task force, Keffe D changed his tune. As detailed in Kading's 2011 book *Murder Rap*—as well as the documentary of the same name—Keffe D, now facing many years behind bars after a drug bust, called his prior story "bullshit." He now claimed that Puffy had offered him a million dollars to murder Tupac and Suge.

Keffe D and his crew hadn't come to Las Vegas that weekend in pursuit of Tupac, he added. They'd come for the Tyson fight. Orlando Anderson arrived in a white Cadillac, which had been rented by the mother-in-law of another member of their party, Keffe D said. But, following Anderson's assault, a man named Eric "Zip" Martin allegedly stepped in. He was an associate of Puffy's also there for the fight, and, according to Keffe D, Zip suggested the occasion might be the perfect opportunity to complete the million-dollar contract. In fact, Keffe D said, Zip even gave them his Glock, which he just happened to have with him.

The group drove to Club 662 and waited for Tupac and Suge for a time, before deciding to venture back out to the streets. They were alerted to Suge's BMW, near the Maxim hotel, by the screaming female fans who joined the caravan. They did a U-turn, and it was Orlando Anderson who pulled the trigger, Keffe D told the investigators: "Orlando rolled down the window, and popped him. If they would have drove on my side, I would have popped them." Then, after escaping the car full of Death Row's enforcers, they parked the Cadillac near their hotel, and went back to the room to drink and smoke weed.

Keffe D and company never did get their half million—for completing half of the job—he said, which is part of the reason he was now giving up Puffy to Kading's investigators. (He'd also been promised immunity for his confession.) Keffe added that Biggie was never involved.

Puffy vehemently denied the allegations. "This story is pure fiction and completely ridiculous," he told *L.A. Weekly* in 2011, after Kading released his book. Indeed, there are many reasons to doubt Keffe D's claims. He'd already changed his story once. He's been imprisoned numerous times, and was bargaining for his freedom. Even if Keffe D was telling the truth, there is no one to validate his claim that the Bad Boy mogul offered him a million for the murders, given that Keffe D said the men were alone when it happened.

However, there were others pointing a finger at Puffy: In the *Murder Rap* documentary, Kading cited a Southside Crip informant who'd told police that Bad Boy had a "standing" million-dollar contract with the Crips set, with which Orlando Anderson and Keffe D were affiliated. (It's unclear if this was allegedly for the murder of Suge and Tupac, or just

Tupac.) Former president of Bad Boy Kirk Burrowes claimed in a 2003 lawsuit that Bad Boy was "suspected" to have hired Tupac's killer, but didn't elaborate.

The case for Orlando Anderson as the triggerman is highly compelling; police reported many anonymous tips suggesting as much, and just about everyone I talked to in the hip-hop community believes he did it. But, even if he were the triggerman, it's possible he shot Tupac as a direct response to his beating—rather than as the result of a wider conspiracy.

One person who cannot weigh in is Orlando Anderson. He was killed in 1998, less than two years after Tupac's murder, following a shootout at a Compton car wash. Police deemed the incident unrelated to Tupac's slaying. But Anderson's name will forever be linked to the rapper, though he was never charged and denied his involvement.

Anderson left four daughters behind. His troubled past included a string of arrests. But he wanted to turn his life around through music, starting a rap label called Success Records with his half-brother Pooh and building a home recording studio. Journalist William Shaw visited the spot and spoke with Pooh, who proclaimed Orlando's innocence in the Tupac case, said he'd segued out of gang life, and called him, "the most charismatic person that I ever knew." Other associates of Anderson's thought his early death was not particularly newsworthy. After all, Anderson, like Eazy-E, attended Dominguez High School in Compton. There, as Shaw points out in his 2000 book *Westsiders*, the yearbook contained a full-page ad for a local mortuary.

TREPIDATION AND BRAVADO

According to his manager Mark Pitts, Biggie Smalls broke into tears at the news of Tupac's death. He could hardly believe it—after all, his onetime mentor had been shot before, and lived to tell the tale. But perhaps there was a bright side to the tragedy. With Tupac dead, could that mean all of this was over?

In 1996 and early 1997, Biggie was working on his second album, *Life After Death*, whose title, he said, alluded in part to Tupac's passing. Biggie had started on the new work a few months before Tupac's murder, and was extremely proud of it. As popular as he'd become, he felt his new album would *really* put him on the map.

But there was stress in Biggie's life, too. By early 1997 his weight had swelled to over 350 pounds. Owing to a recent car accident, he walked with a cane. Weapons and narcotics charges hung over his head—following a July 1996 raid of his Teaneck, New Jersey, home when police found guns and marijuana—and his relationship with Faith Evans was flagging. If that wasn't enough, he was nearly broke. And so it was with a weird mixture of trepidation and bravado that he arrived to California in February 1997. He came to record, shoot a video, do press, and work Hollywood channels in hopes of kicking off an acting career, as Tupac had. But the agenda also included smoking some of that excellent Cali herb beneath palm trees to try to get his mind off things.

For a few weeks, it worked. Puffy put him up at the Los Angeles Four Seasons, and he gave interviews by the pool, just like in "Juicy." He joyously hit the town with his friends; life was too short to live in fear. "We were proceeding like things were back to normal again," said a member of his entourage, speaking anonymously to a *Newsweek* reporter.

Was it too soon? You didn't have to believe Bad Boy orchestrated Tupac's death to think it a tad disrespectful for Biggie and his crew to be acting like they owned the place. "Anybody in their right mind knew they didn't let enough time pass," said promoter Doug Young.

Biggie's mind was unsettled, but he could take solace in a couple of things. For one, he'd found God. Encouraged by Puffy to make things right spiritually, he acquired a Jesus medallion and got a piece of scripture tattooed on his arm. For another, on February 12, 1997, Puffy and Snoop declared a truce in the East Coast–West Coast beef, albeit in the unlikeliest of venues: at a press conference in L.A. before the taping of an episode of Steve Harvey's self-titled WB sitcom. (Employing some rather wooden acting in the show, Puffy and Snoop are brought together by Harvey's teacher character to deliver a message of peace to his class.)

But there were bad omens as well. Boos, surely stemming from the coastal rap rivalry, rained on Biggie when he presented an award to singer Toni Braxton at the Soul Train Awards on March 7, where Tupac's *All Eyez on Me* won album of the year. The less-than-welcoming reception at the show didn't stop Biggie from attending a post-awards party at the Petersen Automotive Museum the following evening, in L.A.'s Miracle Mile neighborhood. He almost didn't come for another reason: Puffy had arranged a London promotional trip for him, but Biggie talked his boss into canceling the trip. "The food is horrible," he explained, in part. He believed the Petersen party might provide some good networking opportunities. Indeed, celebrities crawled the event. The New York–based DJ made everyone comfortable, playing Biggie's new single "Hypnotize" and other Bad Boy songs.

Biggie, in shades and his Jesus piece, chilled at a corner table while Puffy, wearing a bowler hat, got loose on the dance floor. At one point the people around him started chanting, "Bad Boy, Bad Boy." But the West Coast got shout-outs too. When the DJ played "California Love," everyone put their drinks up in the air—even Biggie.

Eventually the fire marshal shut the overcrowded party down. Surrounded by his posse, Biggie limped toward the exit.

"Get Down!"

Located just across the street from the Los Angeles County Museum of Art, the Petersen sits at the corner of two busy streets, Wilshire and Fairfax. The Bad Boy caravan consisted of three vehicles, with Puffy's at the front and the rear car driven by security guard Reggie Blaylock, an Inglewood police officer. The middle vehicle, a GMC Suburban, pulled up to the museum to load Biggie into the front passenger seat.

Though they'd considered attending yet another party, feeling fatigued they decided to turn in. But traffic was jammed, and they inched along. At the corner, just as the light was turning red, Puffy's lead car squeezed through across Wilshire, while the Suburban, blasting *Life After Death*, was forced to stop.

In a scene eerily similar to the one on Flamingo Road in Las Vegas, a car pulled up next to Biggie's vehicle, a green Chevy Impala. A gunman fired about six shots from a 9 mm pistol into the passenger side. "Get down!" yelled Kurupt, a few cars behind with his fiancée, Foxy Brown. Hearing the shots, Puffy jumped out of his car and ran to Big's side, but his star rapper was already losing consciousness. He'd been shot four times, in the arm, back, thigh, and hip, the last proving fatal, as the bullet hit vital organs.

Blaylock chased the Impala but couldn't keep up. Biggie was rushed to Cedars-Sinai, the same hospital where Eazy-E had died two years prior. There, the larger-than-life rapper was pronounced dead shortly after one a.m. He was twenty-four, one year younger than his one-time ally Tupac.

Former New York mayor David Dinkins and rap stars including Dr. Dre attended Biggie's March 18, 1997, funeral on the Upper East Side of Manhattan, where Faith Evans sang gospel and Puffy delivered a eulogy. Mary J. Blige consoled Lil' Kim as they exited. Following the service, thousands gathered to mourn and celebrate him in Brooklyn, as his motorcade, drenched in flowers, passed through the streets where he grew up.

In the wake of Biggie's murder, *Life After Death* took on a horrible and sinister new meaning; in an ad that came out after his passing, he was seen standing next to a tombstone. It became one of the bestselling rap albums ever, going diamond platinum in 2000, fourteen years before *All Eyez On Me* did the same.

Rumors flew in every direction in the weeks that followed Biggie's killing. Many suspected Suge's involvement, despite the fact that he was in prison. But police were instead chasing leads that tied the death to Crips, supposedly over a financial dispute. This theory would maintain a lot of traction over the years, considering Bad Boy's ties to the Southside Crips, and the fact that Keffe D and affiliates were at the Petersen that night. Many explanations were floated: Perhaps Bad Boy owed the gang money for security work, or the gang was simply extorting them. Perhaps the label unceremoniously cut ties with them after Tupac's death, thinking they no longer needed their services, and angering them in the process.

But this hypothesis wilts under scrutiny. For one thing, neither Lil' Cease nor G-Money—members of Biggie's entourage and eyewitnesses to his murder—recognized Keffe D nor any other Crips as the shooter. For another, according to Lil' Cease and Bad Boy bodyguard Eugene Deal, Bad Boy's interactions with the Crips contingency were nothing but cordial that evening.

LAPD detective Russell Poole dismantled this theory, and developed one of his own, with a conspiratorial bent that threatened the entire department. Poole discovered foul-smelling Death Row connections to cops including David Mack, a Compton-bred, Olympics-caliber middle-distance runner whose career was ended by injury. Mack found success as an undercover officer, but was arrested after stealing more than $700,000 from a Bank of America branch in late 1997. Mack's police partner Rafael Perez was also thought to be in cahoots with Death Row. His corruption arrest and testimony would fuel the costly LAPD Rampart scandal of the late nineties, revealing widespread misconduct in its CRASH unit. (The same unit infamous for aggressively rounding up anyone in South Central whom they took to be gang members.)

Poole was shocked to discover David Mack had something of a shrine to Tupac in his garage—right next to his Impala SS, the same model as the one used by Biggie's murderer. But Poole didn't think Mack pulled the trigger. His theory accused a friend and former classmate of Mack's, named Harry Billups. Billups was now a Nation of Islam member who went by Amir Muhammad. This detail seemed especially incriminating, as witnesses said Biggie's killer wore a traditional Muslim suit and bow tie. Information police received from a jailhouse informant seemed to finger Amir Muhammad as well. Further, Bad Boy bodyguard Eugene Deal later said he'd seen Muhammad at the Petersen on the night in question.

The LAPD stymied Poole in his investigation; he believed it was to cover their own. Transferred off the case, he resigned from the department in 1999, and before long went public with his investigation. Poole's theories inform Randall Sullivan's 2002 book *LAbyrinth* and Nick Broomfield's *Biggie & Tupac* documentary that same year. Poole also worked closely with Biggie's mother, Voletta Wallace, on a wrongful death lawsuit she and others filed against the city of Los Angeles in 2002. It was amended five years later to allege police conspiracy in Biggie's murder.

The suit was potentially worth a half billion dollars, the rapper's estimated lifetime earnings, a sum that apparently terrified LAPD brass. That's why the cold case was reopened in 2006, said Detective Greg Kading, who would come to lead a task force investigating both Biggie's and Tupac's murders.

Kading's team soon dismissed Poole's theory. For starters, the Impala murder car was green, rather than black like the one David Mack had.

They also looked more closely at the accusations of the jailhouse informant who had supposedly fingered Amir Muhammad—it turned out the informant described someone with very little in common with Muhammad. As for bodyguard Eugene Deal's alleged sighting of Muhammad at the Petersen that night? Deal had previously IDed someone different, Kading said, and besides, Muhammad's picture had already been published in the media, which might have tainted Deal's recollection. Ultimately, neither Mack nor Muhammad were charged in the matter.

A Theory

Kading's task force hoped Keffe D might be able to break open the Biggie case. Initially, Keffe D wasn't talking. And so, in 2008, they successfully set him up on a massive PCP bust. After offering immunity, they questioned Keffe in great detail about the night at the Petersen. But he soon let them know they were barking up the wrong tree. "That wasn't us," Keffe said, soon unfurling his story about his, Orlando Anderson's, and Puffy's alleged roles in Tupac's killing.

Kading's team was back at square one, when it came to Biggie's murder. They attempted to resurrect an old FBI racketeering case against Death Row, seeking to tie the label to money laundering and drug trafficking. That effort was unsuccessful, but it did connect them with a key witness, the mother of one of Suge's children, named Theresa Swann (a pseudonym given to her by Kading). She, like Keffe D, was successfully leveraged for information by Kading's team, owing to possible charges against her for bankruptcy fraud and involvement in an auto theft ring. They used her to confirm a theory they had.

That theory? That Suge had Biggie murdered because he believed, erroneously, that Biggie had given to the Crips the gun used to kill Tupac. Kading's team believed an associate of Suge's named Wardell "Poochie" Fouse killed Biggie. A jailhouse letter from a gang member named Roderick Reed (whose codefendant had been close to Suge) espoused as much. Adding fuel to the theory was that, before Biggie's murder, Suge was believed to have purchased a green Impala for Poochie—the model and color of the murder car.

The investigators weren't able to talk to Reed, but they were able to turn the screws on Theresa Swann. They did so by creating a fake confession letter from Poochie, which purported to lay out his arrangement with Suge: murder Biggie in retaliation for the killing of Tupac. The letter also implicated Swann herself as a conspirator in the crime. "To make it look more authentic, we put a fake law firm letterhead, and redacted out certain sections," Kading said in the *Murder Rap* documentary. They dated it April Fool's Day.

Of course, getting Swann to turn against Suge was no small matter, owing both to her personal loyalty to him and his fearsome reputation. But after being assured that the department would do their best to protect her, she broke down. "What Poochie said, that's what happened," she told them. She added that, at Suge's behest while he was behind bars, she met with Poochie to discuss the plan and arrange his payment of $13,000. Death Row security head Reggie Wright Jr. told Kading that he was correspondingly asked by Death Row's general manager about a way to get a large quantity of cash to "one of Suge's female friends."

Swann told investigators she attended the Petersen party, but did not witness the murder herself. Not long afterward, when she met Poochie to give him some of the money, his Impala looked like it had been repainted, she said.

Poochie himself could not be part of Kading's investigation. In July 2003 he was murdered in Compton while riding his motorcycle. That case also remains unsolved.

Greg Kading's task force produced compelling leads in the murders of both Tupac and Biggie. The case for Suge's involvement in Biggie's murder seemed solid, and they were attempting to link Puffy more directly to Tupac's murder as well.

To do so, they were hoping to set up Puffy's associate Eric "Zip" Martin; he was the alleged link between Keffe D and Puffy, and the man believed to have given the .40 caliber Glock to Keffe D and Orlando Anderson in Las Vegas—the same gun that killed Tupac. Since Zip was a narcotics dealer with whom Keffe D had previously done deals, the task force planned to have Keffe D try to set up a new drug deal with him. Then, with Zip's back to the wall, the thinking went, he might be willing to cooperate and testify against Puffy. Zip's loyalty to Puffy likely wasn't what it once was, considering the two of them had reportedly fallen out.

But it was not to be. In 2009 superiors removed Kading from the task force. He claimed it was owing to an LAPD Internal Affairs investigation of his work on a different case that year, against grocery store–chain owner George Torres. Torres's federal murder and racketeering convictions were overturned owing in part to police misconduct; the judge ruled that Kading threatened and bribed witnesses. Though Kading was ultimately cleared by Internal Affairs, he said he felt disenchanted about how the events surrounding the Torres case played out, and retired from the department in 2010.

Still, even without Kading, the Tupac and Biggie investigations could have continued. But LAPD brass put the task force on the shelf. "The LAPD said we're going to take everything we have on Tupac's murder and just give that to Las Vegas PD and let them decide what they want to do for that case," Kading told me in 2016, adding that they simply reassigned the remaining Biggie investigators to work on other murders.

Kading can only speculate as to why the LAPD gave up. He believes it was because his task force had debunked the "cop conspiracy" theory at the heart of Voletta Wallace's lawsuit, the one advanced by Russell Poole. And since the department had thus insulated itself from the lawsuit, the task force was deemed nonessential. They might also be worried, Kading speculated, that a savvy defense lawyer would play up the witness tampering charges against him to tar any case the LAPD brought. At the end of the day, he said, the LAPD no longer desired to commit the energy and resources to proving and prosecuting the cases; the fact that they failed to put to bed the biggest murders in rap history wasn't much of a concern. "They just made a decision on the immediate circumstances and didn't really think, 'Well, how do we look down the road?'" Kading said.

I reached out to LAPD for their side of the story multiple times, through numerous channels, but did not receive a response. A spokesperson for the department told *People* in 2016 that they wouldn't comment on the findings of Kading's film *Murder Rap*.

Travesty of Justice

Every year that passes, more potential leads dry up. The Biggie and Tupac murders are growing increasingly difficult to solve, because the key players keep dying:

- In 1996 Yaki Kadafi of the Outlawz, Tupac's childhood friend and a witness to his slaying, was murdered in New Jersey, not long after Tupac. (It was deemed unrelated.)
- In 1997 Heron, one of Suge's closest associates, and one of the participants in the Orlando Anderson stomping, was killed.
- In 1998 alleged Tupac triggerman Orlando Anderson was killed.
- In 2002 Buntry and Hen Dog, two more of Suge's closest friends and Death Row employees, were killed. Buntry also participated in the Anderson stomping, and was in the car that followed and exchanged gunfire with the white Cadillac following Tupac's shooting.
- In 2003 alleged Biggie triggerman Wardell "Poochie" Fouse was killed.
- 2003 also saw the murder of Anthony "Wolf" Jones, Puffy's bodyguard, and the man believed by some to have murdered Suge's friend Jake Robles, whose death escalated East Coast–West Coast tensions.
- In 2012 Eric "Zip" Martin, the associate of Puffy's who allegedly provided the Glock that killed Tupac, died of natural causes.
- In 2013 Tupac's bodyguard Frank Alexander killed himself.
- Also in 2013 another Tupac bodyguard, Michael Moore, who was also in Vegas at the time of the murder, died of a drug overdose.
- In 2015 Russell Poole, the former LAPD investigator who alleged a massive police conspiracy in Biggie's death, died from natural causes.

- Also in 2015 Terrence "T-Brown" Brown, who Keffe D said drove the white Cadillac in Vegas, was killed at a medical marijuana dispensary.

"If this was Elvis Presley and Frank Sinatra who got murdered, there would've been arrests a long time ago," Russell Poole told journalist Jeff Weiss, shortly before Poole's death in 2015. "This case can be solved, but needs police follow-up. There are clues sitting right in front of the police. It's a travesty of justice."

Voletta Wallace's wrongful death case was dismissed in 2010. But with the news came a hopeful sign: A lawyer for Biggie's estate claimed the police's case had been "reinvigorated." But Captain Kevin L. McClure of LAPD's robbery-homicide division dumped cold water on that theory. "It's always been considered an open investigation," he said.

When asked if the police were close to catching Biggie's assailant, McClure replied, "Probably not."

While most figures in the hip-hop community were devastated by Biggie's murder, a minority of rap fans were actually pleased, including some in the Bay Area, Tupac's onetime home. "[Some] sadly celebrated Biggie's death claiming that it was just revenge for 'Pac's death," wrote San Francisco radio personality Davey D. "'Now folks back East know how it feels,' was what many said." Others, however, were worried the carnage had only begun.

Behind the scenes, a series of under-the-radar gangland revenge plots had been set in motion even before Biggie's murder. On September 9, 1996, two days after Tupac's shooting, with the rapper clinging to life support, a suspected Southside Crips leader named Darnell Brim was shot in Compton. A ten-year-old girl was also hit by a stray bullet, but both survived. (The shooter was set to finish Brim off, but decided not to upon realizing Brim had fallen atop the girl.)

Over the course of the next five days more than a dozen more people were shot, three of them fatally. The incidents seemed tit for tat. According to a police search warrant, the Mob Pirus aligned themselves with other Blood factions for the battle, and the Southside Crips joined forces with other Crip subsets. The gang truce of 1992 was a distant memory.

There's no evidence that these slayings were sanctioned by anyone from Death Row or Bad Boy. It seems plausible that kids in the streets were simply anguished about Tupac's murder, and the subsequent revenge killings created a sinister domino effect. "There are very few Compton gangs that have leaders," said Reggie Wright Jr. "These youngsters, they kinda respect you and call you OG, but if they're going to do something, they're gonna do it." Soon Compton police, responding to the chaos initiated by Tupac's slaying and working in conjunction with other departments, obtained warrants to raid nearly forty homes in Compton and nearby cities, and locked up dozens of gang members.

"The trouble with what 'Pac was doing, with this East Coast–West Coast thing, was that it was just something got out of hand, a publicity thing, but brothers in the street think something is really going on, and they're gonna die for it," said rapper Big Syke, from Tupac's group Thug Life. "'Pac was like a person starting a fire, and it got out of control."

After Tupac's and Biggie's murders, there was, for a time, probably no more terrifying profession in America than high-profile hip-hop artist. Rumors abounded that Ice Cube, Mack 10, or Puffy could be hit next. Bicoastal supergroup the Firm recorded their debut album in neutral Miami, because no one wanted to go to the other's neck of the woods. Particularly frightened was Snoop Dogg. Though things should have been looking up for the rapper after he beat his murder charge, Snoop was drained of his resources, and his labelmate had been brutally murdered. His own potential enemies seemed to lurk everywhere.

Snoop's role in the East Coast–West Coast conflict was hard to pin down. Following the Red Hook, Brooklyn, shooting during the filming of the Dogg Pound video in 1995, he stomped on Big Apple skyscrapers in the "New York, New York" video. But he also showed love for Biggie and Puffy, appearing on *The Steve Harvey Show* with the latter, and sending a loud message that he wouldn't be involved with Death Row's war. That didn't stop him, however, from siding with the label in its divorce from Dr. Dre. Snoop's sophomore album *Tha Doggfather*, released in November 1996, features the mildest of disses against his former benefactor, asserting that he didn't need Dre's beats to be successful.

It's no *Doggystyle*, but the underrated *Doggfather* offers nice tracks from Daz, DJ Pooh, and others. It hit number one on the Billboard 200, but it would be Snoop's Death Row swan song. Like Dre, he believed the gangland culture was getting out of hand (though he partly blamed his own crew). But it was more than that. He believed Suge didn't tolerate disloyalty, and that things could get ugly quick.

The Summit

Owing to a history of anti-Semitic remarks, Louis Farrakhan gets little respect in the mainstream media. The Nation of Islam leader has long maintained unrivaled admiration throughout the hip-hop community, however. During the 1990s, when national leaders, black and white alike, were distancing themselves from rap music and culture, Farrakhan spoke out on its behalf, offering hospitality, counsel, and protection to embattled stars. Even today, hip-hop celebrities seek him out. In 2015 Kanye West announced he was making a documentary about the minister and his pre-Nation music career.

Shortly after Biggie's death Farrakhan conceived the granddaddy of all rap meetings, helping ensure no less than the very survival of the genre itself. To do so he undertook a seemingly quixotic notion: He sent out invitations to everybody in rap who hated each other. And he invited them to his house.

After a few preliminary regional meetings to set the stage, the players arrived in Chicago on April 3, 1997, for talks at Farrakhan's extravagant home in Hyde Park, called "the Palace." The invited rappers were told to take off their shoes; common practice for Muslim homes. (Those in need were provided socks.) They also met at the Salaam Restaurant, a Nation of Islam–run eatery in Auburn Gresham, which adheres to Muslim dietary restrictions.

The assembled included representatives of the East, West, Midwest, and South, of the old school and the new school. The summit addressed hip-hop beefs including the lingering animosity between Ruthless and Death Row Records, which continued after Eazy died. Bone Thugs-N-Harmony's album *E. 1999 Eternal* took shots at Tha Dogg Pound, who retorted by calling them "Hoes-N-Harmony." *It's easy to find MCs to execute*, Kurupt rapped. Taunted by Death Row members at a club, Bizzy Bone said they nearly came to blows. But tempers were dampened in Chicago. "Kurupt came at me, he was like, 'That was some bullshit,'" Bizzy said, adding that they went on to become tight: "These niggas is my *best friend* right now."

"If the minister wasn't there and it was held somewhere else, someone might have gotten put down," said Kurupt.

Ice Cube had lots of explaining to do. He arrived on a chartered jet from a movie set, with numerous scores to settle. He quickly quashed disputes with his affiliates Kam and Shorty. But many New Yorkers were pissed about his album with Westside Connection, *Bow Down*, which had come out in the fall. Bronx rapper Fat Joe, in particular, couldn't understand why Cube was antagonizing people in a city where he'd previously had so much love, dating back to *Amerikkka's Most Wanted*, and even his N.W.A work.

"When I heard you were gonna be here, I got in my car and drove fifteen hours just to see the whites of your eyes," Fat Joe reportedly told Cube. "I wanted to see you face-to-face and ask you why you did what you did."

Cube, flanked by his Westside Connection colleagues Mack 10 and WC, asserted that New York media didn't show L.A. rappers proper respect, and that its artists tarred gangsta rap as a bastardization of true hip-hop (ignoring the fact that New York artists like Wu-Tang Clan and Fat Joe himself made hard-edged rhymes). Cube admitted stirring up some controversy on purpose—after all, battling is an essential part of hip-hop. He and Joe hashed things out, with Cube ultimately admitting that, considering the current volatility, perhaps it was time to tamp things down a bit.

It wasn't Cube's only beef. He also faced hometown hero Common, whom he insulted on *Bow Down* track "Hoo-Bangin' (WSCG Style)": *I'm bombin' on Common Sense / Chicago is mine, nigga hit the fence*. But they reconciled as well; Cube stood up and gave him a hug.

"It was a great thing," Cube told me in 2015, adding that, as a measure of how far they've come, Common stars in the latest version of Cube's

Barbershop franchise. Common credited an atmosphere where they could speak one-on-one, without yes-men and hangers-on in their ears "talking crazy."

At his summit, Farrakhan sought to put the hip-hop acrimony in historical perspective. He handed out copies of the so-called Willie Lynch letter, a guide purportedly written by an eponymous white slave owner in the early eighteenth century, advocating pitting slaves against each other as a method to control them.

Though its historical efficacy is in great doubt, the document served as an effective metaphor for the state of the rap industry, where black artists' beefs with each other were driving sales in the largely white-controlled music and publishing industries. Hip-hop magazines in particular were accused of perpetuating coastal beef, including *Vibe*, which published a 1995 issue with Biggie and Puffy on the cover, alongside the headline "East vs. West." *Vibe*'s president Keith Clinkscale admitted to not giving proper consideration to community concerns, though he defended their journalism. (Puffy couldn't be in Chicago for the meeting, but pledged his support.)

Geto Boys rapper Willie D condemned the mainstream media's ongoing, breathless critique of his art form. Famed activist Kwame Ture also spoke to the group—a heroic effort, considering he had prostate cancer and would die a year later. He talked on J. Edgar Hoover's attempts to infiltrate and disrupt black activist groups, and suggested the same tactics were still at work today.

Other rap notables present at the summit included Chuck D, Goodie Mob's CeeLo Green, Too $hort (who did some soul-searching about his lyrics), and Harlem beatboxing legend Doug E. Fresh, who lamented the state of a genre whose initial goal was to spread unity and good times. Another crucial organizer of the event was Def Jam cofounder Russell Simmons, who discussed leading a bicoastal concert tour. Both he and Farrakhan went on to host subsequent truce meetings, and Simmons founded the Hip-Hop Summit Action Network, which works with the rap industry to effect social change.

"The East and the West have come together, and they have agreed that as of this day, all of the insults that have been heaped on one by the other will cease, and each have forgiven each other," Farrakhan announced at the press conference that concluded the summit. Though the meetings didn't generate much mainstream coverage, that wasn't the main point. The point was to extinguish hip-hop violence. Considering its marked decline since then, the event was an unqualified success.

"The proof is in the history," said Kurupt.

No Limit

At the press conference Snoop stood behind Farrakhan, before delivering a passionate address himself. But the Chicago summit didn't end his troubles with Death Row.

He came to loggerheads with his agent and manager, Sharitha Golden (then known as Sharitha Knight). As Suge's wife, she was in a decidedly difficult position to represent Snoop. Golden declined my request for an interview for this book, but in 2016 she told S. Leigh Savidge, "I'm very open and honest with everybody," in regards to her management style.

In 1997 Sharitha sued Snoop for $1.6 million in unpaid agent commissions—that is, 20 percent of the $8 million he'd earned since she began working for him four years earlier. Snoop claimed to be blindsided. He, along with Dr. Dre, David Kenner, and Suge, sued their accounting firms—the same ones who employed Death Row's embattled accountant Steve Cantrock—and he claimed he was unaware that signing with Death Row meant the boss's wife got one dollar out of every five he made.

He extracted a sizable settlement. But buried in Sharitha's lawsuit was the eye-raising claim that Snoop was deathly afraid for his life. "The defendant presently owns and often times travels in an armored van equipped with gun ports," it read, adding that Snoop was paying "large sums of money to have twenty-four-hour armed security force and maintains a large entourage to travel with him." Snoop denied this was the case. But he had cause for worry. According to an interview he later did with police, he believed Suge was responsible for Tupac's murder. He'd also surely heard the rumor that Suge ordered Biggie's hit.

Could Suge be coming for Snoop next?

Into this uncertainty, Master P came riding in like a white knight. A son of the New Orleans's Calliope Projects, the man born Percy Miller established his No Limit record label in the Bay Area, before returning to Louisiana to kick off one of the most remarkable runs in hip-hop history. No Limit sold grimy, street-centric albums as fast as they could print them, and in 1998 Master P pulled off the seemingly impossible: He signed Snoop away from Death Row.

It helped that Suge was behind bars and financially pinched. It also helped that Master P, a fearsome child of poverty himself, wasn't afraid of him. In Master P's recollection, the negotiations were surprisingly simple: He asked Suge how much Snoop was worth on the open market, and then offered him "a little bit more."

"That's it," Master P said. "The money will be there in the morning."

Snoop promptly relocated, joining Master P and artists including Mystikal in a Baton Rouge gated community called the Country Club of Louisiana. Considering Snoop's parents had grown up in Mississippi, the South wasn't new to him. Though the Country Club denied the No Limit guys memberships to use the tennis courts, Snoop was nonetheless comforted by his new surroundings, about as far from coastal animosity as he could be, physically and psychically. "Master P was willing to step up," Snoop said. "I needed that more than a record label. I needed a friend."

Snoop's three albums with No Limit sold well, though they aren't particularly well remembered. But his Louisiana stint helped him successfully transition to the satisfying next phase of his career, reuniting with Dre on the blockbuster *Chronic 2001* album, and starting a label of his own, which kicked off with the appropriately named *Paid tha Cost to Be da Boss*.

Despite his relocation, Snoop's relationship with Suge continued to disintegrate. Sure, as required, Snoop denied that he lived in fear. "Never was afraid of him," he said of Suge. "I was afraid I was gonna have to kill him." Still, he had reason to believe the Death Row leader was coming for him. Suge called Snoop a government informant, and made thinly veiled threats. Not long before Suge's 2001 release from prison, Death Row's website proclaimed: "2001, the year of fear. All dogs run & hide. Suge is coming home." The message was followed by a dog barking, then a gunshot.

But a funny thing happened. Instead of fighting fire with fire, Snoop chose nonviolence. Having witnessed firsthand what headstrong, armed devotion to your set (be it a gang, record label, or even a coast) entailed, he sought a different path.

Going to Be OK

Following the Farrakhan peace treaty, Ice Cube also began to reassess his priorities. Somewhere along the way he concluded that he didn't always have to be the hardest guy in the room. During his early twenties Cube made a habit of pissing people off. The years since have shown a full reversal: Nowadays Cube seems to thrive off diverse friendships and business pursuits.

The first time I talk with Cube, it's at the Westwood W hotel in 2013, an interview hosted by his new sponsor, Coors Light. Like many of his film roles, his commercials for the brand trade on his tough-guy persona for comedic purposes; in one he faces off against a bottle of the suds over who is the "coldest," and ends up with a face full of frost. In person he's polite and deferential. His bulky frame housed in all black, from his skate shoes to his Dodgers hat, he quickly commences with the beer shilling and indicates he's down to talk about whatever.

We hit many topics, including his ESPN documentary on the Raiders, for which he interviewed owner Al Davis shortly before his passing ("He looked great for a man that was about to die"); his own work ethic ("My wife will tell you when I'm not busy, I'm antsy"); and why gangsta rap gets a bad rap ("How many serial killers listen to classical music? They never blame classical music"). He talks about his love for midcentury designers

Charles and Ray Eames, whom he learned about in his Phoenix architectural drafting studies, and whom he celebrated in a 2011 video for the Getty Institute.

His career continues to evolve, even as he continues to draw snickers from some for having transitioned from hardcore hip-hop to soft multiplex fare. The punch line of Cube jokes almost always involve *Are We There Yet?*, a 2005 family comedy in which his character battles pissing, barfing children. (In one scene a deer karate chops him.) The film was a huge success, earning $82 million at the box office and inspiring a sequel and a television series, but is just one spoke in Cube's Hollywood empire, which also includes the *Friday, Barbershop, 21 Jump Street*, and *Ride Along* franchises.

I once read someone speculate that, had Cube been killed instead of Tupac, the former would have been the hardcore martyr, while the latter would have eventually segued into PG movies. Sooner or later one has to ease off the throttle. To reinvent yourself is no small thing, and Cube's mogul status gave him the platform to push the *Straight Outta Compton* film, which did more to revive N.W.A's legacy than anything else.

Jerry Heller has called N.W.A the "black Beatles." Their meager output makes it hard for me to cosign this characterization, although it's fun to think about. (Cube is John, Dre is Paul, Ren is George, and Yella is Ringo, but who is Eazy? George Martin?) Perhaps a better comparison is with N.W.A's contemporaries Guns N' Roses, with whom they shared mutual appreciation and an L.A. fan base. Lead singer Axl Rose was often spotted wearing an N.W.A ballcap, and the rappers' song "Appetite for Destruction" was inspired by GN'R's album of the same name. Both acts pushed boundaries and were considered politically incorrect—even harbingers of doom—in their times. In the end they remade their respective genres, and today are radio staples.

"We thought we were so badass," said Axl Rose in 2006. "Then N.W.A came out rapping about this world where you walk out of your house and you get shot. It was just so clear what stupid little white-boy poseurs we were."

Oddly, N.W.A's leader Eazy-E doesn't command near-universal appreciation like rappers Notorious B.I.G., Nas, Jay-Z, Tupac, Eminem, and Dr. Dre, most of whose styles can be directly traced to what Eazy started with "The Boyz-N-the Hood." "He is the founder of gangsta rap," Krayzie Bone said.

If you ask me, he deserves iconic status beyond his genre, along the lines of, say, Bob Marley or Kurt Cobain. But unlike those artists, the rough edges of Eazy's image have never been smoothed over. It's easy to forget that Cobain was a moody heroin addict, or that Marley was a womanizer who mistreated his wife. But Eazy's still seen as a volatile ghetto kid with a Jheri curl and a gun. When it comes to keeping his name part of today's culture, his estate hasn't been able to match the efforts of Tupac's estate, which has constantly reinvented the artist posthumously, across all forms of media.

Other surviving N.W.A members MC Ren and DJ Yella have been even less in the public eye, though the group's film and their 2016 induction into the Rock and Roll Hall of Fame put them back in the spotlight. As a result, DJ Yella's services behind the turntables have been in high demand around the world—perhaps a satisfying change from his previous line of work: porno director. Following Eazy's death he made many adult films, including one called *DJ Yella's Str8 Outta Compton*. "I gave that up in like '07," Yella told me, about his porn career. "The internet killed it."

MC Ren, meanwhile, today lives far from the streets of Compton where he grew up. In June 2014 I meet him in Palm Springs, the sweltering resort town two hours inland from Los Angeles, where he moved to be closer to his parents. It's unfortunate that he no longer puts out albums regularly. N.W.A wouldn't have been what it was without his songwriting and commanding flow, and he was one of Eazy-E's main ghostwriters. As revealed by his solo work, he could excel at more than just playing a role; he was a visionary artist in his own right.

He still goes as hard as ever when he does make new music—*Fuck your money, fuck your cars, nigga spit some hot bars*, he raps on a 2014 track called "Rebel Music." But he does it on his own terms, on his own release schedule. He can afford it, flush with N.W.A royalties that never run dry, and an assured legacy. *Who's your top ten? Is it MC Shan? Is it MC Ren?* Nas rapped in 2006.

We meet at the Hard Rock Hotel. In tow is his wife of twenty-one years, Yasmen, and their nine-year-old daughter, who wears a neon green T-shirt reading, "My Dad Thinks I'm Awesome." Ren himself wears a white taqiyah on his head. After joining the Nation of Islam in 1993, he became an orthodox Muslim two years later. His conversion was influenced by his friend DJ Train, an N.W.A affiliate and DJ for J. J. Fad, who died in a 1994 house fire. Before his death Train and Ren planned to travel to Egypt, and so Ren made the trip solo the next year. As we sit down to eat, Ren's daughter orders macaroni and cheese, but he ends up sending it back because it has bacon.

Ren is a bit shorter than I'd expected, but bulkier, and wears no jewelry other than a silver wedding ring. He seems a bit uncomfortable at times and doesn't display an effervescent charisma, which perhaps makes sense, considering he's always fashioned himself as an anti-Hollywood type who calls bullshit while others play industry games.

True to his straight-talking self, MC Ren told the *Goin Way Back Show* that the film *Straight Outta Compton* was about "80 percent" accurate. He complained publicly when the initial marketing largely excluded him and DJ Yella. Today, we also discuss the sale of Dr. Dre's headphones company Beats to Apple, which netted Dre hundreds of millions of dollars. "That's a blessing," Ren says, without a trace of jealousy. "That's dope!" He has critical words for a different figure from his past, however. "When I told my math teacher in high school I was gonna be a hip-hop star he clowned me every day," Ren wrote on Twitter in 2016, "now I'm in the Rock and Roll Hall of Fame."

After N.W.A split, group ghostwriter D.O.C. continued working with Dr. Dre, and even mounted something of a solo comeback in 2015. Out of nowhere, his voice—which failed him after his car accident more than twenty-five years earlier—suddenly started to improve. It's not back to its original strength, but he felt confident enough to perform in his hometown Dallas in October 2015. Backed by platinum R&B singer Erykah Badu, who's the mother of his daughter Puma, and Scarface from the Geto Boys, the show was rapturously received.

No Ruthless Records alums, however, have seen success like Dr. Dre. Beyond the windfall of the Beats sale and the ongoing success of his Aftermath label—which spawned the careers of world-beating rappers Eminem, 50 Cent, the Game, and Kendrick Lamar—Dre remains relevant as a performer, and as a producer he's still setting trends. His personal life, meanwhile, is stable. Married for more than two decades, his wife Nicole supported him through the tragic 2008 death of his son Andre Young Jr., from an overdose of heroin and morphine.

Still, even as he moved to extradite himself from the hard-knock lifestyle, Dre hasn't been able to fully escape his past. Like Snoop, he's been taunted by Suge after leaving Death Row. Dre even took out a restraining order against Suge, which was why the latter was turned away from a production lot during the filming of an ad for the *Straight Outta Compton* film on January 29, 2015. After Suge left the scene, an on-set security guard followed him to the parking lot of a Compton restaurant, where Suge non-fatally ran him over, and Suge killed another man in the process. (Suge was charged with murder, though he claimed the death was accidental.)

Ten years earlier, Suge was accused of paying a man to hurt Dre at the November 15, 2004, Vibe Awards, held in a hangar in the Santa Monica Municipal Airport. Shortly before receiving a career achievement award that night, Dre was asked for an autograph and then sucker punched, setting off a melee. The assailant, Jimmy James Johnson, received a year in jail; he claimed Suge Knight paid him $5,000 for the assault, which Suge denied. Dre wasn't hurt in the incident.

Following the Vibe Awards incident, according to Lisa Johnson, Dre showed up at her home in the middle of the night. Johnson is the mother of three of Dre's children, and has accused him of beating her. The pair had only intermittent contact since they stopped seeing each other in the early nineties, according to Johnson, which included court battles over child support and a home he purchased for her. But this night, arriving at Johnson's house, Dre insisted he had something important to tell her and the three girls. The middle daughter La'Toya was not there, so he sent a cab to retrieve her. With the whole family assembled, Dre promised monies totaling half a million dollars to be split among the four of them, though he later added stipulations, and ultimately never gave it to them, Johnson and La'Toya said. (Dr. Dre had no comment.)

That night, Johnson said Dre, clearly shaken by the evening's assault, opened up to her.

"He asked me, 'What did I see?' Did I see harm coming towards him? Did I see anything wrong?" she recalled. "I gave him a kiss on his forehead and told him that he was going to be OK."

He then put on a movie—*The Ladies Man*, Johnson said. He sat down, watched it, and ate a bowl of cornflakes.

Survival

Among this legendary cohort of gangsta rappers, it is perhaps Snoop who had the most intriguing transformation of all. He managed to fully stamp out his differences with Suge. The two were even photographed together at a club in 2013. "My relationship with him is where it's supposed to be. It's respectful on both ends," Suge told *Rolling Stone* that year.

Snoop didn't stop there. Pledging to take his music in a more positive direction—even if it meant he sold fewer records—he worked to mend fences. Snoop hinted at this new direction during the Chicago peace treaty. In 1997 he and Kurupt reconciled with B.G. Knocc Out and Dresta, the Ruthless brothers who spoke out against Death Row in the "Real Compton City G's" era. They even made a record together, though it never came out. In 2005, Snoop hosted a summit at a Universal City hotel called Protect the West. In attendance were California rappers representing various territories and factions, everyone from the Game to Young MC, who pledged to end disputes and increase their collective earning potentials.

Call him Uncle Snoop, the trustworthy old-timer who fixes problems. "You could look at me as like a counselor, a doctor, a psychologist, a priest, a big brother, a warden, a mayor," he told me in 2013. "They didn't create this lane for us to hate each other and fight each other and be mad at each other. They created this lane for us to have an outlet to do something with our lives."

Having racked up firearm and drug charges over the years, he's not everyone's idea of a role model. But he founded a youth football league in 2005, and has worked the streets to quell dangerous gang beefs. His 2006 unity song "Gangbangin' 101" paired him with Bloods MC the Game, who rapped: *Red and blue rag tied in a knot.* And as the years passed, Snoop's music has gotten more groovy. He pilgrimaged to Jamaica to create the reggae-influenced 2013 album *Reincarnated* under his Snoop Lion alias, which includes the moving anthem "No Guns Allowed." Soon after, as Snoopzilla, he teamed up with Dâm-Funk to make an old-school funk album.

As promised these albums weren't violent, and (as he suspected) they didn't sell much, either. But the man still lives well. He's got countless endorsement deals, and countless artists happy to have him on their songs. The key word in all of this? He *lives*.

"Survival is what I'm here to do," he said at the press conference for the Swedish socks, while sitting on a throne. "I teach people how to survive, through my experience."

Hard-edged hip-hop, of the style inspired by Ruthless and Death Row Records, hasn't just survived. It's taken over. It's become the defining musical movement of a generation, largely remaking pop in its image. These days, even teen idols like Justin Bieber and Taylor Swift are expected to be hip-hop literate. As shown by Snoop, Cube, and others, the same credentials that qualify you to be a hardcore rapper now qualify you to be a brand ambassador. The tropes and fashions brought in by gangsta rap are routinely adopted by content creators wanting to appear edgy and cool.

What has gangsta rap ultimately left us with? I'd say a popular culture with fewer restrictions, for better or for worse. On the downside, TV, music, and movies have become coarser: more cursing, more sex, and more violent images. Gangsta rap—and its offshoot incarnations, hip-hop subgenres with names like trap, ratchet, and drill—isn't solely to blame for this, of course, but it's hard to argue that Eazy and his disciples' glamorization of gunplay and derogatory names for women, for example, haven't spread outward.

But gangsta rap has also helped disenfranchised people gain a voice. Alonzo Williams, the leader of World Class Wreckin' Cru, was initially against N.W.A's plan to tell it like it was on the streets of Compton, because he didn't think listeners were ready. The prevailing wisdom was that black entertainers were supposed to act *proper*, and that same logic applied to black people generally. Even if the situations they grew up in were marked by poverty, crime, injustice, and squalor, they were expected to present themselves as if nothing was wrong. N.W.A, Ice-T, and Tupac encouraged African-Americans to speak up. The Black Lives Matter movement that began in 2013 likely wouldn't be what it is without "Fuck tha Police" and "Straight Outta Compton." Ice Cube's expression of the daily terrors felt by black people everywhere, on an album heard by millions, was liberating and empowering.

The L.A. gangsta rappers—or, as they preferred, reality rappers—didn't just fight oppression. They showed pride for a culture, celebrating their people in all their messy glory, and with little regard for what anyone else thought. It was shocking to many, including white people and older black people, but it was timely and necessary. Inside the Trojan horse of catchy beats and clever rhymes, Dr. Dre and his brethren smuggled in the hopes, dreams, and fears of those who were otherwise mostly ignored. They took the experience of the inner city and made it understandable to people who had never set foot there. Gangsta rap, more than any other art form, made black life a permanent part of the American conversation.

ACKNOWLEDGMENTS

Thanks first to my wonderful, beautiful wife for her support throughout this process, and for always believing in me. Also to our boys Good Guy and Little Face. Thanks to my super agent Ethan Bassoff and super editor Paul Whitlatch for making this project happen, and everyone at Hachette Books, including Justine Gardner, Hallie Patterson, Michelle Aielli, Betsy Hulsebosch, Lauren Hummel, Yasmin Mathew, Grace Hernandez, and Mauro DiPreta. I'm especially grateful to Jeff Weiss for guiding me in the L.A. scene upon my arrival there in 2011, as well as his friendship. Amin Eshaiker heroically gave me access to his archived interviews, many conducted with Andrew Arellano, and Chad Kiser went above and beyond helping me get access to subjects. Michael Namikas gave me amazing background info on Tupac and Death Row, and Linda Leseman and Imade Nibokun did fantastic transcription work. Thanks also to my dad for his help, as well as to the great music analysts Jake Paine, James "Nocando" McCall, Chaz Kangas, Wendy Day, Dennis Romero, Nate Jackson, Kris Ex, Tim Sanchez, Rodney Carmichael, Martin Cizmar, Clint Mayher, Ronin Ro, Jeff Liles, Andrew Noz, Brian Coleman, Scott Bejda, Martin Cizmar, and Peanut Butter Wolf. I would have gotten nowhere without the kind assistance of Raoul Juneja, Abesi Manyando, Kevin Hoffman, Richie Abbott, Craig and Todd Schweisinger, Margaret Weir, Bruce Johnson, Vibert White Jr., Nancy Byron, Stephanie Frederic, and Ryan Gattis. Much love to my mom, sister, brother, Jay, and Sean.

A big shout-out to the journalists Davey D, Chuck Philips, Kevin Powell, Sway, Brian Cross, Matthew McDaniel, Jonathan Gold, S. Leigh Savidge, Harris Rosen, Jeff Chang, Jeff Weiss, Dan Charnas, Tim Sanchez, Paul Arnold, and Greg Kading, whose reporting and interviews I kept going back to. Savidge and Susan Self were kind to let me look at *Welcome to Death Row* notes, and Kading and Mike Dorsey of the *Murder Rap* documentary were absolute mensches as well. The publications *Vibe*, *Los Angeles Times*, *L.A. Weekly*, *Spin*, *Rap Pages*, and *The Source* did amazing real-time reporting on the events described in this book, and *XXL*, *Rolling Stone*, ThaFormula.com, WestCoastPioneers.com, HipHipDX.com, VladTV.com, *Murder Master Music Show*, and *Goin Way Back Show* have done great work with artists from the era since then. Sergio Hernandez's documentary *Ruthless Memories*, about Eazy-E, is a must-see. *N.W.A: The World's Most Dangerous Group* and *Uprising: Hip Hop and the L.A. Riots*, both directed by Mark Ford, were great resources. The sites discogs.com, whosampled.com, and genius.com were tremendously helpful as well.

Thanks to Kristi Cooper and Tyler Busik for helping facilitate my interview with J-Dee, and to J-Dee himself for hosting me.

A toast to my fabulous editors, Sarah Fenske, Lanre Bakare, Andy Hermann, Justin Hunte, and Andy Van De Voorde.

Thanks also to my friends Sarah Bennett, Ben Welsh, Katie Bain, Brook Perdigon, Tessa Stuart, Shea Serrano, Joe Kessler, Ben Bloom, Dave Schwartz, Eric Royce Peterson, Mary Carreon, Sam Ives, Emily Berkey, Gene Maddaus, Jeff Smith, and Nick Lucchesi for their greatly varied help through all of this.

Most importantly, thanks to my interview subjects. I interviewed 112 people for this book (who's counting?), some of them multiple times, many for many hours. They were all unfathomably generous with their time, but I'd like to offer particular kudos to Alonzo Williams, Charis Henry, Barry "Shakespeare" Severe, Marq "Cli-N-Tel" Hawkins, Tracy Jernagin, David "Rhythm D" Weldon, Marvin Kincy, Anthony "Sir Jinx"

Wheaton, Steffon, DJ Speed, Greg Mack, Lil Eazy-E, Chris "The Glove" Taylor, Anthony "A.W." Williams, Doug Young, David Faustino, Shorty from Da Lench Mob, Bigg A, and MC J.B.

RIP Afeni Shakur, Mark "Big Man" Rucker, and Joe Fierro, aka KJ Mustafa.

NOTES

Chapter One: The Stash

1. **"Eric had stashes of cash everywhere"**: Arnold "Bigg A" White, author interview, June 19, 2014.
2. **"They would catch you with crack and just give you a slap on the wrist"**: Mark "Big Man" Rucker, *Ruthless Memories Part I*, directed by Sergio Hernandez, 2013.
3. **"Then everybody's trying to expand out"**: Vince "CPO Boss Hogg" Edwards, author interview, April 16, 2015.
4. **"He had all the tight cars, clothes and all of that"**: MC Ren, author interview, June 1, 2014.
5. **"community dick"**: Mark Rucker, author interview, August 11, 2014.
6. **Joyce threw a lunchbox at Eric's head**: Dismost, author interview, July 15, 2015.
7. **"I was hearing, from everyone—that's your boyfriend"** (and story about smashing Eric's BMW that follows): Tracy Jernagin, author interview, October 18, 2015.
8. **"baby races"**: Mark Rucker, author interview, August 11, 2014.
9. **"When we had an outing or a weekend together"**: Eric Wright Jr., *OC Weekly*, "DNA Project: Straight Outta OC," by Nate Jackson, September 5, 2013.
10. **squirting lighter fluid on the gopher**: Bigg A, *Ruthless Memories Part I*, directed by Sergio Hernandez, 2013.
11. **"Heeyyyy Charlie"**: MC Ren, author interview, June 1, 2014.
12. **civil service test**: MC Ren, *Rolling Stone*, "N.W.A: American Gangstas," by Brian Hiatt, August 27, 2015.
13. **"I hate workin' for somebody else"**: Eazy-E, *Rap Pages*.
14. **glass house description**: Bigg A, author interview, June 19, 2014.
15. **"'I can cleanse the neighborhood of all these, you know, marauding gangs'"**: Stanley "Tookie" Williams, *Democracy Now!* "A Conversation with Death Row Prisoner Stanley Tookie Williams from his San Quentin Cell," by Amy Goodman, November 30, 2015.
16. **"Raymond would take his shirt off"**: Ronald "Kartoon" Antwine, *L.A. Weekly*, "Tookie's Mistaken Identity," by Michael Krikorian, December 15, 2005.
17. **Bloods took red as their color**: Marvin Kincy, author interview, March 2, 2015.
18. **"If someone saw you were a hustler"**: Da Sean "J-Dee" Cooper, author interview, March 7, 2015.
19. **Horace Butler invited Eric for a ride** (and details about truck in following paragraph): Mark Rucker, author interview, August 11, 2014.

20. **Horace Butler shot seven times**: Los Angeles County Coroner's Report, August 21, 1984.

21. **"Me and him used to be together every day"**: Eazy-E, *Rap Pages.*

22. **"Man, where'd you get this from?"**: Mark Rucker, author interview, August 11, 2014.

23. **Compton police among the most corrupt**: *Murder Rap,* by Greg Kading, 2011.

24. **Eric Wright's parents from Greenville, Mississippi**: Eric Wright Jr., author interview, June 10, 2014.

25. **Compton was hit harder by racial segregation**: KCET.org, "A Southern California Dream Deferred: Racial Covenants in Los Angeles," by Kelly Simpson, February 22, 2012.

26. **"respectable men turn into crackheads"**: Ice Cube interview outtake with Jeff Weiss, early 2015.

27. **"I can have nice cars, I can have a house"**: "Freeway" Rick Ross, author interview, August 6, 2014.

28. **"They swallow the dope or throw it away"**: As told anonymously to civil rights attorney Connie Rice in her book, *Power Concedes Nothing*, 2012.

29. **"Because my wife at the time was Hispanic"**: Greg Mack, author interview, March 7, 2012.

30. **Mixmaster Spade learned DJing in New York**: Raptalk.net, "Raptalk Remembers the Legendary Mix Master Spade," by Tim Sanchez, March 15, 2016.

31. **"It was a race riot"**: Rodger Clayton, CantStopWontStop.com, "An Interview with Uncle Jamm's Army," by Jeff Chang.

32. **Latino gangs gave Lonzo Williams a pass**: Alonzo Williams, author interview, July 19, 2014.

Chapter Two: Sir Romeo

1. **Andre Young pop-locked during halftime at Fremont High School football games**: Laylaw, HipHopDX.com, "Laylaw Discusses His History with Dr. Dre, 2Pac, Ghost-Producing 'California Love (Remix)'," by Paul Arnold, June 7, 2011.

2. **customized Sir Romeo jacket**: Lisa Johnson, author interview, August 21, 2015.

3. **"Before they leave they'd wrap it back up"**: Alonzo Williams, author interview, July 19, 2014.

4. **Andre's mother would drop him off at Eve After Dark**: *Long Road Outta Compton*, by Verna Griffin, 2008.

5. **Andre began talking to fourteen-year-old Lisa Johnson**: Lisa Johnson, author interview, August 21, 2015.

6. **Andre and Johnson met secretly**: Ibid.

7. **"the call that all moms of teenagers dread"**: *Long Road Outta Compton*, by Verna Griffin, 2008.

8. **"My brother was my best friend"**: Dr. Dre, MTV.

9. **"We would all model"**: Warren G, author interview, July 10, 2014.

10. **Kibbles 'N Bits**: Ibid.

11. **"Everybody in my neighborhood loved music"**: Dr. Dre, *Los Angeles Times*, "The Dr.'s Always In," by Robert Hilburn, September 23, 2007.

12. **"We can put rappers on no more than two minutes a night"**: Rodger Clayton, *Los Angeles Times*, "Uncle Jam's Army: Mobile Disco Dances to a Different Beat," by Don Snowden, October 30, 1983.

13. **"like Disco Stu from *The Simpsons*"**: Unknown DJ, WestCoastPioneers.com, 2008.

14. **"You might hear 'Oh Sheila' by Ready for the World"**: Greg Mack, author interview, March 7, 2012.

15. **"I used to put on a serious show"**: Dr. Dre, *Rolling Stone*, "Day of the Dre," by Jonathan Gold, September 30, 1993.

16. **"The Bloods loved pop-locking to that song"**: Anthony Williams, author interview, August 26, 2014.

17. **"When I was coming up"**: Dr. Dre, author interview, May 15, 2013.

18. **"He struggled getting money for her"**: Cli-N-Tel, author interview, May 19, 2015.

19. **"People back East didn't know much of what was going on in the West"**: Chris "The Glove" Taylor, AllHipHop.com, "Chris 'The Glove' Taylor Talks Death Row, Aftermath, and Dr. Dre (Part 1)," by Tim Sanchez, January 28, 2012.

20. **"They looked at us like we was a bunch of faggots"**: Alonzo Williams, *Welcome to Death Row*, directed by S. Leigh Savidge and Jeff Scheftel, 2001.

21. **"Some people from the East Coast wouldn't respect nobody at the time"**: Afrika Bambaataa, author interview, September 24, 2014.

22. **DJ Yella was originally called Bric Hard**: *N.ot W.ithout A.lonzo*, by Alonzo Williams, 2015.

23. **DJ Yella took his name from a 1981 new wave song called "Yella"**: The band who performed the song was called Mr. Yellow, featuring members of the Talking Heads.

24. **DJ Yella performed *Purple Rain* moves**: Alonzo Williams, author interview, July 19, 2014.

25. **Shirley Dixon did World Class Wreckin' Cru's makeup**: Ibid. Shirley Dixon was the daughter of blues legend Willie Dixon.

26. **"no motherfucking lace on"**: Dr. Dre, *The Source*, by Ronin Ro, November 1992.

27. **"We was appealing to the women back then"**: DJ Yella, VH1.

28. **"They wouldn't do my songs"**: Dr. Dre, Death Row Records biography.

29. **" 'This is gonna be a hit. You gotta push these records' "**: Susan Yano, author interview, August 10, 2015.

30. **"Next thing I know"**: Steve Yano, *Los Angeles Times*, "Parental Advisory: Explicit Lyrics," by Terry McDermott, April 14, 2002.

31. **"Dre's in jail"**: Eazy-E, *Rap Pages*.

32. **"We didn't want to just make mixtapes"**: DJ Pooh, *The Pharmacy* Beats 1 Apple Music show, July 4, 2015.

33. **"we used to keep money in our pockets"**: Horace "Mr. Sheen" Taylor, author interview, September 7, 2014.

34. **"I seen that it wasn't really worth it"**: Eazy-E, *BAM Magazine*, "N.W.A: Art or Irresponsibility?" by Davey D and Keith Moerer, April 21, 1989.

Chapter Three: We'll Pull Your Card

1. **Description of Sir Jinx's garage**: Sir Jinx, author interview, December 11, 2014.

2. **Ice Cube's first rap**: Ice Cube, VH1, *Behind the Music: Ice Cube*, June 30, 2011.

3. **How Ice Cube got his nickname**: Ice Cube, interview with the Google service Autocomplete, April 2016.

4. **O'Shea admonished weed smokers**: Laylaw, HipHopDX.com.

5. **Cube was good at storytelling**: Doug Young, author interview, August 14, 2013.

6. **"a gang infested neighborhood"**: Dane Webb, author interview, November 24, 2014.

7. **"that's when you hear the gunshots"**: Ice Cube, interview with filmmaker Matthew McDaniel.

8. **"There were shells that the police had to pick up, right in the grass"**: Ice Cube, author interview, August 30, 2015.

9. **"Man, you don't have to do that"**: Ice Cube, *Bomb* magazine, 1993.

10. **Cube's first rapping name was Purple Ice**: K-Dee, *Murder Master Music Show* internet radio program, November 24, 2015.

11. **"Man, I don't want to fuck with them"**: Cli-N-Tel, author interview, July 19, 2014.

12. **"I used to ditch school and run around the corner"**: Ice Cube, *Bomb* magazine, 1993.

13. **"Jheri curl was popular"**: Greg Mack, author interview, March 7, 2012.

14. **"The smell of mold was so thick"**: Craig Schweisinger, author interview, January 27, 2015.

15. **"you'd better get up and rock"**: Dr. Dre, *Rolling Stone*, "Day of the Dre," by Jonathan Gold, September 30, 1993.

Chapter Four: OG

1. **"buy the mic"**: Ice-T interview on the podcast *The Combat Jack Show*, September 10, 2014."

2. **"Madonna drew us up on stage"**: Chris "The Glove" Taylor, author interview, June 18, 2015.

3. **"She was really good on her feet"**: Ben Caldwell, author interview, July 2, 2015.

4. **Ice-T should abandon his "costume"**: Ice-T, author interview, June 7, 2012.

5. **"Badd Mann Dann Rapp"**: Stones Throw Records founder Peanut Butter Wolf firmly believes this was the first West Coast gangsta rap record.

6. **Schoolly D once brandished a firearm at a record plant employee**: *Los Angeles Times*, "A Tongue-lashing from Schoolly D," by Craig Lee, June 5, 1987.

7. **"Schoolly D didn't initially feature such strong language in his songs"**: Ibid.

8. **"I rap about what I know"**: Ice-T, interview with filmmaker Matthew McDaniel, 1986.

9. **"It shocked people"**: Afrika Islam, *Check the Technique*, by Brian Coleman, 2007.

10. **"These were the only records we were playing"**: Dr. Dre, *Rhythm & Rhyme* documentary, January 20, 1997. https://www.youtube.com/watch?v=DOsLMpphQ_M.

11. **Laylaw was in the drug business**: Laylaw, HipHopDX.com, "Laylaw Discusses His History with Dr. Dre, 2Pac, Ghost-Producing 'California Love (Remix),'" by Paul Arnold, June 7, 2011.

12. **"What Dre wanted to do"**: *Los Angeles Times*, "Twenty-seven Years Later, N.W.A Still Rubs a Raw Spot," by Jonathan Gold, September 5, 2015.

13. **Eric paid Cube a couple hundred dollars and a Suzuki Sidekick for "Boyz"**: Ice Cube, author interview, August 30, 2015.

14. **"They was like, 'Yo, man, we ain't doing that song'"**: Dr. Dre, *The Source*, by Ronin Ro, November 1992.

15. **"I looked at Dre in amazement"**: Ice Cube, *N.W.A: The World's Most Dangerous Group*, directed by Mark Ford, 2008.

16. **"You're thinking, like, 'Damn, how's he gonna get radio play?'"**: MC Chip, *Phoenix New Times*, "MC Chip: What Happened After N.W.A. and the Posse?" by Martin Cizmar, March 24, 2010.

17. **"The line 'Cruising down the street in my '64' created gangsta rap"**: Terrence "Punch" Henderson, *Vibe*, "Eazy-E: The Ruthless Life of an American Gangsta," by Keith Murphy, August 19, 2015.

18. **"I was very blue-eyed"** (and subsequent recollections): Don Macmillan, author interview, March 3, 2015.

19. **"Macola was an open-door policy"**: Ray Kennedy, unpublished interview with documentarians Amin Eshaiker and Andrew Arellano, February 14, 2004.

20. **Macmillan costumed Broussard**: *Billboard*, "Presser Plays Many Roles," March 16, 1985.

21. **"He couldn't tell a good record from a bad record"**: Gerald Weiner, author interview, January 14, 2015.

22. **"I would imagine Don was selling records out the back door"**: Chuck Fassert, unpublished interview with Amin Eshaiker, December 14, 2003.

23. **Maulkie claims credit for the name Ruthless Records**: *Ruthless Memories Part I*, directed by Sergio Hernandez, 2013.

24. **"You knew by listening to it what would happen with the record"**: Violet Brown, author interview, February 5, 2015.

25. **Little-known fact about Young MC**: He helped rewrite Tone Lōc's "Wild Thing" to make it suitable for radio.

26. **"KDAY was the one station"**: Ice-T, author interview, June 7, 2012.

27. **Arabian Prince originally called himself DJ Prince** (and subsequent recollections): Arabian Prince, author interview, January 20, 2015.

28. **"He was like, 'This is corny'"**: MC J.B., author interview, February 19, 2015.

29. **"Black people taking that word and trying to use it"**: Ice Cube, VH1, *Behind the Music: Ice Cube*, June 30, 2011.

30. **"If you rose to the bait, you were a racist"**: *Los Angeles Times*, "Twenty-seven Years Later, N.W.A Still Rubs a Raw Spot," by Jonathan Gold, September 5, 2015.

31. **"That shit was like some whack shit"**: MC Ren, ThaFormula.com, 2004.

32. **"I was blown away"**: Dr. Rock, author interview, January 27, 2015.

33. **Tracy Curry originally called himself Doc**: D.O.C., author interviews, June 17, 2011, and June 2, 2015.

34. **"If you come out to the West Coast, I guarantee you we will be rich"**: D.O.C., ThaFormula.com.

Chapter Five: I'm Not Giving You Shit

1. **Heller sat in Macola's lobby and tried to "pick up artists" to offer manager services**: Don Macmillan, unpublished interview with Amin Eshaiker, December 14, 2003.

2. **"I got a money tree in my backyard"**: *Ruthless: A Memoir*, by Jerry Heller, 2006.

3. **"they're going to be real street with it"**: Doug Young, author interview, August 14, 2013.

4. **"It's either us or Eazy"**: *N.ot W.ithout A.lonzo*, by Alonzo Williams, 2015.

5. **"Every dollar comes into Ruthless, I take twenty cents"**: *Ruthless: A Memoir*, by Jerry Heller, 2006.

6. **"Why you got a white man as your manager?"**: Eazy-E, *Rap Pages*.

7. **"Eazy loved his dad, but they didn't communicate a lot"**: Charis Henry, author interview, November 14, 2014.

8. **Dr. Dre was initially impressed with Jerry Heller**: *N.ot W.ithout A.lonzo*, by Alonzo Williams, 2015.

9. **"We're about to go to Chicago, then we fly to Atlanta"**: Ice Cube, *The Washington Post*, "The Warm and Fuzzy Side of Ice Cube," by Sean Daly, January 19, 2005.
10. **"We had to rap so fast. It was fucked up"**: MC Ren, author interview, June 1, 2014.
11. **"Who the fuck is y'all"**: MC Ren, ThaFormula.com, 2004.
12. **Capitol Records' board chairman told Heller N.W.A wouldn't sell**: Jerry Heller, VH1 interview.
13. **"David Geffen expressed concern over how N.W.A was 'talking about gays'"**: Chuck Fassert, unpublished interview with Amin Eshaiker, December 14, 2003.
14. **Eazy put his Air Jordans up onto the table, while Ren mean mugged** (and other details of the Priority meeting): *L.A. Weekly*, "Eazy Does It," by Jonathan Gold, December 11, 2003.

Chapter Six: A Little Bit of Gold and a Pager

1. **"I think we all was thinking about making a name for Compton and L.A."**: MC Ren, *Have Gun Will Travel*, by Ronin Ro, 1998.
2. **"it just felt silly yelling 'South Central' when everyone else was yelling Compton"**: Ice Cube, author interview, August 30, 2015.
3. **"Chuck D gets involved in all that black stuff, we don't"**: Eazy-E, *Spin*, "Hanging Tough," by Frank Owen, April 1990.
4. **"the best song of that album"**: DJ Yella, *Straight Outta Compton*, DVD extras, directed by F. Gary Gray, 2015.
5. **"We're giving them reality"** (and subsequent MC Ren quote in the next paragraph): Eazy-E, *Los Angeles Times*, "The Rap Reality: Truth and Money : Compton's N.W.A. catches fire with stark portraits of ghetto life," by Dennis Hunt, April 2, 1989.
6. **"To this day I can't stand that album"**: Dr. Dre, *Rolling Stone*.
7. **"Back then I thought the choruses were supposed to just be me scratching"**: Dr. Dre, *Rolling Stone*, August 27, 2015, "N.W.A: American Gangstas," by Brian Hiatt.
8. **"If you have a sample, you can't bring the bass guitar up"**: Stan "The Guitar Man" Jones, author interview, October 2, 2015.
9. **"Dre was like the main ear"**: MC Ren, *Los Angeles Times*, "Parental Advisory: Explicit Lyrics," by Terry McDermott, April 14, 2002.
10. **Ice Cube apologized profusely to Charles Wright**: *L.A. Weekly*, "Watts Soul Legend Charles Wright's 'Mistake' Turned into 'Express Yourself,'" by Jeff Weiss, December 17, 2014.
11. **"I'd be on the board, and he'd be on the drum machine"**: DJ Yella, HipHopDX .com, "DJ Yella Reveals Aborted Eazy-E Tracks & Why Dr. Dre Shelved 'Detox,'" by Joe Jeffrey, March 11, 2014.
12. **"Yella was good at the technical part"**: Dr. Dre, MTV.
13. **Yella was more like Dre's assistant**: MC Ren, ThaFormula.com, 2004.
14. **"he did the tedious shit"**: D.O.C., author interview, June 2, 2015.
15. **"a bunch of thugs"**: *L.A. Weekly*, "N.W.A: A Hard Act to Follow," by Jonathan Gold, May 5, 1989.
16. **"My album poster being on Bud's wall"**: Nas, author interview via email, November 9, 2011.
17. **"We'd go to the Foot Locker in KC"**: Ice Cube interview outtake with Jeff Weiss, early 2015.

Chapter Seven: All Hell Breaks Loose

1. **"I wear my pants like this for easy access, baby"**: Eazy may have cribbed the line from Morris Day, who says almost the same thing on The Time's song "The Walk."
2. **"In the world N.W.A's records described"**: The piece from which this quote is taken, "Poison the Hood," by John Mendelshon, was originally written for *Playboy*, but ultimately was published in the 2003 collection *The Sound and the Fury*.
3. **"We just showed your City Council"**: Ice Cube, *Village Voice*, "The FBI Hates This Band," by Dave Marsh and Phyllis Pollack, October 10, 1989.
4. **N.W.A kicked off of their first flight for arguing with a flight attendant**: *Ruthless: A Memoir*, by Jerry Heller, 2006.
5. **"These guys are buying automatic and semi-automatic weapons"**: Alonzo Williams, *Welcome to Death Row*, directed by S. Leigh Savidge and Jeff Scheftel, 2001.
6. **"'local gangsters' came calling and 'the assault rifles came out'"**: Ice Cube, ShortList .com, "Clooney's a Motherf*cker," by Tom Ellen, February 26, 2014.
7. **N.W.A didn't know how to properly handle guns**: Joe Fierro, author interview, September 19, 2014.
8. **"fake ass Jheri curl wearing preachers"**: MC Ren, ThaFormula.com, 2004.
9. **"Way too many police out here"**: DJ Speed, author interview, September 26, 2014.
10. **"We were strategically placed"**: Sergeant Larry Courts, mlive.com, "Retired Detroit sergeant recalls telling N.W.A. they couldn't play 'F*** tha Police' at 1989 concert," by John Counts, August 27, 2015.
11. **N.W.A was besieged by fans asking them to perform "Fuck tha Police"** (and Cube's subsequent account of the Detroit show, including Atron Gregory's quote): Ice Cube interview with David Mills, 1989.
12. **eighteen concertgoers were arrested**: *Detroit Free Press* account, 1989.
13. **"I guess they were fighting and they fell"**: Dr. Dre, MTV.
14. **"After my brother passed away, I had started boozing"**: Dr. Dre, *Rolling Stone*, "N.W.A: American Gangstas," by Brian Hiatt, August 27, 2015.
15. **"Oh, I didn't know they [the FBI] were buying our records, too!"**: Ice Cube, *Village Voice*, "The FBI Hates This Band," by Dave Marsh and Phyllis Pollack, October 10, 1989.
16. **"It made them even more dangerous"**: Bryan Turner, *Rolling Stone*, "N.W.A: American Gangstas," by Brian Hiatt, August 27, 2015.
17. **"For two weeks I walked around with a pacifier around my neck"**: Michel'le, author interview, July 6, 2015.
18. **"When my mom and my grandma died, he came into my son's life"**: Michel'le, WWPR interview, 2015.
19. **"It seemed like the day before a video, I would get a black eye"**: Michel'le, interview with *R&B Divas: L.A.* host Wendy Williams in 2013.
20. **"during another argument he shot at her and missed her by inches"**: Michel'le, VladTV.com, March 30, 2015.
21. **"You never saw me in the early videos, never heard about me"**: D.O.C., author interview, June 2, 2015.
22. **"I took about five thousand dollars in jewelry"**: D.O.C., *Murder Dog*, "Interview with D.O.C.," by Charlie Braxton, volume 10, issue 1.

23. **Making of "The Formula"**: D.O.C. interview with ThaFormula.com, which incidentally was named for the song.
24. **"I was a young man completely out of control"** (and other accident details): D.O.C., author interviews on June 17, 2011, and June 2, 2015.
25. **"I used to ask Dre for five grand every three or four days"**: D.O.C. interview with ThaFormula.com.
26. **Eazy-E's toilet fellatio**: *Ruthless: A Memoir*, by Jerry Heller, 2006.
27. **" 'Cube, that's the girl you're trying to talk to!' "**: T-Bone, author interview, April 15, 2015.
28. **"over for every other chick in the city"**: J-Dee, author interview, March 7, 2015.
29. **"I think that he got what someone at his stage of his career would have gotten"**: Jerry Heller, VH1, *Behind the Music: Ice Cube*, June 30, 2011.
30. **"Eazy's royalty statement came in"**: Ice Cube, *Beef*, directed by Peter Spirer, 2003.
31. **"I needed that money, I wanted that money"**: Ice Cube, *N.W.A: The World's Most Dangerous Group*, directed by Mark Ford, 2008.
32. **"Jerry told me that lawyers were made to cause trouble"** (and subsequent quote from lawyer Michael Ashburn): Ice Cube, *Spin*, "Hanging Tough," by Frank Owen, April 1990.
33. **"If I've been fuckin' everybody, why aren't they suin' me?"**: Eazy-E, *Rap Pages*.
34. **other N.W.A members made fun of Cube**: One Ruthless employee who asked not to be named said Cube eventually left the group because he was teased so badly.
35. **"Everybody was like, 'Go ahead nigga. Be like Arabian Prince' "**: Ice Cube, *Da Bomb* magazine.
36. **"All the money and all the fame creates a fog"**: Ice Cube, *Billboard*, "Ice Cube Remembers Eazy-E on 20th Anniversary of N.W.A Partner's Death," by Joe Lynch, March 26, 2015.
37. **"It's just too dangerous because of the gangsters"**: Rodger Clayton, *Los Angeles Times*, "L.A.—The Second Deffest City of Hip-Hop," by Cary Darling, February 7, 1988.

Chapter Eight: Most Wanted

1. **Backstage at an Anaheim N.W.A show in 1989** (and her account of signing with Ruthless and her altercation with Dr. Dre, unless otherwise noted): Tairrie B, author interview, September 5, 2014.
2. **"Dre has the Midas touch"**: Linda Martinez, author interview, April 11, 2015.
3. **"People ask me how I come up with these hits"**: Dr. Dre, *Rolling Stone*, "Rolling in Compton with Snoop and Dre," by Jonathan Gold, 1993.
4. **"You'll hear him bark out odd orders"**: *Rollin' with Dre*, by Bruce Williams (with Donnell Alexander), 2008.
5. **"He had been drinking"**: Both Tairrie B and Linda Martinez recalled these details in author interviews.
6. **"I heard your fucking track"**: Tairrie B, author interview, September 5, 2014.
7. **"next thing you know our music would end up on N.W.A.'s records"**: Laylaw, HipHopDX.com, "Laylaw Discusses His History with Dr. Dre, 2Pac, Ghost-Producing 'California Love (Remix),' " by Paul Arnold, June 7, 2011.
8. **"We created Above the Law with street money"**: Cold 187um, author interview, September 7, 2014.

9. **"Hutch came at him with a two-piece chicken wing in the jaw"**: Kokane, author interview, September 18, 2014.

10. **"They were throwing punches"**: Krazy Dee, author interview, August 28, 2014.

11. **"I was a little naïve on that tip until I saw that there was true venom there"**: Ice Cube, *Vibe*, "Eazy-E: The Ruthless Life of an American Gangsta," by Keith Murphy, August 19, 2015.

12. **"I figured he'd be coming into the studio with women and drinking forties"**: Eric Sadler, *Check the Technique, Volume 2*, by Brian Coleman, 2014.

13. **"the America that we were dealing with [during] Reaganomics"**: Ice Cube, *XXL*, "The Making of Ice Cube's *AmeriKKKa's Most Wanted*," June 7, 2010.

14. **"If you're a bitch, you're probably not going to like us"**: Ice Cube, *Rolling Stone*, "N.W.A: American Gangstas," by Brian Hiatt, August 27, 2015.

15. **"I don't think the East Coast and West Coast have ever been as glued"**: Chuck D, *Check the Technique, Volume 2*, by Brian Coleman, 2014.

Chapter Nine: Me and Allah Go Back like Cronies

1. **"I'm on parole, and I'm black"**: Rodney King, *Uprising: Hip Hop and the LA Riots*, directed by Mark Ford, 2012.

2. **"Being an LAPD cop is like being in a gang"**: As told anonymously to civil rights attorney Connie Rice in her 2012 book *Power Concedes Nothing*.

3. **"All black people are going to be faced with things like that"**: Ice Cube, author interview, August 30, 2015.

4. **"nonviolent movement"**: *Creem*, "Ice Cube Lets Off Steam," by Robert Gordon, 1991.

5. **"The only way you're gonna be respected"**: Shorty, author interview, April 14, 2015.

6. **"We sent Cube out. We told him disappear"**: J-Dee, author interview, March 7, 2015. Shorty remembered it differently, saying Cube was already speaking on the panel when the brawl went down.

7. **"bullshit excuse"**: Ice Cube, VH1, *Behind the Music: Ice Cube*, June 30, 2011.

8. **"That was kind of a misunderstanding we had"**: Bryan Turner, VH1, *Behind the Music: Ice Cube*, June 30, 2011.

9. **"There was a knock on the glass door"**: Dave Weiner, *Beef*, directed by Peter Spirer, 2003.

10. **"I swear to God, man, I remember him looking around the room"**: Bryan Turner, *Rolling Stone*, "N.W.A: American Gangstas," by Brian Hiatt, August 27, 2015.

11. **only Cube took John Singleton's offer seriously**: John Singleton, *N.W.A: The World's Most Dangerous Group*, directed by Mark Ford, 2008.

12. **"The only difficult scene was the one where I had to cry"**: Ice Cube, *The New York Times*, "Ice Cube Melts in Front of the Camera," by Kristine McKenna, July 14, 1991.

13. **"cut off Cube's Jheri curl"**: Kam participated in the haircut according to J-Dee, author interview, March 7, 2015.

14. **"[I]t probably hurt and affected me more than anything"**: Jerry Heller, *N.W.A— The Aftermath* by Harris Rosen, 2015.

15. **"I'm pro-black. I'm not anti-anything but anti-poor"**: Ice Cube, *Creem*, "Ice Cube Lets Off Steam," by Robert Gordon, 1991.

16. **"I was ready to mash"**: MC Ren, ThaFormula.com, 2004.

Chapter Ten: Like Winning the Lottery

1. **"You could come over on Sunday morning"**: Dr. Dre, *The Guardian*, "The Rap Trap," by Ekow Eshun, May 26, 2000.
2. **"You wanna move in?"**: Steffon, author interview, September 7, 2014.
3. **"I've seen that little stomp Briseno does on the video"**: Eazy-E, *Los Angeles Times*, "Rapper Takes Officer's Side," by Chuck Philips, April 6, 1993.
4. **Eazy later regretted standing by the officer**: Toker, author interview, November 1, 2015.
5. **"Dre has a lot of space in his music"**: Dawaun Parker, author interview, May 21, 2009.
6. **Yella's contributions**: Colin Wolfe told *Wax Poetics'* Tony Best in 2014 that Yella's creative contributions to *Efil4zaggin* included scratching and live drums.
7. **"We were trying to see how far we could push the envelope"**: Dr. Dre, *N.W.A: The World's Most Dangerous Group*, directed by Mark Ford, 2008.
8. **"my mom is going to kill me"**: Jewell, Dubcnn.com, by Chad Kiser, November 2011.
9. **"She tried to make us look stupid"**: MC Ren, MTV.
10. **"He grabbed me by my hair"**: Dee Barnes, MTV.
11. **Barnes hired a member of the Boo-Yaa Tribe:** As reported in *The Source*.
12. **"She's going through a lot of emotional turmoil"**: Joan Barnes, *The Philadelphia Inquirer*, "As N.W.A Member Awaits Trial, Rap World Reassesses Violent Lyrics," by Ann Kolson, August 6, 1991.
13. **"People think I was paid millions"**: Gawker.com, "Here's What's Missing from Straight Outta Compton: Me and the Other Women Dr. Dre Beat Up," by Dee Barnes, August 18, 2015.
14. **"I think that triggers it because he turns into somebody else"**: Michel'le, author interview, July 6, 2015.

Chapter Eleven: The Enforcer

1. **"His dad used to pay him for every sack"**: Sharitha Golden interview with S. Leigh Savidge on Straight Outta the Podcast, in 2016.
2. **"I used to go to football practice in college and see how many teammates I could hurt"**: Suge Knight, *Esquire: The Meaning of Life*, edited by Brendan Vaughan, 2004.
3. **Suge "wasn't a problem guy at all"**: Wayne Nunnely, *Las Vegas Sun*, "Former coaches portray Knight in positive light," by Rachael Levy, September 10, 1996.
4. **Suge offered contract with 49ers, but lost it following altercation with friend**: Sharitha Golden interview with S. Leigh Savidge on Straight Outta the Podcast, in 2016.
5. **Crockett convicted on drug charges, but Knight found guilty only of gun possession**: *Suge Knight: The Rise, Fall and Rise of Death Row Records*, by Jake Brown, 2001.
6. **"Sometimes you end up in the wrong place at the wrong time"**: Suge Knight, *Spin*, "The Big Mack," by Chuck Philips, August 1994.
7. **Suge helped D.O.C. get into clubs**: D.O.C., author interview, June 2, 2015.
8. **"They were bigger than my bodyguards"** (and Vanilla's other accounts of dealing with Suge): Vanilla Ice, ABC, *Primetime Live*, 1996.
9. **"We knew where he was staying"**: Chocolate, *Welcome to Death Row*, directed by S. Leigh Savidge and Jeff Scheftel, 2001.
10. **Chocolate said his side subsequently sued**: Ibid.

11. **"I investigated and found out"**: Suge Knight, Stephanie Frederic archive.

12. **Suge eventually began managing Dre and Above the Law**: Suge became Dre's manager according to Suge's then-wife Sharitha Golden in her interview with S. Leigh Savidge on Straight Outta the Podcast, in 2016. Suge also managed Above the Law, according to Cold 187um's author interview.

13. **"He was an aggressive person"**: Dr. Dre, VH1.

14. **"We found out that Cube was right"**: Suge Knight, *Spin*, August 1994, "The Big Mack," by Chuck Philips.

15. **"[Turner] was obviously trying to induce Dre to leave Ruthless"**: Jerry Heller, *Moguls and Madmen*, by Jory Farr, 2001.

16. **"The thing I like most about him"**: Snoop Doggy Dogg, *Spin*, "The Big Mack," by Chuck Philips, August 1994.

17. **"It's gonna be called Death Row"**: Dismost (a member of an early Death Row group called Menace to Society), author interview, July 15, 2015. Another name considered for the label was "Def Row." Singer Jewell claims to have coined "Death Row."

18. **The fax said Dre was available** (and Wayne Smith quote below): Michael Bourbeau, *Moguls and Madmen*, by Jory Farr, 2001.

19. **"Nobody messed with him"**: Rhythm D, author interview, December 22, 2014.

20. **"a martial arts expert who also took the Ruthless team to the gun range"**: In their author interviews, Joe Fierro said Klein was a martial arts expert, while Charis Henry said Klein took them for target practice.

21. **"muscle and tactics when you talked to people"**: Tomica Woods, *Vibe*, "It Ain't Eazy," by RJ Smith, June–July 1998.

22. **"We was like, 'Awww, shit'"**: Krayzie Bone, author interview, January 5, 2016.

23. **"Israeli soldiers wielding Uzi machine guns at the office"**: *Welcome to Death Row*, by S. Leigh Savidge, 2015.

24. **"[Dre] said, 'I'm leaving. You wanna come?'"** DJ Yella, *Rolling Stone*, "N.W.A: American Gangstas," by Brian Hiatt, August 27, 2015.

25. **MC Ren claimed Ruthless wasn't paying him properly**: MC Ren, ThaFormula .com, 2004.

26. **"He didn't write checks, he didn't sign nothin'"**: Bruce Williams, *Rollin' with Dre*, by Bruce Williams (with Donnell Alexander), 2008.

27. **Suge's wife Sharitha says she wrote out Suge's $25,000 check**: Sharitha Golden interview with S. Leigh Savidge on Straight Outta the Podcast, in 2016.

28. **Lydia Harris facilitated Michael Harris's prison dealings with Death Row**: The account of Suge's meetings and dealings with Lydia and Michael Harris comes from accounts given by the Harrises, including in the film *Welcome to Death Row*. Suge disputed their roles in helping start Death Row, but a judge ultimately ruled in favor of the Harrises.

29. **David Kenner "had a habit of getting very close to his clients"**: Sam Gideon Anson, *Welcome to Death Row*, directed by S. Leigh Savidge and Jeff Scheftel, 2001.

30. **"Mike thought everybody should look good"**: John Payne, *Welcome to Death Row*, directed by S. Leigh Savidge and Jeff Scheftel, 2001.

31. **Lydia Harris claimed credit for helping convince Death Row to put out Snoop**: *Vanity Fair*, "Meet the 'Real' Cookie Lyon," by Devon Maloney, December 3, 2015.

32. **Big Mike said Lydia Harris invited him to record for Death Row** (and the subsequent quote): Big Mike interview with Charlie Braxton.

33. **Los Angeles judge ordered Death Row to pay Lydia Harris $107 million**:

Monterey County Weekly, "How $107 Million of West Coast Rap King Suge Knight's Money Got Divvied up in a Monterey Courtroom," by Ryan Masters, April 27, 2006.

34. **"You are hereby ordered to appear before the honorable Dr. Dre"**: Norman Winter, *Welcome to Death Row*, directed by S. Leigh Savidge and Jeff Scheftel, 2001.

35. **"I didn't want to be killed"**: D.O.C., author interview, June 2, 2015.

Chapter Twelve: L.A.'s On Fire

1. **"It's like you're paying $10 for a whole lifestyle of game"**: Tupac Shakur, *Beef*, directed by Peter Spirer, 2003.

2. **"My great-grandmother was a slave"**: Afeni Shakur, ABC, *Primetime Live*, February 5, 1997.

3. **"He'd sleep with me sometimes. He'd sleep with her"**: Afeni Shakur, *Afeni Shakur: Evolution of a Revolutionary,* by Jasmine Guy, 2005.

4. **"This child stayed in my womb through the worst possible conditions"**: Afeni Shakur, *Esquire*, by Veronica Chambers, December 1996.

5. **"She always raised me to think I was the Black Prince of the revolution"**: Tupac Shakur, from a 1995 deposition.

6. **"He was always, like, 'peace, peace'"**: Teresa Altoz, *Baltimore Sun*, "Be4 He Was 2Pac," by M. Dion Thompson, September 21, 1996.

7. **"There was a time when I was like, 'Just kiss me!'"**: Jada Pinkett, *The Howard Stern Show*, June 3, 2015.

8. **"He was just on all the time"**: Donald Hicken, *Biggie & Tupac*, directed by Nick Broomfield, 2002.

9. **"He was the sloppiest, messiest person I've ever lived with"** (and "Fuck tha Police" anecdote): Leila Steinberg, *Tupac Shakur: Thug Angel*, directed by Peter Spirer, 2002.

10. **Leila Steinberg wouldn't accept much money from Tupac**: *XXL*, "Changes," by Nicole Lopresti, September 2011.

11. **"When you're going through poverty, everybody dibbles and dabbles"**: Mopreme Shakur, author interview, January 30, 2016.

12. **"He just had an aura"**: Tom Whalley, *Tupac Remembered*, by Molly Monjauze, Gloria Cox, and Staci Robinson, 2008.

13. **Jinx's friends arrived at the studio, carrying armfuls of beer**: Sir Jinx, author interview, December 11, 2014.

14. **"'Pac was expressing his sense of anger, for the verdict"**: Kool G Rap, VladTV.com, February 10, 2011.

15. **"shooting up motherfucking Chinese takeouts"**: Tupac Shakur, *Tupac Shakur: Thug Angel*, directed by Peter Spirer, 2002.

16. **Tupac and Laylaw brutally beat a random man**: Laylaw interview on internet show *The Goin Way Back Show*, September 1, 2013.

17. **"The early response to the riots"**: Russell Poole, *LAbyrinth*, by Randall Sullivan, 2003 edition.

18. **"The mayhem kicked off at a Korean-owned deli"** (and other riot details): *Official Negligence*, by Lou Cannon, 1997.

19. **"Most of the policemen had no helmets"**: Lieutenant Moulin, *Official Negligence*, by Lou Cannon, 1997.

20. **"We got people in there right now that's sitting in there talking about peace"**: *Birth of a Nation 4*29*1992*, directed by Matthew McDaniel.

21. **"We said, 'Y'all need to chill out'"**: Shorty, author interview, April 14, 2015.
22. **Snoop Dogg and friends drove to South Central "and got ours"**: Snoop Dogg, *Uprising: Hip-Hop and the L.A. Riots*, directed by Mark Ford, 2012.
23. **"Get the other end of this couch!"**: Snoop Dogg, *Huffington Post Live*, April 22, 2013.
24. **"It was kinda strange, surreal"**: Ice Cube, author interview, August 30, 2015.
25. **"Bloods walked up to me and was like, 'What's up, Kurupt, blood?'"**: Kurupt, VladTV.com, June 15, 2015.
26. **to use the gym at Jordan Downs, you contacted the Grape Street Crips**: *Power Concedes Nothing*, by Connie Rice, 2012.
27. **"If we could just put a governor on the greed"**: Mopreme Shakur, author interview, January 30, 2016.
28. **"I got people in the penitentiary"**: Tupac Shakur, *Tupac: Resurrection*, directed by Lauren Lazin, 2003.
29. **"LAPD only checked themselves when the people demanded it"**: Ice-T, author interview, June 7, 2012.
30. **Dre was working on *The Chronic* when the verdict came down**: It's not clear what Dre was doing during the riots. Michel'le said she and Dre "bunkered down," but Kurupt said he and Dre witnessed the chaos firsthand, including the burning of a Tower Records.
31. **"With every revolution, there's violence and murder"**: Eazy-E interview with radio host Gil Gross.

Chapter Thirteen: Silencing the Messenger

1. **Body Count included Ice-T's Crenshaw High School buddies**: Ice-T interview on the podcast *The Combat Jack Show*, September 10, 2014.
2. **"Everything was good. Life was perfect"** (and other "Cop Killer" controversy details): Ibid.
3. **"If you've never been out on the streets"**: Ice-T, VH1.
4. **Time Warner presented Ice-T with a visual metaphor**: Ice-T interview on the podcast *The Combat Jack Show*, September 10, 2014.
5. **"If you feel injustice, make a record about it"**: Ice-T, author interview, June 7, 2012.
6. **"He and I wanted to be a West Coast EPMD"**: DJ Slip, author interview, February 3, 2015. Slip's coproducer was Unknown DJ, who was everywhere in early L.A. rap, from the World Class Wreckin' Cru to Ice-T's "6 in the Mornin'."
7. **"We went to damn near every record company"**: Dr. Dre, *Spin*, "The Big Mack," by Chuck Philips, August 1994.
8. **"And all this shit broke out"**: Dr. Dre, *The Source*, by Ronin Ro, November 1992.
9. **"One of the neighbors came over"**: Ibid.
10. **"We was talking 'bout this girl that came up"**: Ibid.
11. **"1992 was not my year"**: Dr. Dre, *Los Angeles Times*, "The Violent Art, Violent Reality of Dr. Dre," by Chuck Philips, December 15, 1992.

Chapter Fourteen: The Funk

1. **Snoop went by Cordozar**: According to Snoop's high school yearbook and his mother in her interview with *Behind the Music: Snoop Dogg*, 2000.
2. **Snoop resembled a puppy, which is partly why they called him Snoopy**: Vernall Varnado (Snoop's father), *Spin*, "Sir Real," by Charles Aaron, October 1993. Varnado

had once been a musician himself, doing a bit of recording for a Mississippi label with his brothers in a gospel group called the Varnado Bros.

3. **Snoop's mom still calls him Snoopy**: Snoop Dogg, VH1, *Behind the Music: Snoop Dogg*, 2000.

4. **Snoop's mother would buy them Schlitz**: Ibid.

5. **Snoop was originally discovered by Above the Law's Cold 187um**: Cold 187um, author interview, March 5, 2016.

6. **Snoop said Dre gave him the song's opening lyrics** (and Snoop quote at the end of the paragraph): Snoop Dogg, *The Source*, by Ronin Ro, November 1992.

7. **"Tomorrow, I'm gonna be famous"**: Chris "The Glove" Taylor, author interview, June 18, 2015.

8. **" 'Deep Cover' was the soundtrack to our lives at that moment"**: Dâm-Funk, author interview, November 9, 2013.

9. **details of Kurupt's battle with Snoop outside the Roxy Theatre**: Kurupt, author interview, September 9, 2014.

10. **"serving all my homies, like a Chinese karate movie"**: Snoop Dogg, *GGN Hood News*, April 2, 2013.

11. **"The first time I heard RBX rap I was high on mushrooms"**: D.O.C., ThaFormula .com.

12. **"Rage would start eating these niggas alive"**: Kurupt, author interview, September 9, 2014. Kurupt said he doesn't remember being a part of the Nickerson Gardens battle, however.

13. **Snoop had a pet roach called Gooch**: *Welcome to Death Row*, directed by S. Leigh Savidge and Jeff Scheftel, 2001.

14. **Lady of Rage and Jewell shared an apartment in the same building**: Rhythm D, author interview, December 22, 2014.

15. **"The best records came out when we were starving"**: Nate Dogg, *Welcome to Death Row*, directed by S. Leigh Savidge and Jeff Scheftel, 2001.

16. **"We would see reels with the old records and old songs"**: Snoop Dogg, author interview, November 9, 2013.

17. **"When it comes to cannabis"**: David Bienenstock, *East Bay Express*, "Why California Weed Is Still the Best," by David Downs, January 29, 2014.

18. **"That's why we made *The Chronic*"**: Snoop Dogg, *Welcome to Death Row*, directed by S. Leigh Savidge and Jeff Scheftel, 2001.

19. **"G-funk was our style of music"**: Kokane, author interview, September 18, 2014.

20. **Cold 187um's argument with Warren G**: As remembered by Cold 187um, author interview, March 5, 2016.

21. **"There were fifteen of them, and about twenty-five to thirty of us"** (and subsequent details about the standoff): Charis Henry, author interview, November 14, 2014.

22. **"So he called in, and I taped the receiver of the phone to the mic"**: Dr. Dre interview with Big Boy, *Big Boy's Neighborhood*, KRRL, March 26, 2015.

23. **"A free-for-all broke out"**: Wendy Day, *Sweet Jones: Pimp C's Trill Life Story*, by Julia Beverly, 2015.

Chapter Fifteen: The Heir and the Janitor

1. **"The music was up as loud as it could go"**: Ronald Ray Howard, *Los Angeles Times*, "Rap Defense Doesn't Stop Death Penalty," by Chuck Philips, July 15, 1993.

2. **"There isn't a doubt in my mind"**: Linda Sue Davidson, *Los Angeles Times*, "Testing the Limits," by Chuck Philips, October 13, 1992.

3. **"They ain't even judged the dude that shot the cop yet"**: Tupac Shakur interview with Chuck Philips, chuckphilipspost.com, August 10, 1993.

4. **"[Interscope's] owners believed in the artist"**: Jeffrey Jolson-Colburn, *Welcome to Death Row*, directed by S. Leigh Savidge and Jeff Scheftel, 2001.

5. **"A lot of this [criticism of rap] is just plain old racism"**: Ted Field, *Los Angeles Times*, "They Sure Figured Something Out," by Robert Hilburn and Chuck Philips, October 24, 1993.

6. **"He's a heat-seeking missile"**: Bono, *Rolling Stone*, "Jimmy Iovine: The Man with the Magic Ears," by David Fricke, April 12, 2012.

7. **"Who produced this?"**: Jimmy Iovine, *Rolling Stone*, "Jimmy Iovine: The Man with the Magic Ears," by David Fricke, April 12, 2012.

8. **"If this was a white artist"**: Jimmy Iovine, *Los Angeles Times*, "The Violent Art, Violent Reality of Dr. Dre," by Chuck Philips, December 15, 1992.

9. **"[N]obody wanted to take a chance on me because of all that legal shit"**: Dr. Dre, *Rolling Stone*, "Rolling in Compton With Snoop and Dre," by Jonathan Gold, 1993.

10. **"Who are you, Blood?"**: DJ Speed, author interview, September 26, 2014.

11. **"Don't start no problems"**: *Have Gun Will Travel*, by Ronin Ro, 1998.

12. **"I don't give a fuck what Dre says, Dre ain't payin' no bills"**: Dick Griffey, *Welcome to Death Row*, directed by S. Leigh Savidge and Jeff Scheftel, 2001.

13. **"He shot through the wall to scare 'em"**: Ibid.

14. **"Suge is the kind of dude to piss on your leg"**: D.O.C., ThaFormula.com.

15. **"We can't get it played on the radio"**: Jimmy Iovine, *Rolling Stone*, "Jimmy Iovine: The Man with the Magic Ears," by David Fricke, April 12, 2012.

16. **no difference between people buying Dre and Guns N' Roses**: Marc Benesch, *Rolling Stone*, "Rolling in Compton with Snoop and Dre," by Jonathan Gold, 1993.

17. **"Gangsta rap was highly financed and endorsed more than Afrocentric rap"**: Chuck D, *Addicted to Noise*, "For Public Enemy's Chuck D, Keeping It Real Means Keeping It Virtual," by Gil Kaufman, December 1, 1999.

18. **"Making money is more important to me than talking about killing police"**: Dr. Dre interview with Matthew McDaniel.

Chapter Sixteen: It's On

1. **"Your songs don't match the energy of your freestyles"**: will.i.am, *Vibe*, "Eazy-E: The Ruthless Life of an American Gangsta," by Keith Murphy, August 19, 2015.

2. **Rhythm D smelled the stench of defeat** (and entire anecdote at Eazy's house): Rhythm D, author interview, December 22, 2014.

3. **"He would say, 'Burn a brown one'"**: Steffon, author interview, September 7, 2014.

4. **"an N.W.A album is not gonna work without Dre doing the beats"**: MC Ren, ThaFormula.com, 2004.

5. **"He only did ["Real Muthaphuckkin G's"] because Dre came at him first"**: DJ Yella interview with Davey D, 1996.

6. **"[W]hen the mayor of Compton goes to New York, he's a joke"**: Omar Bradley, *Los Angeles Times*, "City Orders Rap Video Straight Out of Compton," by Emily Adams, October 13, 1993.

7. **"This is going in a different direction now"**: Kevin Powell, *Beef,* directed by Peter Spirer, 2003.

8. **When Eazy heard about this he laughed**: Julio G, *Ruthless Memories Part I,* directed by Sergio Hernandez, 2013.

9. **"like three hundred deep"** (and other anecdote details): B.G. Knocc Out, *Ruthless Memories Part I,* directed by Sergio Hernandez, 2013.

10. **"We were waiting for Suge"**: Kurupt, author interview, September 9, 2014.

11. **"I had on brand-new shoes for one"** B.G. Knocc Out, HipHopDX.com, "B.G. Knocc Out Alleges Eazy-E Was Murdered, Recalls Showdown with Nate Dogg," by Paul Arnold, August 17, 2011.

Chapter Seventeen: What's My Name?

1. **Carmelitos Housing Project, where a postal worker once refused to deliver mail**: *Los Angeles Times*, "Housing Project Is a Study in Contrasts," by Bettina Boxall, September 19, 1989.

2. **Cameron Diaz "pretty sure" she once bought weed from Snoop**: TBS, *Lopez Tonight,* January 19, 2011.

3. **"Long Beach is like the next step to getting out of the ghetto"**: Vince Staples, *Complex*, "Who Is Vince Staples?" by Dharmic X, October 7, 2013.

4. **"We were insane, and we were going to live up to the name"**: Tray Dee, VladTV.com, March 20, 2015.

5. **"When the other set come by to rock"**: Snoop Dogg, *The Arsenio Hall Show*, 1994.

6. **"I didn't want to be no damn police"**: Nate Dogg, *Vice*, "How to Grow Up in Long Beach," by Busta Nut, December 1, 2004.

7. **"He would dip off in the other room"**: Warren G, author interview, July 10, 2014.

8. **"Warren was coming at me in a crazy way about his group 213"**: Dr. Dre, VH1, *Behind the Music: Snoop Dogg*, 2000.

9. **"'Cause we were having a bunch of fun"**: Ibid.

10. **"We would stay up to two or three in the morning at his house"**: Snoop Dogg, *Welcome to Death Row*, directed by S. Leigh Savidge and Jeff Scheftel, 2001.

11. **"Atomic Dog" sampled on over two hundred different songs**: Information comes from the website WhoSampledWho.com.

12. **"it would cost them $42,000 for every hour"**: Chris "The Glove" Taylor, AllHipHop .com, "Chris 'The Glove' Taylor Talks Death Row, Aftermath, and Dr. Dre," by Tim Sanchez, January 28, 2012.

13. **"A fight broke out on the main deck"**: Chris "The Glove" Taylor, author interview, June 18, 2015.

14. **Snoop almost missed his plane to be on *Saturday Night Live***: DJ Speed, author interview, September 26, 2014.

Chapter Eighteen: Negative Rap

1. **Philip Woldemariam came to the U.S. from Ethiopia** (and other Woldemariam details): *Los Angeles Times*, "A Cry for Justice," by Michael Quintanilla and Chuck Philips, May 4, 1994.

2. **"Either he was going to die or I was going to die"**: McKinley "Malik" Lee, VH1, *Behind the Music: Snoop Dogg*, 2000.

3. **"Natural Born Killaz"**: This song was originally intended for a joint Cube-Dre

album called *Heltah Skeltah*, but that never saw the light of day, and eventually D.O.C. grabbed the title for an ill-fated 1996 comeback attempt.

4. **"It was probably the worst two and a half years of my life"**: Snoop Dogg, VH1, *Behind the Music: Snoop Dogg*, 2000.

5. **"My heart was beating like I was smoking crack"**: Ibid.

6. **"It put everything in the right perspective"**: Ibid.

7. **"I'd do the little bitty shit"**: Warren G, author interview, July 10, 2014.

8. **"Someone quoted me saying that I built Death Row"**: Warren G, *Pitchfork*, "Gangsta Sermon: Warren G's *Regulate... G Funk Era*," by Jeff Weiss, May 23, 2014.

9. **"'It would be so different to do a hip-hop song over this'"**: Warren G, *Rolling Stone*, "Warren G and Nate Dogg's 'Regulate': The Oral History of a Hip-Hop Classic," by Mosi Reeves, December 19, 2014.

10. **"[T]aking some gangsta shit and putting a melody to it"**: Warren G, HipHopDX .com, "Warren G Remembers Nate Dogg, Claims Pioneering G-Funk Sound," by Matt Caputo, May 4, 2011.

11. **"Nate was different"**: Snoop Dogg, author interview, June 24, 2014.

12. **"My family don't listen to R&B—never have, never will"** (and Nate Dogg's first lyrics): Nate Dogg, *Vice*, "How to Grow Up in Long Beach," by Busta Nut, December 1, 2004.

13. **"He had a special voice"**: Mike Dean, Montreality, August 10, 2015.

14. **Nate Dogg lost the ability to talk**: *Long Beach Press-Telegram*, March 15, 2011, "Rapper Nathaniel Hale—Nate Dogg—dies at 41," by Greg Mellen.

15. **"He was getting into gospel music"**: Warren G, HipHopDX.com, "Warren G Remembers Nate Dogg, Claims Pioneering G-Funk Sound," by Matt Caputo, May 4, 2011.

Chapter Nineteen: The One by His Side

1. **"He treated us like princesses"**: MC J.B., author interview, February 19, 2015.

2. **"He was fully engaged"**: Elise Kim, author interview, February 16, 2015.

3. **Eazy had a crush on Jada Pinkett**: Charis Henry, author interview, March 4, 2016.

4. **"the largest child-support order handled by the Los Angeles district attorney's office"**: *Orlando Sentinel* (Associated Press), "Eazy-E Must Pay $58,000 a Year for Child Support," July 2, 1993.

5. **"It didn't seem he had any preference"**: Rebekka Armstrong, author interview, September 27, 2014.

6. **Eazy knocked out a three-hundred-pound man**: Gary Ballen, *Murder Master Music Show* internet radio program, August 27, 2015.

7. **FBI said Eazy's "safety was not endangered"**: *Los Angeles Times*, "More Suspects Sought in White Supremacist Plot," by Jim Newton and David Freed, July 17, 1993.

8. **MC Ren complained that his recording budgets kept getting slashed**: MC Ren, ThaFormula.com, 2004.

9. **"You guys are on a militant tip"**: Benyad, *Swindle* magazine.

10. **Lowriders arrive at Ruthless** (and the signing of Brownside): Toker, author interview, November 1, 2015.

11. **Bone Thugs phone conversation with Eazy-E**: Krayzie Bone, B.E.T.com, "Krayzie Bone Remembers Eazy-E on the 20th Anniversary of His Death," by Jake Rohn, March 26, 2015.

12. **Eazy admired that Bone Thugs went to the bathroom together**: Krayzie Bone, *Vibe*, "Eazy-E: The Ruthless Life of an American Gangsta," by Keith Murphy, August 19, 2015.

13. **"Just based off of image, I thought he would be kinda disrespectful"**: Tomica Woods interview with Matthew McDaniel.

14. **"I've had a Vanessa Williams experience"**: Tomica Woods, *Vibe*, "It Ain't Eazy," by RJ Smith, June–July 1998.

15. **"She's beautiful and she's ruthless and she's bright"**: Clarence Avant, Ibid.

16. **Tomica laughed at Eazy because he was afraid to open his sunroof**: *XXL*, "Eazy-E Tribute: Tomica Wright, a Gangsta & a Gentleman," by Starrene Rhett, March 26, 2010.

17. **"I was indirectly doing things for Eric at the company"**: Tomica Woods, *BRE Magazine*, by Steven Ivory.

18. **"[Eazy] never told me, 'Me and Tomica are thinking about doing this'"**: Dirty Red, author interview, September 7, 2014.

19. **"I think that toward the end of 1994, a lot of people were in [Eazy's] ear"**: Jerry Heller, *N.W.A—The Aftermath,* by Harris Rosen, 2015.

20. **"What's up with your little buddy?"**: Steffon, author interview, September 7, 2014.

21. **"He had records from where money was missing from the label"**: B.G. Knocc Out, HipHopDX.com, "B.G. Knocc Out Alleges Eazy-E Was Murdered, Recalls Showdown with Nate Dogg," by Paul Arnold, August 17, 2011.

22. **"He never told me Jerry was stealing from him"**: Charis Henry, author interview, November 14, 2014.

23. **"It's the most ridiculous allegation I've ever heard"**: Jerry Heller, author interview, October 2, 2014.

24. **"Klein was wedging Jerry out of the picture"**: Gary Ballen, *Murder Master Music Show* internet radio program, August 27, 2015.

25. **Heller doesn't believe Eazy was in his right mind when he wrote a letter firing him**: Jerry Heller, *N.W.A—The Aftermath,* by Harris Rosen, 2015.

26. **"We told him, 'Man, you going to freeze to death out here'"**: Krayzie Bone, NahRight.com, "First-Hand Accounts of the Night Eazy-E & Ice Cube Ended Their Feud," by Paul Meara, September 11, 2015.

27. **"I told Eazy I was down"**: Ice Cube, author interview, August 30, 2015.

28. **Dre said he and Eazy spoke about maybe putting N.W.A back together**: Dr. Dre interview with Big Boy, *Big Boy's Neighborhood*, KRRL, March 26, 2015.

29. **Eazy was focused on fixing the damage with Dre**: Krayzie Bone, author interview, January 5, 2016.

30. **"All I remember is him coughing a lot"**: MC Ren, author interview, June 1, 2014.

31. **"That day was life changing for me"**: Tairrie B, author interview, September 5, 2014.

32. **Eazy threw Tomica out of the Topanga house**: Vince Caruso, author interview, April 21, 2015. Caruso was, at the time, living in Eazy's Woodland Hills house. His roommates were Steffon and former KDAY programmer Greg Mack.

33. **The Twins phoned Mike Klein, who told them to take Eazy to the hospital**: Ibid.

34. **"Bronchitis runs in our family"**: Patricia Wright, author interview, September 7, 2014.

35. **Eazy was using "huge-ass" inhalers**: B.G. Knocc Out, HipHopDX.com, "B.G. Knocc Out Alleges Eazy-E Was Murdered, Recalls Showdown with Nate Dogg," by Paul Arnold, August 17, 2011.

36. **"He was on the phone crying"**: Tomica Woods, *N.W.A: The World's Most Dangerous Group*, directed by Mark Ford, 2008.

Chapter Twenty: Time to Testify

1. **They were there "to keep everybody from rushing in on him"**: Shaheed Muhammad, author interview, March 2, 2015.
2. **"The baby mamas couldn't get up to see him"**: Gary Ballen, *Murder Master Music Show* internet radio program, August 27, 2015.
3. **Tomica Woods instructed the Nation to keep out practically *everyone***: Tracy Jernagin, author interview, October 18, 2015.
4. ***The Final Call* described low-dose alpha interferon as a cure for AIDS**: *The New York Times*, "AIDS Work at a Nation of Islam Clinic Is Questioned," by Paul Hosefros, March 4, 1994.
5. **"We got married at the hospital because he wasn't sure if he was going to make it through"**: Tomica Woods, *N.W.A: The World's Most Dangerous Group*, directed by Mark Ford, 2008.
6. **Woods called Kemron a "miracle potion," and she and Ron Sweeney removed Shaheed Muhammad from Eazy's security detail**: Shaheed Muhammad, author interview, March 2, 2015. Muhammad believes another reason he was removed from the detail was because of his association with Mike Klein.
7. **"Eric was not a person to get married to anybody"**: Bigg A, author interview, June 19, 2014.
8. **Heller called Jernagin and her daughter E.B. "the longtime true loves" of Eazy's life**: *Ruthless: A Memoir,* by Jerry Heller, 2006. Jernagin told me she agrees with Jerry's assessment, but recognizes other women might feel that way, too.
9. **"I had already given Clarence notice"**: Tomica Woods-Wright, *BRE Magazine*, by Steven Ivory.
10. **Joe Fierro abruptly fired**: Joe Fierro, author interview, September 19, 2014.
11. **Gary Ballen fired by Woods-Wright**: Gary Ballen, *Murder Master Music Show* internet radio program, August 27, 2015.
12. **Eazy "must have contracted AIDS through heterosexual contact"**: William Young, *Park City Daily News* (Associated Press), "Gangsta Rapper Eazy-E Dies of AIDS," by Niki Kapsambelis, March 26, 1995.
13. **"incredible outpouring of sympathy"**: Paula Correia, *Los Angeles Times*, "Hospital Deluged With Calls From Eazy-E's Fans," by Edmund Newton, March 19, 1995.
14. **"We told him we loved him"**: Jacob T., *Vibe*, "Eazy Living," by Carter Harris, June–July 1995.
15. **"I felt real bad"**: Dr. Dre, *N.W.A: The World's Most Dangerous Group*, directed by Mark Ford, 2008.
16. **"It was one of the saddest days"**: DJ Yella, Ibid.
17. **People with AIDS expect to live an average of three years without treatment** (and other HIV/AIDS statistics): Figures according to AIDS.gov.
18. **Heller said Eazy was given a clean bill of health in a physical**: Jerry Heller interview on *Murder Master Music Show* internet radio program, June 30, 2014.
19. **"I can't say they're crazy"**: Ice Cube, author interview, August 30, 2015.
20. **Wish Bone was apoplectic after Eazy's funeral**: Steffon, author interview, September 7, 2014.
21. **"Klein thought he was going to be the person who stepped up"**: Tomica Woods-Wright, *Vibe*, "It Ain't Eazy," by RJ Smith, June–July 1998.

22. **"She a cool person, but I don't feel she know how to run a record company"**: MC Ren interview with WorldWideConnected.com.

23. **"That woman has been to hell and back"**: S. Leigh Savidge, author interview, July 22, 2015.

Chapter Twenty-One: Political Prophet

1. **A Sierra Leone army conquered villages to the tune of "California Love"**: *Vice*, "Gen. Butt Naked vs. the Tupac Army," by Chris Parachini and Peter Cushing, December 1, 2003.

2. **"We do the Tupac cross almost daily"**: Dennis Coelho, *Urban Ink*, "I Tattooed Tupac," by Emmanuel Ureña, no. 21, 2011.

3. **"I was in a choke hold passing out with cuffs on"**: Tupac Shakur, *Davey D's Hip Hop Corner*, "On the Line With...2Pac Shakur: The Lost Interview," by Davey D, 1991.

4. **"not only a rapper but a person who was true to the game"**: Mutulu Shakur, *The New Yorker*, "The Takedown of Tupac," by Connie Bruck, July 7, 1997.

5. **"The camera just happen to catch real emotions"**: Tupac Shakur interview with Chuck Philips, chuckphilipspost.com, August 10, 1993.

6. **"Do you know that we stood on slave ship decks"**: Maya Angelou, ESPN, *30 for 30: One Night in Vegas*, directed by Reggie Rock Bythewood, 2010.

7. **Oakland community members taunted Tupac as he filmed *Poetic Justice***: *Esquire*, by Veronica Chambers, December 1996. Chambers was writing a behind-the-scenes book about *Poetic Justice*.

8. **"I can't take this shit"**: Ibid.

9. **Tupac got to know everyone under the Southern California sun**: Tupac Shakur interview with Chuck Philips, chuckphilipspost.com, August 10, 1993.

10. **Meaning of *Strictly for My N.I.G.G.A.Z***: Mopreme Shakur, author interview, January 30, 2016.

11. **Allen Hughes's account of his fight with Tupac**: Allen Hughes interview with Neal Brennan and Moshe Kasher, *The Champs* podcast, June 5, 2013.

12. **"I'm thugging against society"**: Tupac Shakur interview with Chuck Philips, chuckphilipspost.com, August 10, 1993.

13. **Biggie listened to *Amerikkka's Most Wanted* before recording *Ready to Die***: Ice Cube, *XXL*, "The Making of Ice Cube's *AmeriKKKa's Most Wanted*," by *XXL* staff, June 7, 2010.

14. **"Biggie came out here and studied under King Tee"**: Chris "The Glove" Taylor, author interview, June 18, 2015.

15. **"When I first saw her, she was killing me with those eyes"**: Biggie Smalls, *Vibe*, "Chronicle of a Death Foretold," by Cheo Hodari Coker, May 1997.

16. **Account of Tupac and Biggie's first meeting**: Dan Smalls, *The Fader*, "How Ya Livin Biggie Smalls?" May 25, 2011.

17. **"We all thought he was a dope rapper"**: E.D.I. Mean, author interview, December 18, 2015.

18. **Biggie told Tupac he'd like to be part of Thug Life**. Ibid.

19. **"I trained the nigga, he used to be under me like my lieutenant"**: Tupac Shakur interview with Sway, KMEL, April 19, 1996.

20. **Tupac tells Biggie which sex he should rap for**: Ibid.

21. **Biggie asked Tupac to be his manager, but Tupac told him to stick with Puffy**: E.D.I. Mean, author interview, December 18, 2015. Note that Biggie had two managers, Wayne Barrow and Mark Pitts, but Puffy was most instrumental in guiding his career.

22. **"It irked him when they said, 'Fake gangsta rapper'"**: Mopreme Shakur, *The New Yorker*, "The Takedown of Tupac," by Connie Bruck, July 7, 1997.

23. **Tupac had noticed Haitian Jack at a Manhattan club**: Haitian Jack, HipHopWired .com, "Haitian Jack Speaks on Tupac, Suge Knight & Being Labeled a Snitch," by IPOPPEDOFF, February 5, 2015.

24. **Haitian Jack brought celebrities to a Queens bar**: Little Shawn, HipHopDX.com, "Shawn Pen Speaks About the Quad Studios Attack on Tupac, His History with Bad Boy And Roc-A-Fella Records," by Paul Arnold, December 9, 2011.

25. **"[H]e loved the respect and recognition I got"**: Haitian Jack, HipHopWired .com, "Haitian Jack Speaks on Tupac, Suge Knight & Being Labeled a Snitch," by IPOPPEDOFF, February 5, 2015.

26. **Puffy said he and his crew showed Tupac love and concern**: *Tupac: Resurrection*, directed by Lauren Lazin, 2003.

27. **"It was like they were mad at me"**: Tupac Shakur, *Vibe*, "Ready to Live," by Kevin Powell, April 1995.

28. **"I think the wounds to his head were superficial lacerations"**: Greg Kading, author interview, January 12, 2016.

29. **"A message was being sent to him not to name-drop"**: Bill Courtney, *XXL*, "Pit of Snakes," by Jason Rodriguez, September 2011.

30. **"Nobody came to rob you"**: Jimmy Henchman, *Vibe*, "The Score," by Ethan Brown, December 2005.

31. **"He gave me $2,500, plus all the jewelry I took"**: Dexter Isaac, AllHipHop.com, "Jimmy Henchman Associate Admits to Role in Robbery/Shooting of Tupac," by Grandmaster Grouchy Greg Watkins, June 15, 2011.

32. **"I was *fucked* up"**: Bill Garland, *XXL*, "True Blood," by Vanessa Satten, September 2011.

33. **Payback for Tupac's anticop lyrics?**: Haitian Jack told HipHopWired.com that New York Mayor Rudolph Giuliani and other "very high profile people" were "calling the judge to make sure that they got him." The former mayor did not respond to a request for comment.

34. **Tupac signed autographs for a white supremacist**: Tupac Shakur, MTV.

35. **Tupac read for the part of Bubba**: Keisha Morris, *F.E.D.S.* magazine.

36. **Keisha Morris felt "used" by Tupac**: Keisha Morris, *XXL*, "Love Is Not Enough," by Mariel Concepcion, September 2011.

37. **"He owed me more than to turn his head"**: Tupac Shakur, interview with Rob Marriott, August 1996.

38. **"Suge sent $15,000 and put it on his books"**: Reggie Wright Jr., author interview, November 13, 2015.

39. **"I know I'm selling my soul to the devil"**: According to one of Tupac's managers, Watani Tyehimba, *The New Yorker*, "The Takedown of Tupac," by Connie Bruck, July 7, 1997.

40. **Interscope and Atlantic Records put up the $1.4 million bond**: According to a suit Tupac's mother later filed against Death Row.

41. **"It wasn't a legal contract"**: Charles Ogletree Jr., *The New Yorker*, "The Takedown of Tupac," by Connie Bruck, July 7, 1997.

Chapter Twenty-Two: My .44 Make Sure Y'all Kids Don't Grow

1. **Suge had two Belgian Malinoises trained to attack**: *My Life with the Knight*, by Stormey Ramdhan, 2014.

2. **Death Row's security *was* the police**: As detailed in Randall Sullivan's *LAbyrinth*, 2003 edition, some officers associated with the label even after their bosses specifically told them not to.

3. **Reggie Wright Jr. blamed Snoop for using a "homeboy" as security**: Reggie Wright Jr., author interview, November 13, 2015.

4. **"hardworking, intelligent people who showed an extreme loyalty to Suge"**: *Got Your Back*, by Frank Alexander with Heidi Siegmund Cuda, 1998.

5. **"Every day our phones were busy with irate, frustrated artists"**: ClashMusic.com, "Working at Death Row Records—The Reality, Crazier Than the Myth," by Nina Bhadreshwar, November 17, 2011.

6. **Tupac rapped "Dear Mama" at a Death Row Mother's Day party with his own mother in attendance**: *My Life with the Knight* by Stormey Ramdhan, 2014.

7. **"He would go to a children's hospital"**: Jonathan Wolfson, author interview, November 12, 2015.

8. **"Why would you do that?"**: Nate Dogg, *Welcome to Death Row*, directed by S. Leigh Savidge and Jeff Scheftel, 2001.

9. **Suge invited Notorious B.I.G. to perform at Club 662**: Reggie Wright Jr., author interview, November 13, 2015.

10. **Suge came straight to The Source Awards after visiting Tupac in prison, who told him of his vendetta against Biggie**. Ibid. Reggie Wright Jr. traveled with Suge on this trip.

11. **Puffy enlisted the support of the Southside Crips**: Puffy has denied using Crips as security, but former LAPD detective Greg Kading told me their relationship has been "corroborated on multiple levels, by a variety of people, including those people in the Bad Boy entourage themselves." A Southside Crip named Keffe D told investigators he was Puffy's liaison to the gang; Keffe D and Puffy were put in contact through an associate of Puffy's named Eric "Zip" Martin. Keffe D and Zip had worked together in the drug trade, according to Kading. Keffe D and one of Puffy's bodyguards, Eugene Deal, said Puffy gave the Crips concert tickets for their troubles.

12. **"Just being upset 'cause somebody said they ain't fuckin with your music"**: E-40, *Complex*, 2013.

13. **"We were in defense mode"**: Mark Pitts, B.E.T.com, "Notorious B.I.G.'s Former Manager Speaks Out," by Alex Gale, March 8, 2012.

14. **"'Keep your mouth shut, Big'"**: Biggie Smalls, *Biggie & Tupac*, directed by Nick Broomfield, 2002.

15. **"[H]e was, like, 'I think you had something to do with this'"**: Sean "Puffy" Combs, *Vibe*, "Stakes Is High," by The Blackspot, September 1996.

16. **Daz doesn't get as much shine as many of his colleagues**: Some people claim Dr. Dre has taken credit for some of Daz's beats; Suge asserted that it was actually Daz, not Dre, who did the bulk of *Doggystyle*, though Dre and Chris "The Glove" Taylor, who worked extensively on the album, denied this. "I ain't no fuckin' Milli Vanilli," Dre told Harris Rosen.

17. **"We were just mad"**: Kurupt, author interview, September 9, 2014.

18. **Faith Evans and Tupac recorded "Wonda Why They Call U Bitch"**: Evans's vocals were later replaced by Jewell.

19. **"I saw him at a couple of parties"**: Faith Evans, *Vibe*, May 1996.

20. **Tupac considered titling his album *NC-17***: Tupac Shakur interview with Chuck Philips, chuckphilipspost.com, August 10, 1993.

21. **Tupac, Outlawz, and Tha Dogg Pound planning a group called Thug Pound**: Young Noble, author interview, January 4, 2016. Tupac also gave Kurupt and Daz their nicknames, "Young Gotti" and "Daz Dillinger," respectively.

22. **Tupac told CPO he'd like to record immediately**: CPO Boss Hogg, HipHopDX .com, "CPO Boss Hogg Explains Getting Paid $37,000 for Tupac's 'Picture Me Rollin','" by Jake Paine, June 24, 2013.

23. **"He wouldn't just say 'do your vocals'"**: Natasha Walker, *Welcome to Death Row*, directed by S. Leigh Savidge and Jeff Scheftel, 2001.

24. **"Whatever 'Pac requested, Johnny could do it"**: Mopreme Shakur, *XXL*, "Mourn You 'Til I Join You," September 2011

25. **"run out in the snow, take their clothes off"**: Reggie Wright Jr., author interview, February 4, 2016.

26. **"Suge did not make 'Pac more aggressive"**: E.D.I. Mean, author interview, December 18, 2015.

27. **Bad Boy enlisted Crips for protection that night**: According to multiple sources. Reggie Wright Jr. said the group included Keffe D.

28. **"That was the first time I really looked into his face"**: Biggie Smalls, *Vibe*, "Stakes Is High," by The Blackspot, September 1996.

29. **"Tupac was on Interscope the whole time"**: Suge Knight, *Rolling Stone*, "Suge Knight Reflects on 'Doggystyle' 20 Years Later," by Paul Cantor, November 25, 2013.

30. **"The day this song dropped, New York was quiet"**: Combat Jack, *Complex*, "Combat Jack Presents: True Stories Behind 25 Rap Classics," by Dominic Green, September 21, 2010.

31. **"If honey was to give you that pussy"**: Biggie Smalls, *Vibe*, "Stakes Is High," by The Blackspot, September 1996.

32. **"What it's been right now is a lot of moviemaking"**: Sean "Puffy" Combs, Ibid.

33. **"I made the mistake of saying I was from L.A."**: Russ Parr, *Los Angeles Times*, "L.A.—The Second Deffest City of Hip-Hop," by Cary Darling, February 7, 1988.

34. **"I was selling millions of records"**: Too $hort, VladTV.com, March 12, 2012.

35. **"It was a little heavy-handed"**: Ice Cube, author interview, August 30, 2015.

36. **"Westside Slaughterhouse"**: This song's title is a play on the song "SlaughtaHouse," which mocked Cube's style of gangsta rap and was performed by a group led by Brooklyn stalwart Masta Ace.

Chapter Twenty-Three: Potential Leads

1. **"It felt funny going in the studio"**: Dr. Dre, *The Guardian*, "The Rap Trap," by Ekow Eshun, May 26, 2000.

2. **"Next thing I know I'm surrounded"**: Dr. Dre, MTV.

3. **"In 1995 downtown jeweler B.L. Diamonds received orders including"**: Information taken from court records.

4. **"Are you with us, or are you with Dre?"**: According to Reggie Wright Jr., author interview, February 4, 2016.

5. "[E]ach time we see a East Coast mutherfucka": According to Daz, interview with ThaFormula.com.

6. **Mark Anthony Bell claimed Suge told him to drink urine**: Bruce Williams's account of the incident is different. In his memoir he said it wasn't urine but rather "expensive-ass champagne." Williams also said he stopped Bell from jumping out of a window.

7. "**Tupac never knew me**": Dr. Dre, *N.W.A—The Aftermath*, by Harris Rosen, 2015.

8. "**When I got sentenced, my mom told me**": Dr. Dre, *Los Angeles Times*, "The Doctor, Unmasked," by Chuck Philips, October 13, 1996.

9. "**[I]t turned into a fucking Don Corleone thing**": Dr. Dre, *Blaze*.

10. **Dre cowered inside while an "off-duty cop" answered the door**: Suge Knight, *The Source*.

11. **Suge claimed to be Jimmy Iovine and had "eight or nine motherfuckers" with him**: Dr. Dre, *Vibe*, "Escape From Death Row," by Ronin Ro, October 1996.

12. **saga surrounding Suge and Dre like Othello**: S. Leigh Savidge, sanjivb.com, "The Suge Knight Trial: Don't Forget About Dre," by Sanjiv Bhattacharya, September 7, 2015.

13. "**I was a princess in a castle**": Michel'le, Bossip.com, "Dr. Dre & Suge Knight's Babies Mother, Michel'le, Cries About Alleged Abuse and Fake Marriage!!," August 16, 2013.

14. "**People think they should be the Hatfields and McCoys**": Michel'le, author interview, July 6, 2015.

15. "**They are great fathers and they are there for them**": Michel'le, TV One, 2013.

16. "**even after they beat you, or whatever they do**": Michel'le, Bossip.com, "Dr. Dre & Suge Knight's Babies Mother, Michel'le, Cries About Alleged Abuse and Fake Marriage!!," August 16, 2013.

17. **Dr. Dre's "Been There Done That"**: The song featured RBX, who'd left Death Row following the infamous "chicken incident." Following a Chicago appearance, he began eating some chicken backstage, when, he recalled, Suge angrily insisted that the food had been ordered for some of his guys. "I'm like, *Man*, why you beefin' over some fuckin' chicken!" he told *Vibe*. "That was just one of the last straws."

18. **Nicole encouraged Dre to "get back on that hardcore shit"**: Dr. Dre, *The Guardian*, "The Rap Trap," by Ekow Eshun, May 26, 2000.

19. "**Dre showed me how to do things with my voice**": Eminem, *Los Angeles Times*, "The Dr.'s Always In," by Robert Hilburn, September 23, 2007.

20. "**two hands slammed down on Tupac's shoulders from behind**": Kidada Jones, *Q: The Autobiography of Quincy Jones*, by Quincy Jones, 2002.

21. "**We thought he was trying to get off of Death Row**": Nate Dogg, MTV.

22. "**'Pac was a loyal dude**": Young Noble, author interview, January 4, 2016.

23. **David Kenner abandoned most of his practice to focus on Death Row**: *Los Angeles Times*, "Grand Jury to Probe Origins of Rap Label," by Chuck Philips, July 24, 1997.

24. "**we already run the streets out here**": Tupac Shakur, MuchMusic interview, 1996.

25. **Tyson gave Tupac and Suge a hug** (and other fight night details): ESPN, *30 For 30: One Night in Vegas*, directed by Reggie Rock Bythewood, 2010.

26. "**Fifty blows! I counted them**": According to Frank Alexander, *Got Your Back,* by Frank Alexander with Heidi Siegmund Cuda, 1998.

27. **They were missing bodyguards including Kevin Hackie**: Hackie said he wasn't in Vegas because he was caught up in Compton police work; Reggie Wright Jr., his boss, said it was because they'd had a disagreement about money.

28. **Tupac and company trying to recruit Run-D.M.C. to Death Row East**: Hammer interview with Davey D, June 1997.

29. **Tupac told Kidada she shouldn't come to Club 662**: Kidada Jones, *Q: The Autobiography of Quincy Jones*, by Quincy Jones, 2002.

30. **"I grabbed him and said, 'Get down!'"**: Suge Knight, BET News, interview with Stephanie Frederic, September 1996.

31. **Tupac entourage members asked by police for gang affiliations**: E.D.I. Mean, author interview, December 18, 2015.

32. **The Outlawz took shifts standing watch at the hospital**: E.D.I. Mean told me a member of their crew was on "the roof" with a rifle, though Young Noble disputes this.

33. **"Can I listen to it without crying?"** (and details about putting Tupac's ashes in her garden): Afeni Shakur, *People*, "All Eyes on Her," by Peter Castro, December 1, 1997.

34. **"sprinkle some of the big homie in there"**: Young Noble, *XXL*, "Ashes to Ashes," by Adam Fleischer, September 2011.

35. **"Suge was always kind of running the show"**: Jonathan Wolfson, author interview, November 12, 2015.

36. **Dick Griffey and D.O.C. "had to sue to get [their] pennies"**: Dick Griffey, *Welcome to Death Row*, directed by S. Leigh Savidge and Jeff Scheftel, 2001.

37. **Tupac's interpretation of Machiavelli**: Tupac interview with William Shaw.

38. **"I don't recognize my friend Tupac Shakur on Makaveli"**: Shock G, Stopbeing famous.com.

39. **"I think they went through the motions"**: Greg Kading, author interview, January 12, 2016.

40. **"Keffe added that Biggie was never involved"**: Ibid. Greg Kading noted that there is "absolutely nothing to support the idea that [Biggie] knew about it or acquiesced to" Tupac's murder.

Chapter Twenty-Four: Trepidation and Bravado

1. **Biggie Smalls cried at the news of Tupac's death**: Mark Pitts, *BET*, "Notorious B.I.G.'s Former Manager Speaks Out," by Alex Gale, March 8, 2012.

2. **"Anybody in their right mind knew they didn't let enough time pass"**: Doug Young in an interview posted on EM NINE YouTube channel.

3. **"The food is horrible"**: Biggie Smalls, *Vibe*, "Chronicle of a Death Foretold," by Cheo Hodari Coker, May 1997.

4. **"Get down!"**: Kurupt, author interview, September 9, 2014. Kurupt added that one of the bullets banked off their windshield.

5. **The case for Suge's involvement in Biggie's murder seemed solid**: As for the witnesses who said the shooter wore a Nation of Islam–style suit and bow tie? That's something of an unresolved matter in the Poochie theory. "We don't know Poochie's possible affiliation with the Nation of Islam," Greg Kading told me, adding that during this time in Los Angeles, there were instances where gang members dressed up like Nation of Islam members to commit crimes, hoping to confuse the victims and investigators.

6. **Zip was a narcotics dealer with whom Keffe D had previously done deals**: Greg Kading, author interview, January 12, 2016.

7. **"Torres's federal murder and racketeering convictions were overturned"**: *San Gabriel Valley Tribune*, "Judge cites government misconduct in Numero Uno case then dismisses serious charges against Arcadia man," by Thomas Himes, September 26, 2009.

8. **"They just made a decision on the immediate circumstances"**: Greg Kading, author interview, January 12, 2016.

9. **"It's always been considered an open investigation"**: Kevin L. McClure, *The New York Times*, "Wrongful-Death Lawsuit Over Rapper Is Dismissed," by Ben Sisario, April 19, 2010.

Epilogue

1. **The shooter decided not to finish Brim off**: *Tupac Amaru Shakur 1971–1996*, "All That Glitters," by Rob Marriott, 1997.

2. **"There are very few Compton gangs that have leaders"**: Reggie Wright Jr., author interview, November 13, 2015.

3. **"The trouble with what 'Pac was doing"**: Big Syke, *The New Yorker*, "The Takedown of Tupac," by Connie Bruck, July 7, 1997.

4. **Rumors abounded that Ice Cube, Mack 10, or Puffy could be hit next**: According to reports from Davey D and *The Village Voice*.

5. **The Firm recorded in Miami because of coastal tensions**: Chris "The Glove" Taylor, AllHipHop.com, "Chris 'The Glove' Taylor Talks Death Row, Aftermath and Dr. Dre (Part 2)," by Tim Sanchez, January 30, 2012.

6. **Snoop had mild disses for Dre on *Tha Doggfather***: Dre responded that Snoop "played his-self" because the song in question, "Freestyle Conversation," "sounds like a track that I would have threw away," Dre told Harris Rosen.

7. **"That was some bullshit"**: Bizzy Bone, video interview with CamCaponeNews, posted December 11, 2011.

8. **"When I heard you were gonna be here, I got in my car and drove fifteen hours"** (and other Summit details): Fat Joe, *Davey D's Hip-Hop Corner*, "Nation Of Islam Hip Hop Peace Summit," by Davey D, April 11, 1997.

9. **Common gave credit to an atmosphere without yes-men**: Common, *Beef*, directed by Peter Spirer, 2003.

10. **Keith Clinkscale defended *Vibe's* journalism**: *Vibe's* coverage of hip-hop in the Biggie-Tupac era was unparalleled. And I think it's unfair to call it reckless. For example, reporter Kevin Powell took the extra step of contacting the NAACP over concerns of escalating tensions. Also, when he was in L.A. to write about Death Row, he was shocked to witness Faith Evans—Biggie's wife—outside of the label's studios. But decided to leave her out of his piece for *Vibe*, to "avoid adding more fuel to this fire," he told *Complex*.

11. **Suge said, "The money will be there in the morning"**: According to Master P, interview with Chuck Dizzle and DJ Hed, *Home Grown Radio*, KRRL, November 2, 2015.

12. **"Master P was willing to step up"**: Snoop Dogg, VH1, *Behind the Music: Snoop Dogg*, 2000.

13. **"Never was afraid of him"**: Snoop Dogg, *Rolling Stone*, "Snoop Dogg: America's Most Lovable Pimp," by Touré, December 14, 2006.

14. **Death Row's website featured a dog barking, then a gunshot**: *Biggie & Tupac*, directed by Nick Broomfield, 2002.

15. **"We thought we were so badass"**: Axl Rose, *New York*, "Ex-'White-Boy Poseur,'" by Jada Yuan, September 18, 2006.

16. **Dr. Dre came to Lisa Johnson's house and talked to her and their daughters**: Lisa Johnson, author interview, August 21, 2015. Their daughter La'Toya similarly described this encounter in her 2008 documentary, *Daddy's Shadow*.

17. **Snoop, Kurupt, B.G. Knocc Out, and Dresta made a record together**: B.G. Knocc Out, HipHopDX.com, "B.G. Knocc Out Alleges Eazy-E Was Murdered, Recalls Showdown With Nate Dogg," by Paul Arnold, August 17, 2011.

INDEX